JOHN COUSINS, DENNIS LILLICRAP AND
SUZANNE WEEKES
CONSULTANT EDITOR: ADAM LUCAS

FOOD AND BEVERAGE SERVICE

FOR LEVELS 1 AND 2

HODDER
EDUCATION
AN HACHETTE UK COMPANY

Orders: please contact Bookpoint Ltd, 130 Milton Park, Abingdon, Oxon OX14 4SB. Telephone: (44) 01235 827720. Fax: (44) 01235 400454. Lines are open from 9.00 to 5.00, Monday to Saturday, with a 24-hour message answering service. You can also order through our website www.hoddereducation.co.uk

If you have any comments to make about this, or any of our other titles, please send them to educationenquiries@hodder.co.uk

British Library Cataloguing in Publication Data

A catalogue record for this title is available from the British Library

ISBN: 978 1 471 80791 6

This edition published 2014.

Impression number   10 9 8 7 6 5 4 3 2 1

Year   2014, 2015, 2016, 2017

Hachette UK's policy is to use papers that are natural, renewable and recyclable products and made from wood grown in sustainable forests. The logging and manufacturing processes are expected to conform to the environmental regulations of the country of origin.

Typeset by DC Graphic Design Ltd, Swanley Village, Kent.

Printed in Italy for Hodder Education, an Hachette UK Company, 338 Euston Road, London NW1 3BH.

Contents

Part A Investigating the catering and hospitality industry

Chapter 1 Employability in the catering and hospitality industry

Chapter 2 Developing skills for employment

Part B Underpinning knowledge and skills

Part C Food and beverage product knowledge

Chapter 13 Alcoholic beverages

Part D Service skills

Chapter 14 Service methods, key technical skills and service principles

Chapter 15 Preparation for service

Chapter 16 Taking customer orders

Chapter 17 Bar service skills

Chapter 18 Food and beverage service skills

Chapter 19 Bookings, billing and payments

Introduction

The aim of the book

Food and Beverage Service for Levels 1 and 2 provides the essential guide for the foundation knowledge and skills necessary for those studying and/or working in food and beverage service at Levels 1 and 2.

The book has been fully revised and updated to support:
- the City & Guilds Level 1 Certificate and Level 2 Diploma in Professional Food & Beverage Service
- the City & Guilds Award and Certificate in Professional Food & Beverage Service Skills at Levels 1 and 2
- those wishing to be assessed at NVQ/SVQ Levels 1 to 2 in Food and Beverage Service
- the broader-based study requirements of a range of other qualifications
- a range of in-company training programmes.

Requirements for professionalism in food and beverage service

Food and beverage operations are continuing to improve and develop, together with advances in quality. The demand for food and beverages away from the home has increased and, with a broader spectrum of the population eating out, customer needs are continuing to diversify.

Food and restaurant styles are also continuing to diversify to meet the challenges of the demands being made by increasingly knowledgeable and value-conscious customers. Menu and beverage list contents are constantly being influenced by trends, fads and fashions; the relationship between health and eating; dietary requirements; cultural and religious influences; the advance of vegetarianism and customer acceptance, or otherwise, of irradiation and genetically modified foods. Expansion of the industry also means greater choice. This, together with potential skill shortages and drives for efficiency, has resulted in a streamlining of foodservice operations.

Good food and beverage service in any sector is achieved when customers' needs are met and when management consistently reinforces and supports service staff in the maintenance of clearly identified technical standards and service goals.

The primary aspect of a meal, that enhances the customer's enjoyment and appreciation of it, is where members of the food and beverage service staff have the confidence to provide a professional level of service that is also genuinely welcoming. But this is not something just anyone can do well. Although there is less emphasis on sophisticated service techniques in some sectors, there is now a far greater emphasis throughout the industry on the need for professional food and beverage service personnel that have:
- sound product knowledge
- well-developed interpersonal skills
- technical competence
- the ability to work as part of a team.

However, food and beverage service also represents the ultimate paradox: the better it is, the less it is noticed.

John Cousins, Dennis Lillicrap and Suzanne Weekes, April 2014

Acknowledgements

The preparation of this book has drawn upon a variety of experience and literature. The authors would like to express their sincere thanks to all the organisations and individuals who gave assistance and support in the revision of this text. In particular we would like to thank:

Academy of Food and Wine Service, UK; British Airways plc; Burgess Furniture Ltd, London; City and Guilds of London Institute; Croners Catering, Croners Publications; Anne Dubberley and Julie Bromfield, Petals of Piccadilly, Birmingham; Dunk Ink; Andrew Durkan, Author and Consultant, formally of Ealing College, London; Elia International Ltd, Middlesex; Euroservice UK, Welford, Northants; Foodservice Consultants Society International, UK; Professor David Foskett, Author, Consultant and Dean at the London School of Tourism and Hospitality, Ealing, and the Operations Team at the School; Fullers Brewery Chiswick and The Rose and Crown Public House in Ealing; German Wine Information Service, London; Simon Girling, Restaurant Manager, The Ritz Hotel, London; The Glasgow Hilton Hotel; Gleneagles Hotel, Auchterarder, Scotland; IFS Publications; The International Coffee Organisation; International Standards Organisation; The Langham Hotel, London, Le Columbier Restaurant, London; Louvet Turner Coombe Marketing; Meiko UK Ltd; National Checking Co UK; PalmTEQ Limited UK; The Restaurant Association of Great Britain; Joachim Schafheitle, Senior Lecturer, Bournemouth University; Ashely Shaw House Manager, The Westbury Hotel, London, Six Continents Hotels, London; Louise Smith, Flowers by Louise, Birmingham; Royal Academy of Culinary Arts; Snap-Drape Europe Limited; Steelite International; The Tea Council; United Kingdom Bartenders Guild, Uniwell Systems (UK) Ltd and Williams Refrigeration, UK.

Figures 1.14, 3.2, 7.4, 7.5, 9.1, 11.1, 12.2, 12.3, 12.9, 14.8, 17.3, 17.4, 17.5, 18.1, 18.2, 18.3, 18.4, 18.5, 18.10, 18.11, 18.12, 18.13, 18.14, 18.18, 18.19 and 18.22 were photographed by Ria Osborne at the University of West London. Figures 11.2, 17.9, 17.10, 17.11, 17.14, 17.15 and 17.16 were photographed by Ria Osborne at the Rose and Crown pub, Ealing. Figures 3.2, 3.4, 3.8, 3.9, 3.10, 4.15, 9.2, 9.3, 9.4, 9.5, 9.6, 9.7, 9.8, 9.9, 9.10, 9.11, 9.12, 9.13, 14.2, 14.4, 15.2, 15.6, 15.7, 15.25, 18.7, 18.26 and 18.27 were photographed by Andrew Callaghan. Figures 3.6, 5.1, 12.8, 14.1, 14.3, 14.5, 14.6, 14.7, 14.9, 15.4, 15.5, 15.12, 15.13, 15.14, 15.16, 15.17, 15.18, 17.7, 18.6, 18.8 and 18.9 were photographed by Carl Drury.

Figures 4.4, 13.5, 15.3, 15.8, 15.9, 15.10, 15.11, 15.20, 17.8 and 18.21 were drawn by Mike Humphries, Clifton Graphics. Figures, 7.3, 17.2, 17.6, were drawn by Oxford Designers and Illustrators. Figures 5.3 and 16.1 were drawn by Barking Dog Art

We would also like to thank the following for permission to reproduce copyright photos:

Figure 1.1 © Stockbyte / Getty Images; Figure 1.2 © Imagestate Media; Figure 1.3 ©Alan Lucas – Fotolia; Figure 1.4 ©Roland Nagy/Getty Images/iStockphoto/Thinkstock; Figure 1.5 © Ingram Publishing Ltd.; Figure 1.6 © Ingram Publishing Ltd.; Figure 1.7 © Clover/Amana Images/Photolibrary; Figure 1.8 © Photodisc / Getty Images; Figure 1.9 © senkaya/Getty Images/iStockphoto/Thinkstock; Figure 1.10 © Photodisc / Getty Images; Figure 1.11 ©Stockbyte/Getty Images/Thinkstock; Figure 2.1 © Eric Gevaert –Fotolia; Figure 2.3 ©Paulo Cruz/Getty Images/iStockphoto/Thinkstock; Figure 2.4 © Jeffrey Blackler / Alamy; Figure 2.5 © goodluz – Fotolia; Figure 4.1 ©mino21 – Fotolia; Figure 4.2 © Iain Cooper / Alamy; Figure 5.1 ©Sascha Burkard – Fotolia; Figure 5.9 © Thomas Perkins/ iStockphoto.com; Figure 5.11 © xyno/istockphoto.com; Figure 6.1 ©Evgeny Karandaev/Getty Images/iStockphoto/Thinkstock; Figure 6.3 © Medioimages/Photodisc/Getty/Thinkstock; Figure 6.5 © Scott Rothstein/Getty Images/iStockphoto/Thinkstock; Figure 7.1 © Antonio_Diaz/Getty Images/iStockphoto/Thinkstock; Figure 8.1 © tanjichica7/Getty Images/iStockphoto/Thinkstock; Figure 10.1 © Jacques PALUT – Fotolia; Figure 10.2 © Galina Peshkova/Getty Images/iStockphoto/Thinkstock; Figure 11.3 © xxf/Getty Images/iStockphoto/Thinkstock; Figure 11.4 © matka_Wariatka/Getty Images/iStockphoto/Thinkstock; Figure 12.1 © Khoo Eng Yow/Getty Images/iStockphoto/Thinkstock.

The Academy of Food and Wine

The Academy of Food and Wine is the professional body for front of house service personnel. We focus on helping to provide the hospitality industry with well-trained and qualified employees and on improving the status of front of house service as a rewarding and meaningful career choice.

The Academy is nationally recognised as the industry's leading voice for raising standards in the delivery of food and in service skills. Affiliated to the Association de la Sommellerie Internationale, the Academy is also the official professional body for sommeliers working in the UK.

The Academy is delighted to endorse *Food and Beverage Service for Levels 1 and 2* as a high-quality resource supporting students and tutors in the delivery of the new certificates and diplomas in Professional Restaurant Service.

The United Kingdom Bartenders' Guild

The United Kingdom Bartenders' Guild came into being in 1933 and is a trade association with the prime aim of advancing the professional skills of bar men and women throughout the country.

The Guild promotes a high standard of workmanship and encourages the development

of creative new cocktails through rewarding competitions both at home and abroad. The Guild also maintains a strict code of ethics within the bartending business.

The Guild is very pleased to support the publication of this invaluable resource for students.

The structure of the book and how to use it

Structure of the book

The content of the book has been structured to follow a logical progression from exploring the hospitality industry as a whole, underpinning knowledge and skills of food and beverage operations, service areas and equipment and product knowledge of food and beverages, through to interpersonal and technical service skills and their application.

The book is presented in four parts:

- **Part A Investigating the catering and hospitality industry** provides an overview of the hospitality industry, employment, staff roles, qualifications and the development of skills necessary for working in the industry.
- **Part B Underpinning knowledge and skills** provides foundation knowledge of service areas and equipment, legislation in food and beverage service, food safety, health, safety and security, and customer service and customer relations.
- **Part C Food and beverage product knowledge** covers knowledge of menus and wine and drink lists, and product knowledge of non-alcoholic and alcoholic beverages.
- **Part D Service skills** begins by detailing the various service methods, identifies the essential technical skills needed by service staff and details key service principles. This is followed by the full service sequence from preparing for service, taking bookings, food service skills and bar and beverage service skills. The final chapter covers bookings and payments.

A list of cocktail and mixed drink recipes and methods is provided in **Annex A**.

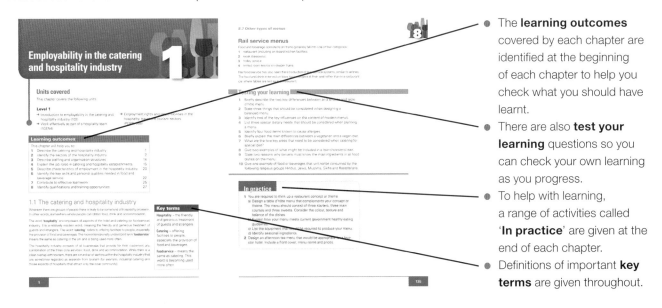

- The **learning outcomes** covered by each chapter are identified at the beginning of each chapter to help you check what you should have learnt.
- There are also **test your learning** questions so you can check your own learning as you progress.
- To help with learning, a range of activities called '**In practice**' are given at the end of each chapter.
- Definitions of important **key terms** are given throughout.

The content of the book, while having its origins in classic cuisine and service (the context and the body of knowledge on which modern foodservice operations are based) is also intended to reflect current practice within the industry. Therefore, while the book gives information and describes various aspects of food and beverage service, it is not intended to be a prescriptive book. Clearly the actual operation of the service will be substantially affected by the style and business needs of the individual operation.

Throughout the book we have referred to job titles and job categories such as manager, waiter, supervisor, bar tender, servers and catering assistants. In all cases these terms, in line with general trends within the industry, refer to both male and female personnel.

How to use this book

The information in the book can be found in four ways:

1   Using the **contents list** at the front of the book (pages iii–vii): this takes account of the various examining and awarding body recommendations and assessment requirements, especially the City & Guilds Certificate and Diploma in Professional Food and Beverage Service, together with the Level 1 and Level 2 NVQs in Food and Beverage Service. Because of the wide variety of hospitality operations, the contents list also indicates the broad range of knowledge and skills that will be relevant to a range of food service operations.
2   Using the **qualification mapping** (pages xiii–xix): this makes it easy to find the information that you will need for a specific qualification unit or standard.
3   The **learning outcomes** identified at the beginning of each chapter: these are identified at the beginning of each chapter together with the page numbers.
4   Using the **index** at the back of the book (pages 358–362): this provides an alphabetical list of key words from the text, together with relevant page numbers.

Within the following qualification maps you will find the chapters that are relevant to specific City & Guilds units and also the NVQ/SVQ standards.

City & Guilds Level 1 and Level 2 – qualification mapping

City & Guilds Level 1 Certificate in Introduction to Professional Food and Beverage Service

Unit title*	Chapters/sections and page numbers
Introduction to employability in the catering and hospitality industry (102)	Chapter 1 Employability in the catering and hospitality industry page 1
Health and safety awareness for catering and hospitality (103)	Chapter 5 Health, safety and security page 78
Legislation in food and beverage service (104)	Chapter 4 Legislation in food and beverage service page 70
Understand menus (105)	Chapter 8 Understanding menus page 125
	Chapter 9 Menu knowledge page 138
Dealing with payments and bookings (107)	Chapter 19 Bookings, billing and payments page 334
Food and beverage service skills (108)	Chapter 3 Service areas and equipment page 49
	Chapter 14 Service methods, key technical skills and service principles page 214
	Chapter 15 Preparation for service page 230
	Chapter 16 Taking customer orders page 259
	Chapter 18 Food and beverage service skills page 292
Bar service skills (109)	Chapter 3 Service areas and equipment page 49
	Chapter 14 Service methods, key technical skills and service principles page 214
	Chapter 16 Taking customer orders page 259
	Chapter 17 Bar service skills page 269
Hot beverage skills (110)	Chapter 12 Hot beverages page 172
	Section 18.4 Service of hot beverages page 307
Food safety in catering (202 Level 2)	Chapter 6 Food safety page 95

* Numbers in brackets are the current City & Guilds unit numbers.

City & Guilds Level 2 Diploma in Professional Food and Beverage Service

* Numbers in brackets are the current City & Guilds unit numbers

Level 1 and Level 2 NVQ/SVQ – qualification mapping

Level 1 NVQ/SVQ Certificate in Food and Beverage Service

Level 1 NVQ/SVQ Units*	Chapters/sections and page numbers
Mandatory units	
Maintain a safe, hygienic and secure working environment (1GEN1, 104)	Chapter 4 Legislation in food and beverage service page 70 Chapter 5 Health, safety and security page 78
Work effectively as part of a hospitality team (1GEN4)	Chapter 2 Developing skills for employment page 32
Maintain customer care (1GEN3, 106)	Chapter 7 Principles of customer service page 109
Maintain food safety when storing, holding and serving food (2GEN4, 204)	Chapter 6 Food safety page 95
Section A Optional units	
Prepare and clear areas for drink service (1BS2, 113)	Chapter 10 Wine and drink lists page 161 Chapter 11 Non-alcoholic beverages page 166 Chapter 13 Alcoholic beverages page 188 Chapter 17 Bar service skills page 269 Chapter 18 Food and beverage service skills page 292
Serve drinks (1BS2)	Chapter 10 Wine and drink lists page 161 Chapter 11 Non-alcoholic beverages (soft drinks) page 166 Chapter 13 Alcoholic beverages page 188 Chapter 17 Bar service skills page 269 Annex A Cocktail and mixed drink recipes page 346
Prepare and clear areas for table/tray service (1FS1, 107)	Chapter 3 Service areas and equipment page 49 Chapter 14 Service methods, key technical skills and service principles page 214 Chapter 15 Preparation for service page 230 Chapter 16 Taking customer orders page 259 Chapter 18 Food and beverage service skills page 292
Clean and store crockery and cutlery (1GEN5, 105)	Chapter 3 Service areas and equipment page 49

* Numbers in brackets are the current National Occupational Standards numbers; the second number is the City & Guilds unit number.

Level 2 NVQ/SVQ Diploma in Food and Beverage Service

Level 2 NVQ/SVQ Units*	Chapters/sections and page numbers
Section A Food service optional units	
Provide a counter/takeaway service (1FS4, 110)	Chapter 3 Service areas and equipment page 49
	Chapter 8 Understanding menus page 125
	Chapter 9 Menu knowledge page 138
	Chapter 14 Service methods, key technical skills and service principles page 214
	Chapter 15 Preparation for service page 230
	Chapter 16 Taking customer orders page 259
	Chapter 18 Food and beverage service skills page 292
Serve food at the table (2FS2, 207)	Chapter 3 Service areas and equipment page 49
	Chapter 8 Understanding menus page 125
	Chapter 9 Menu knowledge page 138
	Chapter 14 Service methods, key technical skills and service principles page 214
	Chapter 15 Preparation for service page 230
	Chapter 16 Taking customer orders page 259
	Chapter 18 Food and beverage service skills page 292
Provide a silver service (2FS8, 208)	Chapter 3 Service areas and equipment page 49
	Chapter 8 Understanding menus page 125
	Chapter 9 Menu knowledge page 138
	Chapter 14 Service methods, key technical skills and service principles page 214
	Chapter 15 Preparation for service page 230
	Chapter 16 Taking customer orders page 259
	Chapter 18 Food and beverage service skills page 292
Provide a buffet/carvery service (2FS4, 209)	Chapter 3 Service areas and equipment page 49
	Chapter 8 Understanding menus page 125
	Chapter 9 Menu knowledge page 138
	Chapter 14 Service methods, key technical skills and service principles page 214
	Chapter 15 Preparation for service page 230
	Chapter 16 Taking customer orders page 259
	Chapter 18 Food and beverage service skills page 292

Level 2 NVQ/SVQ Units*	Chapters/sections and page numbers
Section C Optional units	
Prepare and clear areas for table service (2FS1, 206)	Chapter 3 Service areas and equipment page 49
	Chapter 14 Service methods, key technical skills and service principles page 214
	Chapter 15 Preparation for service page 230
	Chapter 18 Food and beverage service skills page 292
Prepare and clear the bar area (2BS1, 211)	Chapter 3 Service areas and equipment page 49
	Chapter 10 Wine and drink lists page 161
	Chapter 11 Non-alcoholic beverages (soft drinks) page 166
	Chapter 12 Hot beverages page 172
	Chapter 13 Alcoholic beverages page 188
	Chapter 14 Service methods, key technical skills and service principles page 214
	Chapter 17 Bar service skills page 269
Maintain cellar and kegs (2BS5, 215)	Chapter 17 Bar service skills page 269
	Section 17.9 onwards page 284
Clear dispense lines (2BS6, 216)	Chapter 17 Bar service skills page 269
	Section 17.9 onwards page 284
Receive, store and issue drinks stock (2BS9, 219)	Chapter 17 Bar service skills page 269
	Section 17.9 onwards page 284
Resolve customer service problems (2GEN5, 261)	Chapter 7 Principles of customer service page 109
Promote additional services and products to customers (2GEN6, 273)	Chapter 16 Taking customer orders page 259
Maintain and deal with payments (2GEN9, 205)	Chapter 19 Bookings, billing and payments page 334
Employment rights and responsibilities in the hospitality, leisure, travel and tourism sector (PERR, 666)	Chapter 1 Employability in the catering and hospitality industry page 1
	Chapter 2 Developing skills for employment page 32

* Numbers in brackets are the current National Occupational Standards numbers; the second number is the City & Guilds unit number.

Dynamic Learning teaching and learning resources for food and beverage service

Dynamic Learning teaching and learning resources allow you to combine your trusted resources with our quality content and tools. They offer time-saving tools to streamline your planning and outstanding content and lessons for your college network.

Food and Beverage Service teaching and learning resources provides support for users of:

- Food and Beverage Service for Levels 1 and 2
- Food and Beverage Service Ninth Edition.

It is invaluable for students working towards VRQ, S/NVQ, BTEC or Institute of Hospitality qualifications in hospitality and catering at Levels 1, 2 and 3, and can also be used to support in-company training programmes.

Features include:

- PowerPoint presentations
- ready-made lesson plans with ideas on how to deliver each unit
- short videos of key food and beverage service techniques
- knowledge check quizzes to check understanding and provide practice for tests – these can be used to track and monitor progress.
- student activity worksheets and answers
- links to useful websites.

Visit www.hoddereducation.co.uk/dynamiclearning to learn more and to sign up for a free trial.

Employability in the catering and hospitality industry

Units covered

This chapter covers the following units:

Level 1

→ Introduction to employability in the catering and hospitality industry (102)

→ Work effectively as part of a hospitality team (1GEN4)

→ Employment rights and responsibilities in the hospitality, travel and tourism sectors (PERR, 666)

Learning outcomes

This chapter will help you to:

1.1 The catering and hospitality industry

Wherever there are groups of people there is likely to be some kind of hospitality provision. In other words, somewhere where people can obtain food, drink and accommodation.

The word '**hospitality**' encompasses all aspects of the hotel and catering (or foodservice) industry. It is a relatively modern word, meaning the friendly and generous treatment of guests and strangers. The word '**catering**' refers to offering facilities to people, especially the provision of food and beverages. The more internationally understood term '**foodservice**' means the same as catering in the UK and is being used more often.

The hospitality industry consists of all businesses that provide for their customers any combination of the three core services: food, drink and accommodation. While there is a clear overlap with tourism, there are a number of sectors within the hospitality industry that are sometimes regarded as separate from tourism (for example, industrial catering and those aspects of hospitality that attract only the local community).

Key terms

Hospitality – the friendly and generous treatment of guests and strangers

Catering – offering facilities to people, especially the provision of food and beverages

Foodservice – means the same as catering. This word is becoming used more often

1

Figure 1.1 Golf courses usually have bars, serve food and offer a range of other hospitality services

1.2 Sectors of the hospitality industry

A summary of the hospitality sectors is given in Table 1.1 on page 14.

Hotels and other tourist accommodation

Hotels provide accommodation in private bedrooms. Many also offer services such as restaurants, bars and room service. Job roles in a hotel will include reception staff, porters and housekeepers.

The level of service offered by a hotel will depend on what type of hotel it is and how many stars it has. Hotels are rated from five-star (indicating a luxury hotel) to one-star (indicating more basic accommodation).

The hotel sector is mainly independently owned and hotels come in all shapes, sizes and locations. More than three-quarters of them have fewer than 20 rooms and are often family run. There are many international hotel chains, such as Hilton, Radisson, Mandarin Oriental and Intercontinental, in the five-star hotel market. There are also budget hotels, guesthouses and bed and breakfast accommodation.

Figure 1.2 The Savoy is an example of a luxury hotel

To attract a wide a range of guests, many hotels now offer a variety of services, such as office and IT facilities (such as internet access, fax machines and a quiet area to work in), gym and sports facilities, swimming pool, spa, therapy treatments, hair and beauty treatments and so on.

The hotel sector can be divided into distinct categories: luxury, business, resort, town house and budget properties, and each category has its own characteristics.

Business hotels, as the name suggests, are geared to the corporate traveller and the emphasis therefore tends to be on functionality. These hotels will usually have a dedicated business centre, up-to-date communications technology in the bedrooms and ample conference and meeting facilities. Business hotels are more likely to be chain operated, often with a strong brand element. Town houses, meanwhile, are notable for their individuality, intimacy and emphasis on service. These hotels are usually small and, as the name suggests, located in converted town houses with a domestic feel that is emphasised by their décor. The fastest-growing sector is budget hotels (e.g. Travelodge, Premier Inn), where the accommodation is often co-located with a food operation such as Little Chef.

Consortia

'Consortia' is the plural of '**consortium**'. A consortium is a group of independent hotels that make an agreement to buy products and services together. For example, they might all pay a specialist company to do their marketing (advertising and so on). This might mean, for example, that the members of the consortium could then use international reservation systems and compete against the larger hotel chains.

Food and beverage provision

The provision of food and beverage services varies greatly between establishments. Again, some general differences can be seen between the various hotel categories.

- Upmarket hotels are likely to provide a full range of services, usually with at least one à la carte restaurant, 24-hour room service and a well-stocked bar.
- Town house properties generally provide little or no food.
- Budget hotels are characterised by the presence of a family restaurant. This is often a stand-alone, branded outlet that also draws custom from the surrounding area.

Recently many hotels have been re-examining the place of food and beverages in their operations. While many town houses open with no restaurant at all, other hotels believe that food and beverage provision is an essential guest service. This has led them to consider alternative methods of running a restaurant, such as **contracting out** to a third party or introducing a **franchise** operation.

The contracting out of food and beverage services to third parties will continue to be a major trend in the hotel catering sector over the next few years, although it is likely this will be stronger in London than in other areas of the UK. As many hotels remain slow in response to growing consumer demand for food and beverages and there is intense competition from the high street, outsourcing food and beverage services will become increasingly appealing.

Outsourcing is not always a straightforward option for hotels, however. To attract walk-in dining customers, a hotel ideally needs to be located where there is easy access to the restaurant, and the location of the hotel itself (city centre, countryside, etc.) needs to fit with the type of customers being targeted – that is, the product must be attractive to passing trade. Despite these constraints, the number of outsourced restaurants is expected to increase considerably.

With increased consumer interest in food and eating out, hotels are becoming more focused on developing attractive food and beverage facilities in-house. The success of in-house catering depends on the willingness of hotels to deliver a product that is attractive to the outside market, and to maintain this product so that it evolves with changing consumer tastes and trends. According to human resource specialists within the hotel sector, key factors holding back further development are that food and beverage managers in hotels tend to be hoteliers rather than restaurateurs, as well as a shortage of experienced culinary and service staff.

Key term

Consortium – a group of independent hotels that make an agreement to buy products and services together

Key terms

Contracting/outsourcing – to obtain services from an outside supplier

Franchise – an agreement where a person or group of people pay a fee and some set-up costs to use an established name or well-known brand

Country house hotels

Country house hotels are mostly located in attractive old buildings, such as stately homes or manor houses, usually in rural areas or popular tourist areas. They often have a reputation for good food and wine, and offer a high standard of service. Country house hotels may also offer the additional services mentioned on page 2.

Figure 1.3 A country house hotel

Budget hotels

Budget hotels like motels and Travelodges are built near motorways, railway stations and airports. They are aimed at business people and tourists who need somewhere inexpensive to stay overnight. The rooms are reasonably priced and have tea and coffee-making facilities. No other food or drink is included in the price. Budget hotels do not employ many members of staff and there is often no restaurant. They are usually located close to shops, cafés, restaurants or pubs, which are often run by the same company as the hotel.

Guesthouses and bed and breakfasts

There are guesthouses and bed and breakfast establishments all over the UK. They are small, privately owned businesses. The owners usually live on the premises and let bedrooms to paying customers, many of whom are regular customers. Some guesthouses offer lunch and an evening meal as well as breakfast.

Farms

The rural tourism industry is important in the UK. Farmers understand this and have formed a national organisation called the Farm Holiday Bureau. The farms in the organisation usually offer bed and breakfast and holiday cottages. Most members of the organisation have invested money to improve their bedrooms to meet the standards required by the National Tourist Board. The accommodation is usually on or near a working farm.

Youth hostels

The Youth Hostels Association runs hostels in various locations in England and Wales. These establishments cater for single people, families and groups travelling on a limited budget. They mainly provide dormitory accommodation, but some also have private rooms. In some locations they offer a number of sports and leisure facilities. Basic, wholesome meals are provided at

Figure 1.4 Youth hostels provide budget accommodation

a low cost in some hostels, and they all have a kitchen that can be used by visitors to store and prepare their own food.

Restaurants

Restaurants make up approximately 40 per cent of the commercial hospitality market in the UK, while small establishments employing fewer than ten staff make up the majority of the industry. The south-east of England has the highest concentration of catering and hospitality outlets.

The restaurant sector has become the largest in the UK hospitality industry. It includes exclusive restaurants and fine-dining establishments, as well as a wide variety of mainstream restaurants, fast-food outlets, coffee shops and cafés.

Many restaurants specialise in regional or ethnic food styles, such as Asian and Oriental, Mexican and Caribbean, as well as a wide range of European-style restaurants. New restaurants and cooking styles appear and become popular all the time.

Figure 1.5 Restaurants often specialise in regional or ethnic food styles

Moderately priced speciality restaurants are very popular. In order for them to succeed, the manager must understand what customers want and plan a menu that will attract enough customers to make a good profit. A successful caterer is one who gives customers what they want; they will be aware of changing trends and adapt to them. The most successful catering establishments are those that are able to sell food over a long service period, throughout the year.

Chain organisations

Many of the most popular restaurants, coffee shops, stores and shops with restaurants appear on British high streets up and down the UK and are known as chain organisations. Many of these chains have more than one outlet in a city and some have outlets in other countries too. Many of these chains are well-known and advertise widely. They often serve morning coffee, lunches and teas, or they may be in the style of snack bars and cafeterias.

Fast food and takeaways

Many customers prefer the option of popular foods at a reasonable price, with little or no waiting time. Fast-food establishments offer a limited menu that can be consumed on the premises or taken away. Menu items are quick to cook and have often been partly or fully prepared beforehand, often at a central production point.

Drive-ins and drive-thrus

The concept of drive-ins and drive-thrus came from America. As the name suggests, at a drive-in the customer enters a parking area and the server comes to their car to deliver the customer's order. At present there are none of these in the UK. However, drive-thrus appear across the UK, with the most well-known being the drive-thru at McDonald's

restaurants. Customers stay in their vehicles and drive up to a microphone where they place their order. As their car moves forward in a queue, their order is prepared and is ready for them to pick up at a service window.

Figure 1.6 Fast-food is often available as a takeaway

Delicatessens and salad bars

These offer a wide selection of salads and sandwich fillings to go in a variety of bread and rolls at a 'made-to-order' sandwich counter. The choice of breads might include panini, focaccia, pitta, baguette and tortilla wraps. Fresh salads, homemade soups and chilled foods, as well as a hot 'dish of the day' and baked jacket potatoes with a variety of fillings may also be available. With such a variety of choice on offer, these establishments can stay busy all day long, often serving breakfast as well.

Retail

Many retail operations offer catering services alongside the retail operation. This can range from vending machines to takeaway services, through to a full service restaurant. Some retail operations include branches of well-known coffee chains or other popular catering restaurant brands. Independent food and beverage operations are also located within shopping centres and retail parks.

Event catering

Hospitality operations may also have separate event planning departments, while a number of organisations specialise in providing event management services. Event management involves planning and organising weddings, parties, dinners, business meetings and conferences, etc. The event management company will be responsible for hiring a venue, organising staff, food and drink, music, entertainment and any other requests the client may have.

Corporate hospitality

Corporate hospitality is hospitality provided by a business, usually for its clients or potential clients. The purpose of corporate hospitality is to build business relationships and to raise awareness of the company. Corporate entertaining is also used to thank or reward loyal customers.

Leisure

The leisure sector covers a variety of establishments, including cinemas, theatres and sporting events, all of which are likely to offer some form of catering service.

Timeshare villas and apartments

A timeshare owner buys a particular amount of time (usually a few weeks) per year in a self-catering apartment, room or suite in a hotel or leisure club. The arrangement may be for a set number of years or indefinitely. There will usually be a number of restaurants, bars and other leisure facilities within the same complex for timeshare owners to use.

Health clubs and spas

Figure 1.7 A gym café

Health clubs and spas are often luxury establishments or hotels that offer their clients a variety of health and beauty treatments, and they have become very popular in recent years. Many people today have very busy lifestyles and they like to visit a health club or spa to relax. These establishments may offer healthy food, therapies and activities that offer people an opportunity to improve their fitness, health and general wellbeing.

Museums

Museums today provide much more than just interesting exhibitions and most will have at least one café or restaurant catering for visitors. Some run events such as lunchtime lectures, family events and children's discovery days where food is provided as part of the event. Museums are also used as a venue for private events and banqueting during the hours they are closed to the general public. Sometimes outside caterers are employed for the occasion, but many museums have their own catering team to provide a wide range of food.

Theme parks

Theme parks are extremely popular venues for a family day out or even a full holiday. Larger theme parks include several different eating options, ranging from fast food to fine dining. Some include branded restaurants such as McDonald's and Burger King. Theme parks are also used for corporate hospitality and conferences, and many have conference and banqueting suites for this purpose, while larger theme parks may even have their own hotel.

Holiday centres

Holiday centres (sometimes referred to as holiday complexes) around the UK provide leisure and hospitality facilities all on one site and cater for families, single people and groups of people. In recent years, many holiday centres have invested large amounts of money to improve the quality of the holiday experience they offer. Center Parcs, for example, offers sub-tropical pools and other sporting and leisure activities that can be used even if the weather is bad. Holiday centres include a range of different restaurants and food courts, bars and coffee shops. They operate all year round, offering short holidays and weekend breaks throughout the year.

Historic buildings and visitor attractions

Figure 1.8 Hampton Court Palace

Numerous historic buildings and places of interest have food outlets such as cafés and restaurants. Many in the UK specialise in light lunches and afternoon tea for the general public. Some are also used as venues for large private or corporate events.

Hampton Court, Kew Gardens and Poole Pottery are all categorised as visitor attractions and will usually have refreshment outlets serving a variety of food and drinks. Some, like Kew Gardens, also stage large theatrical events and concerts in the summer months.

Motorway service stations

Sometimes referred to as roadside services, motorway service stations provide a variety of services for motorists and other travellers, including fuel, car washing and maintenance facilities and convenience shops. Motorway service stations are becoming increasingly sophisticated, offering baby changing, infant and pet feeding facilities, bathrooms and showers, a variety of branded food outlets (such as Burger King and M&S Simply Food) and sometimes accommodation. The catering usually consists of food courts offering travellers a range of meals 24 hours a day, seven days a week. MOTO is an example of a company that provides motorway services nationwide.

Industrial catering

Catering for business and industry

The provision of staff dining rooms and restaurants in industrial and business settings has provided employment for many catering workers outside traditional hotel and restaurant catering. Working conditions in these settings are often very good. Apart from the main task of providing meals, these services may also include retail shops, franchise outlets and vending machines. They will also provide catering for meetings, special functions and conferences.

In some cases a 24-hour, seven-days-a-week service is necessary, but usually the hours are shorter than in other areas of the hospitality industry. Food and drink is provided for all employees, often in high-quality restaurants and dining rooms. The catering departments in these organisations are keen to retain and develop their staff, so there is good potential for training and career development in this sector.

Many industries have realised that satisfied employees work more efficiently and produce better work, so have spent a great deal of money on providing first-class kitchens and dining rooms. In some cases companies will subsidise (i.e. pay a proportion of) the cost of the meals so that employees can buy food at a price lower than it costs to produce.

Contract food service sector

The contract food service sector consists of companies that provide catering services to other organisations – a sector that has grown in recent years. Contract food service management provides food for a wide variety of people, including those working in business and industry, schools, colleges and universities, private and public healthcare establishments, public and local authorities and other non-profit making outlets such as the armed forces, police or ambulance services.

The sector includes commercial areas, such as corporate hospitality events and the executive dining rooms of many corporations, as well as special events, sporting fixtures and places of entertainment and outlets such as leisure centres, galleries, museums, department stores and DIY stores, supermarket restaurants and cafés, airports and railway stations. Some contractors provide other support services such as housekeeping and maintenance, reception, security, laundry, bars and retail shops.

Welfare catering

Public sector organisations that need catering services include hospitals, universities, colleges, schools, prisons, the armed forces, police and ambulance services, local authorities and many more.

While the aim of catering in hotels, restaurants and other areas of the leisure and travel industry (known as the **private sector**) is to make a profit, the aim of **public sector** catering is to keep costs down by working efficiently. Organisations are often working within the constraints of a given budget, known as the **cost provision**. Often companies will compete to win a contract to provide the catering for these organisations. Many public sector catering **tenders** are won by contract caterers (contract food service providers) which introduce new ideas and more commercialism (promoting business for profit) into the public sector. Because much of the public sector is now operated by profit-making contractors, it is sometimes referred to as the **secondary service sector**.

The type of menu in the public sector may be different from that in the private sector because the food offered must be suitable for the end consumers. For example, school children, hospital patients and soldiers have particular nutritional needs (they may need more energy from their food or more of particular vitamins and minerals, for example), so the menu must meet their needs. Menus may also reflect the need to keep costs down.

Prisons

Catering in prisons may be carried out by contract caterers or by the prison service itself. The food is usually prepared by prison officers and inmates. The kitchens are also used to train inmates in food production and they can gain a recognised qualification to help them to find work when they are released. In addition to catering facilities for the inmates, there are also staff catering facilities for all the personnel (staff) who work in a prison, such as administrative staff and prison officers.

Armed forces

Catering in the armed forces includes providing meals for staff in barracks, in the field and on ships. Catering for the armed forces is specialised, especially when they are in the field, and they have their own well-established cookery training programmes. However, like every other part of the public sector, the armed forces need to keep costs down and increase

Key terms

Private sector – privately owned organisations that aim to make a profit

Public or **secondary service sector** – industries where the provision of accommodation, food and beverages is not the principal business

Tender – when companies compete to win a contract

Cost provision – a budget that an organisation must work within

efficiency, so they also have competitive tendering for their catering services. The Ministry of Defence contracts food service providers to cater for many of its service operations.

National Health Service

Hospital caterers need to provide well-cooked, nutritious and appetising meals for hospital patients and must maintain strict hygiene standards. High standards of food in hospitals can contribute to the recovery of patients.

The scale of catering services in the NHS is enormous. Over 300 million meals are served each year in approximately 1,200 hospitals. NHS Trusts must ensure that they get the best value for money within their catering budget.

As well as providing nutritious meals for patients in hospital (many of whom need special diets), provision must also be made for outpatients (people who come into hospital for treatment and leave again the same day) as well as visitors and staff. This service may be provided by the hospital catering team, but is sometimes allocated to commercial food outlets, or there may be a combination of in-house hospital catering and commercial catering.

Education sector: school meals service

School meals play an important part in the lives of many children, often providing them with their only hot meal of the day. A formal school meals service was first introduced in 1879 and came under government control in 1906. In April 2001, for the first time in over 20 years, minimum nutritional standards were re-introduced by the government. These standards are designed to bring all schools up to a measurable standard set down in law. Since this date, local education authorities (LEAs) have been responsible for ensuring that the minimum nutritional standards for school lunches are met. Schools must provide a paid-for meal, where parents request one, except where children are under five years old and only go to school part time. This does not affect the LEA's or the school's duty to provide a free meal to those children who qualify for one.

Figure 1.9 Counter service

In 2006 the government announced new standards for school food, covering all food sold or served in schools (including breakfast, lunch and after-school meals) as well as tuck shops, vending machines, mid-morning break snacks and anything sold or served at after-school clubs.

Residential establishments

Residential establishments include schools, colleges, university halls of residence, nursing homes, homes for the elderly, children's homes and hostels where all the meals are provided. The food and beverages provided have to satisfy all the residents' nutritional needs, as the people eating these meals may have no other food provision. Many of these establishments cater for children who may lead energetic lives and will be growing fast, so the food must be well prepared using good ingredients as well as nutritious, varied and attractive.

Licensed trade

Licensed house (pub) catering

There are tens of thousands of licensed public houses (pubs) in the UK and almost all offer some type of food. Pub food is ideal for many people as it is usually quite simple, inexpensive and quickly served in a comfortable atmosphere. In recent times many pubs have moved into selling food, revisiting their product offer (i.e. what they have to offer the customer) and the total pub experience for their customers in order to stay in business, for example by adding restaurants, offering more bar snacks and putting on live entertainment.

Figure 1.10 A traditional public house

There is now a great variety of food available in pubs, from those that serve ham and cheese rolls to those that have exclusive à la carte restaurants.

Clubs and casinos

Private clubs are usually run by managers who are appointed by club members. People pay to become members of private clubs and what most members want from a club in Britain, particularly in the fashionable areas of London, are good food and drink, and informal service.

Most nightclubs and casinos are open to the public rather than to members only. As well as selling drinks to their customers, many now also provide food services, such as restaurants.

Transport catering

In addition to providing food and beverage operations at ports, airport terminals and railway stations, there is considerable provision for people on the move, including marine, airline and on-train services.

Ferries and cruise liners

Catering for passengers (and crew) on ferries and cruise liners is becoming increasingly important in today's competitive markets.

There are several ports in the UK where ferries leave every day, making crossings to Ireland and mainland Europe. As well as passengers and their cars, many ferries also carry freight lorries. As well as competing against each other, ferry companies also compete against airlines and, in the case of English Channel crossings, Eurostar and Eurotunnel. In order to win customers ferry companies have invested in their passenger services, with most offering several shops, bars, cafés and lounges on board. Some also have very good restaurant and leisure facilities, fast-food restaurants and branded food outlets. These may be run by contract caterers on behalf of the ferry operator. More recently, well-known chefs have become involved in providing top-quality restaurants on popular ferry routes.

Cruise ships are floating luxury hotels and people are increasingly opting for a cruise when booking their holiday. The food provision on a large cruise liner is of a similar standard

Figure 1.11 An ocean-going cruiseliner

to the food provided in a five-star hotel and is usually high-quality, banquet-style cuisine. Many shipping companies are known for the excellence of their cuisine.

As cruising becomes more popular, cruise companies are investing in increasing numbers of larger cruise liners. On cruises where the quality of the food is of paramount importance, other factors such as the dining room's ambience, refinement and elegance are also of great significance. Ship designers generally try to avoid Las Vegas-style glittery dining rooms, but also those that are too austere. Ships must be designed with easy access to the galley so waiting staff are able to serve food quickly and easily.

Dining is one of the most important selling points for cruise lines. People who take cruises want to dine well and generally they do, though cooking dinner for 800 people per sitting and giving them what they want takes skill and good management.

Many modern cruise liners are giant ships that have many different dining rooms. On such ships passengers can eat in the dining room of their choice, more or less whenever they want, at tables of various sizes, giving passengers maximum freedom.

As well as luxury liners, catering at sea includes smaller cargo and passenger ships and giant cargo tankers. The food provision for crew and passengers on these ships will vary from good restaurants and cafeterias to more industrial-style catering on tankers. On all types of ship, extra precautions have to be taken in the kitchen in rough weather.

Airline services

Air travel continues to increase and so do the opportunities and need for food services catering to the airline industry. Food provision varies greatly from airport to airport and airline to airline.

Airports offer a range of hospitality services catering for millions of people every year. They operate 24 hours a day, 365 days a year. Services include a wide variety of shops along with bars, themed restaurants, speciality restaurants, coffee bars and food courts.

In-flight catering is a specialist service provided by companies located at or near airports in the UK and around the world. The meals provided vary from snacks and basic meals to luxury meals for first-class passengers. Menus are chosen carefully to ensure the food can safely be chilled and then reheated on board the aircraft.

The price of some airline tickets includes a meal served at your seat. Budget airlines usually have an at-seat trolley service from which passengers can buy snacks and drinks.

Rail services

Snacks can be bought in the buffet car on a train and some train operators also offer a trolley service so that passengers can buy snacks from their seat. Main meals are often served in a restaurant car. However, because of a lack of space in a restaurant car kitchen and the movement of the train, it can be quite difficult to provide anything other than simple meals.

Employability in the catering and hospitality industry

Two train services run by separate companies run through the Channel tunnel. One is Eurotunnel's Le Shuttle train, which transports drivers and their vehicles between Folkestone and Calais in 35 minutes. Passengers must buy any food and drink for their journey before they board the train. Eurostar is a passenger-only service that operates between London St Pancras and Paris or Brussels. Eurostar is in direct competition with the airlines, so it provides catering to airline standards for premier and business class passengers. Meals are served by uniformed stewards in a similar service to an airline's business class. The food and beverages are included in the ticket price. Economy travellers usually buy their food separately from buffet cars or trolley services.

Outside (or outdoor) catering (ODC)

When events are held at venues where there is no catering available, or where the level of catering required is more than the caterers can manage, then a catering company may take over the management of the event. This type of catering is known as **outside catering** – in other words, a business providing services in a location that is not its own. Examples of such functions include garden parties, agricultural and horticultural shows, the opening of new buildings, banquets, parties in private houses, military pageants and tattoos, and sporting fixtures such as horse racing, motor racing, football and rugby.

There is a lot of variety in this sort of outside catering work, but standards are very high and people employed in this area need to be adaptable and creative. Sometimes specialist equipment will be required, especially for outdoor jobs, and employees need to be flexible as the work often involves a lot of travel, remote locations and outdoor venues.

Types of customer

Some sectors provide services to the general public while others provide them for restricted groups of people. It is useful to define these different types of market as follows:
- General market
  - Non-captive: customers have a full choice.
- Restricted market
  - Captive: customers have no choice, for example, welfare.
  - Semi-captive: customers have a choice before entering, for example, marine, airline, trains, some hotels and some leisure activities. Customers can choose alternatives to what is offered but, once chosen, have little choice of food and drink other than that on offer.

A general summary of the markets for different sectors is shown in Table 1.1, although the contracting out of catering and other services has blurred the division between profit- and cost-orientated establishments. Defining the market in this way helps us to understand why different methods of organisation may be in operation. For example, in captive markets customers might be asked to clear their own tables, whereas in non-captive markets this is unlikely to be successful.

Key term

Outside catering – off-premises catering

Table 1.1 Summary of sectors in the foodservice industry

Profit orientated (public or private ownership) – foodservice as main or secondary activity		Cost oriented
Restricted market	**General market**	**Restricted market**
Transport catering	Hotels/restaurants	Institutional catering
Clubs	Popular catering	Schools
Industrial (contract)	Fast food/takeaway	University and colleges
Private welfare	Retail stores	Hospitals
	Events/conferences/exhibitions	Armed forces
	Leisure attractions	Prisons
	Motorway service stations	Industrial (in-house)
	Pubs and wine bars	
	ODC (off-premises catering)	

1.3 Staffing and organisation structures

Hospitality companies need a structure for their staff in order for the business to run efficiently and effectively. Different members of staff have different jobs and roles to perform as part of the team so that the business is successful.

In smaller organisations, some employees have to become multi-skilled so that they can carry out a variety of duties. Managers may have to take on a supervisory role at certain times.

A hospitality team will consist of **operational staff**, **supervisory staff**, **management staff** and, in large organisations, senior management. These roles are explained below.

Operational staff

These are usually practical, hands-on staff and include the chefs de partie (section chefs), commis chefs, waiters, apprentices, reception staff and accommodation staff.

Supervisory staff

Supervisors oversee the work of operational staff. In some establishments the supervisors will be the managers for some of the operational staff.

Management staff

Managers are responsible for making sure the operation runs smoothly and within budget. They are accountable to the owners to make sure that the products and services on offer are what the customer expects and wants, and to provide value for money. Managers may also be responsible for future planning for the business. They will be required to make sure that all the health and safety policies are in place and that health and safety legislation is followed. In smaller establishments they may also act as the human resources manager.

A hotel will normally have a manager, assistant manager(s), an accommodation manager, a restaurant manager and a reception manager. Within each section of the hotel there could be a manager with departmental responsibilities – a head chef is a manager, for example.

> **Key terms**
>
> **Operational staff** – practical, hands-on staff, including chefs de partie, section chefs, commis chefs, waiters, apprentices, reception staff and accommodation staff
>
> **Supervisory staff** – oversee the work of operational staff
>
> **Management staff** – responsible for making sure the operation runs smoothly and within budget and may be responsible for future planning. Examples are head chef, restaurant manager and reception manager

Employability in the catering and hospitality industry

1.4 Food and beverage service job roles

Figure 1.12 shows a typical organisation chart for a hotel and identifies various food and beverage job roles. Food and beverage operations not within hotels often have a similar type of organisation, although different terminology may be used for the various job roles depending on the type of establishment. Various job roles in food and beverage service are described below. In smaller operations some of these job roles may be combined.

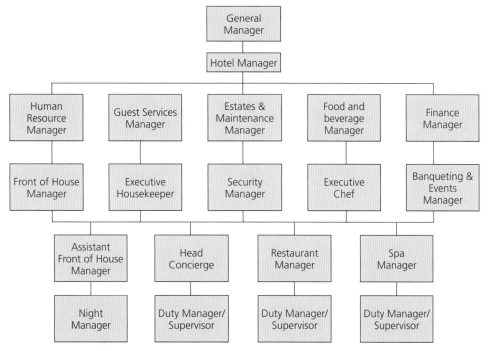

Figure 1.12 Staffing structure of a four-star spa hotel

Food and beverage manager

Depending on the size of the establishment, the food and beverage manager may be responsible simply for implementing agreed policies or they may play a part in determining the organisation's food and beverage policies. The larger the organisation, the less likely the manager is to be involved in policy setting. In general, food and beverage managers are responsible for:

- ensuring that each food and beverage service area makes the required profit
- updating and compiling new wine lists according to availability of stock, current trends and customer needs
- compiling, with the kitchen, menus for the various food service areas and for special occasions
- purchasing all materials, both food and drink
- ensuring that quality in relation to the price paid is maintained
- determining portion size in relation to selling price
- ensuring staff training, sales promotions and maintenance of the highest professional standards
- employing and dismissing staff
- holding regular meetings with section heads to ensure all areas are working effectively, efficiently and are well coordinated.

Food production roles

Head chef/maître chef de cuisine

The head chef has overall responsibility for the organisation and administration of the food production operation. He or she is responsible for managing the food production team, often called a kitchen brigade. The head chef is also responsible for menu planning and development, overseeing sourcing of produce, and setting and maintaining standards for the operation.

Second chef/sous-chef de cuisine

The sous-chef is the second in command to the chef de cuisine and will act as head chef when the head is off duty. The sous-chef may also cover for or assist a chef de partie when required. They often have responsibilities for staff training and staff rotas as well as overseeing stock control. Smaller operations may not employ a sous-chef, while larger operations may have more than one.

Chef de partie/section chef

A chef de partie is also known as a section chef and is usually in charge of a specific area of food production, such as fish, vegetables, roasts, sweets or the larder. In larger kitchens, each chef de partie might have several cooks and/or assistants working with him or her.

Commis chef

A commis is a junior chef who works under a chef de partie in order to gain experience in the section's work. It is common for commis chefs to work in a number of sections as part of their training.

Kitchen assistants

There are often two types of kitchen assistants. Kitchen hands assist with basic food preparation tasks under the section chef's direction. Stewards work in the scullery and carry out washing up and general cleaning duties. In smaller kitchen operations these two duties are often combined.

Food and beverage service roles

Restaurant manager/supervisor

The restaurant manager or supervisor has overall responsibility for the organisation and administration of particular food and beverage service areas. These may include the lounges, room service (in hotels), restaurants and possibly some of the private function suites. The restaurant manager sets the standards for service and is responsible for any staff training that may be required, either on or off the job. They may make out duty rotas, holiday lists and hours on and off duty, and contribute to operational duties (depending on the size of the establishment) so that all the service areas run efficiently and smoothly.

Reception head waiter/receptionist

The reception head waiter or receptionist is responsible for accepting any bookings and for keeping the booking diary up to date. They will take reservations and work with the head waiter to allocate reservations to particular stations. The reception head waiter or receptionist greets customers on arrival and takes them to the table and seats them.

Head waiter/maître d'hôtel/supervisor

The head waiter has overall charge of the staff team and is responsible for ensuring that all the pre-preparation duties necessary for service are carried out efficiently. The head waiter will aid the reception head waiter during service and may take some orders if the station waiter is busy. The head waiter also helps to compile duty rotas and holiday lists and may relieve the restaurant manager or reception head waiter on their days off.

Station head waiter/section supervisor/service captain

For larger establishments the restaurant area is broken down into sections. The station head waiter has overall responsibility for a team of staff serving a number of stations within a section of the restaurant area. Each of the sets of tables (which may range from four to eight in number) within a section of the restaurant area is called a station. The station head waiter will also assist in taking food and beverage orders and with the service if required.

Station waiter/chef de rang

The chef de rang or station waiter provides service to one set of tables (a station) within the restaurant area. The station waiter will take food and beverage orders and carry out service at the table with the help of the demi-chef de rang.

Assistant station waiter/demi-chef de rang

The assistant station waiter or demi-chef de rang is the person next in seniority to the station waiter and assists as directed by the station waiter.

Waiter/server/commis de rang

The waiter or commis de rang acts on instructions from the chef de rang. They mainly fetch and carry, and may do some of the service of either vegetables or sauces, offer rolls, place plates upon the table and so on, as well as help to clear the table after each course. During the pre-preparation period much of the cleaning and preparatory tasks will be carried out by the commis de rang.

Trainee commis/debarrasseur/apprentice

The trainee commis or debarrasseur is an apprentice or learner who has joined the food and beverage service staff and who wishes to take up food service as a career. The debarrasseur will carry out many of the tasks during the pre-preparation periods. During service this person will keep the sideboard well stocked with equipment and may help to fetch and carry items as required for the bar or kitchen. As they develop their skills they will begin to assist with service at the table.

Carver/trancheur

The carver or trancheur is responsible for the carving trolley and the carving of joints at the table as required. The carver will plate up each portion and serve with accompaniments as appropriate.

Floor or room service staff/chef d'étage/floor or room waiter

The floor or room service staff are often responsible for a complete floor in an establishment or, depending on the size of the establishment, a number of rooms or suites. Room service of all meals and beverages throughout the day is normally only offered by a first-class establishment. In smaller establishments room service may be limited to early morning teas and breakfasts with the provision of in-room mini bars and tea and coffee facilities.

Lounge staff/chef de sale

Lounge service staff may be employed only for lounge service within larger establishments. In a smaller establishment it is usual for members of the food service staff to take over these duties on a rota basis. The lounge staff are responsible for the service of morning coffee, afternoon teas, apéritifs and liqueurs before and after both lunch and dinner, and any coffee required after meals. They are responsible for setting up the lounge in the morning and maintaining its cleanliness and presentation throughout the day.

Wine butler/wine waiter/sommelier

The sommelier is responsible for serving alcoholic and non-alcoholic bar drinks during the service of meals. The sommelier must also be a good sales person. This employee should have a thorough knowledge of all drink to be served, of the best wines and drinks to go with certain foods, and of the liquor licensing laws in respect of the particular establishment and area.

Bar staff/bartender/mixologist

The staff working within bar areas must be responsible and competent in preparing and serving a variety of wine, drinks and cocktails. They should have a thorough knowledge of all alcoholic and non-alcoholic drinks offered by the establishment, the ingredients necessary for making cocktails, and understand the requirements of the liquor licensing laws to ensure legal compliance.

Mixology is the art of making mixed drinks and a mixologist is an employee who mixes and serves alcoholic beverages at a bar. The name is often used for people who specialise in creating new mixed drinks. It can also refer to a person who makes cocktails, a cocktail bar person or simply a bartender.

Barista

The word *barista* is of Italian origin. In Italian, a barista is a male or female bartender who typically works behind a counter, serving both hot and cold beverages as well as alcoholic beverages. Barista does not mean specifically a coffee maker, although it is now often used as such. The plural in English is baristas.

Buffet assistant/buffet chef/chef de buffet

The chef de buffet is in charge of the buffet in the room including its presentation and service, and the carving and portioning of food. This staff member will normally be a member of the kitchen team.

Cashier

The cashier is responsible for billing and taking payments or making ledger account entries for a food and beverage operation. This may include making up bills from food and drink checks or, in a cafeteria for example, charging customers for their selection of items on a tray.

Counter assistants

Counter assistants are found in cafeterias where they will stock the counter and sometimes serve or portion food for customers. Duties may include some cooking of call order items.

Table clearers

Table clearers can be found in seating areas where there is no waiter service. They are responsible for clearing tables using trolleys specially designed for the stacking of crockery, glassware, cutlery, etc.

Function catering/banqueting staff/events staff

In establishments with function catering facilities there will normally be a number of permanent staff. These will include the banqueting and conferencing manager, one or two assistant managers, one or two head waiters, a dispense person and a secretary to the banqueting and conferencing manager. All other banqueting, conferencing and events staff are normally engaged as required on a casual basis. In small establishments, where there are fewer events, the manager, assistant manager and head waiter will undertake the necessary administrative and organisational work.

Staffing requirements

Staffing requirements vary for a number of reasons. Table 1.2 shows the types of food and beverage staff that might be found in different types of foodservice operation.

Table 1.2 Examples of staffing requirements for different types of foodservice operation

Medium class hotel	Cafeteria
Hotel manager	Catering manager
Assistant manager	Supervisors
Head waiter	Assistant supervisors
Waiters	Counter service hands
Wine waiter	Clearers
Cashier	Cashier
Popular price restaurant	**Industrial foodservice/welfare catering**
Restaurant manager/supervisor	Catering manager
Waiting staff	Assistant catering manager
Dispense bar assistant	Supervisors
	Assistant supervisors
	Waiter
	Steward/butler
	Counter service staff
	Clearers
	Cashiers

1.5 Employment in the hospitality industry

Working in the food and beverage industry requires a variety of skills and knowledge. It is also important to be aware of the characteristics of working in the industry:

- working in shifts that start at different times of the day, and in some operations, throughout the night
- working on a part-time or full-time basis
- working on fixed-term contracts to cover a specific period when the operation is busy or to replace staff who are on holiday

Sources of information

Information on jobs in the industry can be found in trade magazines and websites such as:

- *Caterer and Hotelkeeper* (www.catererandhotelkeeper.co.uk)
- Caterersearch – www.onrec.com/directory/job-boards/caterersearch
- *Restaurant* (www.william-reed.com/markets-products/hospitality/restaurant-magazine)
- Imbibe (www.imbibe.com)
- advice can also be found from agencies such as Springboard UK Ltd (www.springboard.uk.net).

Legal requirements

Those employed in the hospitality industry are covered by a considerable amount of legislation that regulates both the industry itself and employment in the industry. Employers face stiff penalties if they contravene (break) the law or attempt to undermine the statutory (legal) rights of their workers, for example, by paying less than the national minimum wage or denying them their right to paid annual holidays. Penalties include prosecution and fines and the employer could be ordered by a tribunal or the court system to pay substantial amounts of compensation to their employee.

Both employers and employees have employment rights.

Employer responsibilities

Employers must provide each employee with:

- a detailed job description (see Figure 1.13)
- a contract of employment that gives details of the job itself, working hours, the amount of annual holiday the employee will have and the required notice period.

An essential feature of a contract of employment is the **mutuality of obligation**. This means that the employer will provide the employee with work on specified days of the week for specified hours and, if employed under a limited term contract, for an agreed number of weeks or months. In return, the employee agrees to carry out the work for an agreed wage or salary.

Employers must adhere to laws relating to employment of staff, health and safety, and food safety.

> **Key term**
>
> **Mutuality of obligation** – employer and employee have specific rights and responsibilities

Employee responsibilities

Employees must:

- work in the way that has been agreed to in their contract and job description
- follow all the organisation's policies and practices.

Workers and employees

An **employee** is a person who is employed directly by a company under a contract of employment or service.

A **worker** is someone who works for another company (a **sub-contractor**) that has won a contract to carry out work or provide services, i.e. they are not actually an employee of the company itself.

Workers who are not employees are still protected by the following legislation:

- Health and Safety at Work Act (1974) and other safety legislation
- Working Time Regulations (1998)
- anti-discriminatory laws such as the Sex Discrimination Act (1986) and Equal Pay Act (1970)
- Public Interest Disclosure Act (1998)
- National Minimum Wage Act (1998)
- Part-time Workers (Prevention of Less Favourable Treatment) Regulations (2000).

> **Key terms**
>
> **Employee** – a person who works for the organisation
>
> **Worker** – someone who works within the organisation but is employed by another company
>
> **Sub-contractor** – a company or person who carries out work on behalf of the company

Statutory sick pay

Employers in the UK are liable to pay up to 28 weeks' statutory sick pay to any qualified employee who is unable to work because of illness or injury. Employers who operate their own occupational sick pay schemes may opt out of the statutory sick pay scheme, as long as the payments available to their employees under such schemes are equal to or greater than payments they would be entitled to under statutory sick pay, and so long as these employees are not required to contribute towards the cost of funding such a scheme. Payments made under statutory sick pay may be offset against contractual sick pay and vice versa.

JOB DESCRIPTION

Title of job: Restaurant waiter

Purpose of job: To provide a quality food and beverage service to meet our customers' expectations and to enhance and maintain the reputation of the company.

Reporting to: Restaurant supervisor

Skills, experience and qualifications required:

- Good communication, presentation, time management and social skills
- One year's similar experience
- Wine knowledge useful but not essential as training will be given
- Current Food Handler's Certificate desirable but full training will be provided

Main duties:

- Preparation of the restaurant area ready for service in accordance with the establishment daily duties list.
- Service of food and beverages to customers in accordance with the service specification.
- Ensuring correct charges are made and payment received.
- Clearing of restaurant area in accordance with service specification.
- Ensuring compliance with control procedures for equipment and other stock.
- Following correct health and safety procedures to ensure welfare of both staff and customers.
- Explaining to customers the content, preparation and presentation of all menu and beverage items, and promoting sales through positive selling techniques.
- Additional food and beverage service duties as required in order to meet business demands.

Training requirements

- Induction and company policy as contained in the Staff Handbook
- Menu and beverage list content and updates as required
- Customer care programme
- Basic food hygiene
- Basic fire training at induction and further training every six months
- Basic health and safety at induction and full COSHH every six months
- Manual handling at induction

Performance measures

- Customer feedback
- Management feedback
- Regular knowledge test on foods, wine and other services offered
- Six-monthly appraisals with restaurant supervisor

Figure 1.13 Example of a job description

Working Time Regulations

The Working Time Regulations apply not only to employees but to every worker (part-time, temporary, seasonal or casual) who undertakes to do work or carry out a service for an employer and relate to a worker's statutory rights to rest breaks, rest periods and paid annual holidays. The 1998 Regulations are policed and enforced by employment tribunals and by local authority environmental health officers.

Further information on employment rights and responsibilities is given in Section 2.7, page 44.

1.6 Key factors for success in food and beverage service

Food and beverage service is the essential link between customers and the menu on offer in an establishment. The server is the main point of contact between customers and the establishment and therefore plays an important role. The skills and knowledge of food and beverage service are transferable between establishments, sectors and throughout the world.

To be successful in food and beverage service members of staff must have:

- sound product knowledge
- well-developed interpersonal skills
- a range of technical skills
- an ability to work as part of a team.

Professional and hygienic appearance

How staff look and the first impression they create are a reflection of the hygiene standards of the establishment and the quality of service to come. All staff should be aware of the factors listed below and it is their individual responsibility to ensure that these are practiced in the workplace.

Figure 1.14 Waiter in uniform

- Staff should be clean and use subtle-smelling deodorants.
- Staff should ensure they have sufficient sleep, an adequate and healthy intake of food and regular exercise to maintain good health and the ability to cope with the pressures and stress of work.
- Hands must always be clean, free from nicotine stains, with clean, well-trimmed nails. Hands must be washed immediately after using the toilet, smoking or dealing with refuse.

- Teeth should be brushed immediately before coming on duty and the breath should be fresh smelling.
- Men should normally be clean-shaven or with moustache or beard neatly trimmed.
- Women should only wear light make-up. If nail varnish is worn then it should be clear.
- Earrings should not be worn, with the possible exception of studs/sleepers.
- Uniforms must be clean, starched as appropriate, neatly pressed and in good repair. All buttons must be present.
- Hair must be clean and well groomed. Long hair should be tied up or back to avoid hair falling into food and drink and to avoid repeated handling of the hair.
- Shoes must be comfortable and clean, and of a plain, neat design. Fashion is less important than safety and comfort.
- Cuts and burns must be covered with waterproof dressings.
- If a member of staff is suffering from a cold or other possible infections this must be reported immediately.
- Staff should try to avoid any mannerisms they may have, such as running their fingers through their hair, chewing gum or scratching their face.
- Excessive jewellery should not be worn – the establishment policy should be followed.

Knowledge of food and beverages and technical ability

Staff must have sufficient knowledge of all the items on the menu and wine and drink lists in order to advise and offer suggestions to customers. They must also know how to serve correctly each dish on the menu, what its accompaniments are, the correct cover, the make-up of the dish and its garnish. For beverage service, staff should know how to serve various types of wine and drink, in the correct containers (e.g. glasses, cups) and at the right temperature.

Punctuality

Punctuality is very important. Staff that are continually late on duty show a lack of interest in their work and a lack of respect for both management and customers.

Local knowledge

Staff should have a reasonable knowledge of the local area in which they work so they may be able to advise guests on the various forms of entertainment offered, the best means of transport to places of interest, local transport, parking and so on.

Personality

Staff must be tactful, courteous, good humoured and of an even temper. They must converse with customers in a pleasing and well-spoken manner, and the ability to smile at the right time is helpful.

Cultural awareness

The range of customers that may use specific operations is increasing in their cultural diversity. This is reflected in factors such as language, dress and traditions, which also include dietary requirements based on specific religious following (see Section 8.2, page 126 for more information on specific dietary needs). Members of service staff need to be open-minded, non-judgemental and flexible, and also to be able to appreciate and communicate respect for other people's ways, backgrounds, values and beliefs.

Attitude to customers

The correct approach to the customer is of the utmost importance. Staff should be able to anticipate the customer's needs and wishes without being servile. During service a careful watch must be kept on customers to check the progress of the meal; this allows service staff to anticipate customer needs with minimal intrusion.

Memory

A good memory is an asset to food and beverage service staff. It may help them in various ways in their work if they know the likes and dislikes of regular customers, where they like to sit in the food service area, what are their favourite drinks, and so on.

Honesty

Trust and respect among staff, customers and management leads to an atmosphere at work that encourages efficiency and a good team spirit.

Loyalty

The obligations and loyalty of staff are first to the establishment in which they are employed and its management.

Conduct

Staff conduct should be impeccable at all times, especially in front of customers. The rules and regulations of an establishment must be followed and respect shown to all senior members of staff.

Sales ability

All members of staff reflect the image of the establishment. They are sales people and must therefore have a complete knowledge of all forms of food and drink and their correct service, and so be able to contribute to personal selling and merchandising.

Sense of urgency

In order for an establishment to be profitable and generate the maximum amount of business over the service period, staff must develop a sense of urgency in their work.

Complaints

Staff should never show their displeasure, even during a difficult situation. Staff should never argue with a customer and, if they are unable to resolve a situation, they should refer immediately to a senior member of the team. They should be able to reassure the customer and put right any fault, as loss of time in dealing with complaints only makes the situation worse.

1.7 Importance of teamwork

Figure 1.15 Staff working as a team

Staff must be able to work as part of a team, both within and between departments. The people in a team depend on each other to be successful and, as a member of the food and beverage department, you will need to be able to work as part of a team. Each team will have targets and deadlines and in order to meet these there must be good communication and planning within the team. All members of the team need to understand what deadlines and targets have been set and what is expected of them.

It is also important that you:
- do your job in a professional way
- are punctual for work
- inform your employer, ideally your line manager, if you are ill
- are reliable and courteous because other people depend on you; if one person is away, it puts pressure on the other members of staff and, in some cases, temporary staff may have to be employed as cover
- manage your time and deadlines well and be able to prioritise – food has to be served on time; breakfast, lunch and dinner must be ready when the customer is ready.

Understanding yourself

In order to be a good employee it is important that you try to understand yourself. To do this, ask yourself the following questions:
- What am I capable of doing?
- What development do I need to help the team and myself?
- What are my strengths?
- What are my weaknesses?
- Do I know when to ask for help?
- What training do I need? For example, do I wish to improve my:
  - culinary skills
  - writing skills
  - IT skills
  - equipment skills?

Communication

Listening

Everyone in the team should be working towards the same goals and targets. Listening is an important part of effective communication. You should learn to listen carefully and to understand facial expressions, gestures and body language. Good listeners:
- avoid distractions
- concentrate on what is being said
- think about what is being said
- show interest in the person speaking and do not look bored

- maintain eye contact with the person talking and acknowledge what is being said
- ask sensible questions if necessary
- summarise what has been said in their own words to check they understand what they have been told.

It is important to be an active listener. Show the person you are listening to that you are interested in what they are saying by maintaining eye contact and responding to what they say. Listen before you form your own opinion.

Non-verbal communication

Communication can also be non-verbal, in other words, unspoken. It is important to understand other people's body language. Body language refers to such things as:

- posture
- how close a person stands to another person
- facial expressions
- hand movements and gestures
- eye contact.

Body language is often unconscious and can tell us what people really think and feel. If someone is telling a lie, for instance, their body language will usually give them away because they may be unable to maintain eye contact. By focusing on other people's body language, you can discover their true feelings about you, and how they are reacting to what you are saying. Think about how you approach people and what body language you use. Everyone uses body language, but it can mean different things in different cultures and to different people.

Signs and meanings

Some gestures are open and positive. For example, leaning forwards with the palms of your hands open and facing upwards shows interest, acceptance and a welcoming attitude. On the other hand, leaning backwards, with your arms folded and head down might show that you are feeling closed, uninterested, defensive and negative or rejected.

If someone uses plenty of gestures this may indicate that they are warm, enthusiastic and emotional. If someone does not use many gestures this may indicate that they are cold, reserved and logical.

However, a gesture does not always reveal exactly what a person is thinking. For example, if someone has his or her arms folded this may mean that:

- they are being defensive about something
- they are cold
- they are comfortable.

Barriers to effective communication

In order to communicate effectively:

- speak clearly and slowly
- remember that not speaking the same language can cause difficulties
- avoid using too much unfamiliar terminology and jargon
- speak clearly and slowly to those who have a hearing impairment, as they may be able to lip read
- read through any letters or emails you write to check for grammar and spelling mistakes; if possible use a word processing program and use the grammar and spellchecker.

Try to be confident when you are communicating with other people.

Working with colleagues

It is important to develop good working relationships with your colleagues, work as a team and be supportive of each other. Seek guidance from other team members and your line manager in order to identify suitable role models.

Usually there will be a work plan developed for the day and for the week. Your manager will discuss duty rotas and work schedules with team members to determine who will be covering what duties. The manager will also discuss targets and required outcomes with team members and will be responsible for evaluating your performance and the team's performance. This may be done informally, perhaps through a social occasion by meeting for a drink after work, or formally through a team meeting. Within your own establishment, you should be able to identify how both your performance and that of your team is being monitored and measured.

1.8 Qualifications and training

The hospitality industry provides many opportunities to learn because of its complexity and diversity. There are many different sectors, trends and themes, and there are new developments in training all the time.

Qualifications show that a person has studied a subject successfully and a certificate is usually awarded as proof of the qualification. Successfully achieving a qualification usually involves some sort of assessment, either in the form of examinations, coursework or observation by an assessor, or a combination of these things. The assessor decides whether the student had learned what they were supposed to and whether they have performed the skills to the required standard. Courses without assessment are not viewed very highly by potential employers.

Qualifications inform employers of what you should be able to do. They indicate to the employer whether you have the skills required to do the job. Qualifications differ all over the world and it is often difficult to make comparisons between qualifications in different countries.

Even in the UK there are many different qualifications and that is why some employers ask job applicants to do a practical test before they have an interview. Some employers ask chef applicants to do a trial day or more of work.

Despite this it is important to obtain qualifications as they increase your career prospects and opportunities for personal development. Qualifications also help to boost confidence and self-esteem. There are a number of college-based courses that will help you to develop a range of practical and theoretical skills such as numeracy, language and information technology.

A number of qualifications are described below.

National Vocational Qualification/Scottish Vocational Qualification (NVQ/SVQ)

NVQs and SVQs are work-related, competence-based qualifications that include work experience. There are no age limits or minimum entry requirements. Assessment is normally through on-the-job observation and questioning. Levels for both qualifications range from 1 to 5.

Other vocational qualifications

There is a range of Vocationally Relevant Qualifications (VRQ). These include certificates and diplomas such as the City & Guilds Professional Food and Beverage Service.

BTEC qualifications are work-related. They offer a mix of theory and practice and can include work experience. Qualifications offered by colleges and universities are at different levels, have different entry requirements and can be taken as full-time or part-time courses. BTEC qualifications also include the Higher National Certificate and Higher National Diploma (HNC and HND). Again, these can be taken as a full-time or part-time course.

Apprenticeships

Apprenticeships are a way to learn skills within a workplace setting while also getting a qualification. An apprenticeship can be through a day-release course at college or may be completely work based, where an assessor monitors the apprentice's learning and development. Apprenticeships are available at different levels, with the higher apprenticeships being equivalent to a degree.

Degrees

A foundation degree is designed to give you the skills and knowledge that can lead directly to employment or be part of a route into higher education. It is roughly equivalent to the first two years of an honours degree. You can learn via distance learning, in the workplace or online.

An undergraduate degree (also known as a bachelor's degree, an ordinary or first degree) is an academic qualification that usually takes three or four years to complete full time. This is normally four years if you're doing a sandwich course, which includes a year in industry or abroad. You can also study part time or through flexible learning.

Whichever type of learning you choose, it is important to understand that learning is for life. In order to ensure that you have a job throughout your life you must continue to learn and develop your skills. You can improve your knowledge by reading hospitality journals, books and food magazines, and by searching the internet for food sites. Electronic learning (using CDs, DVDs and the internet) can help you to learn in the way that suits you best and to work at your own pace, testing yourself when you are ready.

Assessment helps you to understand what you have achieved and what you must do to improve and provides the building blocks for further learning and achievement.

An important source of information on routes to employment and qualifications can be found on the Hospitality Guild website: www.hospitalityguild.co.uk/A-Career-in-Hospitality.

1 Name three sectors of the hospitality industry in:
   (a) the private sector
   (b) the public or secondary service sector.
2 Name two types of hotels.
3 As well as accommodation, food and beverages, hotels now offer an increasing range of services and facilities. Name three of these services and facilities.
4 What are the four key requirements of food and beverage service staff?
5 Why is it important to present a professional personal appearance?
6 List two attributes that would be helpful when dealing with customers.
7 What is the main reason for having neat, tidy hair that is tied back?
8 Describe what is meant by body language.
9 State one reason why it is important to work well in a team in the hospitality industry.
10 Identify three principles for handling customer complaints.

In practice

Job search

Using either trade magazines or the internet, identify two job advertisements for one specific type of job – such as a waiter or barperson. Compare the two advertisements in terms of:

- Sector of the industry
- Type of establishment
- Location
- Key responsibilities
- Working patterns
- Salary
- Other benefits

In practice

Visiting and gathering information on two local food and beverage outlets

When working in a food and beverage environment it is important that you have an awareness of what is happening within other operations around you. This helps you to monitor trends and understand changes in prices, food and beverages on offer and the type of customer using the operations, etc.

1 Copy the template below and visit and collect information about two different types of food and beverage (or foodservice) operation. These could be within the building you are currently in.

2 Identify the key similarities and differences between the operations.

Name of establishment:	....	....
Which type of sector of the industry is the operation in? (*Profit orientated or cost provision*)		
What type of market is it aimed at? (*Captive, semi-captive or non-captive*)		
What type of food and beverage is provided?		
What is the type of food and beverage service is offered? (*Fast food, takeaway, table service, self-service*)		
What is the cheapest item on the menu?		
What is the cheapest item on the beverage list?		
What is the most expensive item on the menu?		
Briefly describe how these establishments are staffed		
Briefly describe the uniforms		
Briefly describe the décor and furnishings		

Developing skills for employment

2

Units covered

This chapter covers the following units:

Level 2

→ Developing skills for employment in the catering and hospitality industry (214)

→ Give customers a positive impression of self and your organisation (2GEN1, 201)

→ Employment rights and responsibilities in the hospitality, leisure, travel and tourism sector (PERR, 666)

2.1 The catering and hospitality industry

Travel, tourism and hospitality together make up the world's largest industry. According to the World Travel and Tourism Council (WTTC), the annual gross output of the industry is greater than the gross national product (GNP) of all countries except the USA and Japan. Worldwide, the industry employs over 112 million people. In many countries, especially in emerging tourist destinations, the hospitality and tourism industry plays a very important role in the national economy, being the major foreign currency earner.

The globalisation of the hospitality and tourism industries has advanced under the pressures of increased technology, communication, transportation, deregulation, elimination of political barriers, socio-cultural changes and global economic development, together with growing competition in a global economy. An international hospitality company must perform successfully in the *world's* business environment.

Figure 2.1 An increase in international travel will affect hospitality and tourism

As the world's economies continue to become increasingly interdependent, the amount of business travel, too. With this in mind, it is clear that the global economic environment plays a significant role in the internationalisation opportunities available to hospitality and tourism companies, and that global economic policies and developments play a critical role in the hospitality and tourism industry.

2.2 Key influences on the hospitality industry

The key influences affecting the hospitality industry can be summarised using the **PESTLE** model, which is widely used by businesses to classify potential influences on the future of the business.

- **Political** influences might include issues such as the availability of grants and food and drink subsidies for specific government initiatives.
- **Economic** influences might include exchange rates (because they affect tourism), the availability of credit, and inflation and taxation.
- **Social** issues might concern changing market needs, social/lifestyle trends, **demographic changes**, levels of disposable income and changing patterns of employment. It also includes cultural factors – people using hospitality to celebrate occasions such as birthdays, weddings, etc., and the increasing influence of the media through television, advertising, magazines and celebrity chefs.
- **Technological** issues might concern advances in cooking and service methods as well as improvements in efficiency of plant and premises, together with advances in information technology, channels of distribution (how a business communicates with its customers) and data and information gathering.
- **Legal** issues might mean changes in legislation, such as hygiene and food safety, opening hours, employment contracts and responsibilities, trade descriptions, licensing, taxation and level of VAT.
- **Ecological** might mean the increasing requirements for energy conservation, ensuring the maintenance of **social responsibility** policies or the acceptability (or otherwise) of irradiation and genetically modified (GM) foods.

Key terms

PESTLE – stands for Political, Economic, Sociological, Technological, Legal and Ecological. A model used to classify influences on a business

Demographic changes – differing patterns of population statistics

Social responsibility – concerns about sustainability and the environment

2.3 Size and scope of the UK hospitality industry

The UK hospitality industry employs around 1.7 million people and is growing all the time. The industry provides excellent opportunities for training and employment.

Like all leisure markets, hospitality and catering benefits from improving economic conditions. For many people, real disposable income has grown over the last 20 years, and forecasts suggest that it will continue to grow. In wealthy markets, the leisure and pleasure sectors generally outperform the economy. As people become wealthier, their extra income tends to be spent on pleasure and luxury items. However, whenever there is a downturn in the economy, the leisure sectors suffer disproportionately.

The UK leisure sector includes hospitality as well as travel and tourism, and it employs in the region of 2 million people. Around 7 per cent of all jobs in the UK are in the leisure sector or, to put it another way, the sector accounts for about one in every 14 UK jobs. It is worth about £85 billion to the UK economy and approximately £7.5 billion is spent on accommodation.

There are approximately 181,500 hospitality, leisure, travel and tourism businesses in the UK (Table 2.1). The restaurant industry is the largest within the sector (both in terms of the number of outlets and size of the workforce), followed by pubs, bars and nightclubs and the hotel industry.

Table 2.1 Number of businesses (enterprises) by industry sector (2012)

Industry	Number of businesses	%
Restaurants	75,600	42
Pubs, bars and nightclubs	52,000	29
Hotels	12,400	7
Gambling	11,600	6
Travel and tourist services	6,750	5
Food and service management (contract catering)	6,350	4
Self-catering accommodation, holiday parks and hostels	3,800	2
Events	3,500	2
Tourist services	1,400	1
Visitor attractions	500	>1
Total discounting events and tourists services	176,600	100
Hospitality, leisure, travel and tourism total (inclusive)	181,500	

Source: *Inter-departmental Business Register, 2008–2012*, Office for National Statistics

As measured by the number of employees, the hospitality and tourism sector is predominately made up of small businesses; almost half (46 per cent) employ fewer than five people (see Figure 2.2). In contrast, only 1 per cent of businesses employ 100 people or more.

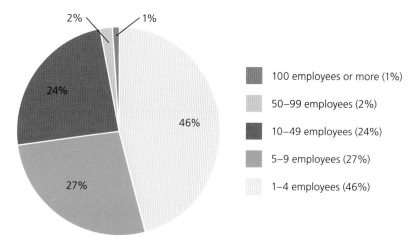

2% 1%

24%

46%

27%

- 100 employees or more (1%)
- 50–99 employees (2%)
- 10–49 employees (24%)
- 5–9 employees (27%)
- 1–4 employees (46%)

Figure 2.2 Hospitality, tourism and leisure business by size (2012).
Source: *State of the Nation Report 2013*, Hospitality Guild

Developing skills for employment

Hotels, restaurants, bars, pubs and clubs are all part of the **commercial sector**. Businesses in the commercial sector need to make a profit so that the business can survive and grow.

Catering provided in places like hospitals, schools, colleges, prisons and the armed services also provides thousands of meals each day. This sort of catering is part of the **public sector** (also known as the secondary service sector). Businesses in the public sector do not need to make a profit but do work within set targets and are often called **cost-provision sectors**, although many catering services in the public sector are now run by profit-making contract caterers.

Figure 2.3 Commercial sector

Despite its complexity, catering represents one of the largest sectors of the UK economy and is fifth in size behind retail food, cars, insurance and clothing. It is also an essential support to tourism, another major part of the economy, and one of the largest employers in the UK.

Types of business

There are three main types of business: **small to medium-sized business enterprises (SMEs)**, **public limited companies** and **private companies**.

SMEs

These have up to 250 employees. In the UK as a whole, SMEs account for over half of all employment (58.7 per cent). SMEs are usually private companies that may become public limited companies if they become very large.

Public limited companies and private companies

The key difference between public and private companies is that a public company can sell its shares to the public, while private companies cannot. A share is a certificate representing one unit of ownership in a company, so the more shares a person has the more of the company they own.

Before it can start in business or borrow money, a public company must prove to Companies House (the department where all companies in the UK must be registered) that at least £50,000 worth of shares have been issued and that each share has been paid up to at least a quarter of its nominal value (so 25 per cent of £50,000). It will then receive authorisation to start business and borrow money.

Other types of business

The types of business in operation in the catering and hospitality industry can be further divided into sole traders, self-employed, partnership and limited liability companies. These are usually private companies.

Sole trader

A **sole trader** is the simplest form of setting up and running a business and is really only suitable for the smallest of businesses. The sole trader owns the business, takes all the risks, is liable for any losses and keeps any profits. The advantage of operating in business as a sole trader is that very little formality is needed. The only official records required are those for HM Revenue and Customs (HMRC), National Insurance and VAT. The accounts are not available to the public.

Self-employed

There is no precise definition of self-employment, although HMRC offers further guidance. It is important to note that a simple agreement with an individual that he or she is regarded as self-employed is insufficient for the purposes of HMRC.

In order to determine whether an individual is truly self-employed, the whole circumstances of his or her work must be considered. This may include whether the individual:

- is in control of their own time, the amount of work they take on and the decision making
- has no guarantee of regular work
- receives no pay for periods of holiday or sickness
- is responsible for all the risks of the business
- attends the premises of the person giving them work
- generally uses their own equipment and materials
- has the right to send someone else to do the work.

Partnership

A **partnership** consists of two or more people working together as the proprietors of a business. Unlike limited liability companies (see below), there are no legal requirements in setting up as a partnership. A partnership can be set up without the partners necessarily being fully aware that they have done so.

A partnership is similar to a sole trader in law, in that the partners own the business, take all the risks, stand any losses and keep any profits. Each partner individually is responsible for all the debts of the partnership. This means that if the business fails, each partner's personal assets are fully at risk. It is possible, though not very common, to have partners with limited liability. In this case, the partner with limited liability must not play any active part in the management or conduct of the business. In effect, he or she has merely invested a limited sum of money in the partnership.

The advantages of operating a business as a partnership can be very similar to those of the sole trader. Little formality is needed, although those contemplating entering into a partnership should consider taking legal advice and having a partnership agreement drawn up.

The main official records that are required are records for HMRC, National Insurance and VAT. The accounts are not available to the public. There may be important tax advantages, too, when compared with a limited company. For example, partners might be able to pay the tax they owe at a later date or treat deductible expenses more generously. These are business expenses that can be claimed against tax, in other words taken away from the business's income so the amount of money taxed is less, which means the amount of tax owed is less.

Limited liability companies

Limited liability companies are incorporated under the Companies Act. This means that the liability of their owners (the amount they will have to pay to cover the business's debts if it fails or is sued) is limited to the value of the shares each shareholder (owner) owns.

Limited liability companies are much more complex than sole traders and partnerships because the owners can limit their liability. As a consequence, it is vital that people investing in them or doing business with them are aware of the financial standing of the company. Company documents are open to inspection by the public. These documents are the memorandum of association and the articles of association (the Constitution):

- The Memorandum of Association: this is the 'outer face' of the company, informing the outside world of its name and purpose.
- The Articles of Association: this is the 'inner face' of the company and is concerned with the detailed conduct of the company, including rules about general meetings, the powers of the directors, accounts, and so on.

Franchising

Many operations in the hospitality industry are run under a **franchise** agreement. A franchise is an agreement where a person or group of people pay a fee and some set-up costs to use an established name or brand that is well known and is therefore likely to attract more customers than an unknown or start-up brand.

An example of this is the contract caterer Compass Group, which buys a franchise in the Burger King brand from Burger King's owner. It pays a fee plus a proportion of the **turnover** (the amount of money it takes). The **franchisor** (the branded company providing the franchise) will normally lay down strict guidelines or 'brand standards' that the **franchisee** (franchise user) has to meet. In this example, these will affect things like which ingredients and raw materials are used and where they come from, as well as portion sizes and the general product and service. The franchisor will use mystery shopping services to regularly check on the brand standards to ensure that the brand reputation is not being put at risk. The franchisor will normally also provide advertising and marketing support, accounting services, help with staff training and development, and designs for merchandising and display materials.

Figure 2.4 An example of a fast food franchise operation

Sources of information

Information about the industry is available from a variety of sources:

- trade magazines such as:
  - *Caterer and Hotelkeeper*
  - *Restaurant*
  - *Imbibe*
  - *Cost Sector Catering*
- various news media

- textbooks
- websites and other publications of the various trade and professional bodies
- government websites
- business links
- People 1st
- Hospitality Guild
- professional trade reports, such as those from Keynote and Mintel.

When seeking information, especially from internet sources, take care to ensure that the source is reputable and up to date.

2.4 Trade and professional associations

The industry has a wide variety of regional, national and international trade and professional bodies.

Trade bodies are associations of employers or can also be for specific types of suppliers. These include:
- British Hospitality Association
- Catering Equipment Distributors Association (CEDA)
- Catering Equipment Suppliers Association (CESA)
- International Hotel and Restaurant Association

Professional bodies draw membership from professions at various levels. These include:

- Academy of Food and Wine Service
- British Institute of Innkeeping
- Club Secretaries and Managers Association
- Court of Master Sommeliers
- Craft Guild of Chefs
- Foodservice Consultants Society International (FCSI)
- Guild of International Professional Toastmasters
- Guild of Professional English Butlers, The
- Hospital Caterers Association
- Institute of Hospitality
- Institute of Masters of Wine
- Local Authority Caterers Association (LACA)
- Royal Academy of Culinary Arts
- University Caterers Organisation (TUCO), The
- Worshipful Company of Innholders

> ### Key terms
>
> **Trade bodies** – associations of employers or specific types of suppliers
>
> **Professional bodies** – draw membership from various professions at various levels and provide a range of support for both their members and the industry

Professional bodies provide a range of support for both their members and the industry. This can include:
- providing recognition for individuals through professional membership
- promoting the profession and the industry
- providing information to members and also to the wider business community
- organising and running a range of competitions to recognise people both at the start of their careers and also those who have achieved over a long period
- providing opportunities for study and the achievement of qualifications.

You can find information on these trade and professional bodies by visiting their official websites.

2.5 Legal requirements to work in the hospitality industry

For those employed in the hospitality industry there is a considerable amount of legislation that regulates both the industry itself and employment in the industry. Both employers and employees have employment rights. For information on legal requirements also see Section 1.5, page 20.

Recruitment and selection

When advertising for new staff it is important to be aware of the relevant legislation:

- Children and Young Persons Act (1933)
- Licensing Act (1964)
- Rehabilitation of Offenders Act (1974)
- Data Protection Act (1998)
- Asylum and Immigration Act (1996)
- National Minimum Wage Act (1998)
- Working Time Regulations (1998)
- Sex Discrimination Act (1986)
- Race Relations Act (1976)
- Disability Discrimination Act (1995)
- Human Rights Act (1998).

Job advertisements

It is unlawful to discriminate against job applicants on grounds of:

- sex, marital status or gender
- colour, race, nationality or ethnic origin
- disability
- sexual orientation
- religion or beliefs
- trade union membership or non-membership.

The following words and phrases should be avoided in a job advertisement as they could be construed (understood) or misconstrued as indicating an intention to discriminate on grounds of sex, race or disability:

- pleasing appearance
- strong personality
- energetic
- articulate
- dynamic
- no family commitments.

Use of job titles associated with a particular sex (e.g. 'barmaid', 'manageress') will also be taken to indicate an intention to discriminate on the grounds of a person's sex, unless the advertisement contains an indication or an illustration to the contrary.

Job applications

Job application forms must be designed with care. If sensitive personal information is needed, such as a health record or disability disclosure, the reason for this should be explained and the candidate reassured that the data will remain confidential and will be used and stored in accordance with the provisions of the Data Protection Act 1998.

Human Rights Act

Candidates must be informed when the application is sent out, and again at interview, that they have to wear a uniform or protective clothing when on duty. Any surveillance or monitoring that the company is likely to carry out must also be disclosed to applicants.

Asylum and Immigration Act

It is an offence under the Asylum and Immigration Act (1996) to employ a foreign national subject to immigration control (i.e. a person who needs a visa or work permit, for example) who does not have the right to enter or remain in the UK, or to take up employment while in the UK. Job application forms should caution future employees that they will be required, if shortlisted, to produce documents confirming their right to be in, and to take up employment in, the UK.

Job interviews

Figure 2.5 A job interview

The purpose of the job interview is to assess the suitability of a particular applicant for the vacancy. The interviewer should ask questions designed to test the applicant's suitability for the job, covering their qualifications, training and experience, and to find out about the individual's personal qualities, character, development, motivation, strengths and weaknesses.

If a job applicant resigned or was dismissed from their previous employment, the interviewer may need to know why. Any health problems, injuries or disabilities the candidate has admitted to may also need to be discussed in order to determine the applicant's suitability for employment – for example, in a high-risk working environment.

Employers may lawfully ask a job applicant if he or she has been convicted of any criminal offence, but must be aware of the right of job applicants, under the Rehabilitation of Offenders Act (1974), not to disclose details of any criminal convictions that have since become 'spent' (i.e. those that occurred so long ago that they have been dealt with and are no longer an issue).

The interviewer should not ask questions about the applicant's sexuality or religion. However, questions on religion may be asked if, for example, aspects of the job may directly affect the beliefs of an individual – an example would be the handling of alcoholic drinks.

Job offers

An offer of employment should be made or confirmed in writing and is often conditional on the receipt of satisfactory references from former employers. Withdrawing an offer of employment once it has been accepted could result in a civil action for damages by the prospective employee.

2.6 Applying for a job

Before reading this section, you should also have read the following sections in Chapter 1:
- 1.3 Staffing and organisation structures (page 14)
- 1.4 Food and beverage service job roles (page 15)
- 1.5 Employment in the hospitality industry (page 20)
- 1.6 Key factors for success in food and beverage service (page 23)
- 1.7 Importance of teamwork (page 25)
- 1.8 Qualifications and training (page 27).

When applying for a job you will often be required to complete an application form or send in your CV (**curriculum vitae**). Then, if the first stage of your application is successful, you will be asked to attend an interview.

Writing a CV

Your CV is a document that lists your educational qualifications and work history, your interests and any other activities in which you participate. Employers will usually want to know where you have demonstrated certain skills, how you have dealt with certain situations in the workplace and whether you carry out any voluntary work.

When preparing a CV, you should bear in mind the following:
- Make sure your CV is up to date and includes details of all your experience, jobs, dates of employment, names of employers and any professional awards you have won (relevant to the employment you are seeking).
- Always check spelling, layout and punctuation.
- Include a short paragraph about yourself that describes your career to date and your personal qualities and skills.
- Give a brief explanation of what inspires you and how you use existing skills.
- Specify what your long-term goals are, as well as your immediate goals and targets.
- Identify how you broaden your outlook, your range of skills and your ability to deal with a range of different people, personalities and cultural diversity.

> ### Key term
>
> **Curriculum vitae (CV)** – lists your contact details, educational qualifications and work history, your interests and any other activities in which you participate. It is used when applying for a job to demonstrate your skills to potential employers

Curriculum vitae

Name

Current position:
Home address:
Telephone:
Home email:
Date of birth:

General career overview:

[*Include bullet point list of key features and achievements of career, including key experience and skills*]

- X years' industry experience in food and beverage operations, including X years at craft and supervisory level.
- Experienced in [*give details*].
- Proven record of achievement recognised through promotion and career advancement.
- Hard working and a good team member.
- Commitment to continuing professional development through undertaking various in-company training programmes [*give details*].

Professional experience:

- Dates [*write as month and year in full and include job title and name of place, name of specific place and indication of level of operation, e.g. 5**]
- Reporting to [*give details*].
- Give some descriptive information, such as services provided, for how many people and how many staff responsible for. [*For example, á la carte and table d'hôte all-day dining for up to 000 people, function catering for up to 000 people, with a staffing of 000 people.*]
- List key responsibilities.
- List other job features and unique experience.

[*Then repeat this format for all employment going back in time. Write in the third person as it is easier to write in that format and much easier for other people to read.*]

Professional activities:

- [*Bullet point list of any professional memberships and any contributions to industry activities.*]

Competitions and awards:
Education, training and qualifications:
Hobbies and interests:
Nationality: [*Include visa status if appropriate.*]

Figure 2.6 An example of a format for a CV.

Writing a covering letter

A **covering letter** will usually accompany a CV. The covering letter:

- introduces you to the company
- explains why you are suitable for the job on offer and the skills and qualities you can bring to it
- gives you an opportunity to say how you would be able to contribute to the establishment and the organisation as a whole.

An example of a covering letter is show in Figure 2.7.

Key term

Covering letter – accompanies a CV and explains why you are suitable for the job on offer

Developing skills for employment

4 Maynard Avenue
Compton
Sturbridge
B20 1SB
Telephone: 0123 456 789
Email:william.johns@xxx.com

Mr James Bryant
Human Resources Manager
Hambury Hotels Ltd
Hertford Road
Birmingham
XXX XX

23 May 2014

Dear Mr Bryant

Re: 55/001: Commis Chef Trainee programme

I am writing to you to apply for the Commis Chef trainee programme, currently advertised on the Hambury Hotels' website. My current CV is enclosed for your consideration.

Having always been interested in cooking, I applied to study a GNVQ Chef and Restaurant Diploma course after my GCSEs. My interest in becoming a chef started when my school attended an openday at University College Birmingham, my local catering college.

Hambury Hotels has an excellent reputation, focusing on high standards and the opportunity to study for higher qualifications while training and contributing to the work of the hotel. At the college's open day in February, I met with current graduate trainees and I was impressed by the friendliness of your employees and the very positive descriptions of working life at the hotel.

As well as completing my current course in May, my practical experience has included working on a three-month chef placement at the Weigh Bridge Hotel, Sturbridge.

I am available for an interview from 1 June onwards. In the meantime, I look forward to taking the opportunity to talk with you further about my application.

Yours sincerely

William Johns

Figure 2.7 Example of a covering letter.

Interview skills

First impressions are important; always make sure you prepare thoroughly for an interview as this will help to ensure that you are in control during the interview. Try to remember the following points:

- Research the job you are applying for and find out about the company.
- Prepare questions in advance.
- Consider how you are going to introduce yourself at the start of the interview.
- Make sure you are well groomed, smart and look professional.
- Practise an interview with a friend or colleague beforehand – this is known as role play.
- Before the interview plan your journey and work out the travelling time – allow yourself plenty of time to get there so you do not feel rushed.

Personal presentation for interview

When you attend an interview you should:

- create a good first impression
- use the correct vocabulary
- know the questions you are going to ask
- demonstrate good communication skills
- show that you understand the importance of time management.

During the interview maintain eye contact with the interviewer and smile occasionally. Be confident and polite. Think about the questions being asked before you answer them and do not waffle! Be clear and concise in your answers. If you do not understand a question, ask the interviewer to repeat it.

When the interview is over, it is useful to reflect on your performance. If you are unsuccessful, ask for feedback and learn from the experience. Assess what you did well and what you did less well to think about how you might improve in the future.

2.7 Developing a personal development plan

Whatever your job role, it is useful to evaluate and check your progress from time to time. Feedback from your peers and managers is a useful way of evaluating your performance. Keeping records (e.g. personal development plans) provides a further way to check your progress, refer back to your **targets** and think about the outcome. Monitoring performance to check whether targets are being met involves three key stages:

- work plans (e.g. personal development plans) – seeking guidance
- targets – evaluating them and taking corrective action when necessary
- outcomes – must be measurable in order to know whether they have been achieved.

Gathering information to improve your workplace skills is useful because, once you have achieved a successful outcome, you can use that information to inform and help others.

A **personal development plan** will help you identify targets and timescales to improve your skills and advance your career for personal and professional success. The next step is to identify which skills you need to develop further. Table 2.4 shows an example of a skills development progress chart that would help someone to assess the skills they currently possess, identify skills they would like to develop and then rank them in order of priority.

> **Key terms**
>
> **Target** – something to be achieved
>
> **Personal development plan** – measuring, improving and monitoring own performance

Table 2.4 Skills development progress chart

Knowledge, skills, qualities and experience	Already experienced	Want to know more	Want to develop further	Order of importance
Preparation skills				
Bar skills				
Wine skills				
Service skills				
Order-taking skills				
Billing skills				
Time management				
Identifying barriers to personal success				

Developing skills for employment

Knowledge, skills, qualities and experience	Already experienced	Want to know more	Want to develop further	Order of importance
Being able to reflect positively				
Knowing what kind of career you want				
Preparing a job application				
Writing a job application covering letter				
Writing an attractive CV				
Understanding what is required to be successful				
Teambuilding skills				
Developing professional relationships				
Being assertive				
Dealing with difficult people				
Developing confidence				
Dealing with basic problem solving				
Being self-motivated				
Evaluating personal competitiveness				
Understanding effective interview techniques				
Preparing for an interview				
Developing personal records				
Recording evidence				

Table 2.5 shows a personal target chart that can be used to identify a skill to be developed. The chart asks you to explain why the skill is important, describe how you will achieve it and provide evidence that it has been achieved successfully.

Table 2.5 Personal target chart

	Target 1	Target 2	Target 3
What is the target?			
Importance of the skill and why you need it			
How you will achieve the skill and what support and guidance you will need			
Evidence that you have achieved your aim			

A personal development plan helps you to evaluate performance feedback from your mentor, manager or tutor and will help you to improve your future performance. An example of an action plan for personal development is shown in Table 2.6.

Table 2.6 Action plan for personal development

Target	Steps to take in milestones	Indicators of successful completion	Start date	Target completion date	Done
1	a				
	b				
	c				
2	a				
	b				
	c				

Testing your learning

1 Briefly explain what is meant by the term 'hospitality industry'.
2 What is meant by each of the following terms?
  (a) Sole trader
  (b) Self-employed
  (c) Partnership
3 Approximately how many people are employed in the hospitality industry in the UK?
4 Give one example of why the hospitality industry is now a global industry.
5 What does franchising mean?
6 Identify two professional bodies and briefly describe what each organisation does.
7 Name three different sources of information on the hospitality industry.
8 List three essential pieces of information that should appear on a CV.
9 Why should you provide a covering letter with a CV?
10 Identify one person that you could go to for help in developing a personal development plan.

Developing skills for employment

In practice

1 Over three practical sessions, copy and complete the table below to check how well you are achieving the standards required. Make a note of how you checked and who you checked your performance with – for example your supervisor or tutor.
In all cases, please give one example of how you met the standards required.

	Session 1	Session 2	Session 3
How did you check your punctuality?			
How did you ensure your uniform was correct?			
How did you ensure your uniform was clean and tidy?			
How did you ensure your personal hygiene?			

2 Copy and use the personal target chart below to identify skills you wish to develop. You need to explain why the skill is important, how you will achieve it and provide evidence that the skill has been achieved.

	Target 1	Target 2	Target 3
What is the target?			
Importance of the skill and why you need it			
How you will achieve the skill and what support and guidance you will need			
Evidence that you have achieved your aim			

3 Copy and use the action plan chart below to identify your targets for personal development. You need to break down each target into milestones and provide an indication of how you will know you have successfully completed your target.

Target	Steps to take in milestones	Indicators of successful completion	Start date	Target completion date	Done
1	a				
	b				
	c				
2	a				
	b				
	c				

4 Identify a job advertisement you may like to apply for (agree it is appropriate with your supervisor or tutor) and prepare:
- your curriculum vitae (CV)
- a covering letter
- a list of preparations that you would make before the interview
- an explanation of how and why you would obtain feedback on your performance at the interview.

Your explanation should demonstrate a clear understanding of the importance of preparation, presentation and evaluation, and your ability to see how an employer makes decisions for business reasons.

Service areas and equipment 3

Units covered

This chapter covers the following units:

Level 1

→ Food and beverage service skills (108)
→ Bar service skills (109)
→ Prepare and clear areas for table/tray service (1FS1, 107)
→ Clean and store crockery and cutlery (1GEN5, 105)
→ Provide a table/tray service (1FS2, 108)
→ Prepare and clear areas for counter/takeaway service (1FS3, 109)
→ Clean and store crockery and cutlery (1GEN5, 105)
→ Maintain a vending machine (1GEN6, 106)

Level 2

→ Food and beverage service skills (209)
→ Provide a counter/takeaway service (1FS4, 110)
→ Serve food at the table (2FS2, 207)
→ Provide a silver service (2FS8, 208)
→ Provide a buffet/carvery service (2FS4, 209)
→ Serve alcoholic and soft drinks (2BS2, 212)
→ Prepare and serve cocktails (2BS3, 213)
→ Prepare and serve wines (2BS4, 214)
→ Prepare and serve hot drinks using specialist equipment (2BS8, 218)
→ Prepare and clear areas for counter/takeaway service (1FS3, 109)
→ Prepare and clear areas for table service (2FS1, 206)
→ Prepare and clear the bar area (2BS1, 211)

Learning outcomes

This chapter will help you to:

1	Explain the importance of design and purchasing factors	49
2	Describe the function of the stillroom	50
3	Describe the function of the hotplate	51
4	Describe the function of the wash-up	52
5	Describe the equipment and set up of the bar	53
6	Explain how furniture contributes to an establishment's success	56
7	Explain how the linen contributes to an establishment's success	58
8	Describe the different types of crockery	59
9	Describe the tableware (flatware, cutlery and hollow-ware)	61
10	Describe the glassware	64
11	Explain what is meant by disposables	65
12	Outline what is meant by automatic vending	68

3.1 Importance of design and purchasing factors

In any establishment a customer's first impressions on entering the service areas are of great importance – a customer may be gained or lost on these impressions alone. Atmosphere, décor, furnishings and equipment are major factors that contribute to the success of the foodservice operation. Careful selection of items in terms of shape, design and colour will enhance the overall décor or theme. The choice of furniture and its layout and choice of linen, tableware, small equipment and glassware will be determined by such factors as:

- the type of customer expected
- the site or location of the establishment
- the layout of the food and beverage service area
- the type of service offered
- the funds available.

General points to be considered when purchasing equipment for a food and beverage service area are:

- flexibility of use
- type of service being offered
- type of customer
- design and colour
- durability
- ease of maintenance
- stackability
- availability of replacements in the future
- storage
- rate of breakage, e.g. for crockery
- shape
- psychological effect on customers
- delivery time
- costs and funds available.

The front-of-house areas must be well designed for operational purposes as these are the busiest areas of a foodservice establishment. Department heads must ensure that all members of staff know exactly how to carry out their duties efficiently and effectively.

The back-of-house areas include the stillroom, hotplate (or pass) area and the wash-up. They are usually between the kitchen and food and beverage service, or front-of-house areas. They are important parts of the design of a foodservice operation, acting as the link between kitchen or food preparation areas and the restaurant or food and beverage service areas. A well-designed layout of these areas is essential to ensure an even flow of work by the various members of staff. These areas need to be well organised, efficient and stocked with well-designed equipment.

3.2 The stillroom

The **stillroom** provides items of food and beverages needed for the service of a meal that are not catered for by the other major departments in a foodservice operation, such as the kitchen, larder and pastry. The duties performed in this service area will vary according to the type of meals offered and the size of establishment concerned.

Equipment

The following items of equipment may be needed in the stillroom:

- refrigerator for storage of milk, cream, butter and fruit juices
- hot and cold beverage-making facilities
- large double sink and draining board for washing-up
- dishwasher of a size suitable for the stillroom but large enough to ensure efficient turnover of equipment
- salamander or toasters
- bread-slicing machine
- worktop and cutting board
- storage space for small equipment such as crockery, glassware, cutlery and tableware
- storage cupboard for all dry goods held in stock and for paper items such as doilies, kitchen papers and napkins
- coffee-grinding machine to ensure the correct grind of coffee for the brewing method to be used
- ice machine.

Figure 3.1 Example of a stillroom

Provisions

As a basic guide, the following food items would normally be dispensed from the stillroom:

- all beverages such as coffee, tea, hot chocolate, tisanes and jugs or bottles of water
- assorted fruit juices: orange, tomato, pineapple and grapefruit
- milk, cream and alternatives
- sugars: loose, pre-wrapped portions, brown coffee crystals, Demerara, etc., and alternatives
- preserves: marmalade, cherry, plum, raspberry, strawberry, apricot and honey. For the purpose of control and to reduce wastage, many establishments now offer pre-portioned jars or pots of jams or preserves at breakfast and for afternoon tea, rather than a preserve dish

> ### Key term
>
> **Stillroom** – provides items of food, beverages and equipment needed for the service of a meal not found in other major departments such as the kitchen, larder and pastry

- butter: either passed through a butter pat machine, curled or pre-wrapped portions, as well as butter alternatives
- sliced and buttered brown, white and malt bread
- rolls, brioche and croissants
- bread substitute items: gluten-free, rye and rice crackers
- dry crackers, digestives and water biscuits for service with cheese; sweet biscuits for service with early morning and afternoon teas and coffees
- assorted breakfast cereals. In many establishments cereals of all types are offered in pre-wrapped, portion-controlled packets
- toasted scones and teacakes
- pastries, gâteaux and sandwiches.

Control

There are two main ways of controlling goods to be issued from the stillroom:

- If a foodservice area requires items such as butter, sugar or preserves in bulk, a requisition signed by a supervisor is required before the stillroom will issue the items.
- Upon receipt of a waiter's check, tea, coffee or any other beverage required in the necessary portions will be dispensed.

3.3 The hotplate

The **hotplate** or **pass** is the meeting point between the service staff and the food preparation staff. Active cooperation and a good relationship between the members of staff of these two areas helps to ensure that the customer receives an efficient and quick service of the meal.

The hotplate is stocked with all the crockery necessary for the service of a meal. This may include some or all of the following items:

- soup plates/soup cups/consommé cups
- fish/joint/sweet plates
- platters.

Food flats and serving dishes are placed on the top of the hotplate, which should be lit/ switched on well in advance so all items are sufficiently heated before service. Care should be taken to ensure that the plates are of a safe temperature before service to prevent injury to staff and customers.

> **Key term**
>
> **Hotplate** or **pass** – the meeting point between the service staff and the food preparation staff

Figure 3.2 Example of a hotplate area

Aboyeur or barker

The **aboyeur**, or **barker**, is in charge of and controls the hotplate (pass) during the service period. The aboyeur will receive the clearly written food check from the waiter. The aboyeur checks that none of the dishes ordered are off the menu. The order from the various 'parties' or 'sections' of the kitchen is then called out.

With the modern use of an EPOS (electronic point of sale) system, the electronic order is sent directly from the restaurant to each section of the kitchen and the aboyeur coordinates the dishes so they arrive on the pass at the same time, checking for quality before releasing the plate to the waiting staff. The control department also use the EPOS information to control sales and revenue.

3.4 The wash-up

Servers should stack same-sized plates together and place cutlery into a plastic bowl filled with hot, soapy water or wire baskets or containers in readiness for washing. The server must place any debris into the bin or bowl provided. All used paper, such as napkins, doilies or kitchen paper, should be placed in separate waste bins to ensure proper recycling. Glassware that has not had grease or fat in it should be taken to a separate glass wash-up point usually located in the bar area.

Dishwashing methods

There are four main methods of dishwashing and a summary of these is shown in Table 3.1.

Table 3.1 Summary of dishwashing methods (based on a chart from *Croner's Catering*)

Method	Description
Manual	Soiled ware washed by hand or brush machine
Automatic conveyor	Soiled ware loaded in baskets and mounted on a conveyor by operators for automatic transportation through a dishwashing machine
Flight conveyor	Soiled ware loaded within pegs mounted on a conveyor by operators for automatic transportation through a dishwashing machine
Deferred wash	Soiled ware collected together, stripped, sorted and stacked by operators for transportation through a dishwashing machine at a later stage

Manual

Dirty crockery is placed into a tank of hot water containing a soap detergent. After washing, the plates are placed into wire racks and dipped into a second sterilising tank containing clean hot water at a temperature of approximately 75°C (179°F). The racks are left for two minutes and then lifted out and the crockery left to drain. If sterilised in water at this temperature the crockery will dry by itself without the use of drying-up cloths. This is more hygienic. After drying, the crockery is stacked into piles of the correct size and placed on shelves until required for further use.

Automatic

Many larger establishments have dishwashing machines. These are necessary because of the high usage of crockery.

Debris is removed from the crockery before it is placed into the wire racks. The racks are then passed through the machine, the crockery being washed, rinsed and then sterilised in turn. Having passed through the machine the crockery is left to drain for two to three minutes and is then stacked and placed on shelves until required for further use. As with the tank method, the plates do not require drying with tea cloths.

Figure 3.3 Rack conveyor dishwasher with stand for loading the racks at the right of the picture and a trolley for collection of completed racks on the left (image courtesy of Maidaid – Halcyon)

3.5 The bar

The bar may be situated within a food and beverage service area and dispense wine or other alcoholic drinks to be served to a customer consuming a meal or using a lounge area. Wine and other alcoholic drinks are sometimes obtained from bars situated outside the food and beverage service area itself, from one of the public bars. All drinks dispensed must be checked for and controlled (see Section 16.2, page 261).

Equipment

All the equipment necessary for correctly making cocktails, decanting wine, serving wine and preparing all other drinks ordered must be available at the bar to ensure efficient service of all forms of wine and drink. The equipment will include the items described below.

Main items

- **Cocktail shaker:** the ideal utensil for mixing ingredients that will not normally blend together well by stirring. A three-part utensil.
- **Boston shaker:** consists of two cones, one of which overlaps the other to seal in the mix. Made of stainless steel, glass or plated silver. The mix is strained using a Hawthorn strainer.
- **Mixing glass:** like a glass jug without a handle, but with a lip. Used for mixing clear drinks that do not contain juices or cream.

- **Strainer:** there are many types, the most popular being the Hawthorn. This is a flat, spoon-shaped utensil with a spring coiled round its edge. It is used in conjunction with a cocktail shaker and mixing glass to hold back the ice after the drink is prepared. A special design is available for use with liquidisers and blenders.
- **Bar spoon:** for use with a mixing glass when stirring cocktails. The flat 'muddler' end is used for crushing sugar and mint in certain drinks.
- **Bar liquidiser or blender:** used for making drinks that require puréed fruit.
- **Drink mixer:** used for drinks that do not need liquidising, especially those containing cream or ice cream. If ice is required, use only crushed ice.

Other items

Examples include:

- assorted glasses
- ice buckets and stands
- water jugs
- cutting board and knife
- coasters
- cork extractor
- small ice buckets and tongs
- ice-crushing machine
- drinking straws
- cocktail sticks
- carafes
- wine and cocktail/drinks lists
- glass cloths, napkins and service cloths
- sink unit
- refrigerator
- ice-making machine
- glass-washing machine
- optics/spirit measures
- wine measures
- bottle opener
- lemon-squeezing machine
- swizzle sticks
- strainer and funnel
- service salvers
- wine knife and cigar cutter
- bin
- hot beverage maker
- juice press
- mini whisk.

Food items

- olives
- Worcestershire sauce
- salt and pepper
- nutmeg
- Angostura bitters
- caster sugar
- eggs
- fresh mint
- oranges
- coconut cream
- Maraschino cherries
- Tabasco sauce
- cinnamon
- cloves
- sugar cubes
- Demerara sugar
- cream
- cucumber
- lemons
- limes
- salted nuts/crisps
- gherkins.

Service areas and equipment

Figure 3.4 (a) Examples of cocktail bar equipment: (1) cocktail shaker, (2) Boston shaker, (3) mixing glass with bar spoon, (4) Hawthorn strainer, (5) jug strainer insert, (6) mini whisk, (7) straws, (8) ice crusher, (9) juice press, (10) ice bucket and tongs

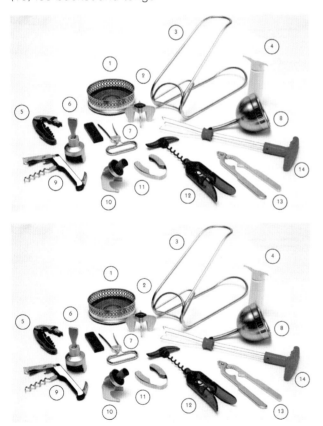

Figure 3.4 (b) Examples of bar equipment: (1) bottle coaster, (2) Champagne star cork grip, (3) wine bottle holder, (4) vacu-pump, (5, 7, 9, 12) wine bottle openers, (6, 10) Champagne bottle stoppers, (8) wine funnel, (11) wine bottle foil cutter, (13) Champagne cork grip, (14) wine cork extractor, (15) appetiser bowls and cocktail stick holder, (16) measures on drip tray, (17) cutting board and knife, (18) cigar cutters, (19, 21) bottle stoppers, (20) bottle pourers, (22) crown cork opener, (23) mini juice press

Safety and hygiene

Great care must be observed to ensure that the materials used in the make-up of the bar are hygienic and safe. Flooring must be non-slip. The bar top should be of a material suited to the general décor that is hard wearing, easily wiped down and has no sharp edges.

The bar area should be cleaned after each service, paying attention to all surfaces, fridges, preparation and dispense equipment, and waste removal. Sinks and glass washers should be emptied and cleaned as required throughout service.

Any perishable items should be correctly covered, labelled, dated and refrigerated as necessary. Good stock rotation will avoid unnecessary wastage.

3.6 Furniture

Furniture must be chosen according to the needs of the establishment. Examples of various dining arrangements are shown in Table 3.2.

Table 3.2 Dining arrangements (based on a chart from *Croner's Catering*)

Type	Description of furniture
Loose random	Freestanding furniture positioned in no discernible pattern within a given service area
Loose module	Freestanding furniture positioned within a given service area to a pre-determined pattern, with or without the use of dividers to create smaller areas within the main area
Booth	Fixed seating (banquette), usually high backed, used to create secluded seating
High density	Furniture with minimum dimensions and usually fixed, positioned within a given service area to create maximum seating capacity
Module	Seating incorporates tables and chairs constructed as one and may be fixed to the floor
In situ	Customers served in areas not designed for service, e.g. aircraft and hospital beds
Bar and lounge areas	Customers served in areas not primarily designed for food and beverage service

By using different materials, designs and finishes of furniture, and by their careful arrangement, the atmosphere and appearance of the service area can often be changed to suit different occasions.

Figure 3.5 Restaurant area with traditional seating and with banquette seating

Tables

Tables come in three main shapes: round, square and rectangular. An establishment may have a mixture of shapes to give variety, or tables of all one shape depending on the shape of the room and the style of service being offered. As a guide, tables are usually found in the following sizes:

Square

- 76 cm (2 ft 6 in) square to seat two people.
- 1 m (3 ft) square to seat four people.

Round

- 1 m (3 ft) in diameter to seat four people.
- 1.52 m (5 ft) in diameter to seat eight people.

Rectangular

- 137 cm × 76 cm (4 ft 6 in × 2 ft 6 in) to seat four people, extensions being added for larger parties.

Sideboards

The sideboard or workstation is used to store spare cutlery and linen, close to the service point, that might be needed during service. It is also an area to place service trays and clearing equipment used during service.

The style and design of a sideboard varies between establishments and is dependent upon:
- the style of service and the food and beverages on offer
- the number of service staff working from one sideboard
- the number of tables to be served from one sideboard
- the amount of equipment it is expected to hold.

It is essential that the sideboard is of a minimum size and portable so that it may be easily moved if necessary. Some establishments use smaller fixed sideboards and also use tray jacks (folding tray stands, as shown in Figure 3.5) when serving and clearing.

After service the sideboard is either completely emptied out or restocked for the next service. In some establishments the waiting staff are responsible for their own equipment on their station. If sideboards are restocked after service, the sideboard will also carry its own stock of linen. In the examples shown in Figure 3.7, the sideboards have everything necessary to equip a particular waiter's station or set of tables.

Figure 3.6 A tray jack

Figure 3.7 Examples of sideboards (images courtesy of Euroservice UK)

3.7 Linen

The type of linen used will depend on the class of establishment, type of clientele, cost involved and the style of menu and service to be offered. The main items of linen normally found are described below.

Tablecloths

- 137 cm × 137 cm (54 in × 54 in) to fit a 76 cm (2 ft 6 in) square table or a round table of 1 m (3 ft) in diameter
- 183 cm × 183 cm (72 in × 72 in) to fit a 1 m (3 ft) square table
- 183 cm × 244 cm (72 in × 96 in) to fit rectangular tables
- 183 cm × 137 cm (72 in × 54 in) to fit rectangular tables.

Slip cloths

- 1 m × 1 m (3 ft × 3 ft) used to cover a slightly soiled tablecloth.

Napkins (serviettes)

- 46–50 cm (18–20 in) square if linen.
- 36–42 cm (14–17 in) square if paper.

Buffet cloths

- 2 m × 4 m (6 ft × 12 ft) – this is the minimum size; longer cloths will be used for longer tables.

Waiter's cloths or service cloths

Servers use these as protection against heat and to help keep uniforms clean.

Tea and glass cloths

These are used for drying items after washing; tea cloths should be used for crockery and glass cloths for glassware.

Service areas and equipment

Use and control of linen

Linen should be used only for its intended purpose in the restaurant and not for cleaning purposes, as this often results in permanent soiling that will render the item unusable in the future. It is also an expensive piece of equipment to launder or replace.

The stock of clean linen is usually issued upon receipt of a requisition signed by a responsible person from the service department. A surplus linen stock is usually held in the food service area in case of emergency.

At the end of each service the dirty linen should be counted, recorded and sent to the issuing department to be exchanged for clean linen.

A range of disposable linen, including napkins, place mats and tablecloths, are available in various colours and qualities. There are also reversible tablecloths with a thin polythene sheet running through the centre that prevents any spillages from penetrating from one side to the other. For more information on disposables, see Section 3.11 (page 65).

3.8 Crockery

The crockery must blend in with the general décor of the establishment and with the rest of the items on the table. An establishment generally uses one design and pattern of crockery, but when an establishment has a number of different service areas it is easier, from a control point of view, to have a different design in each service area.

Foodservice crockery

There are various classifications of foodservice crockery. Although referred to as crockery throughout this book, all glazed tableware is traditionally referred to as china. Items include:

- flatware, for example plates, saucers and serving flats
- cups and bowls, for example tea and coffee cups, soup and sweet bowls, and serving dishes
- hollow-ware, for example pots and vases.

Types of crockery

There are four main types of crockery used in foodservice operations and these are described in Table 3.3 below.

Table 3.3 Types of crockery

Type	Description of crockery
Bone china	This very fine, hard china is expensive. Decorations are only found under the glaze. It can be made to thicker specifications, if requested, for hotel use
Hotel earthenware	Vitrified (or vitreous) earthenware is produced in the UK in vast quantities. It is the cheapest but least durable hotelware, although it is much stronger than regular domestic earthenware
Stoneware	This is a natural ceramic material traditionally made in the UK and fired at a very high temperature, about 1,200–1,315°C (2,200°F). It is shaped by traditional handcrafting techniques so there are a wide variety of shapes and finishes available, from matt to a high-gloss glaze. It is non-porous and extremely durable with high thermal and shock resistance. The price is slightly higher than earthenware due to its long-life guarantee
Porcelain	This is of a different composition with a semi-translucent body, normally cream/grey, and has a high resistance to chipping.

As well as crockery item, contemporary styles now include other materials such as glass, slate, plastic or wood.

Crockery sizes

A wide range of crockery items is available (see Figures 3.11(a) and (b)) and their exact sizes will vary according to the manufacturer and the design produced. As a guide, the sizes are as follows:

- side plate: 15 cm (6 in) diameter
- sweet plate: 18 cm (7 in) diameter
- fish plate: 20 cm (8 in) diameter
- soup plate: 20 cm (8 in) diameter
- joint plate: 25 cm (10 in) diameter
- cereal/sweet bowl: 13 cm (5 in) diameter
- breakfast cup and saucer: 23–28 cl (8–10 fl oz)
- teacup and saucer: 18.93 cl (6⅔ fl oz)
- coffee cup and saucer (demi-tasse): 9.47 cl (3½ fl oz)
- teapot: 28.4 cl (½ pint), 56.8 cl (1 pint), 85.2 cl (1½ pint), 113.6 cl (2 pint).

Other items of crockery required include:

- consommé cup and saucer
- soup bowl/cup
- platter (oval plate)
- salad crescent
- egg cup
- butter dish
- ashtray
- teapot

- hot water jug
- coffee pot
- milk jug
- cream jug
- hot milk jug
- sugar basin
- salt and pepper pots.

Figure 3.8 (a) Selection of crockery – traditional style

Service areas and equipment

Figure 3.8 (b) Selection of tableware – contemporary style

Storage

Crockery should be stored on shelves in piles of approximately two dozen. Any higher may result in their toppling down or damage to plates at the bottom of the stack because of the weight bearing down on them.

Crockery should be stored at a convenient height for placing on and removing from the shelves without fear of accidents occurring. If possible crockery should be covered to prevent dust and germs settling on it.

3.9 Tableware (flatware, cutlery and hollow-ware)

Traditionally **flatware** included spoons and forks, and **cutlery** referred to knives. The modern usage of these terms has changed. All spoons, forks and knives used as eating implements are now referred to as cutlery. The term 'cutlery' is therefore used throughout the rest of this book.

Hollow-ware consists of any other item, apart from flatware and cutlery, for example teapots, milk jugs, sugar basins and serving dishes.

Manufacturers produce varied patterns of flatware, hollow-ware and cutlery in a range of prices to suit all demands. There are also patterns of flatware and cutlery that are scaled down to three-quarters the normal size specifically for tray service.

> ### Key terms
>
> **Flatware** – spoons and forks
>
> **Cutlery** – now refers to all items used as eating implements – spoons, forks and knives
>
> **Hollow-ware** – items other than cutlery, for example teapots, milk jugs, sugar basins and serving dishes

Figure 3.9 Examples of cutlery (left to right: fish fork, sweet (small) fork, joint fork, fish knife, small (side) knife, joint knife, coffee spoon, tea spoon, soup spoon, sweet spoon, table (service) spoon).

Silver

Silver-plated tableware comes in two grades:

1 standard for general use
2 thicker grade for restaurant use and marked with an 'R'.

The minimum thickness of silver plating quoted should give a life of at least 20 years, depending on usage.

Plain cutlery and flatware is more popular than patterned for the simple reason that it is cheaper and easier to keep clean.

Silver cleaning methods

All items of service silver should be cleaned on a rota basis to ensure every item is cleaned regularly. Items that are in constant use will require more attention.

There are various methods of silver cleaning and the method used generally depends on the size and class of establishment. The main methods used are summarised in Table 3.4.

Table 3.4 Summary of silver cleaning methods

Method	Description
Silver dip	Items to be cleaned are completely immersed in dip in a plastic bowl for a very short time, rinsed in clean water and polished with a tea cloth
Burnishing machine	Items to be cleaned are placed in a drum containing ball bearings, soap powder and water. The drum rotates and the tarnish is rubbed off
Polvit	An enamel or galvanised iron bowl within which is the Polvit aluminium metal sheet containing holes, together with some soda. At least one piece of silver needs contact with the Polvit. Boiling water is poured on to the silver and a chemical reaction causes the tarnish to be lifted
Plate powder	Pink powder is mixed with a little methylated spirit to a smooth paste and rubbed well on to the tarnished silver with a clean piece of cloth

(Information based on that obtained from the Cutlery and Allied Trades Research Association (CATRA))

Stainless steel

Stainless steel tableware is available in a variety of grades. The higher-priced designs usually incorporate alloys of chromium (which makes the metal stainless) and nickel (which gives a fine grain and lustre). Good British flatware and cutlery is made of 18/8 or 18/10 stainless steel.

Stainless steel is finished by different degrees of polishing:

- high polish finish
- dull polish finish
- light grey matt, non-reflective finish.

Stainless steel resists scratching far more than other metals and may therefore be said to be more hygienic. Although it does not tarnish it can stain. There are special cleaning products for stainless steel such as a commercial powder that is applied with a wet sponge or cloth and rubbed on the surface before being rinsed off. These products help to keep stainless steel looking clean and polished.

Storage

In larger establishments the silver room, or plate room as it is sometimes known, is a separate service area within which a complete stock of tableware required for the service of meals (plus a small amount of surplus stock in case of emergency) is stored. Tableware for banqueting service may be of a different design and kept specifically for that purpose within the banqueting department. In smaller establishments it is often combined with the wash-up area.

- **Large tableware**: Flats, salvers, soup tureens and cloches – store on shelves, with all the flats of one size together. All shelves should be labelled showing where each item goes. Heavier items should go on lower shelves and smaller, lighter items on higher shelves.
- **Small tableware**: Smaller items such as cruets, butter dishes, special equipment, table numbers and menu holders can be stored in drawers lined with green baize to protect items and reduce noise.

Ideally all tableware should be stored in a room or cupboard that can be locked, as it is a large part of the capital investment of the foodservice operation. Cutlery may be stored in cutlery trolleys or trays ready for use, which can also be locked in a store.

3.10 Glassware

Glassware contributes to the appearance of the table and the overall attractiveness of the service area. All glassware should be clean and well polished. Most manufacturers now supply hotel glassware in standard sizes for convenience of ordering, availability and quick delivery.

Type and sizes of glassware

Glassware is made by various processes. The main ones are shown in Table 3.5.

Table 3.5 Types of glassware

Type of glass	Use
Soda lime glass	For day-to-day use. Relatively inexpensive glassware
Lead crystal	Softer glass of high brilliance where the surface can be left plain or can be cut to produce prismatic effects and sparkle. Expensive
Borosilicate glass	Hard and heat-resistant glass used for flame ware
Tempered and toughened glass	Resistant to the effects of heat; this glass is mostly used as ovenware glass and can also withstand heavy usage

Glassware decoration

The surface of glassware may be decorated by:
- cutting to produce patterns or badging
- sand blasting to texture the surface
- acid etching to make patterns or to add badging
- engraving using grinding wheels to add patterns
- surface printing with patterns from transfers.

Glassware sizes

Examples of sizes for drinking glasses are shown in Table 3.6.

Table 3.6 Examples of sizes for glassware

Glass	Size
Wine goblets	14.20, 18.93, 22.72, 28 cl (5, 6⅔, 8, 10 fl oz)
Champagne flute/tulip	18–23 cl (6–8 fl oz)
Champagne saucer	18–23 cl (6–8 fl oz)
Cocktail glasses	4–7 cl (2–3 fl oz)
Sherry/port glasses	5 cl (1.75 fl oz)
Highball	23–28 cl (9–10 fl oz)
Lowball	18–23 cl (6–8 fl oz)
Worthington	28–34 cl (10–12 fl oz)
Lager glass	28–34 cl (10–12 fl oz)
Brandy balloon	23–28 cl (8–10 fl oz)
Liqueur glass	2.5 cl (0.88 fl oz)
Tumbler/Slim Jim	28.40 cl (½ pint)
Beer	25–50 cl (½–1 pint)

As well as being used for drinking glasses, jugs and vases, contemporary glassware is now used as an alternative to crockery for the presentation and service of food (see Section 3.8, page 59).

Storage and cleaning

Drinking glasses are normally stored in single rows on thin plastic grid matting, upside down to prevent dust settling in them. Plastic racks made specifically for the purpose of stacking and storing glasses are another alternative. These racks are also a convenient method of transporting glassware from one point to another, which reduces breakages. Tumblers and other straight-sided glassware should not be stacked inside one another as this may result in breakages and can cause accidents to staff.

Most day-to-day glassware used in the industry can be washed using dishwashers. However, for certain glassware this is not recommended. This includes lead crystal and other forms of fine glassware, which should be hand washed. Over time most glassware will become milky in appearance and will then need to be replaced. Finer glassware will be affected in this way more quickly, unless hand washed.

3.11 Disposables

There has been considerable growth in the use of disposables, or 'throw-aways' as they are sometimes called, and this is due to a number of factors:

- the need to reduce costs
- the difficulty of obtaining labour for washing up
- to reduce the high cost of laundering
- improved standards of hygiene
- breakage cost minimisation
- reduction in storage space required
- changes in cooking and storage technology, for example, cook/chill and cook/freeze
- the needs of transport caterers on trains, boats and planes
- the development of fast-food and takeaway operations
- increased customer acceptability.

Although many establishments use disposables to reduce costs, they must be attractive, presentable and acceptable to the client and also attractive to customers. The choice of which disposables to use may be determined by:

- necessity because of operational needs for:
  - outdoor catering
  - automatic vending
  - fast food
  - takeaways
- cost considerations such as:
  - traditional forms of service equipment
  - cost of laundry
  - wash-up costs.

Types of disposables

The main varieties of disposables used are as follows:

- for storage and cooking purposes
- service of food and beverages, for example plates, knives, forks, cups
- décor: napkins, tablecloths, slip cloths, banquet roll, place mats
- hygiene: wipes
- clothing: aprons, chef hats, gloves
- packaging: for marketing and presentation purposes.

Disposables that may be used to replace regular restaurant linen include serviettes, place mats, tray cloths, tablecloths and coasters. Today, most forms of disposables are available in a variety of colours and patterns, and can have the house-style motto or crest reproduced on them. The vast range of colours available also allows for changes in a service area with different colours being used for each meal.

Throwaway packs of knives, forks and spoons are more convenient and hygienic where the turnover of custom is very high over very short periods of time, for example in industrial canteens and transport catering. Throwaway packs eliminate delays at service points because the speed of washing-up is inadequate.

A considerable advance in the range of disposables available has been the introduction of disposables whose approximation to crockery tableware is very close. For instance, they may have a high-quality finish and a smooth, hard, white surface. These plates are strong and rigid with no tendency to bend or buckle, while a plasticising ingredient ensures that they are greaseproof and moisture-proof, even against hot fat and gravy. Oval meal plates, snack trays and compartmentalised plates are all available to the caterer.

Figure 3.10 Examples of disposable products used in food service

Environmental issues

When purchasing disposable items it is important to consider products that are environmentally friendly. With the development of new materials many disposable products are now totally compostable and biodegradable, as they are made from renewable resources such as:

- **sugar cane fibre off-cuts**: these are very similar to conventional paper products and are used for bowls, plates and cups
- **clear polylactic acid (PLA)**: made from carbon stored in plants such as corn and used for cups, containers and straws. Not suitable for hot liquids but can be frozen
- **cornstarch cutlery**: made from a starch-based polymer and chalk
- **bamboo ware**: used to make plates, bowls, cups and cutlery from reconstituted bamboo.

Advantages of disposables

- **Equipment and labour**: disposables reduce the need for washing-up equipment, staff and materials.
- **Hygiene**: using disposables improves hygiene standards.
- **Time**: disposables may speed up service, for example for fast food.
- **Properties**: disposables have good heat retention and insulation properties.
- **Marketing**: disposables can be used as a promotional aid.
- **Capital**: usage reduces the amount of capital investment.
- **Transport**: disposables are easily transported.
- **Cost**: disposables may be cheaper than hiring conventional equipment.

Disadvantages of disposables

- **Acceptability**: customer acceptability may be poor.
- **Cost**: disposables can be more expensive than some conventional equipment.
- **Storage**: back-up quantities are required.
- **Supply**: there is heavy reliance on supply and delivery time.
- **Environment**: unless they are made from renewable resources and are completely biodegradable disposables have a negative impact on the environment.

3.12 Automatic vending

Automatic vending is a form of automatic retailing that uses one or more of the following methods of payment:

- coins
- banknotes
- money card
- tokens
- free vend.

Types of foodservice vending machine

Within foodservice operations, automatic vending is used for the supply of a wide variety of food and beverages, both hot and cold. Vending machines used for foodservice operations include:

- **Merchandiser**: Customers view the products for sale, for example, confectionery machines. Also used for refrigerated drinks (bottles and cans) and pre-packaged meals and snacks, as well as for hot meals and snacks through internal heating.
- **Hot beverage vendor**: This mixes powdered ingredients with hot water to produce the product.
- **In-cup system**: Ingredients are already in individual cups to which hot water is added.
- **Cold beverage vendor**: Post-mix syrup mixed with water (carbonated or non-carbonated).
- **Micro-vend system**: Provides a range of hot or cold foods from which the customer may make a selection and heat in an accompanying microwave oven.

Figure 3.11 Examples of foodservice vending machines (image courtesy of Sodexo UK and Ireland)

Maintenance of vending machines

Automatic vending machines are neither self-cleaning nor self-maintaining or filling. Therefore, regular maintenance is required if the vending service is to run smoothly without mechanical breakdown. The type of vending machine and the service demand upon it will determine its service requirements. All vending machines come with instructions about cleaning, maintenance and stocking.

Extreme care must be taken concerning the various aspects of hygiene and food safety of foods and beverages served in this way.

Testing your learning

1 Briefly describe the purpose of the stillroom.
2 What are the main items of equipment that you would expect to find in a stillroom?
3 Describe the role of the aboyeur or barker.
4 How should glasses be stored after washing?
5 List four different styles of glassware.
6 List eight items that you expect to find in a bar.
7 Describe the differences between a coffee pot and a teapot.
8 How should crockery be stored when not being used?
9 Identify two of the four types of crockery that can be used in a food and beverage operation.
10 State two actions that a member of staff should carry out in order to maintain a vending service.

In practice

List ten of the main items of equipment that you would expect to find in a sideboard prior to service.

Legislation in food and beverage service

4

Units covered

This chapter covers the following units:

Level 1

→ Legislation in food and beverage service (104)
→ Maintain a safe, hygienic and secure working environment (1GEN1, 104)

Level 2

→ Legislation in food and beverage service (204)
→ Maintain a safe, hygienic and secure working environment (1GEN1, 101)
→ Maintain food safety when storing, holding and serving food (2GEN4, 204)

4.1 Importance of legal compliance

A wide variety of legal requirements apply to foodservice operations including health and safety law, company law, liquor licensing regulations and employment law. Summaries of the key responsibilities for foodservice operations are given throughout this chapter.

Enforcement bodies

Enforcement bodies include representatives of:

- Trading Standards
- local councils
- police
- weights and measures enforcement
- Information Commissioner's Office
- Equality and Human Rights Commission

Penalties for non-compliance with legislation can be severe, both for the business and for the management and staff. It is important that all members of staff contribute to ensuring compliance with the legal requirements.

4.2 Health, safety and security

An establishment has a common law duty to care for all staff and lawful visitors. In addition establishments must not:

- sell (or keep for sale) food and beverages that are unfit for people to eat
- cause food or beverages to be dangerous to health
- sell food or beverages that are not what the customer is entitled to expect, in terms of content or quality
- describe or present food in a way that is false or misleading.

A foodservice operator must be able to demonstrate that steps have been taken to ensure good food hygiene (this is called **due diligence**).

Figure 4.1 Safe condition sign – exit direction

> ### Key term
>
> **Due diligence** –
> a foodservice operator
> must be able to
> demonstrate that steps
> have been taken to ensure
> good food hygiene

The Health and Safety at Work Act 1974, the Fire Safety Order 2006 and Fire (Scotland) Act 2005 cover areas of safety within the workplace. Key responsibilities under the legislation include ensuring that:

- there is a written health and safety policy
- service standards comply with health, safety, environmental and food hygiene regulations
- adequate arrangements are in place to ensure the safety, security and well-being of staff and customers
- periodic risk assessments are carried out and recorded
- emergency exits are clearly marked and regular fire drills are carried out
- staff are trained in fire procedures and know how to use fire-fighting equipment
- staff are aware of evacuation procedures in the event of a fire or security risk such as a bomb threat
- health and safety notices are displayed in working areas
- staff and customers are trained, as appropriate, on correct usage of equipment and facilities
- all food handlers are trained in safe and hygienic working practices.

In addition the Employers' Liability Act (1969) and Employers' Liability (Northern Ireland) Order (1972) require employers to ensure that they have valid employer liability insurance cover at all times and a notice is displayed to that effect.

Note

More detailed information on health, safety and security is presented in Chapter 5 Health, safety and security (page 78).

4.3 Liquor and other licensing

The sale of alcoholic liquor is subject to the requirements of the Licensing Act (2003), which has four key objectives:

1 the prevention of crime and disorder
2 public safety
3 the prevention of public nuisance
4 the protection of children from harm.

The Act requires a foodservice operation to:

- display a summary of the premises' licence, including the days and times of opening, the name of the registered licence holder, the licence number and a valid date
- display a price list of drinks
- adhere to restrictions on under-aged persons being served alcohol and employed to serve alcohol
- ensure an authorised person (or the personal licence holder) is on site at all times.

Other types of licences include licences for music, both live and pre-recorded – Phonographic Performance Limited (PPL) and Performing Right Society (PRS) – dancing, gambling, theatrical performance and television display. In all cases the supervisor and staff should be aware of the provisions and limitations of the licences to ensure compliance.

In order to retail alcohol the business must have a Premises Licence, a Designated Premises Supervisor and every shift should ideally be supervised by at least one Personal Licence Holder. Without these licence holders the business is in contravention of Licensing Law and will not be able to retail alcohol until the correct licences are in place. These licences are applied for through the Local Licensing Authority and can take several weeks to obtain.

Reasons for refusal of service of alcohol

In England and Wales it is illegal to sell any form of alcohol to anyone under the age of 18. You are, however, allowed to serve beer, wine or cider to under-18s if they are 16 or 17 years of age, sitting having a substantial meal and accompanied by a responsible adult who is also partaking of a meal and is paying for the alcoholic drinks. It is the responsibility of the person serving the drinks to check the ages of the customers if they suspect that they might not be 18 or over, by looking at a photo driving licence, passport or one of the photo hologram age identity cards available from recognised authorities and organisations.

It is the duty of all service staff to prevent the sale and consumption of any alcoholic beverage to a person who appears to be drunk or to the companion of a drunken person if it is suspected that the drunken person may consume the alcohol. It is an offence to allow this to happen, and this also applies to any service staff who were suspicious but failed to do anything about it, even if they did not serve the customers themselves.

Legal measures

To comply with the law, whisky, gin, rum and vodka are sold in measures of 25 ml or 35 ml or multiples thereof. All other spirits do not require measuring under law but, in order to calculate sales and profits, it is usual practise to measure all spirits unless making a cocktail that is a mixture of three or more liquids, which therefore means that the liquids used do not require measuring.

- Beer, wine and cider is sold in measures of ⅓ and ½ pints and multiples thereof.
- Wine by the glass is sold in measures of 125 ml or 175 ml and multiples thereof.
- Wine in a carafe or jug is sold in measures of 25 cl, 50 cl, 75 cl and 1 litre.

Figure 4.2 Part of a back bar fitting

Premises can sell wine in multiples of either 125 ml or 175 ml but they can only sell spirits in *either* 25 ml *or* 35 ml and multiples thereof, but not both sized measures. A sign declaring this must be clearly displayed for any customer to read. All prices must also be clearly displayed for all alcoholic drinks sold on the premises.

Permitted hours

Premises may only serve intoxicating drinks during their permitted hours. At the end of the permitted hours service and consumption must cease immediately. These permitted hours are shown on the premises' licence, a summary of which must be clearly displayed on the premises. These will vary from establishment to establishment and so staff must be made aware by the Premises Licence Holder or the Designated Premises Supervisor of the hours and activities allowed on the premises.

4.4 Misuse of drugs

The Misuse of Drugs Act 1971 lists a number of drugs whose production, possession or supply is illegal. It is therefore important that Premises Licence Holders have a zero-tolerance policy in relation to illegal drug activity on their premises. Staff should be trained in what to look out for and be vigilant at all times.

The police should be contacted for advice if the Premises Licence Holder suspects that drug-related activity may be happening on the premises. The police have the power to close premises down where they suspect that production or supply of drugs is taking place or serious nuisance or disorder is occurring.

4.5 Smoke-free regulations

Figure 4.3 No smoking symbol

The Smoke-free (Premises and Enforcement) Regulations 2006 mean that no one is permitted to smoke in either an enclosed or a substantially closed space where members of the public have access in the course of their work, business or leisure.

The Smoke-free (Signs) Regulations 2007 state that A5-sized signs showing the burning cigarette symbol (Figure 4.3) indicating that smoking is prohibited must be clearly displayed in all public buildings, both in the entrance to the building and in all areas that may be enclosed or a substantially closed space where members of the public have access in the course of their work, business or leisure.

Failure to comply can lead to prosecution of the individual smoking as well as the person in charge of the premises.

4.6 Legal aspects of the sale of goods

The following legislation covers the sale of goods:
- Sale and Supply of Goods Act (1994)
- Trade Descriptions Act (1968)
- Consumer Protection Act (1987)
- Consumer Protection from Unfair Trading Regulations 2008
- Consumer Protection (Northern Ireland) Order (1987).

Broadly, the legislation requires the foodservice operator and members of staff to follow good practice to ensure:
- all food, beverages and other services provided are fit for purpose and of satisfactory quality in relation to price and description
- food, beverages and other services are accurately described in terms of size, quality, composition, production, quantity and standard
- all statements of price, whether in an advertisement, brochure, leaflet, website or given by letter or orally in person or over the telephone are clear and accurate
- pricing and the display of priced items complies with the Price Marking Order (2004)
- the alcohol by volume (ABV) of alcoholic drinks is declared on the drinks list to comply with the Food Labelling Regulations 1996
- food, beverages and other services correspond to their description in brochures/promotional material
- times, dates, locations and nature of service promised are adhered to
- customer billing is fair, transparent and reflects the prices quoted either orally or in writing.

To ensure compliance with legislation, care must be taken when:
- wording menus and wine lists
- describing menu and beverage items to customers
- stating if prices include local and/or government taxes
- describing conditions such as cover charges, service charges or extras
- describing the service provision.

Selling goods by weights and measures

All sales of goods by weight or measure should be in accordance with the legislative requirements of the Weights and Measures Act (1985) and the Weights and Measures (Packaged Goods) Regulations 1986. This usually requires:
- a display of the prices and the measures used for all spirits, wines, beers, ciders and any other alcohol served
- the food and beverage items for sale to be of the quantity and quality demanded by the customer
- the use of officially stamped measures.

Providing services

Generally a food and beverage operator is under no specific requirement to serve anyone. However, it is important that the supervisor and staff are aware of:
- circumstances where there may be a mandatory requirement to provide services
- valid reasons for refusal.

Contracts

A contract is made when one party agrees to the terms of an offer made by another party; this can be written or verbal. In food and beverage service there are essentially two types of customer: those who pre-book and those who do not (often called chance or casual customers).

All foodservice establishments should be clear on how they will deal with these different types of customers, including:

- circumstances where the restaurant may seek compensation from the customer if they do not turn up or pay for their meals or services
- taking care when making contracts with minors (i.e. persons under 18).

Customer property and customer debt

Good practice usually means that supervisors need to ensure care is taken of customers' property in order to minimise potential loss or damage. Notices warning customers of 'no responsibility' may help in defence but do not guarantee exemption from liability for the food and beverage operator.

Clear guidance must be given to staff on the procedures to follow if a customer is unable or unwilling to pay.

4.7 Avoiding discrimination

There are a number of Acts that the foodservice operator and staff should be aware of relating to discrimination on grounds of ethnic origin, race, creed, sex or disability:

- Race Relations (Amendment) Act (2000)
- Race Relations (Northern Ireland) Order (1997)
- Sex Discrimination Act (1975)
- Sex Discrimination (Northern Ireland) Order (Amendment) 1988
- Disability Discrimination Act (1995)
- Equality Act (2010)

Both the foodservice operator and staff must take steps to ensure that discrimination under the terms of these Acts does not occur. There are potentially three ways in which discrimination can take place.

1   **Direct discrimination**: for example, refusing service to customers of particular ethnic origin, race, creed, sex or disability.
2   **Indirect discrimination**: for example, denying consumer services by imposing unjustifiable conditions or requirements that have ethnic origin, sex or disability implications.
3   **Discrimination through victimisation**: for example, by (a) refusal of provision, that is refusal of admission on the basis of ethnic origin, sex or disability; or (b) omission of provision, that is providing services to ethnic or disabled customers that are markedly inferior to those available to the public in general or which may only be available at a price premium.

It is the responsibility of the business and members of staff to ensure that no such discrimination occurs.

Under the legislation there are requirements to ensure:

- a commitment to providing consistently high levels of service to all internal and external customers to ensure they are not discriminated against on the grounds of race, sex, age, disability, sexual orientation, religion or belief
- an equal opportunities policy is available
- job adverts use wording that indicates equal opportunities
- a diversity of staff are employed or considered for employment including mixed sexes, ages and races, and people with disabilities
- reasonable adjustments are made to the way services are delivered to make it easier for disabled guests to use them, including easy wheelchair access for disabled customers and staff, disabled toilet facilities, elevator facilities as an alternative to stairs for disabled customers and staff, and assistance being given to any disabled customer on request.

4.8 Data protection

Under the terms of the Data Protection Act (1998) customers have a right to expect that data about them is kept secure and is only used for the published business purposes. The general requirements for businesses are to ensure that:
- the company is registered with the Data Protection Registrar
- information on customers is kept up to date, fairly, lawfully and securely
- customer information is not passed on to third parties without prior consent from the customer
- staff are aware of the importance of the protection of customer information and the procedures to follow to ensure it is held securely.

Testing your learning

You can test your learning further by looking at the internet to check the current regulations that apply to foodservice operations.

To complete these questions you may also need to read sections in other chapters.
1 There are a wide variety of legal requirements for foodservice operations. Name three enforcement bodies.
2 State one of the objectives of the Licensing Act 2003.
3 Name two items used to legally measure alcohol in licensed premises.
4 A bartender has refused to serve a person who is obviously intoxicated. Which legislation is the bartender following?
5 Identify one possible consequence for the licence holder if a bartender serves a person who is obviously intoxicated.
6 One young person is ordering alcoholic drinks for a group of young-looking people. In order to establish proof of age what should the bartender ask for?
7 What are the legal measures for the sale of gin, rum, vodka and whisky?
8 State the name of the licence that names the person who is legally authorised to sell alcohol on a premises.
9 A customer is smoking within the premises.
    (a) Identify which action should be taken by a member of staff.
    (b) Identify one possible consequence to the member of staff or the customer if no action is taken.
10 Identify one piece of legislation that governs the sale of goods.
11 Identify the legislation that prevents retailers or service industry providers from misleading customers about what they are purchasing.

12 Name one Act that governs the way alcohol and other goods are measured and sold.

13 A customer complains to a server that their food is not as ordered. The server offers to replace the dish with the correct one. Which legislation protects the customer?

14 Name the legislation that states a menu and price list must be displayed at the entrance of a restaurant.

15 State the immediate action that a member of staff must take if they suspect that drugs are being dealt on a premises.

16 Identify four examples where rights are protected under anti-discrimination legislation.

17 A customer asks for the home address of the restaurant supervisor. Which legislation prevents the waiter from providing this information?

18 Identify one provision that a restaurant must make for wheelchair users in order to meet the requirements of the Disability Discrimination Act 1995.

19 There are potentially three types of discrimination. One is direct discrimination. Name one of the other two.

Health, safety and security

Units covered

This chapter covers the following units:

Level 1

→ Health and safety awareness for catering and hospitality (103)
→ Maintain a safe, hygienic and secure working environment (1GEN1, 104)

Level 2

→ Health and safety in catering and hospitality (203)
→ Maintain a safe, hygienic and secure working environment (1GEN1, 101)

Learning outcomes	
This chapter will help you to:	
1 Contribute to maintaining a safe environment	78
2 Contribute to ensuring fire safety	87
3 Contribute to maintaining a secure environment	90

5.1 Maintaining a safe environment

Every day people are injured at work. Some may be permanently disabled and some may even die. It is important to be safe and not let this happen to you or your work colleagues. Foodservice operations can be dangerous places so it is important to work in a safe and systematic way in order to avoid accidents or injury to yourself or anyone else. Over 200 people die in accidents at work each year; accidents can happen in any workplace.

Stress and accidents are currently the two biggest causes of absence from work.

According to a CBI/Pfizer survey report of July 2013, absence due to sickness costs the UK economy approximately £14 billion each year and the average number of sick days taken each year in the UK is approximately 30 million.

Potential benefits of good health and safety practices

- reduction in accidents and ill health
- motivated workers
- enhanced company reputation
- increased productivity
- improved profitability.

Potential costs of accidents in the workplace

- employees absent from work due to illness and stress
- compensation claims
- prosecution
- fines
- legal costs
- damage to the business' reputation
- high staff turnover.

Who is responsible for health and safety?

The simple answer is that everyone is responsible for health and safety. More specifically, the following can be said to have a responsibility:

- employers/employees
- people in control of work premises
- self-employed
- designers
- manufacturers
- suppliers
- local authorities
- Health & Safety Executive (HSE)
- enforcement officers
- environmental health officers
- health and safety inspectors.

Under the terms of the Health and Safety at Work Act (1974), an employer must make sure that all staff are safe while at work. This means that the employer must:

- provide safe equipment and utensils
- train staff in safe working practices
- provide first aid equipment
- keep an accident book
- produce a policy document telling everyone how to work safely
- provide good welfare facilities for staff including rest facilities, drinking water, toilets, washing facilities, changing rooms and lockers.

Essentially safety is a civil duty and negligence is a criminal offence. The implications of the legislation for staff are that they should:

- understand the food hygiene regulations and that it is their responsibility to act within the bounds of these regulations
- notify management of any serious or infectious illness
- perform duties in any area concerned with the handling of food in a hygienic manner, paying attention to food and hygiene regulations
- make themselves familiar with all escape routes and fire exits in the building
- ensure that fire exits remain clear at all times
- participate in fire evacuation drills and practices
- take reasonable care for the health and safety of themselves and of others, and ensure that health and safety regulations are followed
- report to heads of department or duty managers any hazards that may cause injury or ill-health to customers and/or staff.

Managing health and safety

Employers must have appropriate arrangements in place (which must be recorded if there are five or more employees) for maintaining a safe workplace. These should cover the management functions of:

- planning
- organisation
- control.

Avoiding risks

Risk is the chance of somebody being harmed by a hazard. There may be a high risk or a low risk of harm.

Risk assessment

There are five steps to assessing risk:

1. Look for hazards, i.e. things that can cause harm.
2. Identify who could be harmed and how.
3. Work out the risks and decide if the existing precautions are good enough or whether more should be done to prevent harm being caused.
4. Write down what the hazard is and what the risk is and keep this as a record.
5. Re-check the hazard and the risk at regular intervals and go back and change the **risk assessment** (the written record) if necessary.

Table 5.1 Common risks and hazards and ways to minimise them

Common risks and hazards	Ways to minimise risks
Poor design and structure of building	Improved and safe design of building
Poor signage	Correct and clear/visible signage
Poor housekeeping standards	Good housekeeping
Poor lighting and ventilation	Well-lit and ventilated areas
Dangerous working practices	Well-trained staff
Distraction and lack of attention	Strict enforcement of rules
Working too quickly	Concentrating on the work and avoiding distractions
Ignoring rules	
Not wearing protective clothing	Wearing correct protective clothing

Avoiding hazards

A **hazard** is anything that can cause harm, such as:

- extremes of cold and heat
- uneven floors
- excessive noise
- chemicals
- electricity
- working using ladders
- moving parts and machinery
- dust and fumes.

The following aspects of the foodservice environment have the potential to give rise to hazards:

- equipment: liquidisers, food processors, mixers, mincers, etc.
- substances: cleaning chemicals, detergents, sanitisers
- work methods: carrying knives and equipment incorrectly and not following a logical sequence
- work areas: spillages not cleaned up, overcrowded work areas, insufficient work space, uncomfortable work conditions due to extreme heat or cold.

Figure 5.1 A potential hazard

The Health and Safety at Work Act covers all full-time and part-time workers as well as unpaid workers. The Health & Safety Executive (HSE) is responsible for enforcing health and safety in the workplace.

- The HSE has the power to investigate premises, check, dismantle and remove equipment, inspect records, ask questions, seize and destroy articles.
- It can give verbal or written advice, order improvement and prohibition notices and will, if necessary, prosecute, which can result in unlimited fines or even imprisonment.

Employees have a responsibility to themselves, work colleagues and customers to be aware of hazards that may arise when working. Many accidents occur through carelessness or through lack of thought, for example:

- not wearing the correct protective clothing, such as an apron
- not wearing sensible (stable and properly fitted) shoes
- delays in clearing spillages or picking up items of equipment that have fallen on the floor
- not being aware of customers' bags placed on the floor
- items of equipment not stored correctly
- broken glass or crockery not wrapped up sufficiently before being placed in the bin
- forgetting to unplug electrical appliances prior to cleaning
- putting ashtray debris into rubbish bins containing paper (fire hazard)
- forgetting to switch off and unplug an appliance after use, or at the end of service
- not being observant with table lamps or lit candles on a buffet
- over-filling coffee pots, soup tureens, glasses, etc.
- using cups, glasses, soup bowls, etc., for storing cleaning agents
- stacking trays incorrectly
- carrying a mix of equipment on a tray, such as cutlery, crockery and glassware
- carpet edges turned up
- faulty wheels on trolleys or castors on sideboards
- being unaware of customers' walking sticks and crutches
- lack of adequate space for the safe service of food and drink due to bad planning
- lack of knowledge in carrying out certain tasks, for example, opening a bottle of sparkling wine.

Control of substances hazardous to health

The Control of Substances Hazardous to Health (COSHH) Regulations (2002) state that an employer must not carry out any work that might expose employees to any substances that are hazardous to health, unless the employer has assessed the risks of this work to employees. In foodservice establishments there are many chemicals and substances used for cleaning that can be harmful if not used correctly (see Table 5.2).

Substances that are dangerous to health are labelled as very toxic, toxic, harmful, irritant or corrosive. Figure 5.2 shows some hazardous substances symbols. People using these chemical substances must be trained to use them correctly. They must also wear protective clothing such as goggles, gloves and face masks. Hazardous substances can enter the body through the skin, eyes, nose (by inhaling) and mouth (by swallowing).

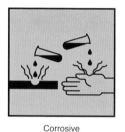
Corrosive

Flammable

Harmful

Toxic

Figure 5.2 Hazardous substances symbols

Preventing accidents

COSHH Regulations state that an employer must assess the risk from chemicals and decide what precautions are needed. The employer should make sure that measures are in place to control the use of chemical substances and monitor their use. Guidelines for using chemical substances include the following:

- inform, instruct and train all staff in their use and safety
- ensure the manufacturer's instructions are followed
- make sure the chemicals are always stored in their original containers, away from heat
- keep lids tightly closed
- do not expose chemicals to heat or naked flames
- read all the labels carefully
- never mix chemicals
- know the first aid procedure
- get rid of empty containers immediately
- get rid of waste chemical solutions safely
- wear safety equipment and clothing.

Hazardous substance monitoring

In order to comply with legal obligations under the COSHH Regulations, all areas should be surveyed to ascertain which chemicals and substances are used. Table 5.2 lists the different work areas and the chemicals and substances likely to be found in them.

Table 5.2 Work areas and the chemicals and substances likely to be found in them

Area	Chemicals and substances
Kitchen	Cleaning chemicals including alkalis and acids, detergents, sanitisers and descalers
	Chemicals associated with burnishing; possibly some oils associated with machines
	Pest control chemicals, insecticides and rodenticides
Restaurant	Cleaning chemicals, polishes, fuel for flame lamps including methylated spirits, LPG
Bar	Beer-line cleaner, glass-washing detergent and sanitisers
Housekeeping	Cleaning chemicals including detergents, sanitisers, descalers, polishes, carpet-cleaning products, floor-care products
Maintenance	Cleaning chemicals, adhesives, solvents, paint, LPG, salts for water softening, paint stripper, varnishes
Offices	Correction fluid, thinners, solvents, methylated spirits, toner for photocopier, duplicating fluids and chemicals, polishes

A COSHH register should be kept by the manager of all substances used in the establishment. Technical data sheets should be attached to the completed COSHH assessment sheet.

Personal protective equipment

According to the Personal Protective Equipment (PPE) at Work Regulations (1992), employees must wear **personal protective equipment** and clothing (e.g. safety shoes, eye protection such as goggles) for tasks that may pose a risk or hazard.

Manual handling

Picking up and carrying heavy or difficult loads can lead to accidents if not done properly. Poor handling of loads is the main cause of back problems in the workplace. The safest way to lift objects is to bend your knees rather than your back (see Figure 5.3). It is also better if two people lift the object together, rather than one person trying to do it on their own. This will help to prevent straining and damage to your back.

Key term

Personal protective equipment (PPE) – protective clothing and equipment used for tasks that may pose a risk or hazard

Figure 5.3 How to lift correctly

Handling checklist

- When you move goods on trolleys, trucks or other wheeled vehicles:
  - load them carefully
  - do not overload them
  - load them in a way that allows you to see where you are going.
- In stores, stack heavy items at the bottom.
- If steps are needed to reach higher items, use them with care.
- Take particular care when moving large pots of liquid, especially if the liquid is hot. Do not fill pots to the brim.
- Use a warning sign to let people know if equipment handles, lids and so on might be hot. This is traditionally done by sprinkling a small amount of flour, or something similar, on to the part of the equipment that might be hot.
- Take extra care when removing a tray from the oven or salamander to avoid burning someone else.

Safety signs

Safety signs are used to control a hazard and they should not replace other methods of controlling risks.

Yellow warning signs

These are warning signs to alert people to various dangers, such as slippery floors, hot oil or hot water. They also warn people about hazards such as a corrosive material.

Figure 5.4 Yellow warning signs

Blue mandatory signs

These signs inform people about precautions they must take. They tell people how to progress safely through a certain area. They must be used whenever special precautions need to be taken, such as wearing protective clothing.

Figure 5.5 Blue mandatory signs

Red prohibition signs – fire fighting signs

Red signs tell people that they should not enter. They are used to stop people from doing certain tasks in a hazardous area. Red signs are also used for fire-fighting equipment.

Figure 5.6 Red prohibition signs

Green safe signs

These are route signs designed to show people where fire exits and emergency exits are. Green is also used for first aid equipment.

Figure 5.7 Green safe signs

Electricity and gas

Great care must be taken when dealing with electricity. If a person comes into direct contact with electricity the consequences can be very serious and sometimes fatal. If a person has an electric shock, switch off the current. If this is not possible, free the person using something that is dry and that will insulate you from the electricity, such as a cloth or something made of wood or rubber. You must take care not to use your bare hands otherwise the electric shock may be transmitted to you. If the person has stopped breathing, call an ambulance and summon a first aider.

In an emergency you should always:
- switch off the electrical current
- raise the alarm
- summon an ambulance/first aid help.

Reporting of Injuries, Diseases and Dangerous Occurrences Regulations (RIDDOR) 2013

The law says that all work-related accidents, diseases and dangerous occurrences must be recorded and reported. Employers must report the following injuries to the Incident Contact Centre (ICC) at the HSE:
- fractures (apart from fractures to fingers, thumbs or toes)
- amputation (cutting off) of limbs – legs, arms, etc.
- dislocation of a hip, knee or spine
- temporary or permanent loss of sight (blindness)
- eye injuries from chemicals getting into the eye, a hot metal burn to the eye or any penetration of the eye
- any injury from electric shock or burning that leads to unconsciousness or the need to resuscitate the person or send them to hospital for more than 24 hours
- any injury resulting in hypothermia (when someone gets too cold), or illness due to heat, that leads to unconsciousness or the need to resuscitate the person or send them to hospital for more than 24 hours (for example, an electric shock or a gas flame blown back and causing burns)

- unconsciousness caused by exposure to a harmful substance or biological agents (such as cleaning products and solvents)
- unconsciousness or illness requiring medical treatment caused by inhaling a harmful substance or absorbing it through the skin (for example, breathing in poisonous carbon monoxide leaking from a gas appliance)
- illness requiring medical treatment caused by a biological agent or its toxins or infected material (for instance, harmful bacteria used in laboratories).

Some diseases are also reportable under RIDDOR and these include:

- dermatitis
- skin cancer
- asthma
- hepatitis

- tuberculosis
- tetanus
- anthrax.

Incident/accident reporting

Health and safety has to be monitored regularly in the workplace by the designated Health and Safety Officer. Any incidents or near misses must be recorded, even if no one is injured.

All accidents should be reported to your line manager, chef or a supervisor. Each accident is recorded in an accident book, which must be provided in every business. Figure 5.8 shows an example of an incident report form showing all the details required.

Full name of injured person:			
Occupation:		Supervisor:	
Time of accident:	Date of accident:	Time of report:	Date of report:
Name of injury or condition:			
Details of hospitalisation:			
Extent of injury (after medical attention):			
Place of accident or dangerous occurrence:			
Injured person's evidence of what happened (include equipment/items and/or other persons):			
Witness evidence (1):		Witness evidence (2):	
Supervisor's recommendations:			
Date:		Supervisor's signature:	

Figure 5.8 An incident report form

Health, safety and security

First aid

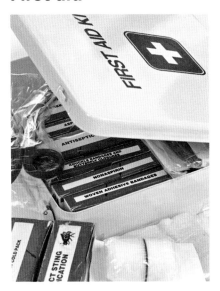

Figure 5.9 A first aid box

When people at work suffer injuries or fall ill, it is important that they receive immediate attention and that, in serious cases, an ambulance is called. The arrangements for providing first aid in the workplace are set out in the Health and Safety (First Aid) Regulations (1981). First aiders and first aid facilities should be available to give immediate assistance to casualties with common injuries or illness.

As the term implies, first aid is the immediate treatment given on the spot to a person who has been injured or is ill. Since 1982 it has been a legal requirement that adequate first aid equipment, facilities and personnel are provided at work. If the injury is serious, the injured person should be treated by a doctor or nurse as soon as possible.

If you are involved in or witness an accident you will be required to give information and/or to complete an accident form (see Figure 5.8). For this reason it is wise to make notes on the event at the earliest opportunity. The information should include:

- the location of the accident
- the time of the accident
- a statement of the event
- details of witnesses
- the treatment administered.

5.2 Ensuring fire safety

Every employer has an explicit duty for the safety of his or her employees in the event of a fire. The Regulatory Fire Safety Order (2005) emphasises that fires should be prevented. It says that fire safety is the responsibility of the occupant of the premises and the people who might be affected by fire, so in catering this will usually be the employer (the occupant) and the employees (who will be affected by fire).

The responsible person must:

- make sure that the fire precautions, where reasonably practicable, ensure the safety of all employees and others in the building
- make an assessment of the risk of and from fire in the establishment; special consideration must be given to dangerous chemicals or substances and the risks that these pose if a fire occurs
- review the preventative and protective measures.

Fire precautions

A fire requires heat, fuel and oxygen – known as 'the fire triangle' (see Figure 5.10). Without any one of these elements there is no fire, so taking precautions to avoid the three coming together will reduce the chances of a fire starting.

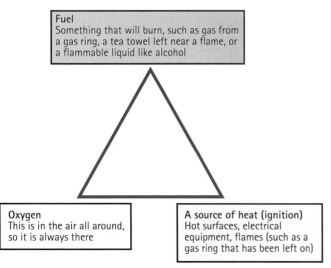

Figure 5.10 The fire triangle

Some fire precaution guidelines are shown below.
- Remove all hazards or reduce them as much as possible.
- Make sure that everyone is protected from the risk of fire and the likelihood of a fire spreading.
- Make sure that all escape routes are safe and used effectively; in other words, ensure they are signposted, easy to access and people know where they are.
- Some way of fighting fires (e.g. a fire extinguisher or fire blanket) must be available on the premises.
- There must be some way of detecting a fire on the premises (e.g. smoke alarms) and instructions on what to do in case of fire.
- There must be arrangements in place for what to do if a fire breaks out on the premises. Employees must be trained in what to do in the event of a fire.
- All fire precaution devices must be installed and maintained by a competent person.

Fire risk assessments

A fire risk assessment will determine how likely it is that a fire might happen and highlight the dangers from fire in the workplace.

You should always report:
- dangerous electrical equipment
- gas leaks
- faulty equipment.

Always use qualified professionals for problems with gas, electricity and water.

There are five steps to complete for a fire risk assessment:
1   Identify the potential fire hazards in the workplace.
2   Decide who will be in danger in the event of a fire, for example, employees, visitors.
3   Identify the risks caused by the hazards. Decide whether the existing fire precautions are adequate or whether more needs to be done, for example to remove a hazard to control the risk.
4   Anything arising from points 1 to 3 above should be written down and a record kept, and all staff should be informed of them.
5   The risk assessment should be reviewed regularly to check that it is up to date. If things change it should be revised as necessary.

Health, safety and security

Fire detection and fire warning

It is important that there is an effective way of detecting a fire and warning people about it quickly enough to allow them to escape before the fire spreads.

In small workplaces, such as small restaurants, a fire will be detected easily and quickly, and is unlikely to cut off the escape routes. In this case, if people can see the exits clearly, shouting 'FIRE!' may be all that is necessary.

In larger establishments fire warning systems are needed. Manually operated call points are likely to be the minimum that is needed. These are the type of fire alarm where you break glass to set off the alarm (as seen on the wall in schools, etc.).

Fire-fighting equipment

Methods of extinguishing fires concentrate on cooling (as in a water extinguisher or fire hose) or depriving the fire of oxygen (as in an extinguisher that uses foam or powder to smother it). Portable fire extinguishers enable people to tackle a fire in its early stages. People should be trained to use the extinguishers and should only use them if they can do so without putting themselves in danger.

Fires are classified in accordance with British Standard EN2 as follows:
- Class A: fires involving solid materials where combustion (burning) normally forms glowing embers (e.g. wood).
- Class B: fires involving liquids (e.g. methylated spirits) or liquefiable solids (e.g. any kind of flammable gel used under a burner).
- Class C: fires involving gases.
- Class D: fires involving metals.
- Class F: fires involving cooking oils or fats.

Different types of fire extinguishers are suitable for different types of fire. Portable extinguishers all contain a substance that will put out a fire. The substance will vary, but whatever it is it will be forced out of the extinguisher under pressure. Generally, portable fire extinguishers contain one of the following five substances (known as extinguishing mediums):
- water
- foam
- carbon dioxide
- dry powder
- vaporising liquids (wet chemical).

Table 5.3 Fire extinguishers and their uses

Contents	Water	Foam	CO$_2$	Dry powder	Wet chemical
Label colour*	White on red	Cream on red	Black on red	Blue on red	Yellow on red
Electrical suitability	Dangerous – electrically conductive		Safe – non-electrically conductive		
Suitable for	Solids	Some liquids	Electrical – do not use in a confined space	Liquid	Liquid, especially cooking fats and oils
Unsuitable for	Oil	Electrical	Solids	Very little	Solids

* Under European Union standards the body of every extinguisher must be coloured red. However, a colour zone is used to indicate what the extinguishing medium is – the

colours used for these mediums are the ones given here, and they are the same as the previous whole body colour coding system.

Procedure in case of fire

All employees should be given fire drill training as part of their induction programme. This initial training should then be followed up by regular training sessions on the procedures to be followed in the event of fire. This training should include:

- fire procedures in employee's own specific area of work
- fire drill instructions for both customers and staff
- the location of fire points (safe places where staff and customers should assemble after an evacuation) nearest to own particular area of work
- the location of the fire exits
- the correct type of fire extinguisher to be used in relation to the type of fire (see Table 5.3)
- identification of employee's own specific responsibilities in the event of fire.

In the event of the fire alarm ringing employees must be aware of the following instructions:

- Follow the fire instructions as laid down for the establishment.
- Usher all customers and staff out of the work area promptly and calmly.
- Pay special attention to customers with special needs such as those with mobility problems.
- Walk quickly but do not run. Display a sense of urgency.
- Do not panic; remain calm as composure will be imitated by others.
- Proceed as promptly as possible to the nearest assembly point.
- Ensure that someone watches to see that there are no stragglers.
- Follow the exit route as laid down in the establishment fire instructions.
- Never use a lift.
- Do not re-enter the building until told it is safe to do so by the fire service.
- Do not waste time to collect personal items.

Employees have a responsibility to assist in fire prevention, control and safety.

They must therefore ensure that:

- fire exits are not obstructed
- fire-fighting equipment is not damaged or misused
- no smoking rules are observed at all times
- as far as is possible all electrical and gas equipment is switched off when not in use
- all doors and windows are closed when not being used for evacuation purposes
- fire doors are not locked or wedged open
- sufficient ashtrays/stands are available for the disposal of cigarette ends and used matches
- the procedure for making an emergency fire call is known.

5.3 Maintaining a secure environment

Security is a major concern these days. The main security risks in the hotel and catering industry are:

- theft: where customers' property, employers' property (particularly food, drink and equipment) or employees' property is stolen
- burglary: where the burglar comes onto the premises (trespasses) and steals customers' property, employers' property or employees' property
- robbery: theft with assault, for example when staff are banking or collecting cash

- fraud: false insurance claims, counterfeit money, stolen credit cards
- assault: fights between customers; assaults on staff by customers (for example if a customer is not happy with the service or is drunk, they may become violent towards staff); attacks on staff while they are taking cash to or collecting cash from the bank
- vandalism: damage to property caused by customers, intruders or employees
- arson: setting fire to the property
- undesirables: having people such as drug dealers on the premises
- terrorism: bombs, telephone bomb threats.

The Health and Safety at Work Regulations now require employers to conduct a risk assessment regarding the safety of staff in the catering business. Preventing crime is better than having to deal with it once it has happened. Here are some ideas for helping to prevent crime.

- The best way to prevent theft is to stop the thief entering the premises in the first place. Reception staff should be trained to spot suspicious individuals. Everyone who comes in should be asked to sign in at reception and, if they are a legitimate visitor, be given a security badge. It is also essential to make sure that any suspicious person does not re-enter the building.
- All contract workers should be registered and given security badges, and they may be restricted to working in certain areas.
- There should be a good security system at the back door, where everyone delivering goods has to report to the security officer.
- Many establishments restrict access to their premises by using a security keypad (see Figure 5.11) which requires staff to enter a numerical code to gain access. The code should be changed on a regular basis to maintain security.
- All establishments should try to reduce temptation for criminals, for example by reducing the amount of cash that is handled. The use of credit and debit cards does cost the establishment a small amount of money (a fee must be paid to credit card companies), but it reduces the amount of cash that is used and therefore the risk of cash being stolen. However, there is also an increase in crime due to fraud (for example, using stolen credit cards).
- Staff who handle money should be trained in simple anti-fraud measures such as checking bank notes, checking signatures on plastic cards and so on.
- It is impossible to remove all temptation, so equipment such as computers, fax machines and photocopiers should be marked with some type of security identification or tag.
- There are many simple and obvious security measures that can also be taken, such as locking doors and windows.

Figure 5.11 A security keypad

- Good lighting is also important – criminals are less likely to come onto the premises at night if people can see them easily. Supervisors and managers should regularly check the lighting in all areas. Leaving lights on in some areas that can be seen by passers-by can also help.
- Closed-circuit television (CCTV) cameras are used as a deterrent against crime.

- With regard to staff, the first step is to appoint honest staff by checking their references from previous employers.
- Some companies include a clause in employee contracts stating their 'right to search'. This means that from time to time the employer can carry out searches of the employees' lockers, bags and so on. This discourages employees from stealing. It is not legal to force a person to be searched even if they have signed a contract agreeing to it, but if they refuse they may be breaking their employment contract.

Personal safety

Below is a personal safety checklist to help you stay safe.
- Wear protective clothing.
- Do not work under the influence of alcohol or drugs.
- Keep hair short, or tied back if long.
- Do not wear jewellery as this, like long hair, can be caught in machinery.
- Walk – do not run.
- Use the gangways provided and never take short cuts.
- Look out for and obey all warning notices and safety signs.
- Back problems can cause a lot of pain and may last a lifetime. Always use trolleys, wheelbarrows or other appropriate lifting equipment if available.
- You must be shown how to lift and carry items correctly. Take care that you:
  - lift or carry only what you can manage
  - can see clearly where you are going
  - get help with anything that you think might be too heavy or awkward to manage on your own.

If in doubt, ask for help!

General procedures

Depending upon the nature of the establishment, the security measures that are laid down may vary considerably. As employees, staff should be aware of all such measures as they relate to their own work environment. Consideration needs to be given to the aspects of security outlined below.
- The importance of wearing some form of recognised identity badge.
- Being observant and reporting 'suspicious' persons and/or packages.
- Not discussing work duties with customers or outside of the workplace.
- Allowing bags, packages and one's person to be searched upon request when either entering or leaving the workplace.
- Being aware of the security procedures for the establishment, should sudden and urgent action need to be taken.
- Ensuring external fire doors are kept shut but not locked, nor left ajar in error.
- Ensuring that all areas have been vacated when responsible for 'locking up' duties. All toilets/cloakrooms must be carefully checked and, at the same time, all windows and doors should be checked to ensure they are locked.
- Keys should only be handled by someone in authority. A signing out book should be available when staff request keys.
- Keys are never to be left unattended.
- When handling cash, all large denomination notes should be checked carefully as well as all cheque and credit card payments, to prevent fraud, the passing of illegal notes and the acceptance of altered credit cards.

- Being alert and observant at all times, and not hesitating in reporting anything suspicious to the immediate superior.

Dealing with a suspicious item or package

All employees should be constantly alert for suspicious items or packages.

- If an object is found then it must immediately be reported to the security officer, manager or supervisor.
- Do not touch or attempt to move the object.
- If there are customers in the immediate vicinity, discreetly attempt to establish ownership of the object.
- If the ownership is established then ask the customer to keep the object with them, or to hand it in for safe keeping.
- If no immediate ownership is established, then the area should be cleared and the authorities notified without delay.

Dealing with a bomb threat

Immediate action needs to be taken as a bomb could go off at any moment. As a result staff should:

- be aware of and follow establishment policy with regard to bomb threats and evacuation procedures
- evacuate the immediate work area
- search the work area to ensure it is cleared, if this is part of their own responsibility
- evacuate the premises and usher all customers/staff through the nearest usable exits to specified assembly areas
- count all persons present to determine their safety and minimise the risk of fatal accidents.

Testing your learning

1. Name three benefits of good health and safety procedures.
2. State four of the potential costs of accidents in the workplace.
3. What does COSHH stand for?
4. A hazard is anything that can cause harm. Identify five examples of potential hazards in the workplace.
5. What are the three things that a fire needs in order to exist?
6. Identify three extinguishing mediums generally found in portable extinguishers and state which fires they should be used on.
7. What is the main Act that covers the health and safety of people in their workplace?
8. Identify two main responsibilities of employees under workplace law.
9. State three responsibilities an employer has under health and safety law.
10. State three communication methods you could use to report an accident in the workplace.
11. What are three common causes of accidents in foodservice operations?
12. Suggest three measures that could help minimise the risk of accidents in foodservice operations.
13. Name four health and safety hazards that may be present in a foodservice operation.
14. What are the first two steps in assessing risks?

15 What is the principal health and safety regulation regarding the provision of first aid in the workplace?

16 Describe the correct procedure for lifting boxes that are not too heavy for you.

17 Which fire extinguisher should be used on electrical equipment fires?

18 What colour are mandatory health and safety signs?

19 Which piece of fire-fighting equipment is most frequently used on deep-fat fryer fires?

20 Suggest two ways to make premises more secure.

In practice

1 Devise your own risk assessment form using the five steps of risk assessment or download a copy of the risk assessment form that can be found in *The five steps to risk assessment* booklet available at www.hse.gov.uk. Print a copy of the form.

2 Go around your building looking for safety signs. Find:
- two yellow warning signs
- two blue mandatory signs
- two red prohibition signs
- two green safety signs.

3 Complete the risk assessment form and for each of the signs:
- make a simple sketch of the sign
- state what it means.

Identify one risk that you see in the area in order to complete the final stage of the form.

Food safety

Units covered

This chapter covers the following units:

Level 1

→ Food safety in catering (202 Level 2)
→ Maintain food safety when storing, holding and serving food (2GEN4, 204)

Level 2

→ Food safety in catering (202)
→ Maintain food safety when storing, holding and serving food (2GEN4, 204)

6.1 The importance of keeping food safe

Everyone consuming food prepared for them by others when they are away from home (for example, in canteens and restaurants) has the right and expectation to be served safe food that will not cause illness or harm them in any way.

Food safety means putting in place all of the measures needed to make sure that food and drinks are suitable, safe and wholesome through all of the processes of food provision, from selecting suppliers and delivery of food through to serving the food to the customer.

Why is food safety important?

Eating 'contaminated' food can cause illness (**food poisoning**) and, in some cases, even death. The number of reported cases of food poisoning each year in England and Wales remains very high, between 70,000 and 94,000 reported cases each year. However, as a large number of food poisoning cases are not reported, no one really knows the actual number.

Key terms

Food safety – putting in place all of the measures needed to make sure that food and drinks are suitable, safe and wholesome through all of the processes of food provision

Food poisoning – an illness of the digestive system that is the result of eating foods contaminated with pathogenic bacteria and/ or their toxins

Food poisoning is an illness of the digestive system that is the result of eating foods contaminated with pathogenic bacteria and/or their toxins. It can be an unpleasant illness for anyone, but it can be very serious or even fatal for some people. High-risk groups include:

- babies and very young children
- elderly people
- pregnant women
- those who are already unwell
- people with a depressed immune system.

It is therefore essential to take great care to prevent food poisoning and the Food Standards Agency has committed to reduce significantly the numbers of reported food poisoning cases in the UK.

Food poisoning may also be caused by eating poisonous fish or plants, allergens or foods contaminated with chemicals, metal deposits or physical contaminants.

Symptoms of food poisoning may include:

- nausea
- vomiting
- diarrhoea
- fever
- dehydration.

What the law says

The latest laws of importance to food businesses took effect from 1 January 2006. Almost all of the requirements in these regulations remain the same as the previous 1990/1995 regulations. These set out the basic food safety requirements for all aspects of a food business, from premises to personal hygiene of staff, with specific attention to temperatures relating to food.

The 2006 laws provide a framework for EU legislation to be enforced throughout the UK and require food establishments to have an approved Food Safety Management Procedure in place, with up-to-date records available.

Food safety legislation

Food safety standards and legislation are enforced by **environmental health officers (EHOs)** – also known as **environmental health practitioners (EHPs)**. They may visit food premises as a matter of routine, after problems have occurred or after a complaint. The frequency of visits depends on the type of business, the food being handled and whether there have been previous problems.

EHOs can enter a food business at any reasonable time, usually when the business is open. The main purpose of inspections is to identify any possible risks from the food business to the consumer, and to assess how well the food safety management systems are working.

> **Key term**
>
> **Environmental health officer (EHO)/environmental health practitioner (EHP)** – responsible for food safety standards and enforcement

Serving of notices

A Hygiene Improvement Notice will be served if the EHO/EHP believes that a food business does not comply with regulations. The notice states the details of the business, what is wrong, why it is wrong, what needs to be put right and the time in which this must be completed (usually not less than 14 days). It is an offence if the work is not carried out in the specified time.

A Hygiene Emergency Prohibition Notice is served if the EHO believes that the business poses an immediate risk to people's health. This includes serious issues such as sewage contamination, lack of water supply, rodent infestation, etc. Serving this notice results in immediate closure of the business for three days, during which time the EHO must apply to magistrates for a Hygiene Emergency Prohibition Order to keep the premises closed. A Hygiene Prohibition Order prohibits a person (i.e. the owner/manager) from working in a food business.

Fines and penalties for non-compliance

Magistrates' courts can impose fines of up to £5,000, a six-month prison sentence or both. For serious offences, magistrates can impose fines of up to £20,000. In a Crown court, unlimited fines can be imposed and/or two years' imprisonment.

Due diligence

'**Due diligence**' can be an important defence under food safety legislation. This means that if there is proof that a business took all reasonable care and did everything it could to prevent food safety problems, legal action may be avoided. Proof would need to be provided in the form of accurate written documents such as pest control reports, staff training records, fridge temperature records, etc.

Food businesses must ensure that all staff who handle food are supervised and instructed and/or trained in food hygiene appropriate to the work they do. Training can take place in-house or with a training provider. All records of staff training must be kept for possible inspection.

> **Key term**
>
> **Due diligence** – ensuring that a business has taken reasonable care and did everything it could to prevent food safety problems

Food Standards Agency

The Food Standards Agency was set up in 2000 'to protect public health and to protect the interest of customers in relation to food'. The agency is committed to putting customers first, being open and accessible, and being an independent voice on food-related matters.

'Scores on the Doors' is a strategy that was introduced by the Food Standards Agency to raise food safety standards and reduce the incidence of food poisoning. Various schemes were piloted and tested, and in 2008 a star-rating scheme was selected for England and Wales. On inspection, food premises can be awarded up to 5 stars (0 stars = very poor food safety; 5 stars = excellent food safety). The intention is that the star-rating certificate given will be placed in a prominent position on the door or window of a premises, but as yet it is not mandatory to do so.

It is expected that the Scores on the Doors scheme will have a positive impact on food safety standards. No matter how good the food in a particular establishment, few people will want to eat there if the food safety score is low!

6.2 Causes of food contamination

There are three main ways that food is contaminated:

1 **Bacteria** are all around us in the environment – on raw food, on humans, animals, birds and insects. When bacteria multiply in food which is then eaten, they can make people ill.
2 **Chemicals** can sometimes get into food accidentally and can make the consumer ill. The kinds of chemical that may get into food include cleaning fluids, disinfectants, machine oil, insecticides and pesticides, etc.

> **Key terms**
>
> **Bacteria** – organisms harmful to humans
>
> **Chemicals** – include cleaning fluids, disinfectants, machine oil, insecticides and pesticides

3 **Physical contamination** is caused when something gets into food that should not be there. This could be anything that a person should not eat, such as glass, pen tops, paperclips, blue plasters, hair, fingernails, etc.

Two further reasons why people can become ill after eating food are allergens and food intolerance:

- **Allergens** cause allergic reactions. An allergy is when someone's immune system reacts to certain foods (allergens). Symptoms of an allergic reaction can include swelling, itching, rashes and breathlessness. In the case of a severe reaction anaphylactic shock can occur, which often causes swelling of the throat and mouth, preventing breathing. Medical help should be sought immediately in such an event.
- **Food intolerance** is different and does not affect the immune system, but there may still be a reaction to some foods.

Foods usually associated with allergies and food intolerances are nuts, dairy products, wheat-based products, eggs and shellfish.

All of these are potentially dangerous and, in the case of the three contaminants, great care must be taken to avoid them, especially bacteria. In the case of allergens and food intolerance, it is important for customers to be aware of what is in their food and drink so they can make an informed choice. For more information on allergens and menus see Section 8.3 (page 129).

For more information on allergens and menus see Section 8.3 (page 129).

Key terms

Physical contamination – when something gets into food that should not be there

Allergen – something that causes an allergic reaction such as swelling, itching or rash

Food intolerance – when a person reacts to eating certain foods

High-risk food

Some foods pose a greater risk to food safety than others and are called high-risk foods. They are usually ready to eat, so do not need to be cooked to the high temperatures that would kill bacteria. Such foods are usually moist, contain protein and need to be stored in the fridge. Examples of high-risk foods include:

- soups, stocks, sauces, gravies
- eggs and egg products
- milk and milk products
- cooked meat and fish, and meat and fish products
- any foods that need to be handled or reheated.

Figure 6.1 Milk and eggs are high-risk foods

Bacteria

Not all bacteria are harmful. In fact, some are very useful and are used in foods and medicines. For example, the processes of making milk into yoghurt and making cheese both use bacteria.

The bacteria that are harmful are called pathogenic bacteria (**pathogens**) and can cause food poisoning. Bacteria are so small that you need to use a microscope to see them – you cannot taste them or smell them on food. This is why pathogenic bacteria are so dangerous – you cannot tell when they are in food. Under the right conditions (food, warmth, moisture and time) they can multiply approximately every 10–20 minutes by dividing in half. This is called binary fission.

Pathogenic bacteria can act in different ways to cause food poisoning. Bacteria may multiply in food until it is heated to very high temperatures, and will then cause infection

Key terms

Pathogen – harmful bacteria

when the food is eaten. Other pathogens use food to get into the body, where they then multiply. Some produce toxins, while others produce spores.

Some pathogens produce **toxins** (poisons) that can survive boiling temperatures for half an hour or more. Because they are so heat resistant, the toxins are not killed by the normal cooking processes that kill bacteria, so remain in the food and can cause illness. Some bacteria produce toxins as they die, usually in the intestines of the person who has eaten the food.

Others produce **spores** to protect themselves. The bacteria form spores when the conditions surrounding them become hostile, for example, as temperatures rise, or in the presence of chemicals such as disinfectant. A spore forms a protective 'shell' inside the bacteria, protecting the essential parts from the high temperatures of normal cooking, disinfection, dehydration, etc. Once spores are formed the cells cannot divide and multiply as before but simply survive until conditions improve, for example the high temperatures drop to a level where multiplication can start again. Normal cooking temperatures will not kill spores. Time is very important in preventing the formation of spores. If food is brought to cooking temperature slowly it allows time for spores to form. To avoid this, bring food up to cooking temperature quickly and cool food quickly.

Common food-poisoning bacteria include:
- Salmonella
- *Staphylococcus aureus*
- *Clostridium perfringens*
- *Bacillus cereus*
- *Clostridium botulinum.*

Some bacteria cause food-borne illnesses but do not multiply in food. Instead, they use food to get into the human gut, where they then multiply and cause a range of illnesses, some of them serious, including severe abdominal pain, diarrhoea, vomiting, headaches, blurred vision, flu symptoms, septicaemia and miscarriage. These organisms may be transmitted from person to person, in water or through the air, as well as through food.

Food-borne pathogens include:
- Campylobacter
- *E.coli* 0157
- Listeria
- Norovirus.

> **Key terms**
>
> **Toxin** – poison
>
> **Spore** – protective shell which allows cells to protect themselves from heat or freezing

6.3 Cross-contamination

Cross-contamination is when bacteria are transferred from contaminated food (usually raw food), equipment or surfaces to ready-to-eat food. Cross-contamination is the cause of significant amounts of food poisoning and care must be taken to avoid it. Cross-contamination could be caused by:
- foods touching each other, such as raw and cooked meat
- raw meat or poultry dripping on to high-risk foods
- soil from dirty vegetables coming into contact with high-risk foods
- dirty cloths or dirty equipment
- equipment (such as chopping boards or knives) used with raw food and then used with cooked food
- hands touching raw food and then cooked food, without being washed between tasks
- pests spreading bacteria from their own bodies around the kitchen.

> **Key term**
>
> **Cross-contamination** – when bacteria are transferred from contaminated food (usually raw food), equipment or surfaces to ready-to-eat food

Controlling cross-contamination

Sources of bacteria include raw meat and poultry, pests, dirty vegetables and unwashed hands. Cross-contamination can be avoided by following hygienic working practices and storing, preparing and cooking food safely.

- Separate working areas and storage areas for raw and high-risk foods are strongly recommended. If this is not possible, keep them well away from each other and make sure that working areas are thoroughly cleaned and disinfected between tasks.
- Vegetables should be washed before preparation/peeling and again afterwards. Leafy vegetables may need to be washed in several changes of cold water to remove all of the soil clinging to them.
- Good personal hygiene practices by staff, especially frequent and effective hand washing, are very important in controlling cross-contamination and will avoid the significant amounts of contamination caused by faecal/oral routes (when pathogens normally found in faeces are transferred to ready-to-eat foods, resulting in cross-contamination and illness). An obvious way that this may happen is when food handlers visit the toilet, do not wash their hands and then handle food.

Colour-coding equipment

Colour-coded chopping boards are a good way to keep different types of food separate. Worktops and chopping boards will come into contact with the food being prepared, so need special attention. Make sure that chopping boards are in good condition – cracks and splits could trap bacteria that could be transferred to food.

As well as colour-coded chopping boards, some kitchens also provide colour coded-knives, cloths, cleaning equipment, storage trays, bowls and even staff uniforms to help prevent cross-contamination.

Figure 6.2 Colour code chart for chopping boards

6.4 Personal hygiene

Because humans are a source of food poisoning bacteria it is very important for all food handlers to take care with personal hygiene and to adopt good practices when working with food. These include:

- Arrive at work clean (bathe or shower daily) and ensure hair is clean.
- Wear approved, clean kitchen clothing and only wear it in the kitchen. This must completely cover any personal clothing.
- Keep hair neatly contained in a suitable hat/hairnet.

- Keep nails short and clean, and do not wear nail varnish or false nails.
- Do not wear jewellery or watches when handling food (a plain wedding band is permissible but could still trap bacteria).
- Avoid wearing cosmetics and strong perfumes.
- Smoking should not be allowed in or near food preparation areas (ash, smoke and bacteria from touching the mouth area could get into food).
- Do not eat food, sweets or chew gum when handling food as this may also transfer bacteria to food.
- Cover any cuts, burns or grazes with a blue waterproof dressing, then wash hands.
- Report any illness to the supervisor as soon as possible. Symptoms such as diarrhoea and/or vomiting; infected cuts, burns or spots; bad cold or flu symptoms must be reported or if illness was experienced while away from work.

Hand washing

Hands are constantly in use in the kitchen and will be touching numerous materials, foods, surfaces and equipment. Contamination from hands can happen very easily so you must take care with hand washing to avoid this.

A basin should be provided that is used only for hand washing. Hands should be washed as follows:

- Wet your hands under warm running water.
- Apply liquid soap.
- Rub your hands together, and rub one hand with the fingers and thumb of the other.
- Remember to include your fingertips, nails and wrists.
- Rinse off the soap under the warm running water.
- Dry your hands on a paper towel and use the paper towel to turn off the tap before throwing it away.

You should always wash your hands:

- when you enter the kitchen, before starting work and handling any food
- after a break (particularly if you have used the toilet)
- between different tasks, but especially between handling raw and cooked food

- if you touch your hair, nose, mouth or use a tissue for a sneeze or cough
- after you apply or change a dressing on a cut or burn
- after cleaning preparation areas, equipment or contaminated surfaces
- after handling kitchen waste, external food packaging, money or flowers.

Figure 6.3 Wash hands thoroughly

6.5 Keeping work areas clean and hygienic

Premises

Suitable buildings with well-planned fittings, layout and equipment allow for good food safety practices. Certain basics need to be available if a building is to be used for food production. There must be:

- electricity and ideally gas supplies
- drinking water and good drainage
- suitable road access for deliveries and refuse collection
- no risk of contamination from surrounding areas and buildings, for example, chemicals, smoke, odours or dust.

Layout

When planning food premises, a linear workflow should be in place, for example: delivery → storage → preparation → cooking → hot holding → serving. This type of workflow means there will be no crossover of activities that could result in cross-contamination.

- There must be adequate storage areas; proper refrigerated storage is especially important.
- Staff hand washing/drying facilities suitable for the work being carried out must be provided.
- Clean and dirty (raw and cooked) processes should be kept apart.
- Cleaning and disinfection should be planned with separate storage for cleaning materials and chemicals.
- All areas should allow for good cleaning, disinfection and pest control.
- Personal hygiene facilities must be provided for staff, as well as changing facilities and storage for personal clothing and belongings.

Cleaning programmes

Maintaining clean work areas plays an essential part in the production of safe food and the team must plan, record and check all cleaning as part of a cleaning schedule. Clean premises, work areas and equipment are important to:

- control the bacteria that cause food poisoning
- reduce the possibility of physical and chemical contamination
- reduce the possibility of accidents (e.g. slips on a greasy floor)
- create a positive image for customers, visitors and employees
- comply with the law
- avoid attracting pests to the kitchen.

The cleaning schedule needs to include the following information:

- *What* is to be cleaned.
- *Who* should do it (name if possible).
- *How* it is to be done and how long it should take.
- *When it is to be done*, i.e. time of day.
- *Materials* to be used, including chemicals and their dilution, cleaning equipment and protective clothing to be worn.
- *Safety* precautions that must be taken.
- *Signatures* of the cleaner and the supervisor checking the work, along with the date and time.

Cleaning products

Different cleaning products are designed for different tasks.

- **Detergent** is designed to remove grease and dirt. It may be in the form of liquid, powder, gel or foam, and usually needs to be added to water before use. Detergent will not kill pathogens (bacteria), although the hot water it is mixed with may help to do this. Detergent will clean and degrease surfaces so that disinfectant can work properly. Detergents usually work best with hot water.

- **Disinfectant** is designed to destroy bacteria when used properly. Make sure you only use a disinfectant intended for kitchen use. Disinfectants must be left on a clean, grease-free surface for the required amount of time (contact time) to be effective.
- **Heat** may also be used to disinfect, for example, using steam cleaners or the hot rinse cycle of a dishwasher. Items that should be both cleaned and disinfected include all items in direct contact with food, all hand contact surfaces, hand wash basins and cleaning equipment.
- **Sanitiser** cleans and disinfects. It usually comes in spray form. Sanitiser is very useful for work surfaces and equipment, especially when cleaning them between tasks.

All food and beverage service staff should be made aware of the importance of cleaning programmes to reduce and minimise the build-up of dust, bacteria and other forms of debris. For this reason, together with the considerations needed for safety and hygiene, full attention needs to be paid by all concerned to cleaning tasks and when they should be carried out. Regular maintenance will make the service area look attractive and will project a positive image for the establishment.

A cleaning programme should be set up for any cleaning tasks that must be done in a particular area. Some tasks are done daily, even twice daily, for instance the washing and polishing of crockery before each service period. Other tasks might be done weekly, monthly or every six months. Certain items of equipment will need cleaning immediately after each service period is finished.

Note

- Always use the correct cleaning materials for the task in hand.
- Clean frequently.
- Rinse all surfaces well.
- Dusters should only be used for dusting and no other cleaning tasks.
- Use cleaning procedures that are adequate and efficient.
- Cloths used for cleaning toilets must not be used for any other purpose.
- Clean and store equipment safely and in its correct place.
- Do not use cleaning cloths for wiping down food preparation surfaces.
- Consider safety at all times and do not stretch or stand on chairs to reach high points – use a stepladder.

Storage of cleaning products

All cleaning products should be stored correctly, kept out of direct sunlight in their original containers and, if necessary, in a lockable cupboard away from heat sources and naked flames. Always follow the manufacturers' instructions for the product's use and dilution. Never mix chemicals together unless you have followed the manufacturer's instructions explicitly. Always wear personal protective safety wear when using cleaning products and ensure all cleaning products are recorded in the COSHH manual. This will need to be updated at regular intervals and when a new product is purchased. (For further information on COSHH see Section 5.1, page 78.)

Waste disposal

Many products can be recycled. Paper, cardboard, glass, metal, food scraps and oil can all be collected by companies to be recycled, and often money can be earned by the business by doing so. Waste that is simply taken away and disposed of contributes to landfill and attracts a Landfill Tax for the business.

Waste items need to be stored in a secure area away from the premises; food waste is especially attractive to pests and rodents, and therefore should be stored in covered containers and removed on a daily basis.

Pests

When there are reports of food premises being forcibly closed down, an infestation of pests is often the reason. As pests can be a serious source of contamination and disease, having them near food cannot be allowed and is against the law. Pests can carry food poisoning bacteria into food premises in their fur/feathers, feet/paws, saliva, urine and droppings. Other problems caused by pests include damage to food stocks and packaging; damage to buildings, equipment and wiring; and blockages in equipment and piping.

Table 6.1 Signs of pest presence and how to keep them out

Pest	Signs that they are present	Ways to keep them out/eliminate them
Rats and mice	Sightings of rodents or droppings; gnawed wires; greasy marks on lower walls; damaged food stock; paw prints; unpleasant smell	Block entry by making sure there are no holes around pipe work Fill all gaps and cavities where they could get in
Flies and wasps	Sighting of flies and wasps; hearing them; sightings of dead insects; sightings of maggots	Use sealed drain covers
Cockroaches	Sightings (dead or alive), usually at night; unpleasant smell	Damage to the building or fixtures and fittings should be repaired quickly
Ants	Sightings, including in food; tiny, pale-coloured Pharaohs ants are difficult to spot but can still be the source of a variety of pathogens	Use window/door screening/netting Check deliveries/packaging for pests
Weevils	Sightings of weevils in stored products, e.g. flour/corn flour; they are tiny black insects that are very difficult to see but can be spotted by their movement in flour, etc.	Use baits and traps Use electronic fly killer Use sealed containers and ensure no open food is left out
Birds	Sighting; droppings in outside storage areas and around refuse	Do not allow build-up of waste in kitchen
Domestic pets	These must be kept out of food areas as they carry pathogens in fur, whiskers, saliva, urine, etc.	Do not keep outside waste too close to the kitchen Arrange professional and organised pest management control, surveys and reports

Note

Pest control measures can also introduce food safety hazards. The bodies of dead insects or even rodents may remain in the kitchen (causing physical and bacterial contamination). Pesticides, insecticides and baits could cause chemical contamination if not managed properly. Pest control is best managed by professionals.

6.6 Safe food handling practices and procedures

Importance of temperature

An important way of controlling bacteria is to ensure that food is kept in controlled temperatures as much as possible.

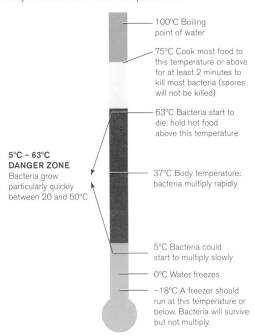

100°C Boiling point of water

75°C Cook most food to this temperature or above for at least 2 minutes to kill most bacteria (spores will not be killed)

63°C Bacteria start to die: hold hot food above this temperature

5°C – 63°C DANGER ZONE Bacteria grow particularly quickly between 20 and 50°C

37°C Body temperature: bacteria multiply rapidly

5°C Bacteria could start to multiply slowly

0°C Water freezes

−18°C A freezer should run at this temperature or below. Bacteria will survive but not multiply.

Figure 6.4 Important food safety temperatures

- Temperatures between 5°C and 63°C are called the **danger zone** because it is possible for bacteria to multiply between these temperatures, with most rapid multiplication at around body temperature (37°C). Keep food held for service above 63°C, or cool it rapidly and keep it below 5°C.
- Thorough cooking is one of the best methods available to control bacteria. Cooking to 75°C and holding that temperature for at least two minutes will kill most pathogens (but not spores and toxins).
- When reheating foods bring the core temperature up to 70°C as quickly as possible and hold this temperature for a minimum of 2 minutes (in Scotland this is 82°C).

> ### Key term
>
> **Danger zone** – temperatures between 5°C and 63°C. It is possible for bacteria to multiply between these temperatures

- Never put hot or warm food into a fridge or freezer as this will raise the temperature in the fridge or freezer and put food into the danger zone.

Using temperature probes

Using a temperature probe is the most effective way of ensuring core temperatures are achieved. The core temperature is taken at the thickest part of the dish or joint as this is the slowest part to absorb heat. The probe needs to be disinfected before and after each insertion to avoid cross-contamination and should be calibrated regularly to ensure the temperature readings are accurate. Follow the manufacturer's instructions as to how to do this correctly for each device. There are however three main methods for checking this:

Figure 6.5 A temperature probe

1. Comparison method: this is carried out by comparing the readings of the device against a device known to be accurate.
2. The ice method: the probe is inserted into a small container containing crushed ice topped up with cold water. When the indicator has stabilised, the calibration may be set to show 0°C.

3   The boiling point method: the probe is inserted into a small container containing boiling water. When the indicator has stabilised, the calibration may be set to show 100°C (at normal altitude).

Food deliveries and storage

Food must be stored correctly for it to remain in the best condition and be safe to eat. This should be planned and the procedures fully understood by staff. Only approved suppliers who can assure that food is delivered in the best condition should be used. Food must be delivered in suitable packaging, properly date coded and at the correct temperature.

General points on storing food in multiuse fridges:
- Ensure the fridge operates at a temperature of 1°C to 4°C.
- All food must be covered and labelled with the name of the item and the date.
- Always store raw food at the bottom of the fridge, with other items above.
- Keep high-risk foods well away from raw foods.
- Never overload the fridge; to operate properly cold air must be allowed to circulate between items.
- Wrap strong-smelling foods very well as the smell (and taste) can transfer to other foods such as milk.
- Record the temperature at which the fridge is operating. Do this at least once a day (this is an example of monitoring) and keep the fridge temperatures with other kitchen records.
- Clean fridges regularly.

'First in – first out'

This term is used to describe stock rotation and is applied to all categories of food. It simply means that foods already in storage are used before new deliveries (providing stock is still within recommended dates and in sound condition). Food deliveries should be labelled with the delivery date and preferably the date by which they should be used. Use this information along with food labelling codes (see below). Written stock records should form part of a 'food safety management system'.

Food labelling codes

- **Use by dates** appear on perishable foods with a short life. Legally, the food must be used by this date and not stored or used after it.
- **Best before dates** apply to foods that are expected to have a longer life, for example, dry products or canned food. A best before date advises that food is at its best before this date; using it after this date is legal but not advised.

Signs of food spoilage

Signs of food spoilage may include an appearance different from the food in its fresh form, such as a change in colour, a change in texture, an unpleasant odour or an undesirable taste. The item may become softer than normal. If mould occurs, it is often visible externally on the item.

Spoilt foods should be recorded in a waste control book and disposed of carefully to avoid any cross-contamination. Excess wastage should be reported to management as this could be a result of poor stock control and should be controlled as part of the food safety management system.

6.7 Food safety management systems

It is good practice for all food businesses to have a food safety management system in place. In line with the Food Standards Agency's commitment to reduce food poisoning cases, it became a legal requirement from January 2006 for all food businesses to operate such a system. When environmental health officers/practitioners inspect the premises of these businesses they will also check that food safety management systems are in place and are working well.

Hazard Analysis and Critical Control Point (HACCP)

All food safety management systems must be based on the Hazard Analysis and Critical Control Point (HACCP) system. This is an internationally recognised food safety management system that aims to identify the critical points or stages in any process. The system must provide a documented record of the stages *all* food will go through right up to the time it is eaten. Once the hazards have been identified, measures are put in place to control the hazards and keep the food safe.

The HACCP system involves seven stages:

1 Identify hazards – what could go wrong.
2 Identify CCP (critical control points), i.e. the important points where things could go wrong.
3 Set critical limits for each CCP, for example, the temperature that fresh chicken should be at when it is delivered.
4 Monitor CCPs and put checks in place to stop problems from occurring.
5 Identify corrective action – what will be done if something goes wrong.
6 Verification – check that the HACCP plan is working.
7 Documentation – record all of the above.

The system must be updated regularly, especially when the menu or systems change (for instance when a new piece of equipment is brought into the kitchen). Specific new controls must be put in place to include any changes.

'Safer food, better business' and 'CookSafe'

The HACCP system described above may seem complicated and difficult to set up for a small business. With this in mind, the Food Standards Agency launched its 'Safer food, better business' system for England and Wales. This is based on the principles of HACCP but is in a format that is easy to understand, with pre-printed pages and charts in which to enter the relevant information, such as temperatures for individual dishes. It is divided into two parts.

- The first part is about safe methods (e.g. avoiding cross-contamination, personal hygiene, cleaning, chilling and cooking).
- The second part covers opening and closing checks. These are checks that procedures are in place (e.g. safe methods, recording of safe methods, training records, supervision, stock control and the selection of suppliers and contractors) to ensure that the operation is working to the standards required to produce safe food. There is a diary entry page for every day that the business is open. Each day, the

pre-set opening checks and closing checks are completed and the diary page signed. Nothing else needs to be recorded unless something goes wrong, for example, a piece of equipment not working would be recorded along with the action that was taken.

A copy of 'Safer food, better business' is available from www.food.gov.uk.

A similar system called 'CookSafe' has been developed by the Food Standards Agency (Scotland) and details of this can also be found at www.food.gov.uk.

Testing your learning

1   Briefly explain what is meant by the term 'food safety'.
2   Identify three of the high-risk groups for whom food poisoning could be very dangerous and even fatal.
3   Give an example of each of the following:
    (a) chemical contamination
    (b) microbiological contamination
    (c) physical contamination.
4   What four conditions are needed by bacteria in order to multiply?
5   Name two of the typical symptoms of food poisoning.
6   What is a food allergy?
7   Suggest three ways that cross-contamination could occur.
8   What is the range of temperature referred to as the 'danger zone' for multiplication of bacteria?
9   Briefly describe what is meant by:
    (a) use by date
    (b) best before date.
10 Suggest three ways that pests can be kept out of foodservice areas.
11 What is meant by HACCP?
12 List the six basic steps for cleaning and disinfection.
13 Complete the following technical terms:
    (a) Bactericide is a substance that…
    (b) Detergent is a chemical that…
    (c) Sanitiser is a chemical used for…
14 Name three common pests.
15 State how each of the following should be stored.

Dry goods	In a
Vegetables	In a
Frozen food	In a _____ at between ___°C and ___°C
Chilled food	In a _____ at ____°C

Principles of customer service

Units covered

This chapter covers the following units:

Level 1

→ Maintain customer care (1GEN3, 106)

Level 2

→ Principles of customer service in hospitality, leisure, travel and tourism (211)
→ Give customers a positive impression of self and your organisation (2GEN1, 201)
→ Resolve customer service problems (2 GEN5, 261)

7.1 Customer needs

There are many different kinds of foodservice operation, designed to meet a wide range of demand. These different types of operation are designed for the needs people have at a particular time, rather than for the type of people they are. For example, a person may be a business customer during the week, but a member of a family at the weekend; they may want a quick lunch on one occasion, a snack while travelling on another and a meal with the family on another occasion. Additionally, the same person may wish to book a wedding or organise some other special occasion.

The main aim of food and beverage operations is to achieve customer satisfaction. In other words, to meet the customers' needs. The needs that customers might be seeking to satisfy include:

- **Physiological**: for example, being hungry or thirsty or the need for special foods such as diabetic or vegetarian.
- **Economic**: for example, the need for good value, rapid service or a convenient location.
- **Social**: for example, going out with friends or business colleagues; attending a function in order to meet others.

- **Psychological**: for example, the need for enhancement of self-esteem; fulfilling lifestyle needs; the need for variety; as a result of advertising and promotion.
- **Convenience**: for example, as a result of being unable to get home (shoppers, workers) or attending some other event (cinema, theatre); the desire for someone else to do the work; the physical impossibility of catering at home (weddings and other special functions).

Figure 7.1 Customers enjoying themselves

Customers may want to satisfy some or all of these needs.

In addition to food and beverage needs, a customer may have special or additional needs due to:
- mobility problems
- blindness or being partially sighted
- communication difficulties as a result of hearing loss, speech loss or because of different languages.

There are also additional considerations when dealing with children (see Section 7.4, page 114).

As the reasons for eating out vary, then so do the types of operation that may be appropriate at the time. It is important to recognise that the specific reasons behind a customer's choice will often determine the customer's satisfaction (or dissatisfaction), rather than the food and beverage service by itself. One example is the social need to go out with friends: if one person fails to turn up or behaves in a disagreeable way, then the customer may be dissatisfied with the meal.

The customer who is not able to satisfy his or her needs will be a dissatisfied customer. The customer may, for instance, be dissatisfied with unhelpful staff, cramped conditions or the lack of choice available. These aspects are the responsibility of the food and beverage operation. However, sometimes the reasons for the customer being dissatisfied are beyond the operation's control, for example, location, the weather, other customers or transport problems.

Not all customers have a full choice. Those that do may be referred to as the **non-captive market**; those that don't may be referred to as being part of a **captive market**.
- **Non-captive market**: the customer has a choice of opportunities for eating out, both in terms of the food and drink to be consumed and the type of operation they may wish to patronise. While it is true that certain types of catering operations might attract certain types of customer, this is by no means true all the time. The same customers may patronise a variety of different operations depending on the needs they have at a given time, for example, a romantic night out, a quick office lunch or a wedding function.
- **Semi-captive market**: Customers may choose, for example, a certain airline, ship or hotel based upon the identification of certain needs they wish to satisfy. However, once the choice has been made, then the food and beverages available become limited to that provided by the location.
- **Captive market**: the customer does not have a choice of operation. This applies, for example, to those in hospital, in prison, in industrial catering, in boarding schools and in care homes. However, there is still a need for customer satisfaction, beyond merely providing food and beverages, through giving attention to the whole experience of the meal.

Promoting features and benefits

To meet specific food and beverage needs, customers tend to view an operation as providing benefits and solutions *not* products. In addition to their need for food and beverages customers may also consider these benefits:

- security/peace of mind
- time saving
- money saving
- health and safety
- status
- convenience
- comfort
- flexibility
- enjoyment
- complies with legislation.

When dealing with customers staff should promote the operation's features and benefits and should know how these compare with those of its competitors. Members of staff can also adopt personal and positive selling techniques when taking food and beverage orders. These are discussed further in Section 16.1, page 259.

7.2 Factors that contribute to the meal experience

It is important to recognise that the customer's needs may vary, so food and beverage operators should be aware of factors that might affect the customer's meal experience. Much research has been carried out in recent years identifying these factors. They range from location to the acceptance of credit cards, and from attitudes of staff to the behaviour of other customers. These factors are summarised in Table 7.1

Table 7.1 Meal experience factors

Factor	Description
Food and beverages on offer	Includes the range of food and beverages, choice, availability, flexibility for special orders and the quality of the food and beverages
Level of service	The level of service sought will depend on the needs people have at a particular time. For example, a romantic night out may require a quiet table in a top-class restaurant, whereas a group of young friends might seek a more informal service. This factor also takes into account the importance to the customer of other services such as booking and account facilities, acceptance of credit cards and the reliability of the operation's product
Level of cleanliness and hygiene	This factor relates to the premises, equipment and staff. Over the last few years this factor has increased in importance in customers' minds. The recent media focus on food production and the risks involved in buying food have heightened awareness of health and hygiene
Perceived value for money and price	Customers have perceptions of the amount they are prepared to spend and relate this to differing types of establishments and operations
Atmosphere of the establishment	This factor takes account of issues such as design, décor, lighting, heating, furnishings, acoustics and noise levels, other customers, the smartness of the staff and the attitude of the staff

Price, cost, worth and value

Customers also make choices by considering their view of the relationship between price, cost, worth and value:

- **Price** is the amount of money required to purchase the product.

- **Cost** includes, in addition to price, the cost of not going somewhere else, the cost of transport and time, the cost of potential embarrassment if things go wrong, the cost of having to look and behave in a required manner and the cost in terms of effort at work to earn the money to pay the required price.
- **Worth** is a perception of the desirability of a particular product over another in order to satisfy a set of established goals.
- **Value** is a perception of the balance between worth and cost.

Good value for a food and beverage operation is where the *worth* is perceived as greater than the *costs*, and poor value is where the *costs* are perceived as greater than the *worth*.

7.3 Providing good customer service

Good customer service is often characterised by:
- meeting/exceeding customer expectations
- being aware of the benefits/features of the services and products on offer
- being able to listen actively
- being friendly and polite
- being able to adapt methods of communication to meet the individual needs of a range of customers, for example those with language difficulties, with health issues, of different age groups, with cultural differences or with learning difficulties
- avoiding the use of jargon
- forming professional relationships with customers
- achieving customer satisfaction.

Benefits of good customer service

The benefits to the operation include:
- Increased sales
- Fewer complaints
- Higher levels of good feedback from customers
- Attracting new customers through increased reputation
- Increases in repeat business and customer loyalty
- Better teamwork.

For individuals working in food and beverages service the benefits of providing good customer service include:
- Achieving job satisfaction, which leads to increased motivation and loyalty
- Training opportunities for advancement
- Recognition by management for promotion and monetary reward.

Defining customer service

The five characteristics of customer service in foodservice operations are:

1 **Service level**: the level of individual personal attention given to customers, for example, being polite and well-mannered and showing respect for the customer. Does the overall service the customer receives meet or even exceed their expectations? Are staff knowledgeable in dealing with requests?

2 **Service availability**: the opening times and variations in the menu and beverage list on offer. For example, knowing the menu, special offers available and forthcoming events, local availability of produce, wine and food harmony.

Principles of customer service

3   **Level of standards**: for example, the food and beverage quality, décor, colour, furnishings, lighting, personal presentation of staff, floral décor, standard of equipment used and professionalism of staff. Do all these factors combine to produce a comfortable atmosphere?

4   **Service reliability**: the extent to which the product (service) is intended to be consistent and its consistency in practice. Does the product (service) bring in repeat business? Is it exceeding expectations? Are customers made to feel 'at home' in this environment?

5   **Service flexibility**: the extent to which alternatives are available and to which there can be variations in the standard products that are offered. For example, does the menu change with the seasons and the seasonal availability of produce? Are special offers by local suppliers promoted?

Figure 7.2 A formal restaurant

Although a foodservice operation is designed to provide customer service, it must also be efficient in its use of resources. The resources used in foodservice operations are:

● **Materials**: food, beverages and short-use equipment (such as paper napkins)
● **Labour**: staffing costs
● **Facilities**: premises, plant and equipment.

The management team must take into account the effect that the level of business has on the ability of the operation to maintain customer service requirements, while at the same time ensuring productivity in all of the resources being used. A foodservice operation will then determine the **customer service specification** of the operation.

Level of service and standards of service

There can be confusion when referring to the level of service and the standards of service.

Figure 7.3 An informal restaurant

The **level of service** in foodservice operations can range from being very limited to complex, with high levels of personal attention.

The **standards of service** are a measure of the ability of the operation to deliver the service level it offers.

An operation might be offering low levels of service, such as a fast-food operation, but may be doing this at a very high standard. Equally, an operation may be offering a high level of service, such as a full service restaurant, but may be doing so with low standards.

Monitoring customer satisfaction

A food and beverage operation must continually monitor its performance and levels of customer satisfaction so that it can take action as appropriate to maintain and improve levels of business. Methods used for monitoring include the following:

- **Informal approaches**: these include asking customers directly for feedback and monitoring the service periods for signs of issues with the service. They can be very effective.
- **Monitoring financial data**: includes both financial performance and sales data, which can indicate changes in customer trends for the business.
- **Customer satisfaction questionnaires**: these can be available or given out within the operation or sent to customers afterwards. The forms usually ask for some rating of the experience with details ranging from factors such as warmth of greeting to value for money and also likelihood of recommending the operation to someone else.
- **Complaint monitoring**: the monitoring of complaints (and compliments) can assist in measuring the achievement of customer satisfaction. However, it is also possible that complaints might be unjustified or the result of some other dissatisfaction, which is not in the control of the operation.
- **Monitoring media**: this includes printed media such as magazines, television, social media and customer-rating websites such as TripAdvisor and OpenTable.
- **Staff focus group sessions**: running staff focus groups can provide a valuable review process, especially when independent people lead the sessions. Opportunities can also be taken to review the customer service specification against the experience of members of staff.
- **Mystery shopper**: this uses an unidentified customer to test the service of the organisation. The individual will check that standards are maintained, working to a brief and check list. Mystery shoppers are not experts; they need by necessity to remain customers so, although the individual shoppers tend not to be professionals, the company they work for is professional.
- **Process reviewer**: the process reviewer differs from a mystery shopper in that the process review is employed to identify problems in how the operation works and also opportunities for improvement.

7.4 Ensuring good customer relations

Customer relations are also referred to as interpersonal skills; in food and beverage service it refers to the relationship between customers (often referred to as the '**external customers**') and the food and beverage service staff.

In food and beverage service operations interaction also takes place with people outside the service areas, such as kitchen staff, bill office staff, dispense bar staff and stillroom staff. These are known as '**internal customers**'.

It is important that the customer can see that the provision of food and beverages and service within an establishment is a joint effort between all departments, with each department understanding the needs of the others in order to meet the customers' demands.

Key terms

Customer relations – the relationship between customers and the food and beverage service staff

External customers – customers from outside the organisation

Internal customers – staff in other service areas, such as kitchen staff, bill office staff, dispense bar staff and stillroom staff

Communication

The three main types of communication are:

1 **Face to face**: the skills used here are maintaining eye contact and active listening. Eye contact may differ across cultures; '**active listening**' is about head nodding, gestures and repeating back phrases to the other person to confirm your understanding of what they are saying.

2 **Telephone communication**: it is important that members of staff are technically able to use the telephone efficiently and effectively. The communications skills for telephone conversations differ because the member of staff is not face to face with the customer. When dealing with a customer by phone it is import to make sure the customer is informed when the member of staff is accessing information and if the customer is to be placed on hold. It is also important to speak clearly and slowly, first to allow for the possibility that reception on the phone line may not be perfect and second to be able to adapt your speech to meet the individual needs of the customer.

3 **Written communication**: for example, letters, emails, memos and reports. Written communication is necessary when a formal response is required. The operation will issue guidelines for staff on when and how to use written communication.

> **Key term**
>
> **Active listening** – head nodding, gestures and repeating back phrases that are heard to ensure confirmation of understanding

Dealing with customers face to face

The starting point for all good customer relations is good manners: saying 'please', 'thank you' and 'I beg your pardon'; being pleasant to people; showing that you care about what they want and apologising for anything that has been unsatisfactory, such as having to wait.

Conversations between customers and staff are of the highest importance and override conversations between staff. Customers should always be made to feel that they are being cared for rather than an intrusion into the operation.

When in conversation with customers, staff should not:

● talk to other members of staff without first excusing themselves from the customer

● interrupt interactions between customers and staff, but should wait until there is a suitable moment to catch the attention of the other member of staff so that they may excuse themselves from the customer first

● serve customers while carrying on a conversation between themselves

● talk across a room, either to each other or to customers.

When addressing customers, 'Sir' or 'Madam' should be used when the customer's name is not known. If the name is known, then the member of staff should also address the customer as 'Mr Smith' or 'Miss Jones', etc. First names should only be used in less-formal operations and where the customer has explicitly indicated that this is acceptable.

Greetings such as 'good morning' and 'good evening' should be used upon receiving customers, or when the member of staff first comes into contact with the customer, for example, when lounge service staff attend people already seated in the lounge.

The list below identifies examples of interpersonal skills and knowledge needed at particular points during the service.

● **Showing customers to their table**: always lead and walk with them at their pace.

● **Seating customers**: ladies first, descending in age unless the host is a lady.

● **Handling coats/wraps**: handle with obvious care.

● **Handing menus/wine lists to customers**: offer the list the right way round, open for the customer and wait for the customer to take it.

- **Opening and placing a napkin**: open carefully – do not shake it like a duster – and place it on the customer's lap after saying 'excuse me' to the customer.
- **Offering water or rolls**: say, for example, 'Excuse me, sir/madam, may I offer you a bread roll?'
- **Offering accompaniments**: only offer them if you have them at the table. Offering them when they are not at the table usually means 'I will get them if you really want them!'
- **Serving and clearing**: always say 'excuse me' before serving or clearing and 'thank you' after you have finished with each customer.
- **Cultural awareness**: customers from a different culture may have different expectations about the ways in which staff should interact with them. In addition, different religious faiths have their own requirements with regard to menu dishes (see Section 8.2, page 126).
- **Explaining food and beverage items**: use terms the customer understands, not technical terms such as turned vegetable or pane. Use terms that make the item sound attractive such as casserole not stew, creamed or purée potatoes not mashed. Do not use abbreviations, for example, 'veg'.
- **Talking to customers**: only talk when standing next to them and looking at them.

Dealing with children

If children are among the customers arriving in the foodservice area then take the lead in how to care for them from the parents, guardian or accompanying adults. Where applicable, the following factors should be determined.

- Are high chairs/seat cushions required?
- Restrictions on the service of alcohol to minors.
- Are children's meal menus required?
- The portion size required if items are ordered from the standard menu.
- The provision of children's 'give aways', such as crayons, colouring books, etc.
- For the safety of both children and others, the staff should be aware of children's movements.
- Should the children be older, then they should be addressed as either 'Sir' or 'Miss'.
- Younger children should be served as promptly as possible as this will lessen the stress on the parents.

Customers with additional needs

Customer mobility

Extra awareness is needed to meet the requirements of customers who may have additional needs, such as mobility difficulties. The following considerations should be made:

- Offer wheelchair users a place at a table where there is adequate space for manoeuvrability.
- Offer wheelchair users a place out of the main thoroughfare of customer/staff movement.
- Offer wheelchair users a place with easy access to cloakrooms, exits and fire exits.
- Always ensure that menus, wine lists and the like are immediately available to any wheelchair user.
- Never move the wheelchair without asking the customer first.
- Crutches/walking sticks should be placed in a safe but accessible and readily available position.
- Customers with dexterity difficulties may be assisted by first asking the customer how best they can be helped. Assistance may include, for example, ensuring that all items served or placed on to the table are near to the customer, offering to fillet/bone fish and meat items, and offering to cut up potato and vegetable items.

Blind and partially sighted customers

Awareness of the needs of those customers who may be blind or partially sighted is also important. The following should be taken into account:

- Talk to and treat the customer as you would any other customer.
- Remember it is by touch that blind people 'see' and are made aware that they are involved in what is happening around them.
- If in doubt ask the person directly how they may best be helped.
- Do not talk to their companions as if the person was not there.
- Offer to read menus or wine and drink lists.
- Immediately prior to taking the customer's order, a gentle touch on the hand or arm will attract his or her attention to you.
- Offer to fillet/bone fish and meat items.
- Offer to cut up potato and vegetable items should it be necessary.
- Never overfill cups, glasses or soup bowls.
- Should you feel it appropriate, use bowls instead of plates for specific food items, but always ask the customer first.
- Ask if you should describe where the food items are on the plate. Use the clock method to explain the location of food on a plate, for example, six o'clock for meat, ten to ten for vegetables and 10 past 2 for potatoes, as shown in Figure 7.4.

Figure 7.4 Standard placement of food items

Customers with communication difficulties

Be aware of communication difficulties that may arise when, for example, customers are hearing impaired or have little understanding of the English language. In such cases the steps shown below may be helpful:

- Speak directly to the customer.
- Stand in such a position that the customer is able to see your face clearly.
- Speak normally but more distinctly.
- Describe food/drink items in simple, precise and plain language.
- Seat customers away from possible excessive noise, as this is uncomfortable for customers wearing hearing aids.
- Always read back the food or beverage order received to confirm all requests.
- Listen attentively to what is being said to you to ensure you understand the customer's requirements.

7.5 Dealing with incidents during service

During service there can be unexpected situations. However, a well-managed operation will have procedures in place to deal with such incidents. It is important to deal with incidents promptly and efficiently without causing more disturbance than is necessary to the other customers. Quick action will usually soothe an irate customer and enable a good impression of the waiting staff and the establishment to be maintained. Complaints, of whatever nature, should be referred immediately to the supervisor; any delay will only cause confusion and very often the situation may be wrongly interpreted if it is not dealt with straight away. In the case of accidents, a report of the incident must be kept and signed by those involved.

Spillages

If during the service of a course a few drops of sauce or gravy have fallen on the tablecloth or a glass of wine has been knocked over, the following steps might be taken:

1 Check immediately that none has fallen on the customer being served. Apologise to the customer.
2 If some has fallen on the customer's clothing, allow the customer to rub over the dirtied area with a clean damp cloth. This will remove the worst of the spillage.
3 If it is necessary for the customer to retire to the cloakroom to remove the spillage then the meal should be placed on the hotplate until he or she returns.
4 Depending on the nature of the spillage the establishment may offer to have the garment cleaned.
5 If the spillage has gone on the tablecloth, the waiter should first of all remove any items of equipment that may be dirtied or in the way.
6 The waiter should then mop or scrape up the spillage with either a clean damp cloth or a knife (Figure 7.5a).
7 An old menu card should then be placed on top of the table but under the tablecloth beneath the damaged area (Figure 7.5b).
8 A second menu should be placed on the tablecloth over the damaged area.
9 A clean rolled napkin should then be brought to the table and rolled completely over the damaged area. The menu will prevent any damp from soaking into the clean napkin (Figure 7.5c).
10 Any items of equipment removed should be returned to their correct position on the table top (Figure 7.5d).
11 Any meals taken to the hotplate should be returned and fresh covers put down where necessary.
12 Again, apologies should be made to the customer for any inconvenience caused.

Figure 7.5 (a)–(d) Example process for covering spillages

Accidents

1   As a more serious spillage usually involves changing the tablecloth, the party of customers should be seated at another table and allowed to continue their meal without delay.

2   If the customers cannot be moved to another table then they should be seated slightly back from the table so that the waiter can carry out the necessary procedures to rectify the fault speedily and efficiently.

3   The customers' meals should be placed on the hotplate to keep warm.

4   All dirty items should be removed on a tray to the waiter's sideboard ready to go to the wash-up area.

5   All clean items should be removed and kept on the waiter's sideboard for relaying.

6   The tablecloth should be mopped with a clean absorbent cloth to remove as much of the liquid as possible (Figure 7.5a).

7   A number of old menus should be placed on the table top but underneath the spillage area of the soiled tablecloth (Figure 7.5b).

8   A clean tablecloth of the correct size should be brought to the table. It should be opened out and held in the correct manner as if one were laying a tablecloth during the pre-service preparation period. The table should then be clothed up in the usual manner except that when the clean tablecloth is being drawn across the table towards the waiter, he or she is at the same time removing the soiled tablecloth. The soiled tablecloth is removed at the same time that the clean tablecloth is being laid to ensure the customers do not see the bare table top at any time. The old menus will prevent any dampness penetrating to the clean tablecloth.

9   When the table has its clean tablecloth on it should be re-laid as quickly as possible.

10 The customers should then be re-seated at the table and the meals returned to them from the hotplate.

Returned food

If, for example, a customer suggests that their chicken dish is not cooked, then the following steps might be taken:

1   Apologise to the customer.

2   The dish should be removed and returned to the kitchen.

3   The customer should be asked if he or she would like another portion of the same dish or would prefer to choose an alternative.

4   The new dish should be collected as soon as possible and served to the customer.

5   Apologies should be made for any inconvenience caused.

6   The policy of the establishment will dictate whether or not the customer is to be charged for the alternative dish.

Lost property

If a waiter finds lost property in a service area that has recently been vacated by a customer, the steps listed below might be taken:

1 A check should be made immediately as to whether or not the customer has left the service area. If they are still in the area, the property may be returned to them.

2 If the customer has left the service area, the waiter should hand the item to the headwaiter or supervisor in charge.

3 The supervisor or headwaiter should check with reception and the hall porter to see if the customer has left the building.

4 If the customer concerned is a resident, then reception may ring their room, stating the property has been found and can be collected at a convenient time.

5 If the customer is a regular customer, it is possible that the head waiter or receptionist may know where to contact them to arrange for them to collect the property.

6 If the customer is a regular customer but cannot be contacted, the property should be kept in the lost property office until the customer's next visit.

7 If the owner has not been found or contacted immediately, the headwaiter or supervisor should list the items found, including the contents if appropriate, with the waiter who found the property. The 'lost property record sheet' (see Figure 7.6) should then be signed by both the headwaiter or supervisor and the finder. This record sheet must be dated and also indicate where the property was found and at what time.

8 A copy of this list should go with the property to the lost property office where the contents of the property must be checked against the list before it is accepted. The details of the find are then entered in a lost property register.

9 Another copy of the list should go to the hall porter in case any enquiries are received concerning the property. Anyone claiming lost property should be passed on to the lost property office.

10 Before the lost property office hands over any lost property, a description of the article concerned and its contents should be asked for to ensure as far as possible that it is being returned to the genuine owner. The office should also see proof of identity of the person claiming ownership.

11 In the case of all lost property, the steps mentioned above should be carried out as quickly as possible as this is in the best interests of the establishment and causes the customer minimum inconvenience. On receipt of lost property, the customer should be asked to sign for the article concerned and to give their address and telephone number.

12 Any lost property unclaimed after three months may become the property of the finder who should claim it through the headwaiter or supervisor.

Lost property record sheet	
Date:	Establishment:
Item description:	
Found by:	
Checked by:	
Where stored:	
Claimed by:	Date:
Contact details:	
Proof of identity seen:	

Figure 7.6 Example of a lost property record sheet

Customer illness

If a customer falls ill in your establishment then the steps below might be taken:

1   As soon as it is noticed that a customer is feeling unwell while in the dining room or restaurant a person in authority should be called immediately.

2   If the customer falling ill is a woman then a female member of staff should attend her.

3   The person in authority must enquire if the customer needs assistance. At the same time they must try to judge whether the illness is of a serious nature or not. If in any doubt it is always better to call for medical assistance.

4   It is often advisable to offer to take the customer to another room to see if they are able to recover in a few minutes. If this happens their meal should be placed on the hotplate until their return.

5   If the illness appears to be of a serious nature, a doctor, nurse or someone qualified in first aid should be called immediately. The customer should not be moved until a doctor has examined them.

6   If necessary the area should be screened off.

7   Although this is a difficult situation to deal with in front of the general public, minimum fuss should be made and service to the rest of the customers should carry on as normal.

8   The medical person will advise whether an ambulance should be called.

9   The customer may have had a sudden stomach upset and wish to leave without finishing their meal. Assistance should be offered in helping the customer leave the restaurant.

10 Payment for the part of the meal consumed and any ensuing travel costs would be according to the policy of the establishment.

11 It is most important that for all accidents (minor or serious) all details are recorded in an accident book. This is in case of a claim against the establishment at a later date.

12 If after a short period of time the customer returns and continues with the meal, a fresh cover should be laid and the meal returned from the hotplate or a new meal served.

Over-consumption of alcohol

If a customer is suspected of having too much to drink the following steps might be taken:

1   If a prospective customer asks for a table and staff believe the client is under the influence of drink, they may refuse them a table, even though there may be one available. It is not always possible, however, to recognise a customer who may prove objectionable later on.

2   If difficulty is found in handling this type of person then assistance in removing the person from the eating area may come from other members of staff (depending on establishment policy; physical contact should be avoided).

3   If a customer is suspected of being drunk this must first of all be ascertained by the headwaiter or supervisor.

4   The customer should then be asked to leave rather than be allowed to become objectionable to other customers.

5   If the customer has already consumed part of the meal ordered but is not being objectionable then the remainder of the meal should be served in the normal fashion, but the headwaiter or supervisor must ensure no more alcoholic beverage is offered.

6   On finishing, the customer should be watched until he or she has left the premises.

7   It is always advisable to make out a report of all such incidents. They should also be brought to the immediate attention of the restaurant manager in case of any claim at a later date concerning a particular incident.

It is an offence to serve alcohol to a customer who appears to be drunk, or to serve their companions if you think the drunken person may receive the alcohol.

Unsatisfactory appearance

If a customer's appearance is not satisfactory according to the policy of the establishment, the following steps might be taken:

1   If a customer's appearance does not meet the dress code policy of the establishment or is likely to give offence to others, then the customer should be asked to correct their dress to the approved fashion required by the establishment.
2   Staff should be made aware of the need for sensitivity towards cultural dress.
3   If the customer will not comply with the request, he or she should be asked to leave.
4   If they have partly consumed a meal then whether they will be charged or not depends on the policy of the house and the discretion of the head waiter or supervisor.
5   A report of this incident must be made and signed by the staff concerned.

Lost children

Should a child be reported lost, the steps listed below must be taken:

1   A complete description of the lost child should be obtained:

- male/female
- name
- age
- where last seen
- clothing worn
- any predominant features
- colour of hair
- whether any accessories were being carried, e.g. a doll.

2   Immediately inform the supervisor/security.
3   Put a constant watch on all entrances/exits.
4   Check all cloakroom/rest areas, play areas and the immediate vicinity where the child has been reported missing.
5   Should nothing result from taking the above actions, immediately inform the police.

Handling complaints

When a problem arises, a customer may make a complaint, for example because:

- service is slow
- food is cold when served
- wine served is at the incorrect temperature
- a reservation is not recorded in the booking diary
- a server has been inattentive
- wrong dish is brought to the table
- explanation of the menu is inaccurate
- poor attitude of staff.

In dealing with a complaint the following steps should be taken:

1   Do not interrupt the customer – let them have their say and make their point.
2   Apologise – but only for the specific problem or complaint.
3   Restate the details of the complaint briefly back to the customer to show you have listened and understood.
4   Agree by thanking the customer for bringing the matter to your attention. This shows you are looking at the problem from the customer's perspective.

5   Act quickly, quietly and professionally, and follow the establishment's procedures for handling complaints.

Never:
- lose your temper
- take it personally
- argue
- lie
- blame another member of staff or another department.

Valid complaints provide important feedback for a foodservice operation and can be used as valuable learning opportunities to improve service.

Recording incidents

When an incident occurs a report should be made out immediately. The basic information that should be included in the report is as follows:

- place
- date
- time
- nature of incident
- individual, signed reports from those concerned
- action taken
- name, address and phone number of the customer involved
- names of the staff involved.

All reports should be kept in case similar incidents occur at a later date. Such reports provide a record in case there is a subsequent complaint from a customer; the record can also be used when revising procedures for dealing with various incidents.

Testing your learning

1   The main aim of food and beverage operations is to achieve customer satisfaction. In other words, to meet the customers' needs. Identify and briefly explain two of the needs that customers might be seeking to satisfy.
2   Briefly explain the difference between a 'captive market' and a 'non-captive market'.
3   A food and beverage operation will determine the customer service specification (or customer service charter) of the operation. This is done by considering the five main customer service factors. Identify and briefly explain two of these factors.
4   Briefly explain the difference between *level of service* and *standards of service*.
5   What is an 'internal customer'?
6   When dealing with children in a restaurant, identify three factors that should be taken into account.
7   Identify two of the additional needs that a customer may have.
8   Identify three of the possible customer incidents that could occur when serving customers.
9   Briefly describe the steps to be taken should a customer make a complaint.
10 Communication is important. Describe four examples of good listening that are essential when dealing with a customer.

In practice

Five meal experience factors can be used to analyse and compare how different food and beverage operations meet customer expectations. It provides a standard template or checklist so that information about an operation can be collected and organised in a specific way. This can then be compared with the same information collected on other foodservice operations.

Using the template shown below, collect information about two different types of food and beverage operation. You may not be able to obtain all of the information but the template will help you to identify what information you need, what you have found out and what information you do not know about each of the operations.

Meal experience factor	Example of what to include under each heading
Food and beverages on offer	The range of foods and beverages offered. The choice, availability, flexibility for special orders and the quality of the food and beverages
Level of service	The level of food and beverage service. Other services such as booking and account facilities, acceptance of credit cards and the reliability of the operation's product
Level of cleanliness and hygiene	The premises, equipment and staff
Perceived value for money and price	Perception of the value for money of the quality of the food and beverages on offer and the service levels in comparison with the price. This also takes account of other costs such as travel
Atmosphere of the establishment	This factor takes account of issues such as design, décor, lighting, heating, furnishings, acoustics and noise levels, other customers, the smartness of the staff and the attitude of the staff

Understanding menus

8

Units covered

This chapter covers the following units:

Level 1

→ Understand menus (105)

Level 2

→ Menu knowledge and design (205)
→ Provide a counter/takeaway service (1FS4, 110)
→ Serve food at the table (2FS2, 207)
→ Provide a silver service (2FS8, 208)
→ Provide a buffet/carvery service (2FS4, 209)

8.1 The purpose of the menu

The menu is primarily a selling aid. The design of the menu should be appealing and interesting to the customer so it encourages them to view its contents. Clear information that is easily found and followed will make the customer feel more at home and will assist in selling your menu.

Design considerations of the menu should include:

- size and shape
- artwork/colour
- ease of handling
- logical flow of information.

Other considerations are:

- providing a clear and accurate description of the dishes
- clear indication of pricing
- stating if a service charge is included or not
- the inclusion of dietary information.

Menus can be presented in a variety of ways:

- single laminated cards
- fold-out cards with inserts from size A5 and above
- iPads
- chalk boards
- white boards
- printed signs, sometimes illuminated from behind
- projections on to table tops.

8.2 Menu development

Menu content, whose origins are traditionally based on classic cuisine, is continually being updated as a result of food trends and fashions. Customers are more aware of different food commodities and cooking methods because of wider exposure to media such as television, the internet and food-related publications.

Principal influences on extent and style of menus

Decisions on the extent and style of the menu will take account of the following:

- The location of the establishment, in terms of access for customers and for obtaining deliveries.
- Available kitchen space and equipment. If space is limited then the storage, preparation and service of menu items will be restricted and a smaller menu will need to be in place.
- Knowledge and ability of kitchen staff to produce the menu to the desired standard.
- Type of service level being offered.
- Opening times of the operation.
- Number of covers to be served in a specific time.

Principal influences on content

The demands and expectations of the customer are influenced by a greater awareness and understanding of:

- the relationship between health and eating
- dietary requirements
- cultural and religious influences
- ethical issues
- seasonality and locally sourced foods.

Relationship between health and eating

Figure 8.1 Raw vegetables

The key issue in the relationship between health and eating is a healthy diet. This means eating a balanced diet rather than viewing individual foods as healthier or less healthy. Customers are increasingly looking for the availability of choices that will enable them to achieve a balanced diet. They also require more specific information on the methods of cooking used, for example, low-fat or low-salt methods.

General consensus suggests that a normal diet should consist of around one-third bread, cereals, rice and potatoes; one-third fruit and vegetables; and the remainder should be dairy foods including low-fat milk, low-fat meats and fish, and small amounts of fatty and sugary food. Figure 8.2 indicates the recommended daily intake for the different food groups.

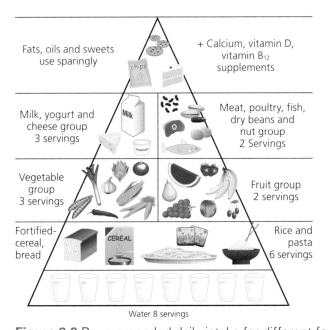

Figure 8.2 Recommended daily intake for different food groups

There is now a greater emphasis on alternatives such as low-fat milk (for example, skimmed or semi-skimmed), non-dairy creamers for beverages, alternatives to sugar such as sweeteners, sorbets alongside ice creams, and polyunsaturated fat and non-animal fats as alternatives to butter. Cooking ingredients and methods are also affected, with the development of lower-fat dishes, lighter cuisine and attractive and decent alternatives for non-meat eaters, including the greater use of animal protein substitutes such as Quorn and tofu.

Dietary requirements

Customers may have a range of dietary requirements because of lifestyle choices or they may require a particular diet for medical reasons (including the prevention of allergic reactions). Such customers will need to know about every ingredient used in a dish, since eating certain ingredients may make them very ill and may even be fatal.

To aid the customer in making the appropriate choice, menu items that are suitable for a vegetarian diet can be identified with 'V' while menu items containing nuts can be identified with 'N' next to their description. Nevertheless, it is important that the server is able to accurately describe the dishes so that the customer can make an appropriate choice. The server should *never* guess and, if in doubt, should seek further information. Some examples of dietary requirements are given in Table 8.1.

Table 8.1 Examples of dietary requirements

Allergies	Food items that are known to cause allergies in some people are called allergens and they include gluten in wheat, rye and barley (known as coeliac); peanuts and their derivatives; sesame seeds and other nuts such as cashew, pecan, brazil and walnuts; as well as milk, fish, shellfish, eggs and tropical fruits. Sometimes these foods can cause anaphylactic shock resulting in the lips, tongue or throat swelling dramatically over a very short period of time. The result can be fatal so prompt medical treatment is needed in such cases
Diabetic	This refers to the inability of the body to control the level of insulin within the blood. An appropriate diet may include foods listed in the low-cholesterol section below and the avoidance of dishes with a high sugar content
Low cholesterol	Diets will include polyunsaturated fats and may include limited quantities of animal fats. Other items eaten may include lean poached or grilled meats and fish, fruit and vegetables, and low-fat milk, cheese and yoghurt
Low sodium/salt	This requires a reduction in the amount of sodium or salt consumed. Diets will include low-sodium/salt foods and cooking with very limited or no salt

Cultural and religious dietary influences

Different religious faiths have differing requirements with regard to the dishes/ingredients that may be consumed, and these requirements often also cover preparation methods, cooking procedures and the equipment used. Examples are given in Table 8.2 below.

Table 8.2 Dietary requirements according to the various faiths

Hindus	Do not eat beef and rarely pork. Some Hindus will not eat any meat, fish or eggs. Diet may include cheese, milk and vegetarian dishes
Jews	Only 'clean' (kosher) animals may be consumed. Jews do not eat pork or pork products, shellfish or animal fats and gelatine from beasts considered to be unclean or not slaughtered according to the prescribed manner. Restrictions are placed on methods of preparation and cookery. The preparation and eating of meat and dairy products at the same meal is not allowed
Muslims	Will not eat meat, offal or animal fat unless it is halal (i.e. lawful, as required under Islamic Dietary Law). Muslims do not consume alcohol, even when used in cooking
Sikhs	Do not eat beef or pork. Some will keep to a vegetarian diet. Others may eat fish, mutton, cheese and eggs. Sikhs will not eat halal meat
Rastafarians	Will not eat any processed foods, pork or fish without fins (e.g. eels). Will not consume tea, coffee or alcohol
Roman Catholics	Few restrictions on diet. Usually will not eat meat on Ash Wednesday or Good Friday. Some keep with the past requirement for no meat to be eaten on Fridays. Fish and dairy products may be eaten instead

Vegetarianism

Vegetarianism may derive from cultural, religious, moral, ethical or physiological considerations. It is therefore important that food descriptions are accurate.

The various forms of vegetarianism are summarised in Table 8.3 below.

Table 8.3 Forms of vegetarianism

Vegetarians: semi	Do not eat red meat, or all meat other than poultry, or all meat. Diet will include fish and may include dairy produce and other animal products
Vegetarians: lacto-ovo	Do not eat meat, fish or poultry but may drink milk, eat milk products and eggs
Vegetarians: lacto	Do not eat meat, fish, poultry and eggs but may drink milk and eat milk products
Vegans	Do not eat any foods of animal origin. Diet will mainly consist of vegetables, vegetable oils, cereals, nuts, fruits and seeds
Fruitarians	More restricted form of vegetarianism. Excluded are all foods of animal origin together with pulses and cereals. Diet may include mainly raw and dried fruit, nuts, honey and olive oil

Ethical influences

Customers have become increasingly aware of ethical issues, such as:
- ensuring sustainability of foods consumed
- Fairtrade
- the acceptability or otherwise of genetically modified foods or irradiated foods
- reducing food packaging and food waste
- reducing the effects that food production and food transportation have on the environment generally.

Seasonality and locally sourced foods

There is now a greater trend towards using more seasonal and locally sourced food and beverage items, when quality, taste, freshness and nutritional value are all at their peak and when supplies are more plentiful and cheaper. For food service businesses, the benefits can also include:
- improved menu planning, as suppliers can give information in advance on what they are able to provide
- more reliable products and service, with greater flexibility to respond to customer needs
- increased marketing opportunities through making a feature of using locally sourced food and beverage items and through special promotions related to local and seasonal food and beverage specialities
- support for training of staff from local suppliers.

8.3 Legal requirements

Menu descriptions

Descriptions of menu items must, by law, be clear and accurate to the customer. For example, the term 'homemade', means that the food must have been made on the premises. The term 'fresh' means that the food did not originate from a can or had been frozen. Some specific considerations relating to the legal requirements of menu items are as follows:
- Dishes that contain genetically modified maize or soya must be clearly identified.

- Steak and burger weights stated should be the approximate uncooked weight.
- Any food that is described as being smoked must have been traditionally smoked and not had chemicals added to it.
- All prices must include Value Added Tax and be correct and easy to read.
- Additional charges such as cover charges must be clearly displayed.
- The service charge should be included in the menu price or clearly itemised on the menu.

Allergen information

At the end of 2014, new legislation will come into force that will require food businesses to provide allergy information on food sold unpackaged, in for example restaurants and cafés, deli counters, bakeries and sandwich bars. Table 8.4 shows the 14 types of allergens that must be tracked and displayed.

Allergen information can be supplied on the menu, on chalk boards, tickets or provided verbally by service staff as well as in other formats made available to the consumer. It must be clear and conspicuous, easily visible and legible. If the information is to be provided by asking a member of staff then this must be made clear on a notice, menu, ticket or label that can easily be seen by customers.

It will not be enough for a food business operator to say that they do not know whether or not a food contains an allergen and deny any knowledge. It will also not be enough to say that all their foods may contain allergens. Allergen information must be specific to the food and complete and accurate. This also applies to food pre-packed for direct sale, such as from takeaways, deli counters, bakeries or sandwich bars.

Table 8.4 The 14 allergens that must be tracked

Celery	Lupin	Peanuts
Crustaceans	Milk	Sesame
Eggs	Molluscs	Soybeans
Fish	Mustard	Sulphur dioxide/sulphites
Gluten	Nuts	

8.4 Classes of menu

Menus may be divided into two classes, traditionally called **table d'hôte** (table of the host) and **à la carte** (from the card).

Table d'hôte menu

The key characteristics of the table d'hôte menu are:
- the menu has a fixed number of courses
- there is a limited choice within each course
- the selling price is fixed
- the food is usually available at a set time.

À la carte menu

The key characteristics of the à la carte menu are:
- the choice is generally more extensive
- each dish is priced separately
- there may be longer waiting times as some dishes are cooked or finished to order.

> **Key terms**
>
> **À la carte** – menu items individually priced
>
> **Table d'hôte** or **menu du jour** – menu with set price for specific number of food courses

Some menus offer combinations of these two classes, with a number of menu items being offered together at a set price and other menu items being priced separately.

Sometimes the term '**menu du jour**' is used instead of the term 'table d'hôte menu'.

Another menu term used is 'carte du jour' (literally 'card of the day') or 'menu of the day', which can also be a fixed meal with one or more courses for a set price. A 'prix fixe' (fixed price) menu is similar. A 'tasting menu' ('menu degustation') is a set meal with a range of courses (often between six and ten). The tasting menu can also be offered with a flight (selection) of wines. Sometimes this can mean a different wine for each course). For all classes of menu the price of the meal might also include wine or other drinks.

8.5 Classic menu sequence

Over the last hundred years the sequence of the European menu has taken on a classical format or order of dishes. This followed the adoption in the late 1800s of what was then called service à la Russe (Russian service). This introduced the principle of serving one course after another, rather than having a range of food dishes all at the same time. The classic format is used to lay out menus as well as to indicate the order of the various

Figure 8.3 Part of an all-day dining menu (courtesy of the Langham Hotel, London)

courses. Although the actual number of courses on a menu, and dishes within each course, will depend on the size and class of the establishment, most follow the classic sequence. A summary of this sequence is shown in Table 8.5.

Table 8.5: Summary of the classic menu sequence

Amuse-bouche	Often offered in fine dining establishments as a small complimentary appetiser. Does not count as a course in the menu
Hors d'oeuvres and other appetisers	Mostly these first three sets of dishes are now grouped together as 'starters'. Sometimes separately presented as 'cold starters' and 'hot starters'.
Soup	
Egg dishes	
Pasta and rice	May be as a starter or main course. Often known as farinaceous dishes
Fish	May be as a starter or main course. May also be a middle course in, for example, a four-course meal
Meats, poultry and game	Often listed just as main courses. Sometimes meats, such as steaks, are listed separately under 'grills'
Potatoes, vegetables and salads	If not included with a main course, these dishes are now often listed as 'sides' (meaning side order) for which there is an additional charge
Cheese	Cheese is shown here after the main course and before the sweet course. However, the sweet course is still sometimes offered before the cheese course
Sweets	
Savoury	Simple savoury dishes served at the end of the meal
Fruit (dessert)	Fresh fruit, nuts and sometimes candied fruits

For a detailed listing of the various courses, accompaniments and service considerations see Chapter 9 Menu Knowledge, page 138.

Note

Beverages are not counted as a course and should not be included when stating the number of courses for a meal. For example, if a meal is stated as having four courses, this means that there are four food courses and that the beverages at the end are an addition to these.

The classic menu sequence outlined in Table 8.5 is based on a logical process of taste sensations. This classic sequence also provides the guide for the compilation of both à la carte and table d'hôte menus, as is evident in many examples of modern menus. The classic menu sequence is also used as a guide for the compilation and the order of courses for event and special party menus (see Section 8.6, page 133).

Note

The modern European classic menu sequence, outlined in Table 8.5, comes from traditional European (mainly Franco-Russian, Swiss and English) cuisine and service influences. The menu structure and menu sequence can change considerably within various world cuisines.

8.6 Event menus

The term 'event' covers a wide variety of occasions that may be requested by customers, such as a wedding anniversary, formal dinner, cocktail party, promotion of a special event or conference.

Following an enquiry about a special event or function to be held, the potential client will receive an 'event sales pack' which will include:

- examples of meal packages, such as a range of set menus, snack menus and conference lunches
- details of the service methods available, such as formal table service, buffets and in-room service.

To assist the customer there should be a varied choice of menus within a wide price range and special menus for specific occasions such as weddings, 21st birthday parties and New Year's Eve.

The number of courses at a banquet is normally four plus beverages, but it can be many more and often includes:

- hors d'oeuvre or other appetisers
- soup or fish
- meat – with a selection of seasonal vegetables
- sweet
- coffee or tea – with a selection of petits fours.

This approach is generally popular, but extra or alternative courses may be added. It is also now common for dishes to be available to meet a variety of dietary needs.

8.7 Other types of menus

Breakfast menu

A variety of terms are used to indicate the different forms in which breakfast may be offered. These terms describe what the customer might expect to receive for their breakfast meal. For example:

Café complet

The term 'café complet' is widely used in continental Europe and means a continental breakfast with coffee as the beverage. The term 'thé complet' is also used, with tea provided as the beverage.

Café simple or thé simple

Café simple or thé simple is just a beverage (coffee or tea) with nothing to eat.

Continental breakfast

The traditional continental breakfast used to consist of hot croissant, brioche or toast, butter and preserves, and coffee as the beverage. The current trend is to offer a wider choice including cereals, fruits, juices, yoghurts, ham, cheese, assorted bread items and a wider selection of beverages.

Full breakfast

A full breakfast menu may consist of from two to eight courses and usually includes a cooked main course. This type of breakfast was traditionally known as an English Breakfast, but is now also known as Scottish, Irish, Welsh or, more simply, British Breakfast. The term 'full breakfast' is also becoming more common.

Afternoon tea menus

Afternoon tea may be classified into three main types:

1 afternoon tea
2 high tea
3 cream tea.

Full afternoon tea

The menu for a full afternoon tea usually consists of assorted sandwiches, bread and butter (including fruit breads), toasted items such as crumpets, warmed scones with jam and cream, cakes and pastries.

High tea menu

A high tea may be available in addition to the full afternoon tea. The menu for this usually includes the regular afternoon tea menu plus items such as grills, toasted snacks, fish and meat dishes, salads, cold sweets and ice creams.

Cream tea menu

A cream tea consists of scones (which may be served warm), clotted cream (although whipped cream can also be offered), and strawberry jam. Butter is generally not included.

Floor/room service menus

Floor or room service varies from basic tea- and coffee-making facilities in the room and possibly a mini-bar, to vending machines on floors, or the service of a variety of meals in rooms. The extent of service in hotel guest rooms will depend on the nature of the establishment.

An example of a room service menu is shown in Figure 8.4. In this establishment full room service is offered on a 24-hour basis.

24 hour menu

---Soups

Tomato and basil soup (v)	£7.00
Cream of chicken soup served with herb croutons	£7.50
Oven baked three onion soup	£8.00
A velouté of green pea soup with croutons (v)	£7.50
Crab and lobster bisque with dill cream topping and cheese straws	£8.50
Soup of the day	£7.00
Mushroom soup (v)	£7.00
Lentil soup (v)	£7.50

Salads

Traditional chicken Caesar salad with garlic croutons, smoked bacon, lettuce, Parmesan cheese and anchovy mayonnaise	£15.00
Greek salad with feta cheese (v)	£12.00
Tomato, avocado and mozzarella salad with balsamic vinaigrette (v)	£12.00
John Ross Scottish smoked salmon salad, baby gem, crispy capers and lemon dressing	£14.00

Omelettes

Four egg omelette served with French fries and salad garnish

Plain	£12.00
Smoked ham, cheese, mushroom, peppers or tuna	£14.00
Open Spanish omelette	£14.50
Smoked salmon or prawn	£15.50

(v) vegetarian dishes

If we cannot tempt you with any of the dishes on our menu, please ask, we will do our utmost to satisfy your requirements

5

Figure 8.4 Example of part of a room service menu (image courtesy of Royal Garden Hotel, London)

24 hour menu

Sandwiches

Brown or white bread, plain or toasted, ciabatta, rye or bagel with your choose of:

Bacon, ham, cheese, egg or tuna	£8.50
Beef, prawns, smoked salmon	£10.00
Royal Garden Deluxe Club: chicken breast, sweet cured back bacon, chorizo, roasted tomatoes, cos lettuce, mayonnaise	£12.00
Steak sandwich: served on toasted ciabatta roll with creamed white onion, horseradish mayonnaise served with French fries	£15.00

Pasta dishes

Fresh egg rigatoni, fettuccine or spaghetti pasta with your choice of sauce:

Bolognese or Carbonara	£13.00
Vine tomato and basil or Arrabbiata (v)	£13.00
Mushroom cream (v)	£13.00
Basil pesto (v)	£13.00

Grills

Royal Garden beef burger: sweet cured back bacon, English cheddar, pickles in a toasted bun served with French fries	£14.00
Grilled or poached salmon steak served with new potatoes and green salad	£16.00
Grilled 200gm Black Leg chicken breast	£16.00
Grilled 250gm Buccleugh Scottish sirloin steak	£24.00
Grilled 200gm Buccleugh Scottish fillet steak	£29.00
Grilled fillet of seabass served with new potatoes and green salad	£16.00
Grilled tiger prawns	M.Q

All grilled meats are served with roasted tomato, grilled mushroom, braised shallot and Béarnaise sauce

6

Lounge service menus

Lounge service may include the service of continental breakfast, morning coffee, luncheon snacks, afternoon tea, dinner or late evening snacks, as well as alcoholic beverages. Although mainly associated with hotels, it is also found in public houses, wine bars and on ships. An example of part of a lounge service menu is given in Figure 8.5.

SANDWICHES

Provençal
Goat's cheese, roasted red peppers, wild rocket,
caramelised onions and black olive tapenade on ciabatta
£13.50

Salt Beef
Salt beef with chopped gherkins, English mustard,
lettuce and mayonnaise on rye bread
£14.50

Classic Club
With grilled breast of chicken, bacon, egg, tomato,
lettuce and mayonnaise
£16.50

Bookmaker
Thin fillet steak sandwich with salsa Verde on
focaccia bread served with a Béarnaise sauce
£18.00

SALADS

Lobster Salad
Half a poached native lobster with fennel,
mango and lobster mayonnaise
£28.50

Beetroot and Feta Cheese
Red and golden beetroot, mixed with seasonal leaves,
feta cheese, basil and aged balsamic
£14.50

Classic Niçoise
Bonito tuna with green beans, vine tomato, Niçoise
olives, potato, egg, lettuce, shallots and anchovy
£16.50

Chicken Caesar
Corn fed chicken breast with baby gem lettuce, crispy
Parma ham, anchovies and a classic Caesar dressing
£19.00

3

SIGNATURE DISHES

Lobster Bisque
Lobster soup with tomato, cream,
Brandy and tarragon
£14.00

Fish and Chips
Line caught fillet of cod in a crisp batter with
hand cut chips, served with tartare sauce
£19.50

Scallop Risotto
Carnaroli rice with chorizo, sweet corn and
pan fried hand dived scallops
£18.50

Duck Ravioli
Homemade, filled with duck confit, chestnut and
mascarpone, sautéed wild mushroom cream
£10.50/£18.50

Beef Bourguignon
Slow cooked beef blade in red wine, with mashed
potato, onions, bacon and mushrooms
£21.50

The Polo Burger
Homemade beef burger with tomato
and rocket served with French fries
£17.50

DESSERTS

Chocolate Mousse
With marshmallow and Grand Marnier
caramelised orange
£8.50

Apple and Pear Crumble
Served with vanilla crème anglaise
£8.00

Cornettos
Filled with cherry and Kirsch bavarois
£14.50

Cheese Plate
A selection of four English cheeses with homemade jams
£12.50

Figure 8.5 Example of part of a lounge and bar menu (image courtesy of The Westbury Hotel, London)

Hospital tray service menus

Hospital catering services have major food service goals, as meals should reach the patient quickly, look attractive and be of specific nutritional value. Patients in hospital often have special dietary needs, too (see Section 8.2, page 126).

The choice of food and beverages for patients in a private ward is usually larger and more varied than in the main wards, and here the service is similar to hotel room service.

Airline tray service menus

On many short-haul routes, only snack-type meals or sandwiches and beverages are offered and for some operators the provision of food and beverages is provided at an additional charge to the customer. On long-haul flights, airlines provide a more extensive service of food and beverages. The airline will also provide dishes to meet its passengers' particular needs, for example, meals that meet specific dietary requirements.

Rail service menus

Food and beverage operations on trains generally fall into one of four categories:

1   restaurant (including on-board kitchen facilities)
2   kiosk (takeaway)
3   trolley service
4   limited room service on sleeper trains.

Rail food service has also seen the introduction of tray service systems, similar to airlines. The food and drink is served on trays to passengers at their seat rather than in a restaurant car where tables are laid as in a restaurant.

Testing your learning

1   Briefly describe the two key differences between an à la carte and table d'hôte menu.
2   State three things that should be considered when designing a balanced menu.
3   Identify two of the key influences on the content of modern menus.
4   List three special dietary needs that should be considered when planning a menu.
5   Identify four food items known to cause allergies.
6   Briefly explain the main differences between a vegetarian and a vegan diet.
7   What are the two key areas that need to be considered when catering for special diet?
8   Give two examples of what might be included in a low-cholesterol diet.
9   State two reasons why servers must know the main ingredients in all food dishes on the menu.
10 Give one example of food or beverages that *will not* be consumed by the following religious groups: Hindus, Jews, Muslims, Sikhs and Rastafarians.

In practice

1   You are required to think up a restaurant concept or theme.
    a) Design a table d'hôte menu that complements your concept or theme. The menu should consist of three starters, three main courses and three sweets. Consider the colour, texture and balance of the dishes.
    b) Explain how your menu meets current government healthy eating guidelines.
    c) List the equipment that would be required to produce your menu.
    d) Identify seasonal ingredients.
2   Design an afternoon tea menu that would be appropriate for a four-star hotel. Include a front cover, menu items and prices.

Menu knowledge

9

Units covered

This chapter covers the following units:

Level 1

→ Understand menus (105)
→ Provide a table/tray service (1FS2, 108)

Level 2

→ Menu knowledge and design (205)
→ Provide a counter/takeaway service (1FS4, 110)
→ Serve food at the table (2FS2, 207)
→ Provide a silver service (2FS8, 208)
→ Provide a buffet/carvery service (2FS4, 209)

9.1 Main cooking terms used in menus

Food production (cooking) may be carried out in a variety of ways. The main cooking methods are:

- **Baking**: cooking in either a fan oven or conventional oven. Often referred to as 'dry' cooking.
- **Boiling**: cooking food in a simmering liquid.
- **Braising**: slow cooking in minimum liquid in a casserole dish with a lid.

- **Deep frying**: cooking by placing into deep fat held at a temperature of about 175–190°C (350–375°F).
- **Grilling**: quick and dry method of cooking food by radiant heat, either over heated charcoal or under electric or gas salamanders.
- **Microwave**: cooking or reheating food using high-frequency radio waves in a microwave oven powered by electricity.
- **Poaching**: cooking in a minimum amount of liquid held at simmering point.
- **Roasting**: cooking with dry convected heat in the oven.
- **Shallow frying**: cooking in the minimum amount of heated fat or oil.
- **Steaming**: cooking heat is transferred from the water vapour (steam) to the food being cooked.
- **Stewing**: very slow cooking of food items in their own juices and using the minimum amount of liquid, such as stock, in the process.
- **Water bath**: technique of vacuum packing ingredients and cooking them at low temperatures in a water bath. This is a slow and gentle process where moisture is not expelled and flavour is retained.

Figure 9.1 Food production area

The nine main **food productions methods** are listed in Table 9.1. In reality, many food and beverage operations combine a number of these food production methods together in order to meet the needs of the operation.

Table 9.1 Food production methods

Method	Description
Conventional	Term used to describe production utilising mainly fresh foods and traditional cooking methods
Convenience	Method of production utilising mainly convenience foods
Call order	Method where food is cooked to order either from customers (as in cafeterias) or from waiters. Production area is often open to customer area
Continuous flow	Method involving production line approach where different parts of the production process may be separated (e.g. fast food)
Centralised	Production not directly linked to service. Foods are 'held' and distributed to separate service areas

Method	Description
Cook-chill	Food production, storage and regeneration method utilising principle of low temperature control to preserve qualities of processed foods
Cook-freeze	Production, storage and regeneration method utilising principle of freezing to control and preserve qualities of processed foods. Requires special processes to assist freezing
Sous-vide	Method of production, storage and regeneration utilising principle of sealed vacuum to control and preserve the quality of processed foods
Assembly kitchen	A system based on accepting and incorporating the latest technological development in manufacturing and conservation of food products

9.2 Basic sauces and food items used in service

Knowledge about the product is at the core of successful food and beverage service. This knowledge enables the server to advise the customer of:

- the content of dishes
- the methods used in making the dishes
- the correct accompaniments to be offered with a selected dish.

The rest of this chapter provides information on the foods, accompaniments and service for a range of menu items by course.

Sauces

Although there appears to be a wide variety of sauces, they are almost always variations on the same base sauces. These base sauces are summarised in Table 9.2.

Table 9.2 Base sauces

Fond brun	Basic brown meat sauce
Velouté	White sauce using fish, meat, poultry or vegetable stock
Allemande	A velouté thickened with cream and egg yolks
Béchamel	Savoury white sauce made with milk
Tomato sauce	Made with fresh, tinned or puréed tomatoes
Mayonnaise	Cold sauce made from egg yolks, oil, vinegar, salt, pepper and mustard
Hollandaise	Hot sauce made from melted butter, egg yolks, shallots, vinegar and seasonings
Vinaigrette	Cold sauce made from mixing oil, vinegar and a selection of seasonings

These sauces provide the base for other sauces by adding a variety of different ingredients.
For example:

- cheese is added to a béchamel sauce to create a Mornay sauce
- whipped cream is added to a Hollandaise sauce to create sauce Mousseline
- tarragon and other herbs are added to Hollandaise to make Béarnaise
- gherkins, capers and fines herbes are added to mayonnaise to form tartare sauce.

Accompaniments

There are a number of dishes where traditional accompaniments are normally served. Accompaniments offered with certain dishes are mainly to improve the flavour and counteract richness. Table 9.3 contains a guide to these accompaniments. However, this is not intended to be prescriptive, as changes are constantly taking place and new accompaniments being tried. The desire for healthier eating has led to a number of changes, for example:

- alternatives to butter, such as margarine, are often provided
- frequently bread is not buttered in advance, allowing the customer to choose their own requirements
- the availability of lower-fat milk, non-dairy creamers and non-sugar sweeteners is also now standard.

A variety of food items are available which support the service of a range of dishes. Some of these items have specific uses for particular dishes and others are used generally across a number of dishes. Table 9.3 shows examples of accompaniments used in food and beverage service.

Table 9.3 Examples of food items used in food and beverage service

Item	Description	Use
Aïoli/ailloli	Garlic mayonnaise	Cold fish dishes and as a salad dip, e.g. for crudités
Apple sauce	Purée of cooking apples, slightly sweetened, served hot but more usually cold	Roast pork, roast duck and roast goose
Balsamic vinegar	Aromatic vinegar; acid product made from sweet grape wine aged in oak	Dressings
Cayenne	Hot, red pepper (actually a species of powdered capsicum)	Oysters, smoked salmon
Chilli sauce	Hot sauce, mostly Chinese made	With Chinese-style foods
Chilli vinegar	Vinegar flavoured with chillies	Oysters
Chutney	Generic name for Indian sauces. Common varieties are sweet mango or hot mango, also piccalilli and others such as the proprietary Branston Pickle	Indian chutneys for tandoori and other Indian dishes. Other chutneys for cold meats, with cheeses and ploughman's lunch
Cider vinegar	Acid product made from cider	Can be used in salad dressings. Viewed by some as a product for the health conscious
Cocktail gherkins	Small gherkins	Appetisers or garnish for charcuterie
Cocktail onions	Small, pearl onions	Appetisers or garnish for charcuterie
Cocktail sauces	Manufactured sauces of mayonnaise with added flavourings, e.g. tomato	Seafood cocktails
Corn oil	Light-flavoured oil made from corn	Dressings
Cranberry sauce	Sauce made from cranberries, usually available as a proprietary sauce. Can be served hot or cold	Roast turkey
Croutons	Small cubes of fried or toasted bread	Garnish for soups and also used in some salad dishes, e.g. Caesar salad
Cucumbers, pickled	Pickled cucumbers	For meats, salad dishes, charcuterie and cheese

Cumberland sauce	Sweet-and-sour sauce including orange and lemon juice and zest, redcurrant jelly and port. Can be kitchen made or proprietary bottled	Game dishes and for charcuterie
Dill pickle	Pickled gherkins or cucumbers flavoured with dill	Meats, salad dishes, charcuterie and cheese
French dressing	Dressing made from oil and usually wine vinegar or lemon juice, with seasoning. Mustards and herbs may be added	Salads
Gherkins	Small pickled cucumbers	Charcuterie
Ginger	Spicy root used in many forms. Ground ginger is most common in restaurants	Melon
Groundnut oil	Bland oil made from groundnuts	Dressings
Horseradish sauce	Hot-tasting sauce made from horseradish root, usually available as proprietary sauce, often needs creaming down	Roast beef and chicken Maryland, and also for cold-smoked fish dishes when creamed down
HP Sauce	Brown proprietary, spicy, vinegar-based sauce	Cold meats and other dishes
Indian pickles	Unsweetened hot pickles, featuring limes, mango, brinjals, etc.	Accompaniment for Indian (and other) savoury dishes
Kasundi	Hot Indian pickle featuring chopped mango	Accompaniment for Indian (and other) savoury dishes
Ketchup, tomato	Sauce of tomato pulp, vinegar and sweetening. Usually available as a proprietary sauce	Grills, fish, burgers
Lemon	Citrus fruit (slices, segments or halves)	Infinite variety of uses, especially smoked fish, fried fish and a range of drinks including tea
Lime	Citrus fruit (slices, segments or halves)	Similar to lemon above
Malt vinegar	Acid product of brewed malted barley	Dressings and traditionally (in the UK) for chips
Mayonnaise	Made from combination of oil and egg yolks, flavoured with vinegar, herbs and seasoning	Dressing for poached fish and sauce for salads
Mint jelly	Sweetish jelly made with mint. Proprietary versions often used	Roast lamb, as an alternative to mint sauce. Also offered with roast mutton
Mint sauce	Vinegar-based sauce with chopped mint and sweetening. Proprietary versions usually used	Roast lamb
Mustard, English	Generally the hottest. Available as powder for making up or as proprietary bottled, sometimes with other ingredients such as whole seeds	Roast beef, boiled beef, grills, cold meats, pâtés and as an ingredient in dressings, e.g. vinaigrette
Mustard, other	Wide variety including French, au poivre, vert, Bordeaux, Meaux, Dijon, Douce, German (senf)	Cold meats, grills, dressings
Mustard sauce	Warm sauce, generally kitchen made, but also available as proprietary sauce	Traditionally grilled herring but is used for other meat and fish dishes
Oil (general)	Many varieties, usually low in unsaturated fats	Dressings and increasingly for cooking
Olive oil	Oil made from olive pressings (cholesterol free)	Dressings
Olives	Black or green fruit lightly pickled in brine	Appetisers but also garnish for food and drinks, or chopped as flavouring
Onions – pickled	Small onions pickled in malt vinegar (brown) or white vinegar (silver skin)	Cold meats, ploughman's lunch
Oriental vinegars	Several varieties	Give character to dressings and food dishes

Menu knowledge

Paprika	Powdered, mild, red capsicum	Garnish on and in seafood cocktails
Parmesan	Italian hard cheese (grated or shredded)	Used in soups, e.g. minestrone, and for pasta dishes
Parsley	Chopped or sprig	Garnish on wide variety of dishes. Sometimes deep fried with fried fish
Pepper	Ground white pepper	Traditional form of pepper in table shaker
Peppercorns – green	Green are usually pickled in brine and soft	In food dishes
Peppercorns – white and black	Dried white and black peppercorns	Black used for the table in pepper mills but sometimes mixed
Piccalilli	Mixed pickle in thickened, spiced sauce (predominantly turmeric and sugar)	Cold meats, ploughman's lunch, buffet, snacks
Piri-piri	Hot chilli sauce of Portuguese/African origin	Prawns, crayfish, chicken
Redcurrant jelly	Proprietary sauce	Traditionally offered with hare. Also traditionally offered with roast mutton but now often offered with roast lamb
Rouille	Provençale sauce made from pounded chillies, garlic and breadcrumbs (or cooked potatoes) blended with olive oil and fish stock	Used as accompaniment to boiled fish and fish soups such as bouillabaisse. If served with chicken bouillabaisse then chicken stock is used
Salt, refined	Ground table salt	Traditionally used as salt in table cellars or shakers
Salt, sea	Salt derived from evaporated sea water	Seasoning, especially with boiled beef and used in table grinders
Soya oil	Oil made from crushed soya beans	Dressings
Soy sauce	Clear, dark brown sauce, usually Chinese, made from soya beans	Chinese and sometimes other dishes
Sunflower oil	Light textured and flavoured oil from sunflower seeds	Dressings
Tabasco sauce	Hot, spicy, pepper proprietary sauce	Oysters, clams, other seafood and in other dishes
Tartare sauce	Mayonnaise-based sauce with addition of chopped gherkins, capers and lemon juice	All deep-fried fish
Vinaigrette	Combination of oil and vinegar or lemon juice with seasoning. May also include mustards and herbs	Dressings
Wasabi	Finely grated root of the Wasabia japonica plant. Extremely strong flavour. Sometimes called Japanese horseradish	Used in paste form as condiment with sushi, sashimi and other oriental dishes
Wine vinegar	Acid product of wine, red or white	Dressings
Worcestershire sauce	Maceration of blend of spices and fruit in vinegar. Often known by the maker's brand name, 'Lea and Perrins'	Tomato juice, Irish stew, Scotch broth, seafood cocktails and in dressings. Also used as a flavouring in a variety of other dishes

9.3 Hors d'oeuvres and other appetisers

Figure 9.2 Example of an appetiser

Traditionally, **hors d'oeuvres** was a selection of salads, fish and meats. Oil and vinegar were also traditionally offered but this has become less common because such foods are usually already well dressed. Buttered brown bread is also offered less often, thereby allowing the customer a choice of breads and butter or alternatives. A selection of common hors d'oeuvre items are shown in Table 9.4. A list of other **appetisers** is given in Table 9.5.

Table 9.4 Common hors d'oeuvre items

Canapés	These are slices of bread with the crusts removed, cut into a variety of shapes, then toasted or fried in oil or butter and garnished. Garnishes can include smoked salmon, foie gras, prawns, cheese, asparagus tips, tomato, egg, capers, gherkins, salami and other meats
Eggs	These can be poached, presented in aspic or mayonnaise, or hard-boiled, cut in two and garnished or stuffed with various fillings, which include the yolk
Fish	May include items such as anchovies, herring (fresh or marinated), lobster, mackerel (marinated, smoked or fresh), smoked eel (filleted or sliced) and prawns (plain, in cocktail sauce or in a mousse)
Meats	Includes pâtés, ham (raw, boiled or smoked) and salamis of all varieties
Salads	Plain or compound. Examples of plain salads include fish and meat salads, cucumber salad, tomato salad, potato salad, beetroot salad, red cabbage and cauliflower. Compound salads include Russian (mixed vegetables in mayonnaise), Andalouse (celery, onions, peppers, tomatoes, rice and vinaigrette) and Italienne (vegetable salad, cubes of salami, anchovy fillets and mayonnaise)

Table 9.5 Other appetisers

Asparagus (Asperges)	Fresh asparagus may be eaten hot with, for example, melted butter or Hollandaise sauce, or cold with vinaigrette or mayonnaise. Generally now eaten with a knife and fork. Sometimes asparagus holders are used
Avocado (Poire d'avocat)	Generally served in halves with a salad garnish on a fish plate. Can be served with vinaigrette (now more likely to be made with a wine vinegar) which is served separately, or with prawns in a cocktail sauce. Brown bread and butter is less common now
Caesar salad	Salad of cos (or Romaine) lettuce, dressed with vinaigrette or other similar dressing (originally containing near-raw egg), garlic, croutons and grated (or shaved) Parmesan cheese. There are a number of variations to these ingredients
Caviar (Caviare)	Served with a caviar knife (broad blade knife) or side knife on the right-hand side of the cover. Accompaniments include blinis (buck wheat pancakes) or hot breakfast toast, butter, segments of lemon, chopped shallots and chopped egg yolk and egg white. Portion size is usually up to about 30 g (1 oz)
Charcuterie	This can include a range of meat (mainly pork) items including Bayonne ham, salamis, smoked ham, Parma ham and also pâtés and terrines. Accompaniments are peppermill and cayenne pepper, gherkins and sometimes onions. Occasionally a small portion of potato salad is offered. Bread is usually offered but brown bread and butter is now less common

Corn on the cob (Maïs naturel)	These are usually served with special corn-on-the-cob holders that are similar to small swords or forks. Hollandaise sauce or melted butter will accompany this appetiser. A peppermill is offered
Fresh fruit	Caster sugar may be offered upon request. Both caster sugar and ground ginger are offered with melon if served alone
Fruit cocktails	Caster sugar is sometimes offered, especially if grapefruit is included in the cocktail
Fruit juices	Caster sugar may be offered should grapefruit juice be ordered. For tomato juice, salt and Worcestershire sauce (shaken) are offered
Globe artichokes (Artichaut)	This vegetable is usually served whole as a starter. The edible portion of the leaves is 'sucked off' between the teeth after being dipped in a dressing (for example, vinaigrette if served cold or melted butter or Hollandaise sauce if served hot). A side knife and sweet fork are laid to enable the 'heart' of the globe artichoke to be eaten. A finger bowl containing lukewarm water and a slice of lemon and a spare napkin are essential as the 'leaves' are eaten using the fingers
Gravlax (Gravadlax)	Salmon pickled with salt, sugar and dill. Traditional accompaniments are a slightly sweetened sauce of mustard and dill and often half a lemon (which may be wrapped in muslin to prevent the juice squirting on to the customer when the lemon is squeezed). A variety of unbuttered breads may be offered, with butter and alternatives served separately
Mousses and pâtés	Hot, unbuttered breakfast toast or bread is offered. Butter or alternatives may be offered and other accompaniments appropriate to the dish itself, for example, lemon segments with fish mousses, although lemon is often offered with meat-based pâtés
Niçoise salad	There are a number of versions of this salad. Generally it includes boiled potatoes, whole French beans, tomatoes, hard-boiled eggs (quartered or sliced), stoned black olives, flakes of tuna fish and anchovy fillets. This salad is usually made up and plated. Vinaigrette is often offered
Other salads	Salads can be made up and served plated or constituted at the guéridon. Dressings vary according to the main ingredient of the salad or upon request from the customer
Oysters (huîtres)	Cold oysters are usually served in one half of the shell on a bed of crushed ice in a soup plate on an underplate. An oyster fork is usually offered but a small sweet fork can also be used. These are placed on the right-hand side of the cover. Oysters are usually eaten by holding the shell in one hand and the fork in the other. Therefore a finger bowl on an underplate containing lukewarm water and a slice of lemon together with an extra napkin may be offered. Accompaniments include half a lemon and the oyster cruet (cayenne pepper, pepper mill, chilli vinegar and Tabasco sauce). Traditionally brown bread and butter is also offered
Potted shrimps	Accompaniments include hot, unbuttered, breakfast toast (there is plenty of butter already in this dish), cayenne pepper, a peppermill and segments of lemon
Seafood cocktails (Cocktail de crevettes)	The traditional accompaniments are a lemon segment, peppermill, sometimes cayenne pepper and traditionally brown bread and butter, although this is less common now
Smoked salmon (saumon fumé)	Traditional accompaniments are half a lemon (which may be wrapped in muslin to prevent the juice squirting on to the customer when the lemon is squeezed), cayenne pepper, peppermill and brown bread and butter. Nowadays a variety of unbuttered bread may be offered with butter and alternatives served separately. Oil is sometimes offered and also chopped onions and capers
Other smoked fish	As well as the accompaniments offered with smoked salmon, creamed horseradish has become a standard offering with all other smoked fish including trout, mackerel, cod, halibut and tuna
Snails (escargots)	Snail tongs are placed on the left of the cover and a snail fork on the right. The snails are served in an escargot dish on its underplate. This dish has six or twelve indentations. A finger bowl containing lukewarm water and a slice of lemon and an extra napkin may also be offered. French bread is offered for mopping up the sauce. Half a lemon (which may be wrapped in muslin to prevent the juice squirting on to the customer when the lemon is squeezed) may also be offered

Service of hors d'oeuvres and other appetisers

Many of these dishes are served plated but they may also be **silver served**. Some can also be prepared and served in the room, for example caviar, pâté, seafood cocktails, smoked salmon, salads and dressings, and melon.

When the dishes are plated the cover usually would be a small knife and fork. Sometimes fish knives and forks are presented with fish dishes. For other dishes usually the lay-up depends of the types of food being presented, for example a prawn cocktail is often presented with a small fork and a teaspoon.

Key term

Silver service – presentation of food by waiting staff, using a spoon and fork, onto a customer's plate, from food flats or dishes

9.4 Soups

Soups are divided into a number of categories, including consommés, veloutés, crèmes, purées, potages, bisques (shellfish soups) and broths. Examples of these are shown in Table 9.6. There are also various national soups and examples of these are shown in Table 9.7.

Figure 9.3 Bowl of soup

Table 9.6 Types of soup

Consommé	Clarified soup made from poultry, beef, game or vegetable bouillon. There are no traditional accompaniments to consommé although warmed Sherry or sometimes Madeira might be added to the consommé in the restaurant just before serving
Veloutés, crèmes and purées	Traditionally croutons were only offered with purées and cream of tomato soup, but they are now commonly offered with a range of soups
Potages, broths and bisques	There are no traditional accompaniments offered here

Table 9.7 National soups

Borscht (Polish)	Duck-flavoured consommé garnished with duck, diced beef and turned root vegetables. The accompaniments are sour cream, beetroot juice and bouchées filled with duck pâté
Bouillabaisse (French)	This is really a form of fish stew. Although a soup plate on its underplate and soup spoon is used, it is common for a side knife and sweet fork to also be laid as part of the cover. Thin slices of French bread dipped in oil and grilled (sippets) are offered as well as rouille
Chowder (USA)	Chowders are thick soups usually containing seafood, potatoes and cream or milk. The most well-known is New England clam chowder made with potatoes, onion, bacon or salt pork, flour and clams. Served with clam cakes, which are deep-fried balls of buttery dough with chopped clam inside
Cock-a-leekie (Scottish)	Veal and chicken consommé garnished with shredded leeks and chicken. Served with prunes which may be put into the soup plate at the service point
Gazpacho (Spanish)	A cold, tomato-based soup. It contains tomatoes, onions, breadcrumbs, peppers, cucumber, garlic, ice water, sugar and spices. Croutons, diced cucumber, peppers, tomato and onion may all be offered as accompaniments

Minestrone (Italian)	Rustic vegetable soup with pasta. Traditional accompaniments are grated (shaved) Parmesan cheese and grilled flûtes
Miso (Japanese)	Miso is a paste made from fermented soya beans. The soup is made by adding this paste to dashi soup stock. The stock itself is made from bonito flakes and konbu seaweed. Ingredients that provide contrasts such as spring onion and delicate tofu, and those that float and sink such as potatoes and seaweed, may be paired together and offered as a garnish at the last moment
Petit marmite (French)	Beef and chicken-flavoured soup garnished with turned root vegetables and diced beef and chicken. Usually served in a special marmite pot, which resembles a small casserole. This marmite pot sits on a doily on an underplate. A sweet spoon is used to eat this soup, as it is easier to get this spoon into the small pot. Accompaniments are grilled flûtes, poached bone marrow and grated (shaved) Parmesan cheese. Sometimes the bread and cheese are added as a croûte on top of the soup before serving at the table
Soupe à l'oignon (French)	French onion soup. May be served with grilled flûtes and grated (shaved) Parmesan cheese but is often topped with a slice of French bread gratinated with cheese

Service of soup

Most soups are plated although they may also be silver served. Soups are usually eaten from a soup plate/bowl, placed on an underplate, and eaten with a soup spoon. However, it is common today to see soup bowls of varying modern designs, together with their underplate, as a set. Consommé is traditionally served in a consommé cup on a consommé saucer and set on a fish plate. It is traditionally eaten with a sweet spoon but a soup spoon is now more common. Consommé may be finished in the room by the addition of warmed (flambéed) sherry.

9.5 Egg dishes

Egg dishes as separate courses have become less common in recent years. Omelettes have retained their popularity while dishes such as eggs *en cocotte* (in pots) occasionally feature on menus. Table 9.8 gives some examples of egg dishes.

Figure 9.4 *Oeuf en cocotte*

Table 9.8 Egg dishes

Oeuf sur la plat	The egg is cooked in the oven in the *oeuf sur la plat* dish (small, round, white earthenware or metal dish with two ears)
Oeuf en cocotte	The egg is cooked in the *cocotte* dish, in a bain-marie in the oven, and served in this dish with various garnishes (see Figure 9.4)
Omelettes	Two- or three-egg omelettes with various fillings. Omelettes can also be made with just egg whites
Savoury soufflés	Various ingredients and fillings, such as cheese, spinach, mushroom

Service of egg dishes

- For *oeuf sur la plat* the cutlery is usually a sweet spoon and fork, with the addition of a small/side knife depending on the garnish.
- Eggs served *en cocotte* (in a small, round earthenware dish with straight sides about the size of a small teacup); the dish is placed on a doily on an underplate and is eaten with a teaspoon.
- As a first course an omelette is eaten usually with a large fork (joint) placed on the right-hand side of the cover. As a main course it would be eaten with a joint knife and fork.
- Savoury soufflés are usually served in the ramekin dish they are baked in. This is placed on a doily on an underplate and the cutlery is a teaspoon and/or a small fork.

9.6 Pasta and rice dishes

Figure 9.5 Pasta dish

These dishes, which are also referred to as **farinaceous** dishes, include all pastas such as:

- spaghetti
- macaroni
- nouilles
- ravioli
- rice dishes such as pilaff and risotto.

Also included are dishes such as:
- gnocchi Piedamontaise (potato)
- gnocchi Parisienne (choux paste)
- gnocchi Romaine (semolina).

Accompaniments

Grated Parmesan cheese is normally offered with all these pasta dishes. Sometimes the Parmesan cheese is shaved from a large piece rather than grated.

Service of pasta and rice dishes

Most pasta and rice dishes are now served plated but may occasionally be silver served, for example gnocchi, pilaff or risotto.

For spaghetti, a joint fork should be laid on the right-hand side of the cover and a sweet spoon on the left. For all other farinaceous dishes a sweet spoon and fork are used, with the sweet spoon on the right and the fork on the left.

9.7 Fish dishes

Figure 9.6 Fish dish

A wide variety of fish and shellfish are available today. They provide a good source of protein and may be cooked and presented in many ways. They are divided into five main groups:

- **Round white fish**: such as bass, bream, cod, coley, haddock, hake, John Dory, monkfish, red mullet and whiting.
- **Flat white fish**: such as brill, dab, flounder, halibut, plaice, skate, sole, lemon sole and turbot.
- **Oily fish**: such as eels, herring, mackerel, pilchards, salmon, salmon trout, sardines, trout, tuna and whitebait.
- **Shellfish**: these are divided into two main groups:
  - Crustaceans, such as crabs, crayfish, lobster, prawns, scampi and shrimps
  - Molluscs, such as clams, cockles, mussels, oysters, scallops and winkles.
- **Cephalopods**: such as the octopus and squid.

The general accompaniments for fish dishes are shown in Table 9.9.

Table 9.9 Accompaniments for fish dishes

Hot fish dishes with a sauce	Usually no accompaniments
Hot fish dishes without a sauce	These often have Hollandaise or another hot butter-based sauce offered. Lemon segments may also be offered
Fried fish which has been breadcrumbed (à l'Anglaise)	These dishes often have tartare sauce or another mayonnaise-based sauce offered, together with segments of lemon
Fried or grilled fish dishes, not breadcrumbed	These dishes are usually offered with lemon. Sometimes sauces such as Hollandaise or tartare are offered
Deep-fried fish which has been dipped in batter (à l'Orly)	A (kitchen-made) tomato sauce is sometimes offered together with segments of lemon. Proprietary sauces can also be offered, as can vinegar if chips are being served
Cold-poached fish dishes	Usually mayonnaise or another mayonnaise-based sauce such as sauce verte is offered, together with segments of lemon
Grilled herring (hareng grillé)	Usually served with a mustard sauce
Sushi and sashimi	Wasabi and soy sauce
Whitebait (blanchailles)	Accompaniments are cayenne pepper, peppermill, segments of lemon and brown bread offered with butter or alternatives
Mussels (moules marinière)	Served with brown bread and butter, or more commonly now a variety of breads offered with butter or alternatives. Cayenne pepper may be offered
Cold lobster (homard froid)	Lemon and sauce mayonnaise are the usual accompaniments

Service of fish dishes

Most main courses are plated but may also be silver served. Some can be finished and served in the room, for example filleting sole or removing the black outer skin and bone from a cutlet of salmon.

For a fish course as a starter then often a fish knife and fork is laid, but a small knife and sweet fork may also be used instead.

Traditionally, main course fish dishes were eaten with a fish knife and fork but this practice is declining. More often now a joint knife and fork are laid.

Oriental dishes are often serviced with chopsticks and sometimes a ceramic spoon. A sweet spoon might also be set.

9.8 Meats, poultry and game

Figure 9.7 Roast duck

Roast meats

In all cases roast gravy is offered. For dishes where the roast is plain (not roasted with herbs, for instance) the main accompaniments are shown in Table 9.10

Table 9.10 Accompaniments for plain roast meats

Roast beef (boeuf rôti)	Horseradish sauce, French and English mustards, and Yorkshire pudding
Roast lamb (agneau rôti)	Traditionally mint sauce, although redcurrant jelly is sometimes also offered
Roast mutton (mouton rôti)	Traditionally redcurrant jelly, although mint sauce is sometimes also offered. An alternative traditional accompaniment is a white onion sauce
Roast pork (porc rôti)	Apple sauce, and sage and onion stuffing
Roast veal	Thickened roast gravy, lemon, parsley and thyme stuffing

Boiled meats

Accompaniments for boiled meats are listed in Table 9.11.

Table 9.11 Accompaniments for boiled meats

Boiled mutton (mouton bouilli)	Caper sauce is traditionally served
Salt beef (silverside)	Turned root vegetables, dumplings and the natural cooking liquor
Boiled fresh beef (boeuf bouilli)	Turned root vegetables, natural cooking liquor, rock salt and gherkins
Boiled ham (jambon bouilli)	Parsley sauce or white onion sauce

Other meat dishes

Figure 9.8 Grilled steak

Table 9.12 Accompaniments for other meat dishes

Irish stew	Accompaniments are Worcestershire sauce and pickled red cabbage
Curry	Accompaniments are poppadums (crisp, highly seasoned pancakes), Bombay duck (dried fillet of fish from the Indian Ocean) and mango chutney. Also offered is a curry tray, which will have items such as diced apple, sultanas, sliced bananas, yoghurt and desiccated coconut
Mixed grill and other grills	These dishes may be garnished with cress, tomato, straw potatoes and parsley butter. Various mustards (French and English) and sometimes proprietary sauces (tomato ketchup and brown sauce) are offered as accompaniments
Oriental dishes	Often served with various types of rice dishes. Accompaniments include wasabi and soy sauce
Steaks	As for mixed grill. Béarnaise sauce is offered with chateaubriand (double fillet) and sometimes with other grilled steaks

Poultry, furred and feathered game

Figure 9.9 Roast chicken

Table 9.13 Accompaniments for poultry, furred and feathered game

Poultry	
Roast chicken (poulet rôti farci)	The accompaniments are bread sauce, roast gravy, parsley and thyme stuffing, game chips, grilled bacon and watercress. Sage and onion stuffing is also used
Roast duck (caneton rôti)	Sage and onion stuffing, apple sauce and roast gravy are served
Wild duck (caneton sauvage rôti)	Roast gravy and traditionally an orange salad with an acidulated cream dressing is offered as a side dish

Roast goose (oie rôti)	Sage and onion stuffing, apple sauce and roast gravy
Roast turkey (dinde rôti)	Cranberry sauce, chestnut stuffing, chipolata sausages, game chips, watercress and roast gravy are the usual accompaniments
Furred game	
Jugged hare	Heart-shaped croutons, forcemeat balls, redcurrant jelly and roast gravy
Venison (venaison)	Cumberland sauce, redcurrant jelly and roast gravy. Sauce poivrade might also be offered
Feathered game	
When roasted	The accompaniments for all feathered game such as partridge (perdreau), grouse (lagopède), woodcock (bécasse), quail (caille) and pheasant (faisan) are fried breadcrumbs, hot liver pâté spread on a croûte on which the meat sits, bread sauce, game chips, watercress and roast gravy

Service of meats, poultry and game

Most main courses are plated although they may also be silver served. Some can also be prepared and served in the room, for example meats carved at the table, steaks cooked, and the preparation of such dishes as steak Diane. The cover is a joint knife and fork. Sometimes steak knives are offered. For oriental dishes, chopsticks and sometimes a ceramic spoon are usually offered. A sweet spoon and fork might also be set.

9.9 Potatoes, vegetables and salads

A wide variety of potatoes and vegetables, including salads, may be served with various main dishes and courses.

Figure 9.10 Potatoes and vegetables

Key terms

Poultry – includes chicken, duck, goose and turkey

Furred game – includes venison and hare

Feathered game – birds such as partridge, grouse, wood cock, quail or pheasant

Potatoes

There are four categories: floury, firm, waxy and salad potatoes, all of which have different uses. Potatoes are from the **tuber** family, which also includes items such as sweet potatoes, yams and Jerusalem artichokes.

Key term

Tuber – vegetable grown beneath the soil

Vegetables

Vegetables fall into a number of categories:
- Roots: such as carrots, parsnips, salsify and beetroot.
- Bulbs: such as onions and fennel.
- Leaf: such as chicory, spinach, cress and the various lettuces.
- Brassicas: such as broccoli, cabbage, cauliflower and pak choi.
- Stems and shoots: including asparagus, bean sprouts, celery, samphire and globe artichokes.
- Fruiting: including aubergine, avocado, cucumber, peppers and tomatoes.
- Plantains: such as ackee and breadfruit.
- Mushrooms and fungi: including field mushrooms, chanterelles, morels and truffles.

Salads

Salads can be offered with a course and may also be eaten separately as a course. There are two main types of salad:

- **Plain salads**, which consist of two main types. These may be either green salads made up of green leaf ingredients or vegetable salads made up of one main vegetable ingredient that will dominate the overall flavour of the dish. Plain salad may often be served with a main course or as a separate course after a main course. Various types of dressings are either included in the salad or offered separately.
- **Compound salads**, which may be a plain salad plus other ingredients, such as meat, fish and mushrooms, or a combination of a number of ingredients, mixed together using specific dressings or sauces.

Table 9.14 Examples of salads

Endive	Hearts of lettuce, endive, sauce vinaigrette
Française	Lettuce hearts, sections of skinned tomato, hard-boiled egg, with vinaigrette offered separately
Mimosa	Lettuce hearts, filleted orange, grapes skinned and stoned, sliced banana, sprinkled with egg yolk, acidulated cream dressing offered separately
Niçoise	French beans, tomato quarters, sliced potatoes, anchovies, capers, olives, vinaigrette
d'orange	Lettuce hearts, in sections, filleted orange, freshly made acidulated cream dressing
Russian	Diced mixed cooked vegetables including potato, often decorated with other ingredients such as tomatoes, eggs, anchovies, lobster, ham and tongue, and bound in mayonnaise sauce
Saison	Lettuce hearts plus other salad vegetables in season, vinaigrette offered separately
Verte	Lettuce hearts, vinaigrette offered separately

Service of potatoes, vegetables and salads

Most often potatoes and vegetables are pre-plated but may also be silver served on to the main plate alongside the main dish. No additional cutlery is required.

Potatoes, vegetables or salads can also be separately pre-plated, or silver served on to a side plate or crescent-shaped dish, separate from the main plate. This is positioned at the top left-hand corner of the cover. A separate sweet fork for the salad, and service spoons and forks for the potatoes and vegetables, may be offered.

Potatoes, vegetables or salads may also be placed on the table in multi-portion serving dishes from which the customers can serve themselves, using service spoons and forks (family service).

Baked potatoes are accompanied by cayenne pepper, peppermill and butter (or substitutes). Butter is not now automatically put on the top of the potato, but is offered separately, together with alternatives.

9.10 Cheese

Cheeses are distinguished by flavour and categorised according to their texture. They differ from each other for a number of reasons, mainly because of variations in the making process. Differences occur in the rind and how it is formed, in the paste and the cooking process (both in the time and temperature at which it is cooked). Cheeses also vary because the milk used comes from different animals such as cows, sheep and goats. The texture of a cheese depends largely on the period of **maturation**.

> **Key term**
>
> **Maturation** – period of time to allow cheese to develop and ripen

Storage

Depending on how they are to be used, cheeses may be purchased either whole or pre-portioned. Cheese should be stored:

- in a cool, dark place, with good air circulation
- in a refrigerator
- with its original wrapping, otherwise it should be wrapped in either greaseproof paper, cling film or aluminium foil to prevent it drying out
- away from food items that absorb flavours/odours, such as dairy produce.

Categories

The recognised categories of cheese are:

- fresh
- soft
- semi-hard
- hard
- blue.

Table 9.15 Examples of cheeses within the five categories

Fresh cheese	
Cottage	Unripened low-fat, skimmed milk cheese with a granular curd. Originated in the USA and now has many variations
Cream	Similar to cottage cheese but is made with full-fat milk. A number of different varieties are available, some made from non-cow's milks
Mozzarella	Italian cheese made from buffalo milk but may now also be made from cow's milk
Ricotta	Italian cheese made from the whey of cow's milk. A number of other Italian varieties are available, made from sheep's milk
Soft cheese	
Bel Paese	This light and creamy Italian cheese has a name that means 'beautiful country' and was first produced in 1929
Brie	Famous French cheese made since the eighth century. Other countries now make this style of cheese, distinguishing it from the original French Brie by the addition of the name of the country or county of origin, e.g. German brie, Somerset brie
Camembert	Famous French cheese which is stronger and often more pungent than Brie
Carré de l'Est	A soft cheese produced in France that is made from pasteurised cow's milk and packed in square boxes. Like Camembert, it softens on ripening and is darker in colour than Brie. When ripe it has a mild flavour

Semi-hard cheese

Caerphilly	Buttermilk-flavoured cheese with a soft paste. Some people will find it almost soapy. Originally a Welsh cheese but now manufactured all over Britain
Cheddar	Classic British cheese now made all over the world and referred to as, for example, Scottish cheddar, Canadian cheddar
Cheshire	Crumbly, slightly salty cheese, available as either white or red. It was originally made during the twelfth century in Cheshire but is now made all over Britain
Edam	A Dutch cheese that is similar to, but harder than, Gouda. It has a fairly bland, buttery taste and a yellow or red wax-coated rind. It is sometimes flavoured with cumin
Emmental	The name of this Swiss cheese refers to the Emme Valley. It is similar to Gruyère, although it is softer and slightly less tasty
Gloucester/ Double Gloucester	Full-cream, classic English cheeses originally made only from the milk of Gloucestershire cows
Gouda	Buttery-textured, soft and mild-flavoured, well-known Dutch cheese with a yellow or red rind
Gruyère	Mainly known as a Swiss cheese, but both the French and Swiss varieties can legally be called by this name. It has small pea-size holes and a smooth, relatively hard texture. The French varieties may have larger holes
Jarlsberg	Similar to Emmenthal, this Norwegian cheese was first produced in the late 1950s. It has a yellow wax coating
Lancashire	Another classic English cheese similar to Cheshire (white Cheshire is sometimes sold as Lancashire)
Leicester	Mild flavoured and orange-coloured English cheese
Monterey	Creamy, soft American cheese with many holes. A harder version known as Monterey Jack is suitable for grating
Pont l'Évêque	Similar to Camembert, but square in shape, this French cheese originates from Normandy
Port Salut	Mild-flavoured cheese with a name meaning 'Port of Salvation', referring to the abbey where exiled Trappist monks returned after the French Revolution
Wensleydale	Yorkshire cheese originally made from sheep or goat's milk but now made from cow's milk. This cheese is the traditional accompaniment to apple pie

Hard cheese

Parmesan	Classic Italian hard cheese, more correctly called Parmigiano Reggiano. It is the grated cheese mainly used in and for sprinkling over Italian dishes, especially pasta, and also minestrone
Provolone	Smoked cheese made in America, Australia and Italy. Now made from cow's milk but originally from buffalo milk. Younger versions are softer and milder than the longer kept and more mature varieties

Blue cheese

Blue de Bresse	Fairly soft and mild-flavoured French cheese from the area between Soane-et-Loire and the Jura
Blue Cheshire	One of the finest of the blue cheeses, which only becomes blue accidentally, although the makers endeavour to assist this process by pricking the cheese and maturing it in a favourable atmosphere
Danish Blue	One of the most well-known of the blue cheeses. Softish and mild flavoured, it was one of the first European blue cheeses to gain popularity in Britain
Dolcelatte	Factory-made version of Gorgonzola. The name is Italian for 'sweet milk' and the cheese is fairly soft with a creamy texture and greenish veining
Dorset Blue	A strong, hard-pressed cheese, being close textured and made from skimmed milk. It is straw-coloured with deep blue veins, rather crumbly and has a rough rind
Gorgonzola	Softish, sharp flavoured, classic Italian cheese with greenish veining, which is developed with the addition of mould culture

Roquefort	Classic, sheep's milk cheese from the southern Massif Central in France. The maturing takes place in caves, which provide a unique humid environment that contributes to the development of the veining
Stilton	Famous and classic English cheese made from cow's milk. So called because it was noted as being sold in the Bell Inn at Stilton by travellers stopping there. According to legend it was first made by a Mrs Paulet of Melton Mowbray. White Stilton has also become popular and is slightly less flavoursome than the blue variety

Accompaniments

Accompaniments set on the table may include:

- cruet (salt, pepper and mustard)
- butter or alternative
- celery served in a celery glass part filled with crushed ice, on an underplate
- radishes (when in season) placed in a glass bowl on an underplate with teaspoon
- caster sugar for cream cheeses
- assorted cheese biscuits (cream crackers, Ryvita, sweet digestive, water biscuits, etc.) or various breads.

Service of cheese

Cheese may be served plated and may also be served from a cheese board or trolley at the table. There should be a separate cheese knife for the service of each of the cheeses on offer. The accompaniments should be placed on the table prior to the cheese selection being offered to the customer. The cover is a side plate with a small/side knife and sweet fork.

9.11 Sweets

The range of possible sweets is very extensive and varied; examples are shown in Table 9.16.

Figure 9.11 Sweets

Table 9.16 Examples of types of sweet dishes

Bavarois, mousses, syllabubs	Either served in individual dishes or glassware, or portioned and served. Various fruit flavours
Charlottes	Moulds lined with sponge and filled with bavarois in various flavours and sometimes with fruits
Coupes and sundaes	Usually ice cream and various fruit combinations, served in coupe dishes or sundae dishes
Creams	Examples include Chantilly (sweetened whipped cream flavoured with vanilla), custard (sauce Anglaise) and dishes such as egg custard or crème brûlée
Fritters (beignets)	For example, beignets de pomme (apple)
Fruit dishes	Examples are fruit salads, poached fruits (compôte) and baked apples

Menu knowledge

Gâteaux	Examples include chocolate and Black Forest
Ices and sorbets	Ices refers to ice cream and frozen yoghurt. Sorbets refers to water ices. Presented in various forms, including bombs (ice cream preparations made into bomb shapes using moulds)
Omelettes	With a variety of fillings and flavourings, for example rum, jam or apple
Pancakes	With a variety of fillings, for example cherries or other fruits
Pies, flans and other pastries	Examples include *flan aux poires* (pear), Bakewell tart, Dutch apple pie
Puddings	Includes bread and butter, cabinet, diplomate and various fruit puddings
Soufflés	Can be served hot or cold and includes *soufflé au citron* (lemon) and *soufflé au café* (coffee)

Accompaniments

There are no particular accompaniments to sweets. Often the customer may require a sugar sifter or, depending on the nature of the sweet selected, sauces such as custard or sauce Anglaise (rich custard) may be offered. Alternatives to this might be Chantilly cream, single cream or whipped double cream.

Service of sweets

Many sweet dishes are plated and some may also be silver served. They may also be portioned and served from a sweet trolley in the room. Other sweet dishes may be prepared and served in the room from the guéridon trolley, for example crêpes suzette, peach flambé and banana flambé.

For most sweets the cover is a sweet spoon laid on the right of the cover and a sweet fork laid on the left of the cover. For other dishes, the lay-up will depend on the type of food being presented, for example sweets being presented in a coupe are often eaten with a teaspoon.

9.12 Savouries

On the lunch and dinner menu a savoury may be served as an alternative to a sweet. In a banquet it may be a separate course served in addition to either a sweet or cheese course. Examples of savouries are given in Table 9.17.

Figure 9.12 A savoury omelette

Table 9.17 Examples of savouries

Barquettes	Filled boat-shaped pastry cases, similar to tartlettes
Bouchées	Filled small, round puff pastry cases. A small edition of a vol-au-vent
Canapés or croûtes	Shaped pieces of bread about 6 mm (¼" inch) thick, brushed with melted butter and grilled, or may be shaped shallow-fried bread. Examples include Scotch woodcock (scrambled egg topped with a trellis of anchovies and studded with capers), devils on horseback (prunes wrapped in bacon) and angels on horseback (poached oysters wrapped in bacon)
Flans	Either single or portioned savoury flans such as quiche Lorraine

Omelettes	Two- and three-egg omelettes with various flavours/fillings such as parsley, anchovy, cheese or mixed herbs
On toast	Usually shaped pieces of toast with various toppings such as anchovies, sardines, mushrooms, smoked haddock and the classic Welsh rarebit (a mature cheese, egg yolk and béchamel sauce mixture, bound together, spread on toast and grilled) or Buck rarebit (Welsh rarebit with a poached egg on the top)
Soufflés	Made in a soufflé dish with various flavours such as mushroom, spinach, sardine, anchovy, smoked haddock or cheese
Tartlettes	Round pastry cases with various fillings such as mushrooms, or cheese soufflé mixtures with various garnishes, or prawns or other fish in various sauces

Accompaniments

- Salt and pepper
- Cayenne pepper
- Peppermill
- Worcestershire sauce (usually only with meat savouries).

Service of savouries

Savouries are usually served plated although occasionally they may be silver served. The cover is a hot fish plate and a small/side knife and sweet fork. Should the savoury take the form of an individual savoury soufflé then it would be eaten from the dish in which it is cooked using either a teaspoon or a sweet spoon and fork.

9.13 Dessert (fresh fruit and nuts)

Dessert may include all types of fresh fruit and nuts according to season, although the majority of the more popular items are now available all year round. Popular items are dessert apples, pears, bananas, oranges, mandarins, tangerines, black and white grapes, pineapple and assorted nuts such as Brazils. Sometimes a box of dates may appear on the fruit basket.

Figure 9.13 Bowl of fruit

Accompaniments

- Caster sugar holder
- Salt for nuts.

Service of fresh fruit and nuts

Fresh fruit may be served plated or presented in a fruit bowl for the customer to make their choice. It may also be presented in a fruit basket from the guéridon at the customer's table. Upon the customer making their selection the fresh fruit might then be prepared, portioned and plated or flambéed and served from the guéridon. The cover is a fruit plate/sweet plate with a fruit knife and fork or small/side knife and fork. Nut crackers are available if required.

Testing your learning

1 Identify one *accompaniment* that could be offered when a customer orders each of the following dishes:
   (a) soups generally
   (b) pasta dishes
   (c) fried or grilled fish dishes, not breadcrumbed
   (d) roast lamb
   (e) roast duck.

2 Identify the *cutlery cover* for a customer who orders the following items:
   (a) soups generally
   (b) plated hors d'oeuvre
   (c) pasta dishes
   (d) fish dishes
   (e) sweet dishes.

3 Describe as you would to a customer:
   (a) croutons
   (b) tartare sauce

4 Which of the following is a clarified soup?
   (a) bisque
   (b) crème
   (c) consommé
   (d) bouillabaisse.

5 Identify two dishes where horseradish sauce would be offered as one of the accompaniments.

6 You have offered sage and onion stuffing, apple sauce and roast gravy to a customer. Which of the following main course dishes is the customer eating?
   (a) roast goose
   (b) roast mutton
   (c) jugged hare
   (d) roast venison.

7 Worcestershire sauce should be offered with:
   (a) chateaubriand
   (b) Irish stew
   (c) beignets de pomme
   (d) oysters.

8 Which of the following is recognised as a 'soft cheese'?
   (a) mozzarella
   (b) Camembert
   (c) Wensleydale
   (d) Roquefort.

9 Identify two dishes that may be prepared and served from a guéridon trolley at the customer's table.

10 List four of the main cooking methods and describe each briefly.

1 A party of three customers have selected food items for their meal. These are listed in the table below. Study the food items and then copy and complete the table.

Customer order	Cover	Accompaniments	Service equipment
First courses			
1 × Cream of tomato soup			
1 × Smoked salmon			
1 × Caesar salad			
Main courses			
1 × Roast pheasant			
1 × Grilled steak			
I × Dover sole			
Sides			
3 × Seasonal vegetables			
3 × New potatoes			
Sweet/cheese			
1 × Fresh fruit salad			
1 × Dutch apple pie			
1 × Cheese plate			

Wine and drinks lists

Units covered

This chapter covers the following units:

Level 1

→ Prepare and clear areas for drink service (1BS2, 113)
→ Serve drinks (1BS2)

Level 2

→ Principles of beverage product knowledge (207)
→ Serve alcoholic and soft drinks (2BS2, 212)
→ Prepare and serve cocktails (2BS3, 213)
→ Prepare and serve wines (2BS4, 214)
→ Prepare and clear the bar area (2BS1, 211)

Learning outcomes

This chapter will help you to:

1	State the purpose of wine and drinks lists	161
2	Describe different types of wine and drinks lists	161
3	Describe the different ways the content of wine and drink lists may be displayed	163
4	State the general information given on wine and drink lists	165

10.1 The purpose of the wine and drink lists

The purpose of a wine and drinks list is similar to that of the food menu: it is a selling aid that provides information to the customer. It should therefore be designed in such a way as to encourage the customer to want to open and explore its contents. Careful thought is also needed in its planning, design, layout, colour and overall appearance to ensure it complements the style of the establishment. The design considerations are similar to those given to food menus (see Section 8.1, page 125). Adequate information that is easy to find and follow will make the customer feel more at home and will assist in selling the wines and drinks on offer.

10.2 Types of wine and drinks lists

Bar and cocktail lists

These lists may range from a basic standard list offering the common everyday apéritifs such as sherries, vermouths, bitters, a selection of spirits with mixers, beers and soft drinks, together with a limited range of cocktails, through to a very comprehensive list offering a good choice in all areas. The format and content of the list will be determined by the style of operation and customer that the establishment wishes to attract. Depending on this, the emphasis may be on:

- cocktails: traditional or fashionable
- malt whiskies
- beers
- New World wines
- non-alcoholic drinks.

Restaurant lists

These lists may take various formats such as:

- a full and very comprehensive list of wines from all countries, with emphasis on the classic areas such as Bordeaux/Burgundy plus a fine wine/prestige selection
- a middle-of-the-road, traditional selection, for example some French, German and Italian wines, together with some New World wines
- a small selection of well-known or branded wines – a prestige list
- predominantly wines of one particular country.

Figure 10.2 iPad-based wine list

Figure 10.1 Traditional wine list

After-meal drink lists (digestifs)

These lists are often combined with the wine list, although sometimes they are presented as a separate liqueur list. The list should offer a full range of liqueurs and may also include a specialist range of brandies and/or malt whiskies. Vintage and Late Bottled Vintage (LBV) port may also be offered here. A range of speciality liqueur/spirit coffees might also be included.

Banqueting and events lists

The length of the list will generally depend on the size and style of operation. In most instances there is a selection of popular wine names/styles on offer and a range of prices from house wines to some fine wines to suit all customer preferences. In some operations the banqueting wine list is the same as the restaurant wine list.

Wine and drinks lists

Room service lists

There may be a mini-bar in the room or the room service menu may offer a choice from a standard bar list. The range of wines offered is usually limited and prices will vary according to the type of establishment.

Lounge service lists

These are often reduced forms of the restaurant list and may also offer a choice from a standard bar list. The range of wines offered is usually limited and prices will vary according to the type of establishment.

10.3 Content of wine and drink lists

The contents of wine and drink lists are commonly listed in the order in which they might be consumed:

- Apéritifs – which alongside sparkling and still wines can include a range of aromatised wines, fortified wines and natural spring and mineral waters.
- Cocktails.
- Spirits and associated mixers such as aerated waters.
- Wines – sparkling and still.
- Beers, cider, aerated waters and squashes.
- Digestifs – which, as well as liqueurs, may also include various spirits such as brandies, malt whiskies and also ports, other fortified wines, sweet table wines and vin doux naturels.
- Speciality coffees.

Listing of wines

Wines are usually listed in three main ways:

1 by place of origin (geographical)
2 by type
3 by grape.

Listing wines by geographical area

The traditional approach is to list wines by geographical area. Wines are presented country by country or region by region, for instance France or Australasia (which includes Australia and New Zealand), and then area by area. It is also usual to have the wines presented under each country, region or area with the white wines first, followed by rosé wines and then red wines. Using this approach the listing of wines within a wine list might be:

1 Champagne and sparkling
2 France
3 Germany
4 Italy
5 Spain
6 Portugal
7 England
8 Other European wine
9 Australia
10 The Americas (Canada, USA, Central and South America)
11 Australasia
12 South Africa
13 Other world wines
14 House wines

Listing wines by type

A modern approach is to have wines listed by type:

- sparkling wines
- white wines
- rosé wines
- red wines
- dessert (sweet) wines.

The wines can then be listed under each type of wine in three main ways:

- country by country
- region by region (similar to the geographical listing described above)
- by the style of the wine.

If the wines are to be listed by type and by style, then the wines may be presented under the following headings:

- sparkling wines
- white wines
  - grapy whites
  - grassy-fruity whites
  - richer whites
- rosé wines
- red wines
  - fruity reds
  - claret-style reds
  - herby-spicy reds.

To help customers choose a wine and to enable staff to make recommendations, it is also useful for each of the groups of wines to be listed in order from the lighter wines to the more full wines.

Listing wines by grape

If the wines are to be listed by grape then one approach is to list the grapes in alphabetical order as follows:

White grapes

- Chardonnay
- Chenin blanc
- Gewürztraminer
- Pinot Blanc
- Pinot Gris/Pinot Grigio
- Riesling
- Sauvignon Blanc
- Sémillon
- Other white grapes

Red grapes

- Cabernet Sauvignon
- Gamay
- Merlot
- Pinot Noir
- Sangiovese
- Shiraz/Syrah
- Tempranillo
- Zinfandel
- Other red grapes

Under each heading the wines made with that grape are listed, as well as the principal blends that are made with that grape as the predominant grape. When the wines are listed under the headings 'Other white grapes' or 'Other red grapes', then the grape(s) of the wine should also be listed next to the name of the wine.

Again, to help the customer choose a wine and to aid staff in making recommendations, it is useful for each of the groups of wines to be listed in order from the lighter wines to the more full wines.

10.4 General information given on wine and drink lists

It is usual to give information on wine and drink lists that help the customer to make a decision and the staff in making recommendations. This information is shown below.

Wines

- bin number
- name of wine
- country and area of origin
- quality indication (e.g. AOC, Qmp etc.)
- shipper
- château/estate bottled
- varietal (grape type(s))

- vintage
- alcoholic strength
- ½ bottle, bottle, magnum
- price
- supplier
- descriptive notes as appropriate.

Other drinks

- type of drink, for example juices, whisky, gin, sherry
- brand name if appropriate, for example Martini
- style (sweet, dry, etc.)

- description, for example for cocktails
- alcoholic strength in percentage by volume as appropriate
- descriptive notes as appropriate.

Test your learning

1 What is the main purpose of a wine and drink list?
2 Briefly describe the difference between a bar list and a restaurant wine list.
3 What are the three main ways in which wine lists can be presented?
4 If listing wines by type, what are the five types that would be listed?
5 What are four pieces of information are required on a wine/drinks list?

In practice

1 Look at a variety of wine lists online to see how different establishments present the content (you can find these by going to a restaurant website and looking for the wine list).
2 Develop a descriptive note that you might use for a cocktail (for a list of cocktails see Annex A, page 346).

Non-alcoholic beverages (soft drinks)

11

Units covered

This chapter covers the following units:

Level 1

→ Principles of beverage product knowledge (207)
→ Prepare and clear areas for drink service
  (1BS2, 113)
→ Serve drinks (1BS2)

Level 2

→ Serve alcoholic and soft drinks (2BS2, 212)
→ Prepare and clear the bar area (2BS1, 211)

A number of terms are used to indicate the alcohol content, or lack of it, within different drinks. However, terms such as 'de-alcoholised' or 'alcohol free' do not actually mean that the drink has *no* alcohol in it. The various terms and definitions are given in Table 11.1.

The drinks covered in this chapter are '**non-alcoholic**' and contain no alcohol. These drinks are also often referred to as 'soft drinks', with alcoholic drinks sometimes being referred to as 'hard' drinks. Drinks described as '**low alcohol**' have a very small percentage of alcohol in them.

Table 11.1 Alcohol content definitions

Term	Alcoholic content – per cent by volume
Reduced alcohol	1.2–5.5%
Low alcohol	0.5–1.2%
De-alcoholised	0.05–0.5%
Alcohol free	Not more that 0.05%
Non-alcoholic	0%

Key terms

Non-alcoholic beverage – drink not containing any alcohol

Low-alcoholic beverage – drink containing between 0.5 and 1.2 per cent alcohol

11.1 Aerated waters

Figure 11.1 Fizzy drinks

These beverages are charged (or **aerated**) with carbonic gas. Artificially aerated waters are by far the most common. The flavourings found in different aerated waters are obtained from various essences.

Examples of aerated waters are shown in Figure 11.1, from left to right:

- *soda water*: colourless and tasteless
- *bitter lemon*: pale, cloudy yellow-coloured with a sharp lemon flavour.
- *dry ginger*: golden straw-coloured with a ginger flavour
- *tonic water*: colourless and quinine flavoured

Key term

Aerated water – a beverage that contains carbonic gas. Examples are tonic water, soda water, dry ginger, bitter lemon, cola and lemonade

Other flavoured waters that come under this heading are:

- 'fizzy' lemonades
- orangeade
- ginger beer
- cola, etc.

Figure 11.2 Post-mix dispenser gun

Aerated waters are available in bottles and cans and many are also available as **post-mix**. The term post-mix indicates that the drink mix of syrup and the carbonated (filtered) water is mixed after (post) leaving the syrup container, rather than being pre-mixed (or ready mixed) as in canned or bottled soft drinks. Post-mix drinks are served from hand-held dispensing guns at the bar. These have buttons on the dispensing gun to select the specific drink.

The key advantage of the post-mix system is that it saves on storage space. Dispensing systems need regular cleaning and maintenance to ensure that they are hygienic and working properly.

The proportions of the mix need to be checked regularly. Too little syrup and the drinks will lack taste, too much syrup and the flavours become too strong.

Key term

Post-mix – aerated water served from a dispensing gun; the carbonated water is added to the syrup after the syrup leaves the container

11.2 Spring and mineral waters

The European Union has divided bottled water into two main types: mineral water and spring water.

- Mineral water has a mineral content (which is strictly controlled).
- Spring water has fewer regulations, apart from those concerning hygiene.

Water can be still, naturally sparkling or carbonated during bottling.

Table 11.2 Examples of mineral waters

Brand name	Type	Country of origin
Appollinaris	Naturally sparkling	Germany
Badoit	Naturally sparkling	France
Buxton	Still or carbonated	England
Contrex	Still	France
Evian	Still	France
Perrier	Naturally sparkling and also fruit flavoured	France
San Pellegrino	Carbonated	Italy
Spa	Still, naturally sparkling and also fruit-flavoured	Belgium
Vichy	Naturally sparkling	France
Vittel	Naturally sparkling	France
Volvic	Still	France

The potential medicinal value of these mineral waters has long been recognised by the medical profession. Where natural spring waters are found, there is usually what is termed a spa, where the waters may be drunk or bathed in according to the cures they are supposed to effect. Many of the best-known mineral waters are bottled at the spring (bottled at source).

Table 11.3 Examples of spring waters

Brand name	Type	Country of origin
Ballygowan	Still or sparkling	Ireland
Highland Spring	Still or carbonated	Scotland
Llanllyr	Still or sparkling	Wales
Malvern	Still or carbonated	England
Strathmore	Still or sparkling	Scotland

Natural spring waters are obtained from natural springs in the ground, the waters themselves being impregnated with the natural minerals found in the soil and sometimes naturally charged with an aerating gas.

Bottle sizes for mineral and spring waters vary considerably from, for example, 200 ml to 2 l. Some brand names sell in both plastic and glass bottles, while other brands prefer either plastic or glass bottles depending on the market and the size of container preferred by that market.

Recently there has been a shift in consumer demand away from bottled waters. The reasons for this include:
- Environmental and sustainability concerns: in some cases demand has reduced considerably. Regular tap water, from safe commercial supplies, has become more popular in food service operations and customers increasingly expect this to be available, chilled or served with ice.

Non-alcoholic beverages (soft drinks)

- The emergence of commercial filter systems being used by food service operations: tap water is filtered at the establishment and then offered either as chilled still or sparking water in branded carafes or bottles, for which the establishment makes a charge.

11.3 Squashes

A squash may be served on its own diluted by water, soda water or lemonade. Squashes are also used as mixers for spirits and in cocktails, or used as the base for drinks such as fruit cups. Examples are:

- orange squash
- lemon squash
- grapefruit squash
- lime cordial.

11.4 Juices

The main types of juices held in stock in the bar are:

Bottled, canned or in cartons

- orange juice
- pineapple juice
- grapefruit juice
- tomato juice.

Fresh

- orange juice
- grapefruit juice
- lemon juice.

Apart from being served chilled on their own, these fresh juices may also be used in cocktails and for mixing with spirits.

Figure 11.3 Fresh orange juice being squeezed

11.5 Syrups

The main uses of these concentrated, sweet, fruit flavourings are as a base for cocktails, fruit cups or mixed with soda water as a long drink. The main ones used are:

- *cassis* (blackcurrant)
- *cerise* (cherry)
- *citronelle* (lemon)
- *framboise* (raspberry)
- *gomme* (white sugar syrup)
- *grenadine* (pomegranate)
- *orgeat* (almond).

Syrups are also available as 'flavouring agents' for cold milk drinks such as milkshakes.

Information on the service of non-alcoholic bar beverages may be found in Section 17.4, page 273.

11.6 Other non-alcoholic beverages

Milkshakes

These are made from:
- chilled milk
- syrups (concentrated flavourings)
- ice cream.

Smoothies

Smoothies have become increasingly popular and are made in a blender. The ingredients required might include fresh fruit or vegetables (these are sweetened if necessary). Also frozen fruit, frozen yogurt, fruit juices, milk and honey may be used in a recipe. Crushed ice is often used to ensure the product is well chilled on serving. Pre-made bottled or carton versions are also available.

Figure 11.4 A strawberry smoothie

Natural vegetable juices

Often known as 'health drinks', these include carrot juice and beetroot juice.

Testing your learning

1   List the six main groups into which non-alcoholic beverages (soft drinks) may be classified, giving two examples of drinks for each group.

2   A party of three guests have ordered one whisky, one gin and one Campari. Identify which of the aerated waters would normally be offered with these drinks.

3   What is the key advantage of the post-mix system when serving aerated waters?

4   Name two French mineral waters and two English spring waters.

5   Give three uses of 'squashes', with examples to explain your choice.

6   What is the flavour of each of the following syrups?
    (a) Cassis
    (b) Gomme
    (c) Grenadine
    (d) Orgeat

7   Discuss the value of mineral waters to the consumer.

8   A customer orders a milkshake. List the basic ingredients required.

9   Describe as you would to a customer a 'smoothie'.

10 Which of the following mineral waters comes from Germany?
    (a) Buxton
    (b) Evian
    (c) Spa
    (d) Appollinaris

Hot beverages

12

Units covered

This chapter covers the following units:

Level 1
→ Hot beverage skills (110)
→ Serve drinks (1BS2)

Level 2
→ Service of hot beverages (208)
→ Prepare and serve hot drinks using specialist equipment (2BS8, 218)
→ Prepare and clear the bar area (2BS1, 211)

12.1 Tea

Figure 12.1 Tea plantation

Tea was discovered by accident over 5,000 years ago, when leaves from a tea bush accidentally dropped into some boiling water and delicately flavoured the liquid. Tea was originally drunk for its medicinal benefits and it was not until the 1700s that it began to be consumed as the beverage known today.

Tea is prepared from the leaf bud and top leaves of a tropical evergreen bush called *Camellia sinensis*. It produces what is regarded as a healthy beverage, containing approximately only half the caffeine of coffee; at the same time it aids muscle relaxation, stimulates the central nervous system and aids digestion.

The tea leaf itself contains a number of chemicals including amino acids, vitamins, caffeine and catechins. A catechin is a type of antioxidant which, in green tea, is thought to be effective in preventing certain cancers such as liver cancer. Green and black teas may also protect against cardiovascular disease.

The leaf particle size is referred to as a **grade**. The main ones are:
- pekoe – the delicate top leaves
- orange pekoe – a rolled leaf with a slim appearance
- pekoe dust – the smallest particle of leaf size.

In between these grades is a set of grades known as '**fannings**', mostly used in tea bags. In tea terminology, a '**flush**' refers to a picking, which can take place at different times of the year.

Tea-producing countries

Tea is grown in more than 25 countries around the world. The crop benefits from acidic soil, a warm climate and where there is at least 130 cm of rain a year. It is an annual crop and its flavour, quality and character is affected by the location, altitude, type of soil and climate. The main tea-producing countries are shown in Table 12.1.

> **Key terms**
>
> **Grade** – particle size of a tea leaf. This is used to describe the quality of tea
>
> **Fanning** – a lower grade of tea, mostly used in tea bags
>
> **Flush** – a picking of tea

Table 12.1 The main tea producing countries

China	The oldest tea growing country; known for speciality blends such as Keemun, Lapsang Souchong, Oolong and green tea
East Africa (Kenya, Malawi, Tanzania and Zimbabwe)	Produces good quality teas, which are bright and colourful and used extensively for blending purposes. Kenya produces teas that are easily discernible and have a reddish or coppery tint and a brisk flavour
India	Largest producer of tea, producing about 30 per cent of the world's tea. Best known are the teas from Assam (strong and full bodied), Darjeeling (delicate and mellow) and also Nilgiri, which is second only to Assam, and produces teas similar to those of Sri Lanka
Indonesia	Produces light and fragrant tea with bright colouring; used mainly for blending purposes
Sri Lanka (formerly Ceylon)	Teas here are inclined to have a delicate, light lemon flavour. They are generally regarded as excellent afternoon teas and also lend themselves to being iced

> **Note**
>
> Most teas are fermented (oxidised) during the process of manufacture, which gives them their black colour. The main exception is the China green tea.

Tea products

Most teas are blended teas sold under proprietary brands or names. Other teas, sometimes called speciality or premium teas, are sold by the name of the specific tea (see Table 12.2, page 175). The word '**blend**' indicates that a named tea may be composed of a variety of different teas to produce one marketable tea, which is acceptable to the average consumer taste. For instance, what is sometimes termed a standard tea may contain somewhere in the region of 15 different teas. These would almost certainly include Indian tea for strength, African tea for colour and China tea for flavour and delicacy.

Tea may be purchased in a variety of forms depending on requirements such as:
- volume of production
- type of establishment
- customer
- the occasion
- method of service

> **Key term**
>
> **Blend** – a tea composed of a variety of different types of tea

- storage facilities available
- cost.

The different means of purchasing are:
- **Bulk**: this is leaf tea (also called loose tea), which allows for the traditional method of serving.
- **Tea bags**: these are heat-sealed and contain either standard or speciality teas. They come in one-cup, two-cup, and pot-for-one or bulk brew sizes up to several litres.
- **String and tag**: this comes as a one-cup teabag with string attached and a tag that remains outside the cup or teapot for easy and quick identification of the type of tea by the customer.
- **Envelopes**: this is again a string-and-tag teabag but in an envelope for hygienic handling. It is used for trays for in-room tea and coffee making facilities.
- **Instant**: instant tea granules, soluble in hot water.
- **Pods**: these are specially designed individual portions of tea that are used in proprietary tea and coffee makers. Each pod makes one portion of tea and the pod is then disposed of.

Storage

Tea should be kept:
- in a dry, clean and covered container
- in a well-ventilated area
- away from excess moisture
- away from any strong-smelling foods as it very quickly absorbs strong odours.

Making tea

The type of tea used will of course depend on the customer's choice, but most establishments carry a varied stock of Indian, Ceylon, China and speciality teas, together with a variety of **tisanes** (fruit-flavoured teas and herbal infusions) available upon request.

The quantities of dry tea used per pot or per gallon may vary slightly with the type of tea used, but the following may be used as an approximate guide:
- 42–56 g (1½–2 oz) dry tea per 4.5 litres (1 gallon) of water for 24 standard tea cups
- ½ litre (1 pint) of milk will be sufficient for 20–24 cups
- ½ kilogram (1 lb) sugar for approximately 80 cups.

When brewing smaller amounts in the stillroom, such as a pot for one or two, it is often advisable to install a measure for the loose tea. This ensures standardisation of the brew and control on the amount of loose tea being used. Alternative methods of pre-portioning tea may also be used, such as tea bags.

Because tea is an infusion, the flavour is obtained by allowing the tea to brew. The following checklist will enable good results.
1   Heat the pot before putting in the dry tea so that the maximum heat can be obtained from the boiling water.
2   Measure the dry tea exactly.
3   Use freshly boiled water.
4   Make sure the water is boiling on entering the pot.
5   Allow the tea to brew for 3–6 minutes (depending on the type of tea) to obtain maximum strength from the brew.
6   Remove the tea leaves at the end of the brewing period if required, but especially if making the tea in multi-pot insulated urns.

> **Key term**
>
> **Tisane** – a flavoured tea or herbal infusion

Hot beverages

7 Ensure all the equipment used is scrupulously clean. Remember hard water resulting in lime scale may affect your equipment and, in turn, your 'brew'. To overcome this safe water softener systems are available.

Figure 12.2 Tea tray

Table 12.2 Characteristics and service of teas

Afternoon tea	Usually a blend of delicate Darjeeling tea and high-grown Ceylon tea to produce a refreshing and light tea. As the name of the blend suggests, this tea is suitable for afternoon tea but may be taken at any time. Served with milk or lemon and sugar offered separately
Assam	Rich, full and malty-flavoured tea, suitable for service at breakfast, usually with milk. Sugar is offered separately
China	Tea made from a special blend of tea that is more delicate in flavour and perfumed than any other tea. Less dry tea is required than for making Indian or Ceylon tea. Traditionally China tea is rarely served with milk. It is made in the normal way and is best made in a china pot. China tea is normally drunk on its own but may be improved, according to taste, by the addition of a slice of lemon. Slices of lemon would be offered on a side plate with a sweet fork. Sugar may be offered separately
Darjeeling	Delicate tea with a light grape flavour and known as the 'Champagne of teas'. Usually served as an afternoon or evening tea with either lemon or a little milk if preferred. Sugar may be offered separately
Earl Grey	Blend of Darjeeling and China tea, flavoured with oil of bergamot. Usually served with lemon or milk. Sugar is offered separately
English Breakfast	Often a blend of Assam and Kenya teas to make a bright, flavoursome and refreshing tea. Usually served as a breakfast tea but may be offered at any time. Usually served with milk but can also be taken with lemon. Sugar is offered separately
Iced tea	This is strong tea that is made, strained and well chilled. The tea is then stored chilled until required. It is traditionally served in a glass, such as a tumbler. A slice of lemon may be placed in the glass and some additional lemon slices served separately on a side plate and with a sweet fork. Sugar may be offered
Indian or Ceylon blend	Indian or Ceylon blend tea may be made in either china or metal teapots. These teas are usually offered with milk. Sugar is offered separately
Jasmine	Green (unoxidised) tea flavoured with dried jasmine blossom; produces a tea with a fragrant and scented flavour
Kenya	Consistent and refreshing tea usually served with milk. Sugar is offered separately
Lapsang Souchong	Smoky, pungent and perfumed tea, delicate to the palate and may be said to be an acquired taste. Usually served with lemon. Sugar is offered separately

Multi-pot	There are many occasions when tea has to be produced in bulk. Such occasions might be a reception tea, tea breaks in an industrial catering concern or for functions catering for large numbers. In these instances tea may be made in multi-pots/urns, which may be described as teapots or urns, varying in capacity from 1 to 25 litres (1 to 5 gallons). These containers have infusers that hold the required quantity of tea leaves for the size of pot/urn being used. The infuser would be placed in the pot/urn and freshly boiled water added. The mix would then be allowed to brew for a number of minutes – a maximum of 10 minutes for a 25-litre urn – and the infuser is then removed to ensure a good-quality product is served. The quantity of tea made should always relate to the number to be served – this will ensure minimum delay in the service and minimum wastage
Russian or lemon tea	Tea that is brewed from a special blend similar to China tea, but is also often made from either Indian or Ceylon tea. It is made in the normal way and is usually served with a slice of lemon. The tea is served in 0.25 litre (half pint) glasses, which stand in a silver holder with a handle and on a side plate with a teaspoon. A slice of lemon may be placed in the glass and a few slices of lemon served separately. Sugar is served separately
Sri Lankan	Makes a pale golden tea with a good flavour. Ceylon blend is still used as a trade name. Served with lemon or milk. Sugar is offered separately
Tisanes	These are fruit-flavoured teas and herbal infusions that are often used for medicinal purposes and are gaining in popularity with trends towards healthier eating and drinking. Often these do not contain caffeine. Examples are: *Herbal teas* • camomile • peppermint • rosehip • mint *Fruit teas* • cherry • lemon • blackcurrant • mandarin orange These teas are usually made in china pots or can be made by the cup or glass. Sometimes served with sugar

Characteristics of good tea

Tea should have:

- good flavour
- good aroma
- good colour when milk or cream are added – not grey
- good body.

Reasons for bad-quality tea

- water not fresh
- water has not reached correct temperature
- infusion time too long or too short
- stale or old tea has been used
- too much or too little tea used
- dirty equipment
- tea reheated
- brewed tea being kept too long before use or kept at wrong temperature.

For further information on the service of tea see Section 18.4, page 307.

12.2 Coffee

Coffee plants were cultivated about 1,000 years ago in the Yemen. The first commercial cultivation of coffee is thought to have been in the Yemen district of Arabia in the fifteenth century. By the middle of the sixteenth century coffee drinking had spread to Sudan, Egypt, Syria and Turkey. Venetian traders first brought coffee to Europe in 1615 and the first coffee house in England was opened in Oxford in 1650. The drinking of coffee spread from Britain to America but, after the Boston Tea Party in 1773, North American tastes changed from drinking tea as a beverage to a preference for coffee.

The shrubs that produce coffee are from *genus Coffea*, which belongs to the *Rubiaceae* family. There are approximately 50 different species, although only two of these are popularly sold. These are known as *Coffea* **arabica** (milder) and *Coffea canephora*, which is usually referred to as **robusta** (harsher, bitter with more caffeine). Arabica accounts for around 75 per cent of world production.

The coffee plant is an evergreen shrub, which reaches a height of two to three metres when cultivated. The fruit of the coffee plant is known as the 'cherry' and these are about 1.5 cm in length and have an oblong shape. The cherry usually contains two coffee seeds. The coffee plant will not begin to produce fruit until it is 3–5 years old and it will then usually yield good crops for up to 15 years.

The coffee bean goes through various stages while it is being processed. These are:
- harvesting
- wet processing (washing, fermenting and drying)
- dry processing (laid out on mats in the sun)
- sorting
- grading
- grinding
- packaging.

Key terms
Arabica – a mild coffee species
Robusta – a harsher, bitter coffee species that contains more caffeine

Coffee-producing countries

Coffee is a natural product grown in many countries of the tropical and sub-tropical belt in South and Central America, Africa and Asia. It is grown at different altitudes in different climates and in different soils, and is looked upon as an international drink consumed throughout the world. Brazil is the world's largest grower of coffee, Columbia is second, the Ivory Coast third and Indonesia fourth.

Figure 12.3 Coffee beans

Coffee products available

The different means of purchasing coffee are:
- **Bulk**: (either as beans or in vacuum packs of pre-ground beans) allowing for the traditional methods of making and serving.
- **Coffee bags**: these are heat-sealed and come in one-cup, two-cup, pot-for-one or bulk brew sizes up to several litres.
- **Instant**: coffee granules, soluble in hot water and available in sizes from one cup to pot size.
- **Individual filters**: vacuum packed and containing one portion.

- **Pods**: specially designed individual portions of pre-ground coffee that are used in proprietary coffee and tea makers. Each pod makes one portion of coffee and the pod is then disposed of.

The blend

Companies who sell coffee have their own blending experts whose task it is to ensure that the quality and taste of their particular coffee brand is consistent, despite the fact that the imported beans will vary from shipment to shipment.

Samples of green coffee beans are taken from bags in the producing countries and the port of arrival. The samples are sent to prospective buyers whose experts roast, brew and taste samples to test their quality before deciding on the type of blend for which a particular coffee is suitable.

The roasting

Most brands of coffee sold in shops are a blend of two or more batches of beans. Because they have no smell or taste, green beans have to be roasted in order to release the coffee aroma and flavour. The roasting process should give a uniform colour. The outputs from different 'roastings' are used to form different blends.

The common degrees of roasting are:
- **Light or pale roastings**: suitable for mild beans to preserve their delicate aroma.
- **Medium roastings**: give a stronger flavour and are often favoured for coffees with well-defined character.
- **Full roastings**: popular in many Latin countries, they have a bitter flavour.
- **High roasted coffee**: accentuates the strong bitter aspects of coffee, although much of the original flavour is lost.

Commercial coffee roasters can either convert the beans into instant (soluble) coffee or prepare them for sale as roasted or ground beans. The higher the roast, the less acidity and the more bitterness there is in the coffee.

Certain coffees also have flavourings added, either in the blend or during the process of making. Examples of these include:
- Turkish coffee – vanilla
- French coffee – chicory
- Viennese coffee – fig.

The grind

Roasted coffee must be ground before it can be used to make the brew. Coffee is ground to different grades of fineness to suit the many different methods of brewing. The most suitable grinds for some common methods of brewing coffee are shown below.

Method	Grinding grade
Cafetière	Medium
Espresso	Very fine
Filter/Drip	Fine to medium
Jug	Coarse
Percolator	Medium
Turkish	Pulverised
Vacuum infusion	Medium-fine to fine

Storage

Tips for storing coffee:

- Store in a well-ventilated storeroom.
- Use an airtight container for ground coffee to ensure that the oils do not evaporate, causing loss of flavour and strength.
- Keep coffee away from excess moisture.
- Do not store near any strong-smelling foods or other substances, as coffee will absorb their odours.

Making coffee

Methods of brewing can vary, ranging from instant coffee brewed by the cup, through to 1½–3 litre (3–6 pint) units and up to machines that may produce large quantities for functions. Coffee beans may be purchased and then ground according to requirements. The beans should not be ground until immediately before they are required as this will ensure maximum flavour and strength from the oils within the coffee bean. Pre-ground coffee normally comes in vacuum-sealed packets in order to maintain its qualities until use. These packets contain set quantities to make 4.5 litres (1 gallon) of coffee and 9 litres (2 gallons) of coffee, and so on.

When making coffee in bulk 283–340 g (10–12 oz) of ground coffee is sufficient to make 4.5 litres (1 gallon) of black coffee.

- Assuming that cups with a capacity of 20 cl (⅓ pint) will be used then 283–340 g (10–12 oz) of ground coffee is sufficient to provide 24 cups of black coffee or 48 cups if serving half-coffee and half-milk.
- When breakfast cups, capacity 28 cl (½ pint), are used then 16 cups of black coffee or 32 cups of half-coffee and half-milk will be available.
- Capacity where demi-tasse (half cups) 10 cl (⅙ pint) cups are used is 48 cups of black coffee or 96 cups half-coffee and half-milk.

The rules to be observed when making coffee in bulk are as follows:

- Use freshly roasted and ground coffee.
- Buy the correct grind for the type of machine in use.
- Ensure all equipment is clean before use.
- Use a set measure of coffee to water: 283–340 g per 4.5 litres (10–12 oz per gallon).
- Add boiling water to the coffee and allow to infuse.
- The infusion time must be controlled according to the type of coffee being used and the method of making.
- Control the temperature since to boil coffee is to spoil coffee (it will develop a bitter taste).
- Strain and serve.
- Offer milk (hot or cold) or cream separately, and sugar and alternatives.
- The best serving temperatures are 82°C (180°F) for coffee and 68°C (155°F) for milk.

Characteristics of good coffee

Coffee should have:

- good flavour
- good aroma
- good colour when milk or cream are added – not grey
- good body.

Reasons for bad-quality coffee

- water not fresh
- water has not reached boiling point
- insufficient or too much coffee used
- infusion time too short or too long or at wrong temperature
- stale or old coffee used
- incorrect grind of coffee used for equipment in operation
- coffee kept too long before use or kept at wrong temperature
- dirty equipment
- coffee not roasted correctly
- sediment remaining in storage or serving compartment
- infusion at too high a temperature.

Coffee-making methods

Coffee may be made in many ways and the service depends on the method used. A description of the various methods is given below.

Figure 12.4 Coffee brewing methods (clockwise from top): pour and serve, filter machine, single filter, Turkish/Greek/Arabic coffee, jug and plunger/ cafetière

Instant

This may be made in individual coffee or teacups, or in large quantities. It involves mixing soluble coffee solids with boiling water. When making instant coffee in bulk, approximately 71 g (2½ oz) to each 4.5 litres (1 gallon) of water should be allowed. This form of coffee may be made very quickly, immediately before it is required, by pouring freshly boiled water onto a measured quantity of coffee powder. Stir well.

Cafetière (coffee maker)

The cafetière, or jug and plunger method, makes coffee simply and quickly by the infusion method and to order. This ensures that the flavour and aroma of the coffee are preserved. The cafetière is a glass container with a lip held in a black, gold or chrome-finished holder and sealed with a lid that also holds the plunger unit in position.

The method of making is completed simply by adding boiling water to the ground coffee, stirring and then placing the plunger unit and lid in position. A guideline to the quantity of coffee to be used might be:

- 2 level sweet spoonfuls for the 3-cup size
- 6 level sweet spoonfuls for the 8-cup size
- 9 level sweet spoonfuls for the 12-cup size.

Infusion time is from 3 to 5 minutes. During this time the coffee grains will rise to the top of the liquid. After this if the plunger is moved slightly the coffee grains will fall to the bottom of the glass container. When the grains have fallen it is easier to push the plunger down.

Filter (café filtre)

This method is used to make coffee individually in the cup or in bulk. The filter method produces excellent coffee. Freshly boiled water is poured into a container with a very finely meshed bottom, which stands on a cup or pot. Within the container is the required amount of ground coffee. The infusion takes place and the coffee liquid falls into the cup/pot below. Filter papers may be used to avoid the grounds passing into the lower cup, but this will depend on how fine or coarse the ground coffee being used is. There are now many electronic units available of differing capacities. Cold water is poured into a reservoir and is brought to boiling point and then dripped on to the ground coffee.

Pour-through filter method

This is an excellent method of making filter coffee, which has increased in popularity over the past few years. Many of these pour-through filter machines are available for purchase, or on loan from a number of the main coffee suppliers.

The principle behind this method is that when the measured quantity of freshly drawn cold water is poured into the top of the pour-through filter machine, this water displaces the hot water already in the machine. This hot water infuses with the ground coffee and runs into the serving container as a coffee liquid ready for immediate use. It takes approximately 3 to 4 minutes to make one brew.

When coffee is made by this method, ensure that:

- the machine is plugged in and switched on at the mains
- the brew indicator light is on. This tells the operator that the water already held in the machine is at the correct temperature for use
- the correct quantity of freshly ground coffee, which will usually come in the form of a vacuum-sealed pack, is used. A fresh pack should be used for each new brew of filter coffee being made
- a new clean filter paper is used for each fresh brew.

Individual filter

This is an alternative way of making single cups of coffee. It uses a disposable plastic individual filter, bought with the required amount of coffee already sealed in the base of the filter. Each individual filter is sufficient for one cup and, after use, the whole filter is thrown away.

When making a cup of coffee by this method, the individual filter is placed on to a cup. Freshly boiled water is then poured into the individual filter to the required level. The liquid then infuses with the ground coffee within the individual filter and drips into the cup. A lid should be placed over the water in the filter to help retain the temperature. Time of making is approximately 3 to 4 minutes.

Espresso

Figure 12.5 Espresso machine

This method is Italian in origin. Machines used to make this form of coffee can provide cups of coffee individually in a matter of seconds, with some machines being capable of making 300 to 400 cups of coffee per hour.

The method involves passing steam through the finely ground coffee and infusing under pressure. The advantage is that each cup is made freshly for the customer. Served black, the coffee is known as espresso and is served in a small cup. If milk is required, it is heated for each cup by a high-pressure steam injector. As an approximate guide, from 12 kg (1 lb) of coffee used, 80 cups of good-strength coffee may be produced. The general rules for making coffee apply here, but with this special and delicate type of equipment extra care should be taken in following any instructions.

The process for making espresso coffee can be summarised as follows:
1　Process sufficient coffee beans to the correct grind.
2　Insert correct dose into group handle.
3　Insert group handle into group head.
4　Use temper to level and compact ground coffee.
5　Place cup under group head.
6　Select correct programme for hot water dispense.
7　Place cup on saucer with correct accompaniments.

Still-set

Figure 12.6 Modern still-set

This method normally consists of a small central container into which the correct sized filter paper is placed. A second, fine-meshed metal filter with a handle is then placed on the filter paper and the ground coffee placed on top of this. There is an urn on either side of varying capacities according to requirements. The urns may be 4½, 9, 13 or 18 litres (1, 2, 3 or 4 gallons) in size.

These still-sets are easy to operate, but must be kept very clean at all times and regularly serviced. The urns should be rinsed before and after each brew until the water runs clear. This removes the thin layer of cold

Hot beverages

coffee that clings to the side of the urn that, if left, will spoil the flavour and aroma of the next brew.

Boiling water is passed through the grounds and the resultant coffee liquid then passes into the urn at the side. Infusion should be complete in 6 to 8 minutes for 4½ litres (1 gallon) of coffee when using medium-ground coffee. The milk is heated in a steam jacket container. It should be held at a constant temperature of 68°C because, if held at too high a temperature or boiled or heated too soon, on coming into contact with the coffee it will destroy its flavour and taste. At the same time, the milk itself becomes discoloured. The coffee and milk should be held separately, at their correct temperatures ready for serving.

Decaffeinated

Coffee contains caffeine, which is a stimulant. Decaffeinated coffee is made from beans after the caffeine has been extracted. The coffee is made in the normal way.

Figure 12.7 Examples of insulated jugs and dispensers for coffee and tea service (images courtesy of Elia®)

Iced coffee

Strong black coffee should be made in the normal way. It is then strained, chilled well and stored in the refrigerator until required. It may be served mixed with an equal quantity of cold milk for a smooth beverage, or with cream. Often served in a glass tumbler set on a doily/coaster, on an underplate, and with a teaspoon.

Turkish or Egyptian coffees

These are made from darkly roasted mocha beans, which are ground to a fine powder. The coffee is made in special copper pots, which are placed on top of a stove or lamp, and the water is then allowed to boil. The sugar should be put in at this stage to sweeten the coffee, as it is never stirred once poured out. The finely ground coffee may be stirred in or the boiling water poured onto the grounds. The amount of coffee used is approximately one heaped teaspoonful per person.

Once the coffee has been stirred in, the copper pot is taken off the direct heat and the cooling causes the grounds to settle. It is brought to the boil and allowed to settle twice more and is then sprinkled with a little cold water to settle any remaining grains. The coffee is served in small cups. While making the coffee it may be further flavoured with vanilla pods but this is optional.

For the service of coffee see Section 18.4, page 307.

Table 12.3 Modern coffee styles

Americano	Espresso with added hot water to create regular black coffee. May also be regular black coffee made using filter method
Café crème	Regular coffee prepared from fresh beans, ground fresh for each cup, resulting in a thick cream-coloured, moussy head
Cafetière	Popular method of making and serving fresh coffee in individual or multi-portion jugs. Often served with hot or cold milk or cream
Caffè (or café) latte	Shot of espresso plus hot milk, with or without foam
Caffè mocha (or mochaccino)	Chocolate compound (syrup or powder) followed by a shot of espresso. The cup or glass is then filled with freshly steamed milk topped with whipped cream and cocoa powder
Cappuccino	Espresso coffee topped with steamed frothed milk, often finished with a sprinkling of chocolate (powdered or grated)
Decaffeinated	Coffee with caffeine removed. Can be used as alternative to prepare the service styles listed above
Espresso	Traditional short, strong black coffee
Espresso con panna	Espresso with a spoonful of whipped cream on top
Espresso doppio	Double espresso served in larger cup
Espresso macchiato	Espresso spotted with a spoonful of hot or cold milk or hot milk foam
Espresso ristretto	Intense form of espresso, often served with a glass of cold water in continental Europe
Filter (filtre)	Traditional method of making coffee. Often served with hot or cold milk or cream
Flat white	Double shot of espresso topped with frothed milk which has been stirred together with the flat milk from the bottom of the jug, to create a creamy rather than frothy texture
Iced coffee	Chilled regular coffee, sometimes served with milk or simply a single espresso topped up with ice-cold milk
Instant coffee	Coffee made from processed powder (often freeze dried). Regular and decaffeinated styles are available
Latte macchiato	Steamed milk spotted with a drop of espresso
Turkish/Egyptian	Intense form of coffee made in special jugs with finely ground coffee

Irish and other speciality coffees

Speciality coffees are often completed and served at the table using the following equipment:

- service salver
- tray cloth or napkin
- 20 cl (7 fl oz) stemmed glass on a side plate
- teaspoon
- jug of double cream
- 25 ml measure
- coffee pot containing black coffee
- sugar basin of coffee sugar with a teaspoon
- bottle of the spirit or liqueur being used.

The procedure for making Irish coffee is:

1 A Paris goblet, or other suitable stemmed glass, of about 20 cl (7 fl oz) capacity is used.
2 Brown sugar is added first (a certain amount of sugar is always required when serving this form of coffee, as it is an aid to floating the double cream on the surface of the hot coffee).
3 The teaspoon is then placed in the goblet before the hot black coffee is poured into the glass. This is so the spoon will help to conduct the heat and avoid cracking the bowl of the glass as the hot, strong black coffee is poured in.
4 The coffee should then be stirred well to dissolve the sugar and to ensure the ingredients are blended. The liquid should now be within 2.5 cm (1 in) of the top of the glass. The liquid may still be swirling but not too much, as this will tend to draw the cream down into the coffee as it is poured.

5 One measure of Irish whiskey added and stirred in to blend all ingredients together.

6 The double cream should now be poured slowly over the back of a teaspoon on to the surface of the coffee until it is approximately 1.9 cm (¾ in) thick. The coffee must not be stirred. The best flavour is obtained by drinking the whiskey-flavoured coffee through the cream

7 As an alternative to six above, the double cream may be poured into the 'cup' of the teaspoon until full and then allowed to fall gently over the edges on to the surface of the coffee

8 When the Irish coffee has been prepared, the glass should be put on a doily on a side plate and placed in front of the customer.

Other forms of speciality, or liqueur, coffees include:

- *Café Royale* or *Café Parisienne*: brandy
- *Monk's coffee*: Bénédictine
- *Russian coffee*: vodka
- *Seville coffee*: Cointreau
- *Jamaican coffee or Caribbean coffee: rum*
- *Calypso coffee: Tia Maria*
- *Highland coffee: Scotch whisky*
- *Swiss coffee: kirsch.*

Figure 12.8 Tray laid for the service of Irish coffee

12.3 Chocolate

Chocolate and cocoa come from the fruit of the plant *Theobroma cacao* in the form of beans containing up to 25 to 30 white seeds. This cocoa plant is grown in countries as far afield as Mexico, Central and South America, West Africa and Asia.

Production process

The seeds are fermented, dried, shipped abroad and then roasted, blended and then pressed, ground and sieved for use as powdered or solid products. They then become cocoa powder, drinking chocolate, eating chocolate and couverture chocolate used for decorating purposes.

Beverage preparation

Hot chocolate is very popular and may come sweetened or non-sweetened and as a powder or soluble granules. It may be mixed with hot water or hot milk. Whipped cream from a whipped cream dispenser, marshmallows or a sprinkling of powdered chocolate may be added upon request. There are also flavoured chocolates available such as ginger, hazelnut and chilli. Continental-style chocolate is of a thicker

Figure 12.9 Hot chocolate served in a glass

consistency while American-style chocolate is lighter. Usually offered as large, medium or small and served in a tall glass or mug.

Product characteristics

The characteristics of chocolate beverages may vary according to the exact ingredients used and in what proportions. This has an impact on:

- flavour
- consistency
- sweetness/bitterness
- milkiness/smoothness
- overall presentation.

Some products on the market only have to be mixed with hot water as dried skimmed milk and milk proteins are among the ingredients making up the product.

Chocolate products and storage

Drinking chocolate products may come in individual vacuum-sealed packs or pods for use with electronic beverage making machines, or in containers of varying sizes to suit demand and turnover. When not in use, these containers should be kept airtight, in cool, dry and well-ventilated conditions and away from excess moisture and sunlight.

Incorrect beverage-making procedures

Any problems arising concerning the quality of the beverage produced may be due to:

- incorrect amount of drinking chocolate (powder or granules) to liquid (water or milk) affecting consistency and strength
- temperature of the liquid used is insufficient to dissolve the powder or granules
- poor storage has affected the commodity being used
- dirty equipment and no regular cleaning or maintenance.

12.4 Checking and cleaning beverage-making equipment

All equipment used in the making and service of hot beverages must be kept spotlessly clean and sterilised at regular intervals, in order to meet standards of health, safety and hygiene, as well as ensuring efficiency in the production of a product that meets the customer's expectations. Checklists are essential to ensure continuity of the cleaning process as staff will change due to shift work and they all need to work to the same level of competence.

Common faults in hot beverage-making equipment might be:

- lack of power – fuses
- lack of pressure – no steam
- leaks
- filter basket scaled up
- blocked pipes due to build-up of coffee grounds
- dirty small equipment due to faulty dishwasher
- lime scale build up.

Large equipment such as dishwashers, glass-washing machines, still-sets, espresso machines and pour-through machines should all be maintained on a regular monthly/

three-monthly schedule and according to the maker's instructions. Where applicable equipment should be sterilised on a daily basis.

On these occasion's equipment may have to be stripped down, soaked, seals checked, new washers fitted, stains and excess lime scale build-up removed, and temperature gauges checked to ensure they are functioning correctly. This is most important because if these checks are not carried out regularly then this, in turn, can affect all your small equipment and the product you wish to produce.

Daily checks on espresso machines at the start of service include:
- steam valves opened
- steam wand(s) clean
- seals on group handles clean and undamaged
- steam pressure
- exterior of machine cleaned and polished.

On a daily basis all small equipment must be checked for cracks, chips, incorrectly fitting lids, broken hinges and chipped teapot spouts. Anything not in order should be put to one side to be repaired as soon as possible.

Small equipment covers the following items:

- teacups
- tea saucers
- coffee cups
- coffee saucers
- hot milk jugs
- cold milk jugs

- hot water pots
- coffee pots
- teapots
- sugar bowls
- sugar tongs
- slop basins

- tea strainers
- side plates
- service salvers
- trays
- teaspoons.

Testing your learning

1 What is the largest tea-producing country? Name two teas produced there.
2 Explain the term 'blend' in relation to tea and describe what it indicates.
3 What are the key points to consider when storing tea?
4 You are required to make 4.5 litres (1 gallon) of tea for a small function. What quantity of dry loose-leaf tea would you use to ensure a good-quality product?
5 Describe as you would to a customer the meaning of the word 'tisanes' and give three examples.
6 State the flavouring which gives Earl Grey tea its distinctive taste.
7 Why should you not store coffee near any strong-smelling foodstuffs?
8 How many ounces of ground coffee would be sufficient to make 4.5 litres (1 gallon) of black coffee?
9 A customer orders café latte. What is he or she expecting to receive?
10 Which grinding grade for coffee beans is most suitable for pour-through equipment; a cafetière and an espresso machine?
11 Identify four common roasting terms for coffee.
12 Give three reasons why coffee might be too bitter.
13 How would you make a single espresso using an espresso machine?
14 State one additional flavouring that can be added to hot chocolate.
15 Identify a reason why hot chocolate may not be dispensing from a machine. What is the solution to this problem?
16 Identify three types of waste that can occur in the service of hot beverages.

Alcoholic beverages

13

Units covered

This chapter covers the following units:

Level 1

→ Prepare and clear areas for drink service
   (1BS2, 113)
→ Serve drinks (1BS2)

Level 2

→ Principles of beverage product knowledge (207)
→ Serve alcoholic and soft drinks (2BS2, 212)
→ Prepare and serve cocktails (2BS3, 213)
→ Prepare and serve wines (2BS4, 214)
→ Prepare and clear the bar area (2BS1, 211)

13.1 Alcoholic strength

Although there are various types of alcohol, the two main ones are methyl alcohol (methanol) and ethyl alcohol (ethanol). Methanol is used for various industrial purposes but is a dangerous poison when drunk; alcoholic beverages are drinks that contain ethanol. Alcoholic beverages are divided into three general classes: beers, wines and spirits.

The two main scales of measurement of alcoholic strength may be summarised as:
- OIML Scale (European): range 0% to 100% alcohol by volume.
- American Scale (USA): range 0° to 200°.

The Organisation Internationale Métrologie Légale (OIML) Scale (previously called Gay Lussac Scale) is directly equal to the percentage of alcohol by volume in the drink at 20°C. It is the universally accepted scale for the measurement of alcohol. This by-volume measurement indicates the amount of pure alcohol in a liquid. For example, a liquid measured as 40% alcohol by volume will have 40 per cent of the contents as pure alcohol (under the American Scale, alcoholic strength of 80° equals 40 per cent by volume). The alcoholic content of drinks, by volume, is now almost always shown on the label. Table 13.1 gives the approximate alcoholic strength of a variety of drinks.

Table 13.1 Approximate alcoholic strength of drinks (OIML scale)

0%	non-alcoholic
not more that 0.05%	alcohol free
0.05–0.5%	de-alcoholised
0.5–1.2%	low alcohol
1.2–5.5%	reduced alcohol
3–6%	beer, cider, FABs* and 'alcopops'** with any of these being up to 10%
8–15%	wines, usually around 10–13%
14–22%	fortified wines (liqueur wines) such as sherry and port, aromatised wines such as vermouth, vin doux naturels (such as Muscat de Beaumes de Venise) and sake***
37.5–45%	spirits, usually at 40%
17–55%	liqueurs, very wide range

* FABs is a term used to describe flavoured alcoholic beverages, for example, Bacardi Breezer (5.4%)
** 'Alcopops' is a term used to describe manufactured flavoured drinks (generally sweet and fruity) which have had alcohol, such as gin, added to them. They are also known as alcoholic soft drinks or alcoholic lemonade. Usually 3.5 to 5% but can be up to 10%
*** Sake is a strong (18%), slightly sweet, form of beer made from rice

13.2 Safe, sensible drinking

Most people who drink alcohol do so for many reasons: to quench a thirst, as a relaxant or simply because it is enjoyable. A small amount of alcohol does no harm and can even be beneficial. However, the more you drink and the more frequently you drink, the greater the health risks.

Alcohol depresses the brain and nerve function, affecting a person's judgement, self-control and skills. The four general stages of becoming drunk are:

- Stage 1: happy (relaxed, talkative and sociable).
- Stage 2: excited (erratic and emotional; movement and thinking affected).
- Stage 3: confused (disorientated, loud, out of control).
- Stage 4: lethargic (unable to stand, talk or walk).

Most of the alcohol consumed passes into the bloodstream from where it is rapidly absorbed. This absorption may be slowed down if drink is accompanied by food, but the amount of alcohol consumed will be the same. The liver must then burn up almost all the alcohol consumed, with the remainder being disposed of in urine or perspiration (sweat).

It takes approximately one hour for the liver to burn up one unit of alcohol; if it has to deal with too much alcohol over a number of years, it will inevitably suffer damage.

Sensible limits

So what are the sensible limits to avoid damage to health? Of course, not drinking alcohol cuts out any risk. Medical opinion in the UK has set the limit at 21 units spread throughout the week for men and 14 units spread throughout the week for women (excluding pregnant women). Drinking in excess of these limits is likely to be damaging to health.

One unit of alcohol is equal to 10 ml (liquid) or 8 g (weight) of alcohol. This is roughly equivalent to:
- ½ pint of ordinary beer or lager
- one glass of wine (125 ml)
- one glass of sherry (50 ml)
- one measure of vermouth or other apéritif (50 ml)
- one measure of spirits (25 ml).

It is important to note the following, however:
- Some extra-strength lagers and beer have two or three times the strength of ordinary beers.
- The number of units required to reach the maximum permitted levels for driving varies between individuals.
- Some alcohol remains in the bloodstream for up to 18 hours after consumption. This should be considered in relation to the legal limits for alcohol in the blood when driving.
- There are about 100 calories in a single unit of alcohol. The amount of calories quickly adds up and can lead to weight gain. Replacing food with alcohol as a source of calories denies the body essential nutrients and vitamins.

Calculating alcohol intake

To calculate the number of units of alcohol in a bottle of wine, the specific percentage of alcohol by volume is multiplied by the amount of the wine in millilitres (ml) and then divided by 1000 ml. This can be shown as:

$$\text{The number of units} = \frac{\text{the specific percentage of alcohol by volume x the amount of the wine in millilitres (ml)}}{1000 \text{ ml}}$$

For example, for a 75 cl bottle of wine at 12% alcohol by volume, the calculation will be:

$$\text{Number of units of alcohol} = \frac{12\% \text{ ABV} \times 750 \text{ ml}}{1000 \text{ ml}} = 9 \text{ units}$$

Therefore, this 75 cl (750 ml) bottle of wine will give 6 x 125 ml individual glasses of wine and each glass will contain 1.5 units of alcohol (9 units in the whole bottle divided by the 6 glasses).

Further examples for calculating the alcohol unit intake for other drinks are:
- Lager at 5% alcohol by volume x 50 cl measure = 5 x 500 ml ÷ 1,000 = 2.5 units per half-litre measure.
- Spirit at 40% alcohol by volume x 25 ml measure = 40 x 25 ml ÷ 1,000 = 1 unit per 25 ml measure.
- Sherry at 18% alcohol by volume x 50 ml measure = 18 x 50 ml ÷ 1,000 = 0.9 unit per 50 ml measure.

For information on liquor licensing and law relating to underage drinkers, times that alcohol can be served, reasons for use of legal measures, and when to refuse service of alcohol, see Section 4.3, page 72.

13.3 Cocktails and mixed drinks

A modern **cocktail** is normally a short drink of up to about 10 cl (3½–4 fl oz) – anything larger often being called a 'mixed drink' or 'long drink'. However, the term cocktail is now generally recognised to mean all types of mixed drinks. Table 13.2 gives the range of drinks that can be included under the heading cocktails.

> ### Key term
>
> **Cocktail** – a short drink up to 10 cl. Often used to describe all types of mixed or long drinks

Figure 13.1 Cocktails (image courtesy of Six Continents Hotels)

Table 13.2 Types of cocktails

Blended drinks	Made using a liquidiser
Champagne cocktails	For example, Bucks Fizz, which has the addition of orange juice
Cobblers	Wine and spirit based, served with straws and decorated with fruit
Collins	Hot-weather drinks, spirit-based, served with plenty of ice
Coolers	Almost identical to the Collins but usually containing the peel of the fruit cut into a spiral; spirit or wine-based
Crustas	May be made with any spirit, the most popular being brandy; edge of glass decorated with powdered sugar and crushed ice placed in glass
Cups	Hot-weather, wine-based drinks
Daisies	Made with any spirit; usually served in tankards or wine glasses filled with crushed ice
Egg noggs	Traditional Christmas drink; rum or brandy and milk-based; served in tumblers
Fixes	Short drink made by pouring any spirit over crushed ice; decorated with fruit and served with short straws
Fizzes	Similar to a Collins; always shaken and then topped with soda; must be drunk immediately
Flips	Similar to egg noggs, containing egg yolk but never milk; spirit, wine or sherry-based
Frappés	Served on crushed ice
Highball	American; a simple drink that is quickly prepared with spirit and a mixer
Juleps	American; containing mint with claret, Madeira or bourbon base
Pick-me-ups	To aid digestion
Pousse-Café	Layered mix of liqueurs and/or spirits using differences in the specific densities of drinks to create layers – heaviest at the bottom, lightest at the top

Smashes	Smaller version of a julep
Sours	Always made with fresh juices to sharpen the flavour of the drink
Smoothies	Blended, chilled and sometimes sweetened, beverage usually made from fresh fruit or vegetables
Swizzles	Take their name from the stick used to stir the drink; 'swizzling' creates a frost on the outside of glass
Toddies	Refreshers that may be served hot or cold; contain lemon, cinnamon and nutmeg

Cocktail making

The art of making a good cocktail is to blend all the ingredients together so that upon tasting no one ingredient is predominant. The making of cocktails has become very popular and the professionalism of cocktail making is increasing. Cocktail making is often called **mixology** and cocktail makers are called **mixologists**.

There are four main methods for making cocktails and mixed drinks: **shaken**, **stirred**, **built** and **layered**.

Shaken

Ice is placed in a shaker together with the ingredients to combine them and chill them down. The lid is placed on the cocktail shaker, or Boston shaker, and then shaken hard until the outside is very cool and condensation has appeared. The mixture is then strained into the serving glass using a Hawthorne strainer to remove the ice and other solid ingredients.

Stirred

The ice and ingredients are placed into a mixing glass and then gently stirred with a bar spoon to mix the ingredients and chill them down. The mixture is then strained into the serving glass, using a Hawthorne strainer, to remove the ice and other solid ingredients.

Built

The drink is created in the serving glass by putting the ingredients and the ice into a service glass, one after the other. Drinks made in this way often including the process of **muddling**: this is crushing together ingredients, such as fruit, leaves and sugar, at the bottom of a glass before adding other ingredients. Muddling is carried out using the flat end of a bar spoon as the muddler (see Section 3.5, page 53 for a picture of a bar spoon), or another specially designed tool.

Layered

Liquids, which can be alcoholic and non-alcoholic, that have different specific densities are floated one on top the other in the serving glass. These drinks can also be referred to as **poured** drinks.

More recently **smoothies** have become popular and are often seen as healthy drinks. These are made in a blender. In addition to fresh fruit or vegetables these are sometimes sweetened. The recipe may also include crushed ice, frozen fruit, honey or frozen yogurt. Pre-made bottled or carton versions are also available.

In all cases the presentation of a cocktail is paramount. Presentation should match the description of the cocktail. This is especially important if it is one of the classic and

Alcoholic beverages

internationally known cocktails. The customer should feel that the cocktail has been specially made for them individually.

Note

For examples of bar equipment see Section 3.5, page 53.

For more information on the service of cocktails see Section 17.5, page 274.

For a listing of cocktail recipes and methods see Annex A, page 346.

13.4 Wine

Wine is the alcoholic beverage obtained from the fermentation of the juice of freshly gathered grapes. Fermentation takes place in the district of origin, according to local tradition and practice.

Only a relatively small area of the world is wine producing. This is because grapes will only provide juice of the quality necessary for conversion into a drinkable wine where the climate is right. The two conditions needed are:

- sufficient sun to ripen the grapes
- winters that are moderate yet sufficiently cool to give the vine a chance to rest and restore its strength for the growing and fruiting season.

These climatic conditions are found in two main wine-producing zones, which lie between the latitudes 30° and 50° north of the equator and between 30° and 50° south of the equator.

Three-quarters of the world's wine is produced in Europe (often referred to as **Old World**) and just under half in the EU. France and Italy produce the most wine, with Italy being the largest producer followed by Spain, Germany and Portugal. Outside Europe (often referred to as **New World**), the largest producer is the USA followed by Australia, Argentina, Chile and South Africa.

Vinification

The process central to **vinification** (wine making) is **fermentation** – the conversion of sugar by yeast to alcohol and carbon dioxide. This conversion process is necessary for making all alcoholic beverages – not only for still, sparkling and fortified wines, but also as the starting point for making spirits, liqueurs and beers (although some variations and further processes will be applied for the different types of beverages).

Vine species

The process of cultivating grapes is known as 'viticulture'. The vine species that produces grapes suitable for wine production, and which stocks most of the vineyards of the world, is named *Vitis vinifera*. Most varieties now planted in Europe and elsewhere have evolved from this species through cross-breeding to suit local soils and climates. The same grape in different regions may be given a different name, for example, Grenache in the Rhône region is also known as Garnacha, which produces fine Spanish wines. There are a number of grapes that have become known for their distinctive characteristics. Examples of these principal grapes of the world, and their general characteristics, are given in Table 13.4.

Key terms

Old World wines – wine produced in Europe

New World wines – wines produced outside of Europe, in countries such as the USA, Australia, Argentina, Chile and South Africa

Vinification – wine making

Fermentation – the conversion of sugar into alcohol and carbon dioxide

Viticulture – the process of cultivating grapes

Table 13.4 Principal white and red grapes used for wine making

White grapes	Where grown	General characteristics of the wine
Chardonnay	Worldwide	The white grape of Burgundy, Champagne and the New World. Aromas associated with chardonnay include ripe melon and fresh pineapple. The fruity, oaky New World wines tend to be buttery and syrupy, with tropical fruits and richness. In Burgundy the wines are succulent but bone-dry, with a nutty intensity. Chablis, from the cooler northern Burgundy, produces wines that have a sharp, steely acidity that may also be countered by the richness of oak. Also one of the three grapes used to make Champagne
Chenin Blanc/ Steen	Loire, California, South Africa	Variety of styles: bone-dry, medium-sweet, intensely sweet or sparkling wines, all with fairly high acidity making the wines very refreshing. Aroma association tends to be apples
Gewürztraminer	Alsace, Australia, Chile, Eastern Europe, Germany, New Zealand, USA	One of the most pungent grapes, making wines that are distinctively spicy, with aromas like rose petals, grapefruit and tropical fruits such as lychees. Wines are aromatic and perfumed and are occasionally off-dry
Muscat	Worldwide	Mainly sweet, perfumed wines, smelling and tasting of grapes and raisins, and made in styles from pale, light and floral to golden, sweet and orangey, or brown, rich and treacly. Often fortified (as in the French vins doux naturels, e.g. Muscat des Beaumes de Venise). Also principal grape for sparkling Asti
Pinot Blanc/ Weissburgunder	Alsace, Eastern Europe, northern Italy, Germany, USA	Dry, neutral, fresh and fruity wines with the best having appley and soft spicy and honeyed aromas
Pinot Gris/Pinot Grigio/Ruländer/ Tokay-Pinot Gris	Alsace, Canada, Germany, Hungary, Italy, New Zealand, Slovenia, USA	Generally full-bodied spicy white wines, often high in alcohol and low in acidity. Wines are crisp and neutral in Italy and aromatic and spicy in Alsace and elsewhere, with a hint of honey. Also used to make golden sweet wines, especially from Alsace
Riesling	Alsace, Australia, Canada, Germany, New Zealand, South Africa, USA	Range of wines from the steely to the voluptuous; always well perfumed with good ageing potential. Aromas tend towards apricots and peaches. Germany makes the greatest Riesling in all styles. Piercing acidity and flavours ranging from green apple and lime to honeyed peaches, to stony and slate-like. Styles can range from bright and tangy to intensely sweet
Sauvignon Blanc	Worldwide	Common aroma association with gooseberries, the wines are green, tangy, fresh and pungent. When made with oak, it can be a different wine: tropical fruits in the Californian examples, while the classic Bordeaux wines are often blended with Sémillon and begin with nectarine hints and then become more nutty and creamy with age. May be called Blanc Fumé
Sémillon	Mainly Bordeaux but also Australia and New Zealand	Lemony, waxy dry whites; when oaked they can gain flavours of custard, nuts and honey. Luscious golden sweet wines when grapes are affected by *Botrytis cinera* (Noble Rot), e.g. Sauternes
Viognier	Rhône Valley and southern France, Australia, USA	Rhône wines, e.g. Condrieu, are aromatic, with hints of apricots and spring flowers; wines from other areas tend to be less perfumed

Red grapes	Where grown	General characteristics of the wine
Cabernet Sauvignon	Worldwide	Principal grape of Bordeaux, especially in the Médoc. New World wines deliver big wines with upfront blackcurrant fruit; Bordeaux wines need time to mature. Generally benefits from being blended, e.g. with Merlot, Cabernet Franc, Syrah, Tempranillo, Sangiovese. Also used to make aromatic rosé wines
Gamay	Beaujolais, Loire, Savoie, Switzerland, USA	The grape of Beaujolais, making light and juicy wines. Characteristic-pear-drop aroma association indicating wine made using the *macération carbonique* method. Makes lighter wine in the Loire Valley in central France and in Switzerland and Savoie. Known as 'Napa Gamay' in California
Grenache/ Garnacha	Southern France and Rhône, Australia, Spain, USA	Makes strong, fruity but pale wines, and fruity rosé wines. Important grape as part of blends, e.g. for Châteauneuf-du-Pape in the Rhône and for Rioja in Spain. Characteristics of ripe strawberries, raspberries and hints of spice
Malbec	South-West France, Argentina	French wines tend to be plummy and tannic. In Bordeaux it is used for blending. The Argentinean wines tend to be rich and perfumed
Merlot	Worldwide	Principal grape of Saint-Emilion and Pomerol in France. Aromas tend towards plums and damsons. The wines are low in harsh tannins and can be light and juicy, smooth and plummy or intensely blackcurrant
Nebbiolo	Italy	One of Italy's best red grapes, used in Barolo and Barbaresco. Fruity and perfumed wines with a mixture of tastes and flavours of black cherry and sloes, tar and roses. Aroma association tends towards prunes. Traditionally tough and tannic when young, with good plummy flavours as they develop
Pinot Noir/ Spätburgunder/ Pinot Nero	Worldwide	Principal grape of Burgundy's Côte d'Or. Aromas can be of strawberries, cherries and plums (depending on where grown). Silky and strawberry-like; simple wines have juicy fruit; the best mature wines, such as the great red wines of Burgundy, are well perfumed. Loire and German wines are lighter. Also one of the three grapes used to make Champagne and used elsewhere (e.g. California and Australia) for making white, sparkling or red and very pale pink wines
Sangiovese	Italy, Argentina, Australia, USA	Principal grape of Chianti. Also known as Brunello and Moreluno. Mouth-watering, sweet-sour red fruit in young wines, reminiscent of juicy cherries, which intensifies in older wines
Shiraz/Syrah	Worldwide	Warm, spicy, peppery wines with aromas of raspberries; French Syrah tends to be smoky, herby and packed with red fruits (raspberries, blackberries or blackcurrants); Australian Shiraz has sweeter black cherry fruit and often black chocolate or liquorice aromas. Very fruity rosé wines are also made
Tempranillo	Spain, Portugal, Argentina	Early ripening, aromatic Rioja grape (Ull de Liebre in Catalonia, Cencibel in La Mancha, Tinto Fino in Ribera del Duero, Tinta Roriz in Douro and Aragonez in southern Portugal). Wines are light and juicy with hints of strawberries and plums, silky and spicy with hints of prunes, tobacco and cocoa. Wines in cooler climates are more elegant and those in warmer climates are more beefy
Zinfande/Pimitivo	California, Italy	Aromas of blackberries, bramble and spice. In California wines have blackberry flavours, which are sometimes slightly metallic. Can be structured and lush and also used to make the pale pink 'blush' white wine. Genetically linked and known as Primitivo in Southern Italy, where it makes big, rustic wines

The grape

The grape consists of:

- skin – which provides tannins and colour
- stalk – which provides tannins
- pips – provide bitter oils
- pulp – contains sugar, fruit acids, water and pectins.

The yeast required for the fermentation process is found on the outside of the grape skin in the form of a whitish bloom. The colour in wine comes mainly from the skin of the grape, being extracted during the fermentation process. Red wine can only be made from red grapes. However, white wine can be made from white or red grapes, provided that, in the case of red grapes, the grape skins are removed before fermentation begins.

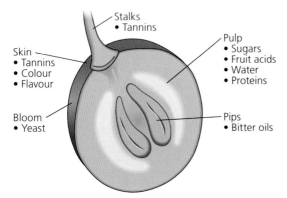

Figure 13.2 Wine-making grape

Factors that influence the quality and final taste of wine

The same vine variety, grown in different regions and processed in different ways, will produce wines of differing characteristics. The factors that affect the quality and final taste of wines include:

- climate and microclimate
- nature of the soil and subsoil
- vine family and grape species
- method of cultivation – viticulture
- composition of the grape(s)
- yeast and fermentation
- method of wine making – vinification
- luck of the year – vintage
- ageing and maturing process
- method of shipping or transportation
- storage temperature.

Wines may be identified as **vintage** wines. These are wines grown and made in a particular year and this is stated on the bottle. Non-vintage wines are those where the bottle may contain a blend of wines from different years. No date will be shown on the bottle.

Key term

Vintage – wines grown and made in a particular year

Pests and diseases

Vines are subject to pests and diseases in the form of birds, insects, fungi, viruses and weeds. The main ones include *phylloxera vastarix*, grey rot (*pourriture gris*) and noble rot (*pourriture*, noble or *Botrytis cinerea*).

Faults in wine

Faults occasionally develop in wine as it matures in bottles. Nowadays, because of improved techniques and attention to detail regarding bottling and storage, faulty wine is a rarity. Some of the more common causes of faulty wine are shown in Table 13.4.

Table 13.4 Faults in wine

Corked wines	These are wines affected by a diseased cork caused through bacterial action or excessive bottle age. TCA (trichloroanisole) causes the wine to taste and smell foul. This is not to be confused with cork residue in wine, which is harmless
Maderisation or oxidation	This is caused by bad storage leading to too much exposure to air, often because the cork has dried out. The colour of the wine browns or darkens and the taste slightly resembles that of Madeira, hence the name. The wine tastes 'spoilt'
Acetification	This is caused when the wine is over exposed to air. The vinegar microbe develops a film on the surface of the wine and acetic acid is produced, making the wine taste sour, resembling wine vinegar
Tartare flake	This is the crystallisation of potassium bitartrate. These crystal-like flakes, sometimes seen in white wine, may cause anxiety to some customers as they spoil the appearance of the wine, which is otherwise perfect to drink. If the wine is stabilised before bottling, this condition should not occur
Excess sulphur dioxide (SO_2)	Sulphur dioxide is added to wine to preserve it and keep it healthy. Once the bottle is opened, the smell will disappear and, after a few minutes, the wine is perfectly drinkable
Secondary fermentation	This happens when traces of sugar and yeast are left in the wine in the bottle. It leaves the wine with an unpleasant, prickly taste that should not be confused with the *pétillant* or *spritzig* (slightly sparkling) characteristics associated with other styles of healthy and refreshing wines
Foreign contamination	Examples include splintered or powdered glass caused by faulty bottling machinery or re-used bottles which previously held some kind of disinfectant
Sediment, lees, crust or dregs	This is organic matter discarded by the wine as it matures in the cask or bottle. It can be removed by racking, fining or, in the case of bottled wine, by decanting
Cloudiness	This is caused by suspended matter in the wine that disguises its true colour. It may be an example of unfiltered wine, which is fine, but can also be caused by extremes in storage temperatures

Classification of wine types

Still (or light) wine

This is the largest category. The alcoholic strength may be between 9% and 15% by volume. The wines may be:

- **Red**: produced by being fermented in contact with grape skins (from which the wine gets its colour). Normally dry wines.
- **White**: usually produced from white grapes, but the grape juice (must) is usually fermented away from the skins. Can be dry to very sweet.
- **Rosé**: can be made in three ways – from black grapes fermented in the skins for up to 48 hours; by mixing red and white wines together; or by pressing grapes so that some colour is extracted. Rosé wine may be dry or semi-sweet. Rosé wines are called 'blush' wines in the USA when made wholly from red grapes.

Sparkling wines

Sparkling wines are available from France, Spain (Cava), Italy (Prosecco), Germany (Sekt) and many other countries.

The most famous sparkling wine is Champagne, which is made in an area of north-eastern France. It is created by the secondary fermentation in the bottle (known in Champagne as *méthode champenoise* and elsewhere as *méthode traditionelle*).

Effervescent wines made outside this area are called *vins mousseux* or sparkling wines. A summary of the four methods for making sparkling wines is given in Table 13.5.

Table 13.5 Key differences in methods of production of sparkling wines

Method	Fermentation and maturation	Removal of sediment
Méthode traditionelle	In bottle	By the processes of *remuage* and *dégorgement* (moving the sediment to the neck of the bottle and then opening the bottle to remove it, topping up the bottle with more wine and then resealing)
Méthode transvasement or transfer method	In bottle	By transfer under pressure to a vat and then filtering before rebottling
Charmat or *méthode cuve close*	In tank	By filtration process
Méthode gazifié or carbonation method	Sometimes termed 'impregnation', where carbon dioxide is injected into a vat of still wine that has been chilled and which is then bottled under pressure. Least expensive method	

Other sparkling wine terms

French
- *Vin mousseux*: sparkling wine other than Champagne.
- *Méthode traditionelle*: sparkling, made by the traditional method.
- *Pétillant/perlant*: slightly sparkling.
- *Crémant*: less sparkling than *mousseux*.

German
- *Spritzig*: slightly sparkling.
- *Flaschengarung nach dem traditionellen Verfahren*: sparkling wine made by the traditional method.
- *Sekt*: sparkling (also used to mean the wine itself).
- *Schaumwein*: sparkling of lesser quality than Sekt.
- *Perlwein*: slightly sparkling.

Italian
- *Prosecco*: name of the northern Italian village where the grape is believed to have originated; the term is now often used as the generic name for Italian sparkling wines.
- *Frizzante*: semi-sparkling.
- *Spumante*: sparkling.
- *Metodo classico/tradizionale*: sparkling wine made by the traditional method.

Portuguese
- *Espumante*: sparkling.
- *Vinho verde*: meaning 'green wine', slightly sparkling.

Spanish
- *Espumosos*: sparkling.
- *Metodo tradicional*: sparkling, made by the traditional method.
- *Cava*: sparkling, made by the traditional method; also used as generic name for Spanish sparkling wines.

Organic wines

These wines, also known as 'green' or 'environmentally friendly' wines, are made from grapes grown without the aid of artificial insecticides, pesticides or fertilisers. The wine itself will not be adulterated in any way, save for minimal amounts of the traditional preservative, sulphur dioxide, which is controlled at source.

Alcohol-free, de-alcoholised and low-alcohol wines

These wines are made in the normal way and the alcohol is removed either by hot treatment – distillation – which unfortunately removes most of the flavour as well, or, more satisfactorily, by a cold filtration process, also known as reverse osmosis. This removes the alcohol by mechanically separating or filtering out the molecules of alcohol through membranes made of cellulose or acetate. At a later stage, water and a little must are added, thus attempting to preserve much of the flavour of the original wine. The definitions for these wines are:
- alcohol free: maximum 0.05% alcohol
- de-alcoholised: maximum 0.50% alcohol
- low alcohol: maximum 1.2% alcohol.

Fortified (liqueur) wines

Fortified wines such as sherry, port and Madeira have been strengthened by the addition of alcohol, usually a grape spirit. These are now known within the EU as liqueur wines or *vins de liqueur*. Their alcoholic strength may be between 15% and 22% by volume. Examples are:
- *Sherry* (from Spain) 15–18% – Fino (dry), Amontillado (medium), Oloroso (sweet).
- *Port* (from Portugal) 18–22% – ruby, tawny, vintage character, late bottled vintage, vintage.
- *Madeira* (made on the Portuguese island of Madeira) 18% – Sercial (dry), Verdelho (medium), Bual (sweet), Malmsey (very sweet).
- *Marsala* (dark sweet wine from Marsala in Sicily) 18%.
- *Málaga* (from Málaga, Andalusia, Spain) 18–20%.

Aromatised wines

These are flavoured and fortified wines, often referred to as vermouths.

The main types of vermouth are:
- *Dry vermouth*: often called French vermouth or simply French (as in 'gin and French'). It is made from dry white wine that is flavoured and fortified.
- *Sweet vermouth/bianco*: made from dry white wine flavoured, fortified and sweetened with sugar or mistelle.
- *Rosé vermouth*: made in a similar way to bianco, but it is less sweet and is coloured with caramel.

> ### Key terms
>
> **Fortified wine** – wines such as sherry and port, which have been strengthened by adding alcohol
>
> **Aromatised wine** – wine that has been flavoured and fortified

- *Red vermouth*: often called Italian vermouth, Italian, or sometimes just 'It' (as in 'gin and It'). It is made from white wine and is flavoured, sweetened and coloured with a generous addition of caramel.

Other aromatised wines include:
- *Chamberyzette*: made in the Savoy Alps of France. It is flavoured with the juice of wild strawberries.
- *Punt-e-Mes*: from Carpano of Turin. This is heavily flavoured with quinine and has wild contrasts of bitterness and sweetness.
- *Dubonnet*: made in France and is available in two varieties: blonde (white) and rouge (red) and is flavoured with quinine and herbs.
- *St Raphael*: red or white, bittersweet drink from France flavoured with herbs and quinine.
- *Lillet*: popular French apéritif made from white Bordeaux wine and flavoured with herbs, fruit peel and fortified with Armagnac brandy. It is aged in oak casks.
- *Pineau des Charentes*: although not strictly an aromatised or fortified wine, Pineau des Charentes has gained popularity as an alternative apéritif or digestif. It is available in white, rosé or red, and is made with grape must from the Cognac region and fortified with young Cognac to about 17% alcohol by volume.

Quality control for wines

The majority of the world's wine-makers must ensure that their products conform to strict quality regulations covering aspects such as the location of the vineyards, the variety of grape used, how the wine is made and how long it is matured.

Many countries now give the name of grape varieties on the wine label. Within the EU, if a grape variety is named on the label then the wine must contain at least 85 per cent of that variety. For EU wines, any number of grapes may be listed as part of descriptive text, but only a maximum of two may appear on the main label. For most countries outside of the EU, the wine must contain 100 per cent of the named variety, although there are exceptions. These include Australia and New Zealand who are permitted 85 per cent and the USA who are permitted 75 per cent. Australia allows up to five varieties, provided each is at least 5 per cent of the blend.

European Union

EU directives lay down general rules for quality wines produced in specified regions (QWPSR) or, in French, *vin de qualité produit en regions determinés* (VQPRD).

Countries outside the EU

Developments in the international wine business, especially in the New World, have led to a more marketing-led approach to wines. Simpler information is given on the labels and also on detailed back labels, including the identification of grape varieties (or the use of the Californian term 'varietals') and straightforward advice on storage, drinking and matching the wine with food.

Although most countries have a category for wines that is similar to EU Table Wine, this is mainly sold locally. On the international markets the wines are classified as Wine with Geographical Description. Each country has its own system for dividing its vineyard areas into regions, zones, districts and so on, and controlling the use of regional names. Where regions, vintages and varieties are named on the label, these wines may also have a small proportion of wine from other regions, vintages and varieties blended with them. All countries have their own legislation covering production techniques and use of label terms to prevent consumers from being misinformed.

Reading a wine label

The EU has strict regulations that govern what is printed on a wine bottle label. These regulations also apply to wine entering the EU. In addition, standard sized bottles of light (or still) wines bottled after 1988, when EU regulations on content came into force, must contain 75 cl.

Examples of taste and colour terms that appear on wine labels are given in Table 13.7.

Table 13.7 Examples of wine label terms indicating colour and taste

Term	France	Germany	Italy	Spain	Portugal
Wine	vin	wein	vino	vine	vinho
Dry	sec	trocken	secco	seco	seco
Medium	demi-sec	halbtrocken	abboccato	abocado	semi-seco
Sweet	doux/moelieaux	süß	dolce	dulce	doce
White	blanc	weißwein	bianco	blanco	branco
Red	rouge	rotwein	rosso	tinto	tinto
Rosé	rosé	rosé	rosato	rosado	rosado

The label on a bottle of wine can give a lot of useful information about that wine. The language used will normally be that of the country of origin. The information always includes:

● the name of the wine
● the country where the wine was made
● alcoholic strength in percentage by volume (% vol)
● contents in litres, cl or ml
● the name and address or trademark of the supplier.

It may also include:

● the varietal(s) (name of the grape(s) used to make the wine)
● the year the grapes were harvested, called the vintage, if the wine is sold as a vintage wine
● the region where the wine was made
● the property where the wine was made
● the quality category of the wine
● details of the bottler and distributor.

An example of the kind of information that is given on a wine label is shown in Figure 13.3. This example shows a guide to a French wine label.

Domaine de Dionyses —————— Winery name
2010 —————— Vintage
CAIRANNE —————— Village
CÔTES DU RHÔNE VILLAGES ⌐
Appelation Côtes du Rhône Villages Contrôlée ⌐ —————— Appellation title

Grenache · Syrah · Mourvèdre · Vieux · Carignan —————— Grape varieties

Mis en bouteille au Domaine —————— Domaine-bottled
14.5% PAR EARL DIONYSOS – 84100 UCHAUX – FRANCE 750ML —————— Produce name and location

Figure 13.3 Guide to the French wine label (source: wine-searcher.com)

13.5 Spirits

Production

All spirits are produced by **distillation**. The history of distillation goes back over 2,000 years when it is said that stills were used in China to make perfumes and by the Arabs to make spirit-based drinks.

The principle of distillation is that ethyl alcohol vaporises (boils) at a lower temperature (78°C) than water (100°C). Thus, where a liquid containing alcohol (alcoholic wash) is heated in an enclosed environment the alcohol will form steam first and can be taken off, leaving water and other ingredients behind. This process raises the alcoholic strength of the resulting liquid.

There are two main methods of producing spirits:
1 The **pot still** method, which is used for full, heavy flavoured spirits such as brandy.
2 The **patent still** method (also referred to as the 'column still', 'continuous still', or the 'Coffey still' after its inventor), which produces lighter spirits such as vodka.

Types of spirit

The main types of spirits are shown in Table 13.7.

Table 13.7 Types of spirit

Aquavit	Made in Scandinavia from potatoes or grain and flavoured with herbs, mainly caraway seeds. To be appreciated fully, Aquavit must be served chilled
Arrack	Made from the sap of palm trees. The main countries of production are Java, India, Sri Lanka and Jamaica
Brandy	Brandy may be defined as a spirit distilled from wine. The word brandy is more usually linked with the names Cognac and Armagnac, but brandy is made in almost all wine-producing areas

> **Key terms**
>
> **Distillation** – process used to increase the alcoholic strength of a liquid
>
> **Pot still** – method used to produce heavy flavoured spirits, e.g. brandy
>
> **Patent still (continuous, column or Coffey still)** – method used to produce light spirits, e.g. vodka

Calvados	Apple brandy made from the distillation of cider from the French region of Basse-Normandie or Lower Normandy – also see eau de vie.
Eau de vie	Eau de vie (water of life) is the fermented and distilled juice of fruit and is usually water-clear in appearance. The best eau de vie comes from the Alsace area of France, Germany, Switzerland and Eastern Europe. Examples are: • *Calvados*: from apples and often known as apple brandy (France) • *Himbergeist*: from wild raspberries (Germany) • *Kirschwasser*: from cherries (Alsace and Germany) • *Mirabelle*: from plums (France) • *Quetsch*: from plums (Alsace and Germany) • *Poire William*: from pears (Switzerland and Alsace) – sometimes known by the brand name Williamine • *Slivovitz*: from plums (Eastern Europe) • *Fraise*: from strawberries (France, especially Alsace) • *Framboise*: from raspberries (France, especially Alsace)
Gin	The term 'gin' is taken from the first part of the word Genièvre, which is the French term for juniper. Juniper is the *principal botanica* (flavouring agent) used in the production of gin. The word 'Geneva' is the Dutch translation of the botanical, juniper. Maize is the cereal used in gin production in the UK. However, rye is the main cereal generally used in the production of Geneva gin and other Dutch gins. Malted barley is an accepted alternative to the cereals mentioned above. The two key ingredients (botanicals) recognised for flavouring purposes are juniper berries and coriander seeds. Types of gin: • *Fruit gins*: as the term implies, these are fruit-flavoured gins that may be produced from any fruit. The most popular are sloe, orange and lemon • *Geneva gin*: this is made in Holland by the pot still method alone and is generally known as 'Holland' gin • *London dry gin*: this is the most well-known and popular of all the gins. It is unsweetened • *Old Tom*: this is a sweet gin made in Scotland. The sweetening agent is sugar syrup. As the name implies, it was traditionally used in a Tom Collins cocktail • *Plymouth gin*: this has a stronger flavour than London dry and is manufactured by Coates in Devon. It is most well-known for its use in the cocktail Pink Gin, together with the addition of Angostura Bitters
Grappa	An Italian-style brandy produced from the pressings of grapes after the required must – unfermented grape juice – has been removed for wine production. It is similar in style to the French marc brandy
Marc	Local French brandy made where wine is made. Usually takes the name of the region, for example, Marc de Borgogne
Pastis	Pastis is the name given to spirits flavoured with anis and/or liquorice, such as Pernod. The spirit is made in many Mediterranean countries and is popular almost everywhere. It has taken over from absinthe, once known as the 'Green Goddess'.
Quetsch	A colourless spirit with plums being the main ingredient. The key countries of production are the Balkans, France and Germany. It has a brandy base. Also see eau de vie
Rum	This is a spirit made from the fermented by-products of sugar cane (molasses). It is available in dark and light varieties and is produced in countries where sugar cane grows naturally, for example Jamaica, Cuba, Trinidad, Barbados, Guyana and the Bahamas
Schnapps	A spirit distilled from a fermented potato base and flavoured with caraway seed. The main countries of production are Germany and Holland
Tequila	A Mexican spirit distilled from the fermented juice (pulque) of the agave plant. It is traditionally drunk after a lick of salt and a squeeze of lime or lemon
Vodka	A highly rectified (very pure) patent still spirit. It is purified by being passed through activated charcoal, which removes virtually all aroma and flavour. It is described as a colourless and flavourless spirit

Whisk(e)y	Whisky, or whiskey, is a spirit made from cereals: Scotch whisky from malted barley; Irish whiskey usually from barley; North American whiskey and bourbon from maize and rye. The spelling *whisky* usually refers to the Scotch or Canadian drink and *whiskey* to the Irish or American.
	• Scotch whisky is primarily made from barley, malted (hence the term malt whisky) then heated over a peat fire. Grain whiskies are made from other grains and are usually blended with malt whisky
	• Irish whiskey differs from Scotch in that hot air rather than a peat fire is used during malting, thus Irish whiskey does not gain the smoky quality of Scotch. It is also distilled three times (rather than two as in the making of Scotch) and is matured longer
	• Canadian whisky is usually a blend of flavoured and neutral whiskies made from grains such as rye, wheat and barley
	• American whiskey is made from various mixtures of barley, maize and rye. Bourbon is made from maize
	• Japanese whisky is made by the Scotch process and is blended

13.6 Liqueurs

Liqueurs are defined as sweetened and flavoured spirits. They should not be confused with liqueur spirits, which may be whiskies or brandies of great age and quality. For instance, a brandy liqueur is a liqueur with brandy as a basic ingredient, while a liqueur brandy may be defined as a brandy of great age and excellence.

Production

Liqueurs are made by two basic methods:

1 Heat or **infusion** method: best when herbs, peels, roots, etc., are being used, as heat can extract their oils, flavours and aromas.
2 Cold or **maceration** method: best when soft fruits are used to provide the flavours and aromas.

The heat method uses a pot still for distillation purposes. The cold method allows the soft fruit to soak in the spirit in oak casks over a long period of time.

For all liqueurs a spirit base is necessary and this may be brandy, rum or a neutral spirit. Many flavouring ingredients are used to make liqueurs.

Types of liqueurs

Table 13.8 lists some of the more popular liqueurs. The service of liqueurs is discussed in Section 17.8, page 284.

Table 13.8 Popular liqueurs

Liqueur	Colour	Flavour/spirit base	Country of origin
Abricotine	Red	Apricot/brandy	France
Avocaat	Yellow	Egg, sugar/brandy	Holland
Anisette	Clear	Aniseed/neutral spirit	France, Spain, Italy, Holland
Amaretto	Golden	Almonds	Italy
Archers	Clear	Peaches/schnapps	UK
Arrack	Clear	Herbs, sap of palm trees	Java, India, Sri Lanka, Jamaica
Bailey's Irish Cream	Coffee	Honey, chocolate, cream, whiskey	Ireland

Bénedictine	Yellow/green	Herbs/brandy	France
Chartreuse	Green (45% abv) Yellow (55% abv)	Herbs, plants/brandy	France
Cherry brandy	Deep red	Cherry/brandy	Denmark
Cointreau	Clear	Orange/brandy	France
Crème de cacao	Dark brown	Chocolate, vanilla/rum	France
Disaronno	Amber	Almonds with herbs and fruits soaked in apricot kernel oil	Italy
Drambuie	Golden	Heather, honey, herbs/whisky	Scotland
Galliano	Golden	Herbs/berries/flowers/roots	Italy
Frangelico	Golden	Hazelnut	Italy
Grand Marnier	Amber	Orange/brandy	France
Glayva	Golden	Herbs, spices/whisky	Scotland
Kahlúa	Pale chocolate	Coffee/rum	Mexico
Kümmel	Clear	Caraway seed/neutral spirit	East European countries
Malibu	Clear	Coconut/white rum	Caribbean
Maraschino	Clear	Maraschino cherry	Italy
Parfait amour	Violet	Violets, lemon peel, spices	France/Holland
Sambuca	Clear	Liquorice/neutral spirit	Italy
Southern Comfort	Golden	Peaches/oranges/whiskey	United States
Strega (The Witch)	Yellow	Herbs/bark/fruit	Italy
Tia Maria	Brown	Coffee/rum	Jamaica
Van Der Hum	Amber	Tangerine/brandy	South Africa

13.7 Beer

Beer in one form or another is an alcoholic beverage found in all bars and areas dispensing alcoholic beverages. Beers are fermented drinks deriving their alcoholic content from the conversion of malt sugars into alcohol by brewer's yeast. The alcoholic content of beer varies according to type and is usually between 3.5% and 10% alcohol by volume.

Types of beer

There are a number of different types of beer, as shown in Table 13.9.

Table 13.9 Types of beer

Abbey-style	Ale brewed in the monastic tradition of the Low Countries but also by secular brewers, often under license from a religious establishment
Barley wine	Traditionally an all-malt ale. This beer is sweet and strong and sold in small bottles or nips (originally ⅓ of a pint, now 190 ml)
Bitter	Pale, amber-coloured beer served on draft. May be sold as light bitter, ordinary bitter or best bitter. When bottled it is known as pale ale or light ale depending on alcoholic strength

Burton	Strong, dark, draft beer. This beer is popular in winter when it is mulled or spiced and offered as a winter warmer
Fruit beers and flavoured beers	Variety of beers with additional flavourings such as heather or honeydew, or fruit beers, which have fresh fruits such as raspberry or strawberry introduced during the making process to add flavour
IPA (India Pale Ale)	Heavily hopped strong pale ale, originally brewed in the UK for shipping to British colonies. The modern style is a light-coloured, hoppy ale
Lager	The name comes from the German *lagern* (to store). Fermentation takes place at the bottom of the vessel and the beer is stored at low temperatures for up to six months and sometimes longer. Sold on draft, in a bottle or can
Mild	Can be light or dark depending on the colour of the malt used in the brewing process. Generally sold on draft and has a sweeter and more complex flavour than bitter
Old ale	Brown, sweet and strong. Can also be mulled or spiced
Pilsner	Clear, pale lagers (originally from Pilsen in the Czech Republic, hence the name). Modern styles are characterised by a zesty hop taste and bubbly body
Porter	Brewed from charred malt, highly flavoured and aromatic. Its name comes from its popularity with market porters working in Dublin and London
Reduced-alcohol beer	There are two categories of beer with reduced alcohol levels: • Non-alcoholic beers (NABs) which, by definition, must contain less than 0.5% alcohol by volume • Low-alcohol beers (LABs) which, by definition, must contain less than 1.2% alcohol by volume The beer is made in the traditional way and then the alcohol is removed
Smoked beers	Beers made with grains that have been smoked as part of the malting process. Various woods are used, including alder, cherry, apple, beech or oak. Sometimes the process uses peat smoke
Stout	Made from scorched, very dark malt and generously flavoured with hops. Has a smooth, malty flavour and creamy consistency. Sold on draft or in bottles and was traditionally not chilled (although today it often is). Guinness is one example
Strong ale	Colour varies between pale and brown, and taste between dry and sweet. Alcoholic content also varies
Trappist beer	Beer brewed in Trappist monasteries, usually under the supervision of monks. Six Belgian breweries produce this beer, which is strong, complex and unpasteurised, and often includes cane sugar in the recipe
White beer	Traditional beers made with a high proportion of wheat, sometimes known as wheat beers

Cask-conditioned beers

Cask-conditioned beer is ale that has its final fermentation in the cask (or barrel) from which it is dispensed.

Bottle-conditioned beers

Also known as sediment beers, bottle-conditioned beers tend to throw a sediment in the bottle while fermenting and conditioning takes place. These beers need careful storage, handling and pouring. Available in bottles only.

Draught beer in cans

These draft-flow beers have an internal patented system that produces a pub-style, smooth creamy head when poured from the can. A range of beers are available in this format.

Faults in beer

Although thunder has been known to cause a secondary fermentation in beer, affecting its clarity, faults are usually as a result of poor cellar management. The common faults in beer are described below.

- **Cloudy beer**: this may be due to too low a temperature in the cellar or, more often, may result from the beer pipes not having been cleaned properly.
- **Flat beer**: flat beer may result when a wrong spile has been used – a hard spile builds up pressure, a soft spile releases pressure. When the cellar temperature is too low, beer often becomes dull and lifeless. Dirty glasses, and those that have been refilled for a customer who has been eating food, will also cause beer to go flat.
- **Sour beer**: this may be due to a lack of business resulting in the beer being left on ullage for too long. Sourness may also be caused by adding stale beer to a new cask or by beer coming into contact with old deposits of yeast that have become lodged in the pipeline from the cellar.
- **Foreign bodies**: foreign bodies or extraneous matter may be the result of production or operational slip-ups.

Beer measures

- Nips: 7–8 fl oz (about 22.72 cl)
- Half pint: 10 fl oz (about 28.40 cl)
- Pint: 20 fl oz (about 56.80 cl)
- Half litre
- Litre

Draught beer containers

- Pin: 20.46 litres (4½ gallons)
- Firkin: 40.91 litres (9 gallons)
- Kilderkin: 81.83 litres (18 gallons)
- Barrel: 163.66 litres (36 gallons)
- Hogshead: 245.48 litres (54 gallons)
- 2½ barrel tanks: 205 litres (45 gallons)
- 5 barrel tanks: 410 litres (90 gallons)

Mixed beer drinks

A selection of beverages based on beer is given below:

- mild and bitter
- stout and mild
- brown and mild
- light and mild
- shandy: draught bitter or lager and lemonade or ginger beer
- black velvet: Guinness and champagne
- black and tan: half stout and half bitter
- lager and lime
- lager and blackcurrant.

13.8 Cider and perry

Cider is an alcoholic beverage obtained through the fermentation of apple juice, or a mixture of apple juice and up to 25 per cent pear juice. **Perry** is similarly obtained from pear juice and up to 25 per cent apple juice.

Key terms

Cider – alcoholic beverage obtained through the fermentation of apple juice, or a mixture of apple juice and up to 25 per cent pear juice

Perry – obtained from pear juice and up to 25 per cent apple juice

Cider and perry are produced primarily in England and Normandy, but may also be made in Italy, Spain, Germany, Switzerland, Canada, the USA, Australia and New Zealand. The main areas of production in England are the counties of Devon, Somerset, Gloucester, Hereford, Kent and Norfolk where the best cider orchards are found.

Cider

The characteristics of the apples that are required for making cider are:

- the sweetness of dessert apples
- the acidity of culinary apples
- the bitterness of tannin to balance the flavour and help preserve the cider.

Main types of cider

- **Draught**: this is unfiltered. Its appearance, while not cloudy, is also not 'star-bright'. It may have sugar and yeast added to give it condition. Draught cider may be completely dry (known as 'scrumpy') or sweetened with sugar. It is marketed in oak casks or plastic containers.
- **Keg/bottled**: this cider is pasteurised or sterile filtered to render it star-bright. During this stage, one or more of the following treatments may be carried out:
    - it may be blended
    - it may undergo a second fermentation, usually in a tank, to make it sparkling
    - it may be sweetened
    - its strength may be adjusted
    - it will usually be carbonated by the injection of carbon dioxide gas.

The characteristics of keg and bottled ciders are:

- medium sweet (carbonated): 4% vol alcohol.
- medium dry (carbonated): 6% vol alcohol.
- special (some carbonated): 8.3% vol alcohol – some special ciders undergo a second fermentation to make them sparkling.

Perry

Perry is usually sparkling; it may be carbonated or the sparkle may come from a second fermentation in sealed tanks. In the production of perry the processes of filtering, blending and sweetening are all carried out under pressure.

Perries were traditionally drunk on their own, chilled and in saucer-shaped sparkling wine glasses. Today the tulip-shaped sparkling wine glasses are more commonly used.

13.9 Tasting techniques

The tasting, or evaluation, of wine and other drinks is carried out to:

- develop learning from experience
- help to assess the quality of a wine in terms of value (the balance between price and worth) when making purchasing decisions
- monitor the progress of a wine which is being stored, to determine the optimum selling time
- assist in the description of a wine when explaining its qualities or deficiencies to customers
- provide a personal record of wines tasted, which helps to reinforce the experience and the learning.

To appreciate the tasting of wine to the full it should be carried out in an environment that supports the wine evaluation process:

- no noise to distract the taster
- good ventilation to eliminate odours
- sufficient light (daylight rather than artificial if possible), preferably north facing in the northern hemisphere (south facing in the southern hemisphere), as the light is more neutral
- a white background for tables so as not to affect the perception of the colour of the wine
- a room temperature of about 20°C (68°F).

A wine glass with a stem and of sufficient capacity should be chosen (see Figure 13.5) when tasting wine. The glass should be fairly wide but narrowing at the top. This allows the elements making up the **bouquet** to become concentrated and therefore better assessed. The wine-tasting glass should never be filled to more than one-third capacity. This allows the taster to swirl the wine round the glass more easily. It goes without saying that the tasting glass should be spotlessly clean.

Figure 13.5 Wine taster's glass (image courtesy of International Standards Organisation)

> **Key term**
>
> **Bouquet** – aroma/smell

Professional approach

The purpose of wine tasting is to attempt to identify characteristics that describe the wine, which are then used to assess its quality. The professional tasting, or evaluation, of wines includes three key stages:

1. Recording the details of each individual wine.
2. Looking at, smelling and tasting the wine.
3. Recording the findings.

Approaching the process in this way ensures the development of confidence and the ability to make sound judgements.

Recording wine details

To ensure a complete record of the tasting of each wine, it is important to record the following details:

- name of wine
- country and area of origin
- quality indication (e.g. AOC, Qmp etc.)
- shipper
- château/estate bottled
- varietal(s) (grapes)
- vintage
- alcohol level
- ½ bottle, bottle, magnum
- price
- supplier.

Looking at, smelling and tasting the wine

Professional wine tasting is really an analysis and evaluation of qualities of the wine by the senses. This includes:

- looking at the wine to assess its clarity, colour and intensity, and the nature of the colour by identifying the specific shade of white, rosé or red

- smelling, or nosing, the wine to assess the condition of the wine, the intensity of aroma or bouquet, and to identify other aroma characteristics. Taste is 80 per cent smell!
- tasting the wine to assess the sweetness/dryness, acidity, tannin, body, length and other taste characteristics
- touch, to feel the weight of the wine in the mouth, the temperature, etc.
- hearing, to create associations with the occasion
- drawing conclusions about the evaluation (summing up) and making a judgement of the quality of the wine (poor, acceptable, good, outstanding).

Examples of the terms that might be used as part of the evaluation of wine are given in Table 13.10

Table 13.10 Examples of wine evaluation terms

Sight	*Clarity*: clear, bright, brilliant, gleaming, sumptuous, dull, hazy, cloudy *Colour intensity*: pale, subdued, faded, deep, intense *White wine*: water clear, pale yellow, yellow with green tinges, straw, gold, deep yellow, brown, Maderised *Rosé wine*: pale pink, orange-pink, onion-skin, blue-pink, copper *Red wine*: purple, garnet, ruby, tawny, brick-red, mahogany
Smell (nose, aroma, bouquet)	*Condition*: clean to unclean *Intensity*: weak to pronounced *Other aroma descriptors*: fruity, perfumed, full, deep, spicy, vegetal, fine, rich, pleasant, weak, nondescript, flat, corky
Taste	*Sweetness/dryness*: bone dry, dry, medium dry, sweet, medium sweet, sweet, luscious *Acidity*: low to high *Tannin*: low to high *Body*: thin, light, medium, full-bodied *Length*: short to long *Other taste descriptors*: fruity, bitter, spicy, hard, soft, silky, floral, vegetal, smooth, tart, piquant, *spritzig/pétillant* (slightly sparkling)
Conclusion	*Summing up*: well-balanced, fine, delicate, rich, robust, vigorous, fat, flabby, thick, velvety, harsh, weak, unbalanced, insipid, for laying down, just right, over the hill *Overall quality/value*: poor – acceptable – good – outstanding

Tasting technique

1 After assessing the clarity, colour and the smell, take a small amount of the wine in the mouth together with a little air and roll it around so that it reaches the different parts of the tongue.
2 Now lean forward so that the wine is nearest the teeth and suck air in through the teeth. Doing this helps to highlight and intensify the flavour. (Fortified wines, spirits and liqueurs are often assessed by sight and smell without tasting.)

When tasting the following should be considered:
- The taste-character of the wine is detected in different parts of the mouth but especially by the tongue: sweetness at the tip and the centre of the tongue, acidity on the upper edges, saltiness on the tip and at the sides, sour at the sides and bitterness at the back.
- Sweetness and dryness will be immediately obvious.
- Acidity will be recognised by its gum-drying sensation but, in correct quantities, acidity provides crispness and liveliness to a drink.

Alcoholic beverages

- Astringency or tannin content, usually associated with red wines, will give a dry coating or furring effect, especially on the teeth and gums.
- Body, which is the feel of the wine in your mouth, and flavour, the essence of the wine as a drink, will be the final arbiters as to whether or not you like it.
- Aftertaste is the finish the wine leaves on your palate.
- Overall balance is the evaluation of all the above elements taken together.

Note

It is important that you make up your own mind about the wines you taste. Do not be too easily influenced by the observations of others.

General grape and wine characteristics

There are a number of grapes that have distinctive characteristics. Examples of these grapes are listed in Table 13.4 (page 194) and information on their general characteristics is also given.

Recording the findings

Whenever wine is being evaluated a written record should be kept. These notes should be made at each stage of the process, otherwise it is possible to become muddled and confused. The process of writing down the findings helps to reinforce the discipline of the approach and leads, over time, to the development of greater confidence and skill, and also provides a record of wine tastings over time.

13.11 Matching food with wine and other drinks

Food and its accompanying wine/drink should harmonise well together, with each enhancing the other's performance. However, the combinations that prove most successful are those that please the individual.

When considering possible food and wine partnerships there are no guidelines to which there are not exceptions. However, general guidelines on matching wine and food are summarised in Table 13.11.

Table 13.11 General guidelines for matching wine and food

Characteristic	Food considerations
Acidity	Can be used to match, or to contrast, acidity in foods, for example, crisp wines to match lemon or tomato, or to cut through creamy flavours
Age/maturity	As wine ages and develops it can become delicate with complex and intricate flavours. More simple foods, such as grills or roasts, work better with older wines than stronger tasting foods, which can overpower the wines
Oak	The more oaked the wine then the more robust and flavoursome the food needs to be. Heavily oaked wines can overpower more delicate foods
Sweetness	Generally the wine should be sweeter than the food or it will taste flat or thin. Sweet dishes need contrast for them to match well with sweeter wines, for example, acids in sweeter foods can harmonise with the sweetness in the wines. Savoury foods with sweetness (e.g. carrots or onions) can match well with ripe fruity wines. Blue cheeses can go well with sweet wines. Also sweeter wines can go well with salty foods

Tannin	Tannic wines match well with red meats and semi-hard cheeses (e.g. cheddar). Tannic wines are not good with egg dishes and wines with a high tannin content do not work well with salty foods
Weight	Big, rich wines go well with robust (flavoursome) meat dishes, but can overpower lighter-flavoured foods

Some general guidelines when selecting and serving wines are given below.

- Dry wines should be served before sweeter wines.
- White wines should be served before red wines.
- Lighter wines should be served before heavier wines.
- Good wines should be served before great wines.
- Wines should be at their correct temperature before serving.
- Wine should always be served to customers before their food.

Beers and food

Recently there has been an increasing trend to offer beers with food, either alongside or as an alternative to wine. As with wine it is a question of trial and error to achieve harmony between particular beers and foods. Generally the considerations for the pairing of beers and foods are similar to those for matching wines with foods, as shown in Table 13.13, and in particular, taking account of acidity, sweetness/dryness, bitterness, tannin, weight and the complexity of the taste.

Making recommendations to customers

A few general pointers are set out below that may be followed when advising the customer on which beverage to choose to accompany a meal. However, customers should at all times be given complete freedom in their selection of wines or other drinks.

- Apéritifs are usually alcoholic beverages that are drunk before the meal. If wine will be consumed with the meal, then the apéritif selected should be a grape (wine-based) rather than a grain (spirit-based) apéritif, since the latter can potentially spoil or dull the palate.
- The apéritif is usually a wine-based beverage. It is meant to stimulate the appetite and therefore should not be sweet. Dry and medium dry sherries, dry vermouths and Sercial or Verdelho Madeira are all good examples of apéritifs.
- Starter courses are often best accompanied by a dry white or dry rosé wine.
- National dishes should normally be complemented by the national wines of that country, for example, Italian red wine with pasta dishes.
- Fish and shellfish dishes are often most suited to well-chilled dry white wines.
- Red meats, such as beef and lamb, blend and harmonise well with red wine.
- White meats, such as chicken and pork, can be paired with medium white wines.
- Game dishes require the heavier and more robust red wines to complement their full flavour.
- Sweets and desserts are served at the end of the meal and chilled sweet white wines are often offered, which may come from the Loire, Sauternes, Barsac or Hungary. These wines also harmonise best with dishes containing fruit.
- The majority of cheeses blend well with port and other dry robust red wines. However, cheese can also be served with sweet whites. Port is the traditional wine harmonising best with Stilton cheese.
- Grain- and fruit-based spirits and liqueurs all harmonise well with coffee.

Testing your learning

1 What are the UK sensible limits of weekly alcohol consumption, in units, to avoid damage to health for men and for women?
2 What is a mixologist?
3 Describe the four main methods for making cocktails and mixed drinks.
4 The climatic conditions to support the production of wine are found in two main wine-producing zones. Geographically where do they lie?
5 What are the three main classifications for wine?
6 Identify four factors that can affect the quality and final taste of wines.
7 Name four of the main white grape varieties used in making white wine.
8 Name four of the main red grape varieties used in making red wine.
9 Explain the terms 'viticulture' and 'vinification'.
10 Describe the cause of each of the following faults found in wine:
   (a) Corked wines
   (b) Maderisation or oxidation
   (c) Sediment, lees, crust or dregs
   (d) Cloudiness
11 Name and state the country of origin of three fortified (liqueur) wines.
12 Identify three pieces of information that you would always expect to find on the label of a bottle of wine.
13 All spirits are produced by the distillation of alcoholic beverages. What are the alcoholic beverage bases for each of the following five spirits?
   (a) Brandy
   (b) Calvados
   (c) Rum
   (d) Tequila
14 What is the main botanical used in the production of gin?
15 List the four main ingredients used in the making of beer.
16 List three of the serving measures used for beer, cider and perry.
17 Identify one possible cause of the following three faults found in beers:
   (a) Cloudy beer
   (b) Flat beer
   (c) Sour beer
18 State the recommended order for the three steps in wine tasting.
19 Identify a type/style of wine that would match each of the following dishes:
   (a) Fish and shellfish dishes
   (b) Red meats such as beef and lamb
   (c) White meats such as veal and pork
   (d) Game dishes
   (e) Sweets and desserts
   (f) Cheeses

Service methods, key technical skills and service principles

Units covered

This chapter covers the following units:

Level 1

→ Food and beverage service skills (108)
→ Bar service skills (109)
→ Prepare and clear areas for table/tray service (1FS1, 107)
→ Provide a table/tray service (1FS2, 108)
→ Prepare and clear areas for counter/takeaway service (1FS3, 109)
→ Clean and store crockery and cutlery (1GEN5, 105)

Level 2

→ Food and beverage service skills (209)
→ Provide a counter/takeaway service (1FS4, 110)
→ Serve food at the table (2FS2, 207)
→ Provide a silver service (2FS8, 208)
→ Provide a buffet/carvery service (2FS4, 209)
→ Serve alcoholic and soft drinks (2BS2, 212)
→ Prepare and serve cocktails (2BS3, 213)
→ Prepare and serve wines (2BS4, 214)
→ Prepare and serve hot drinks using specialist equipment (2BS8, 218)
→ Prepare and clear areas for counter/takeaway service (1FS3, 109)
→ Prepare and clear areas for table service (2FS1, 206)
→ Prepare and clear the bar area (2BS1, 211)

Learning outcomes

This chapter will help you to:

14.1 Food and beverage service methods

In food and beverage service, the customer is central to the process and is also an active participant within it. Understanding customers' involvement in the process and identifying the experience they are likely to have, and should expect, has become critical to the business success of food and beverage operations.

It is also now recognised that food and beverage service actually consists of two aspects operating at the same time. These are:

1   The **service sequence** – which is concerned with the delivery of the food and beverages to the customer.
2   The **customer process** – which is concerned with the experience that the customer undertakes so that they can order, be served, consume and have the area cleared.

Key terms

service sequence – stages in the service of a meal

customer process – the experience the customer undertakes

The service sequence

The service sequence is essentially the bridge between food production, beverage provision and the customer process (or customer experience). The service sequence may consist of a number of stages. Each of these stages may be carried out by a variety of ways. These are described in the Chapters 15 to 19 of this book. Table 14.1 gives various stages of the service sequence and where they are covered in this book.

Table 14.1 Food and beverage service sequence

Stages of the service sequence	Covered in:
1 Preparation for service	Chapter 15, page 230
2 Taking food and beverage orders	Chapter 16, page 259
3 Providing bar and beverage service	Chapter 17, page 269
4 Serving food and beverages	Chapter 18, page 292
5 Taking bookings	Chapter 19, page 334
6 Billing	
7 Dealing with payments	

The rest of this chapter identifies and describes the various food and beverage service methods, covers the essential technical service skills required when working in food and beverage service, and highlights the key service principles and the reasons for them.

The customer process

The customer receiving the food and beverage product is required to undertake or observe certain requirements: this is the customer process. Essentially, a customer enters a food and beverage service area, orders or selects his or her choice and then is served (the customer may pay either at this point or later). Food and beverages are then consumed, following which the area is cleared.

When considering food and beverage service from a customer process perspective, **five categories of food and beverage service methods** can be identified. These are summarised in Table 14.2.

Table 14.2 The five main categories of food and beverage service methods

Service method	Service area	Ordering/ selection	Service	Dining/ consumption	Clearing
Table service	Customer enters and is seated	From menu	By staff to customer	At a laid cover	By staff
Assisted service	Customer enters and is usually seated	From menu, buffet or passed trays	Combination of both staff and customer	Usually at a laid cover	By staff
Self-service	Customer enters	Customer selects items on to a tray	Customer carries	Dining area or takeaway	Various
Single-point service	Customer enters	Orders at single point	Customer carries	Dining area or takeaway	Various
Specialised or in situ *service*	Where the customer is located	From menu or predetermined	Brought to the customer	Served where the customer is located	By staff or customer clearing

Table service: the customer is served at a laid table. This type of service, which includes plated service or silver service, is found in many types of restaurant, cafés and in banqueting.

Assisted service: the customer is served part of the meal at a table and is required to obtain part through self-service from some form of display or buffet. This type of service is found in carvery-type operations and is often used for meals such as breakfast in hotels. It may also be used for events.

Self-service: the customer is required to help him or herself from a buffet or counter. This type of service can be found in cafeterias and canteens.

Single-point service: the customer orders, pays and receives the food and beverages, for instance at a counter, at a bar in licensed premises, in a fast-food operation or at a vending machine.

Specialised service (or service *in situ*): the food and drink is taken to where the customer is. This includes, for example, tray service in hospitals or aircraft, trolley service, home delivery, lounge and room service.

A detailed listing of all the modern food and beverage service methods is given in Table 14.3.

In **table service, assisted service self-service**, and **single-point service** the customer comes to where the food and beverage service is offered and the service is provided in areas primarily designed for that purpose, such as a restaurant or takeaway. In **specialised** or *in-situ* service, the service is provided in another location, where the area is not primarily designed for the purpose, for example in a guest room, lounge or hospital ward.

The level of complexity of food and beverage service, in terms of staff skills, tasks and duties, reduces from **table service** (the most complex) to **single-point service**. **Specialised service** contains specialised forms of service, which require an additional range of service skills. For a particular service method, such as waiter service, a number of tasks and duties are undertaken during the actual service of food and beverages. However, there are other tasks and duties that contribute to the service. These may be identified under the headings given in the service sequence outlined in Table 14.1.

Table 14.3 Food and beverage service methods

Table service: service to customers at a laid cover		
Waiter	Silver/English	Presentation and service of food by waiting staff, using a spoon and fork, on to a customer's plate from food flats or dishes
	Family	Main courses plated (but may be silver served) with vegetables placed in multi-portion dishes on tables for customers to help themselves; sauces offered separately
	Plate/American	Service of pre-plated foods to customers. Now also widely used for banqueting
	Butler/French	Presentation of food individually to customers by food service staff for customers to serve themselves
	Guéridon	Food served on to customer's plate at a side table or trolley; may also include carving, jointing and fish filleting, the preparation of foods such as salads and dressings and flambéing
Bar counter		Service to customers seated at bar counter (often U-shaped) on stools
Assisted service: combination of table service and self-service		
Assisted	Carvery	Some parts of the meal are served to seated customers; other parts are collected by the customers. Also used for breakfast service and for banqueting
	Buffets	Customers select food and drink from displays or passed trays; consumption is either at tables, standing or in lounge area
Self-service: self-service of customers		
Cafeteria	Counter	Customers queue in line formation past a service counter and choose their menu requirements in stages before loading them on to a tray (may include a 'carousel' – a revolving stacked counter, saving space)
	Free-flow	Selection as in counter (above) but in food service area where customers move at will to random service points; customers usually exit area via a till point
	Echelon	Series of counters at angles to the customer flow within a free-flow area, thus saving space
	Supermarket	Island service points within a free-flow area
Single-point service: service of customers at a single point – consumed on premises or taken away		
Takeaway	Takeaway	Customer orders and is served from single point, at a counter, hatch or snack stand; customer consumes off the premises; some takeaway establishments provide dining areas
	Drive-thru	Form of takeaway where customer drives vehicle past order, payment and collection points
	Fast food	Term originally used to describe service at a counter or hatch where customers receive a complete meal or dish in exchange for cash or ticket; commonly used nowadays to describe a type of establishment offering a limited menu, fast service with dining area and takeaway facility
Vending		Provision of food service and beverage service by means of automatic retailing
Kiosks		Outstation used to provide service for peak demand or in specific location; may be open for customers to order and be served or used for dispensing to staff only
Food court		Series of autonomous counters where customers may either order and eat (as in bar counter described above) or buy from a number of counters and eat in separate eating area or takeaway
Bar		Term used to describe order, service and payment point, and consumption area, in licensed premises

Specialised (or *in situ*): service to customers in areas not primarily designed for service		
Tray		Method of service of whole or part of meal on tray to customer *in situ*, e.g. at hospital beds or at aircraft seats; also used in event catering
Trolley		Service of food and beverages from a trolley, away from dining areas, e.g. for office workers at their desks and customers at aircraft seats or train seats
Home delivery		Food delivered to customer's home or place of work, e.g. 'meals on wheels', pizza home delivery or sandwiches to offices
Lounge		Service of variety of foods and beverages in a lounge area, e.g. hotel lounge
Room		Service of variety of foods and beverages in guest bedrooms or in meeting rooms
Drive-in		Customers park their motor vehicle and are served at their vehicles

Note

With the exception of fast-food operations, there is no particular link between a specific service method and a specific food production method. It is also possible that the production and service may be separated by distance or time, or both, as for example in off-premises catering.

Banquet/function is a term used to describe catering for specific numbers of people at specific times in a variety of dining layouts. Service methods also vary. In these cases banquet/function catering refers to the organisation of service rather than a specific service method.

14.2 The importance of technical skills

Developing good technical skills is essential for three main reasons:
- helps to develop greater confidence in undertaking technical service tasks
- allows servers to concentrate on their social skills and increases their contribution to achieving excellence in the service
- increases efficiency and reduces the risks of accidents.

There are six basic technical food and beverage service skills. These are identified in Table 14.1 below, together with examples of their application. The rest of this chapter provides further information on the application of these skills.

Table 14.4 Technical service skills and their application

Technical skill	Examples of application
Holding and using a service spoon and fork	Service of food at a customer's table, especially for silver service, and for serving at a buffet or from a trolley
Carrying plates	When placing and clearing plates from a customer's table
Using a service salver (round tray)	For carrying glasses, carrying tea and coffee services, as an under liner for entrée dishes and for potato and vegetable dishes
Using a service plate	For carrying items to and from a table, including clean cutlery, clearing side plates and knives, crumbing down and clearing accompaniments
Carrying glasses	Carrying clean glasses by hand or on a salver and for clearing dirty glasses from a service area
Carrying and using large trays	For bringing equipment or food and beverage items to the service area and for clearing used equipment from the service area

These basic technical skills are used specifically for table service and assisted service. However, these skills are also used when providing other forms of service, for example, when carrying trays for room service or using a service salver for bar service.

14.3 Holding and using a service spoon and fork

Expertise in this technique can only be achieved with practice. The purpose of the service spoon and fork is to enable the waiter to serve food from a flat or dish on to the customer's plate quickly and to present the food on the plate well.

Holding a service spoon and fork

1 The service fork should be positioned above, or on top of, the service spoon. The key to developing this skill is the locking of the ends of the service spoon and fork with the small finger and the third finger.

2 The spoon and fork are manoeuvred with the thumb and the index and second fingers. Using this method food items may be picked up from the serving dish in between the service spoon and service fork.

3 Alternatively, the service fork may be turned to mould to the shape of the items being served, for example when serving bread.

There are occasions where two service forks may be used, for example when serving fillets of fish, as this makes the service of this food item easier.

When using a service spoon and fork for serving at a sweet or cheese trolley, or at a buffet or guéridon, the spoon and fork are held one in each hand.

Other service equipment that may be used includes serving tongs, fish slices and gâteaux slices, serving spoons, scoops, small sauce ladles and larger soup ladles, as shown in Figure 14.2.

Figure 14.2 Examples of service equipment

14.4 Carrying plates

Clean plates can be carried in a stack, using both hands or using a tray. When carrying clean plates that are to be placed on the customer's table, a single hand is used to hold the plates (usually the left hand) and the right hand is used to place the plates at each cover on the customer's table. If the plates are hot then the plates are held with a service cloth placed on the palm of the left hand. A separate service cloth is then used in the right hand to hold the hot plates when placing them in front of the customer.

When carrying plates of pre-plated foods and when clearing plates from a customer's table, a single hand is used to hold the plates (usually the left hand) and the right hand is used to place plates on, and remove plates from, the customer's table.

Service methods, key technical skills and service principles

Hand positions when carrying plates of pre-plated food and when clearing plates

1 Initial hand position for the first plate. Care must be taken to ensure that the first plate is held firmly as succeeding plates are built up from here.

2 The second plate positioned on the left (holding) hand. The second plate will rest firmly on the forearm and the third and fourth fingers.

Clearing plates properly means that the waiting staff work efficiently, avoid accidents and create the minimum of inconvenience to customers. It also means that more items can be cleared from tables, in less time and in fewer journeys between the sideboard or workstation and the customer's table. Clearing properly also allows for the stacking of dirties neatly and safely at the sideboard or workstation. (See also clearing skills in Section 18.3, page 302.)

14.5 Using a service salver (round tray)

A **service salver** is a round, often silver or stainless steel, tray (wood or plastic may also be used). A napkin (folded flat) or non-slip mat is placed on the tray to help prevent items slipping on it as they are being carried. Some trays are made with non-slip surfaces. The service salver is often used to:

- carry clean glasses to, and remove dirty glasses from, a customer's table
- carry clean cutlery to and from a customer's table
- place clean cutlery on the table
- place clean cups and saucers on the table
- provide an underflat when silver serving vegetables.

Carrying clean cutlery

In order to be more efficient, hygienic, safer and more professional, clean and polished items to be placed on or removed from a table should be carried on a service salver rather than carrying these items in bunches in the hand.

On occasions when setting up for larger parties or functions, the blades of the knives may be placed under the arch in the middle of the forks and, if carrying sweet spoons and forks, the prongs of the fork should go under the arch in the middle of the sweet spoon. The reason for this is to help hold the items steady on the service salver. Bearing in mind that the handles of the cutlery are generally the heaviest parts, this method prevents them sliding about too much.

> **Key term**
>
> **Service salver** – a round, often silver or stainless steel tray used to carry glasses and cutlery

Figure 14.4 Cutlery positions when carrying on a service salver

Clean cutlery is placed on to the service salver after the final polish and then carried to the table on the salver. The cutlery is then placed on the table by holding the item of cutlery between the thumb and forefinger at the side. This is done in order to reduce the possibility of finger marks on already polished cutlery.

Carrying cups and saucers

Tea and coffee cups are carried to the table using a service salver. They are arranged on the service salver by stacking the saucers, cups and teaspoons separately. Before placing the cup, saucer and teaspoon on the table, the cup is put on to a saucer, together with a teaspoon, and then the whole service is placed in front of the customer from their right-hand side. This is a speedier and safer method, especially when larger numbers are involved, than carrying individual cups, saucers and teaspoons to the table one by one. (For further information see Section 18.4, Figure 18.13 (a) and (b), page 307.)

As an underflat

When silver serving some food dishes and potatoes or vegetables at the table, an **underflat** should be used. This is to hold either one large vegetable dish or a number of smaller ones, depending on the customer's order. The purpose of using a service salver as an underflat is to:

- add to the presentation of the food being served
- give the waiter more control when using the service spoon and fork to serve from the food dishes on to the customer's plate
- provide greater protection in case of spillage, therefore not detracting from the presentation of the food on the plate or the overall table presentation
- give the waiter added protection against heat and possible spillage on the uniform.

For examples of where underflats are used during silver service see Section 18.2, page 298.

> **Key term**
>
> **Underflat** – also called an underliner

14.6 Using a service plate

A **service plate** is a joint plate with a napkin on it. During the meal service it can be used for:

- placing clean cutlery on and removing it from the table
- clearing side plates and side knives

> **Key term**
>
> **Service plate** – used by the server during service

- crumbing down after the main course or any other stage of the meal if necessary
- clearing accompaniments from the table.

Carrying clean cutlery

When placing on or removing clean cutlery from a table, the items can be carried on a service plate. The reasons for this are the same as given under using a service salver above.

Clearing side plates and knives

When clearing dirty side plates and side knives from the customer's table, the use of a service plate means that the waiter has a larger area on which to stack the side knives and any debris. Using the hand positions shown on page 305, the side plates may be stacked above the service plate and all the debris in a separate pile, together with the side knives laid flat on the service plate (this is shown in Section 18.3, page 302). This is a much safer and speedier method, especially when larger numbers are involved.

Clearing accompaniments

The service plate is also used to clear such items as the cruet, peppermill or other accompaniments.

Crumbing down

The service plate is used in the **crumbing down** process. The purpose here is to freshen up the appearance of the tablecloth prior to laying the sweet covers and serving the sweet. For further information on crumbing down see Section 18.3, Figure 18.10 and Figure 18.11, page 306.

> **Key term**
>
> **Crumbing down** – removing bread crumbs and other debris from the customer's table

14.7 Carrying glasses

There are two basic methods of carrying glasses in food and beverage service areas: by hand or on a service salver.

Carrying by hand

Figure 14.5 Carrying clean glasses by hand

Wine goblets should be positioned between alternate fingers as far as is possible. The wine goblets should only be carried in one hand, allowing the other hand to remain free to steady oneself in case of emergencies.

This method allows wine goblets that are already polished to be handled. They can be carried about the room and set in their correct position on the table without the bowl of the glass being touched. This should only be done if there are no customers present, otherwise a service salver should be used. Clean glassware is always handled by the stem and for non-stemmed glassware by the base.

Carrying glasses on a service salver

The method of carrying clean wine glasses about the restaurant during service using the service salver is illustrated in Figure 14.6.

A service cloth is placed on the palm of the hand, with the service salver placed upon it. This allows the service salver to be rotated more easily in order to remove each upturned wine glass, in turn, by the stem and to set it on the table.

Figure 14.7 shows the use of the service salver for clearing dirty wine glasses from a table. A service cloth would be used as mentioned above. The first dirty wine glass cleared should be placed on the service salver nearest to the server. As the dirty glasses are cleared, they should be placed on the service salver to ensure a better and more even distribution of weight, to lessen the likelihood of accidents occurring. Again, dirty glassware is always handled by the stem and, for non-stemmed glassware, by the base. This is more hygienic as it avoids touching where the customer has been drinking from the glass.

Figure 14.6 Carrying clean, upturned, wine glasses on a service salver

Figure 14.7 Carrying dirty glasses on a service salver

Carrying glasses using glass racks

Glass racks, usually made of plastic, are often used to carry glasses during the setting up of the restaurant and for functions. These racks enable the transportation of glasses in bulk once they have been washed and polished at a central point. Glass racks are also used for dirty glasses and may be put through a glass-washing machine.

Figure 14.8 Carrying glasses using a glass rack

Service methods, key technical skills and service principles

14.8 Carrying and using large trays

Trays are used for:

- carrying food from the kitchen to the restaurant
- service in rooms and lounges
- clearing from sideboards/workstations
- clearing from tables at functions or when the customer is not seated at the table in the restaurant
- carrying equipment.

The correct method of holding and carrying an oblong tray is to position the tray lengthways on to the forearm and to support it by holding the tray with the other hand (see Figure 14.9). Note that the tray is organised so that the heaviest items are nearest the carrier. This helps to balance the tray. Also note that one hand is placed underneath the tray and the other at the side.

Figure 14.9 Carrying a loaded oblong tray

14.9 Importance of standard service principles

There are traditional ways of doing things that have become established over time within food and beverage service. These are known as the 'service principles' (sometimes also known as service conventions) and have proved to be effective and efficient ways in which to carry out the service.

Having agreed service principles for an establishment ensures standardisation in the service sequence and the customer process (see Section 14.1, page 214, for the definition of these terms), both for staff and for customers. The service principles detailed in this chapter are only a guide. Different establishments may have variations on the service principles listed here, but for food and beverage service to operate efficiently and smoothly it is important that all members of staff follow the same service principles. Otherwise the service will be inefficient, and potentially chaotic, and customers will feel that the operation is not well managed or coordinated.

14.10 Traditional service principles

The various service principles may be broken down into a number of groups:

- personal service
- service preparation
- order taking
- general service
- when serving
- general working and clearing following service.

Examples of these groups of service principles, and the rationale for them, are given in the tables below:

Table 14.5 Personal service principles

Principle	Rationale
Always work as part of a team	All members of the team should know and be able to do their own job well, to ensure a smooth, well-organised and disciplined operation
Work hygienically and safely	For the protection of other staff and customers from harm and to avoid accidents
Pass other members of staff by moving to the right	Having an establishment rule about each member of staff always moving to the right (or left) when passing each other avoids confusion and accidents
Avoid contact between fingers and mouth or hair	If contact between fingers and mouth or hair, etc., is unavoidable, then hands must be washed before continuing with service. Always wash hands after using the toilet
Cover cuts and sores	Covering cuts and sores with waterproof plasters or dressings is an essential health and safety practice

Table 14.6 Service preparation principles

Principle	Rationale
Use checklists for preparation tasks	Using checklists ensures that all members of staff complete all preparatory tasks in the same way
Prepare service areas in sequence	Ensure service areas are laid out and housekeeping duties have been completed before the preparation for service begins. This can save time and unnecessary duplication of effort afterwards
Consider using white gloves	In some establishments members of staff wear white cotton gloves when carrying out various preparation tasks. Gloves help to prevent the soiling of clean service items and avoid putting finger marks on cleaned and polished service equipment. White gloves are also sometimes used during service, instead of using service cloths, when serving plated foods that are presented on hot plates
Use a model lay-up	Lay one initial full place setting (cover) to use as a model for all staff to measure against. A place setting is usually about 60 cm wide
Hold glasses or cups by the stem, the base or the handle	This is hygienic practice. Service staff should not hold glasses or cups, etc., by the rim
Hold cutlery in the middle at the sides between the thumb and forefinger	This is safer, makes for more accurate placing of items on the table and also helps to prevent finger marking on clean cutlery items

Service methods, key technical skills and service principles

Principle	Rationale
Lay table place settings (covers) from the inside out	This makes table laying easier. Place a centre to the cover (a table mat or side plate for instance) then lay tableware in order from the inside of the cover outwards. When laying a number of covers it is more efficient to lay each piece of tableware for all covers in sequence, i.e. all side plates, then all side knives, etc.
Use of standard lay-ups	Indicates the type of meals being taken, the sequence of the courses and also what stage customers are at within a meal
Fully or partly lay the table before a meal begins	Most often tables are fully laid before a meal but this may vary, for instance, if the table is likely to become excessively cluttered where there is not sufficient equipment to fully pre-lay all the tables, or if the style of service is à la carte
Place items on the table consistently	Make sure that any crested or patterned crockery or glassware is always placed the same way round on the table and that it is evenly spaced, i.e. crests or badges at the head of the cover

Table 14.7 Order-taking principles

Principle	Rationale
Take food, wine and drink orders through the host	This is common courtesy – agreement needs to be obtained for any items that are to be served. For larger parties, where there may be a choice, orders may be taken individually, but it is useful to confirm what has actually been ordered with the host as this may save any disagreements later
Use order notation techniques	Use of such techniques helps any server to identify which member of a party is having a particular item of food or beverage
Be aware of customers who may have additional needs	Look out for, and be prepared to deal with, people with sight, hearing, speech, mobility and language difficulties. Also be prepared and able to deal with children

Table 14.8 General service principles

Principle	Rationale
Use checklists for all aspects of service	These help to ensure that all information is complete and that all managers and staff carry out procedures in the same way
Avoid leaning over customers	This shows courtesy and respect for personal physical space. Remember that no matter how clean service staff members are, food and beverage smells do tend to cling to service uniforms
Place items low to high	Lower items should be placed near to the customer and taller items behind or to the side of these. This makes items easily accessible by the customer and helps to avoid accidents
Place items according to the customer's position at the table	Items placed on a table should be within reach of the customer. Handles, etc., should be set for the customer's convenience
Use underplates (liners)	These are used (cold) for four main purposes: to improve presentation on the table; to make carrying of soup plates, bowls and other bowl-shaped dishes easier; to isolate the hand from hot dishes; to allow cutlery to be carried along with the item
Use service salvers or service plates (with napkins or mats on them to prevent items slipping)	Service salvers or service plates are used for five main purposes: to improve presentation of items to be served; to make carrying of bowl-shaped serving dishes easier and more secure (also avoids the thumb of the server being inside a service dish); to allow for more than one serving dish to be carried at a time; to isolate the hand from hot dishes; to allow service gear to be carried along with the item(s)

Principle	Rationale
Hold flats, food dishes and round trays on the palm of the hand	This is safer and ensures that the food items are best presented for the customer. It also makes for easier carrying and avoids the server's thumb or service cloth being seen on the edge of flats, dishes and round trays. If the flats or dishes are hot then the service cloth can be underneath, folded and laid flat on to the palm to protect the hand.
Use doilies/dish papers on underplates (liners)	Doilies, dish papers (or linen or paper napkins) on underplates are used to improve presentation, to reduce noise and to prevent the dish from slipping on the underplate. Use doilies for sweet food items and dish papers for savoury food items

Table 14.9 Principles when serving

Principle	Rationale
Serve cold food before hot food	When the hot food is served the service is complete and customers can enjoy the meal without waiting for additional items to be served. For the same reason, accompaniments should be automatically offered and served at the same time as the food item
Serve wine before food	Similar to above. Customers will wish to enjoy the wine with their meal. They will not want to wait for the wine service, as their hot food will go cold
Start service from the right-hand side of the host, with the host last	Honoured guests are usually seated on the right of a host. The principle is to serve a table by first serving the principal guest and then moving anti-clockwise for plated service (and clockwise for silver service) to each customer, as this ensures that members of the serving staff are walking forwards to serve the next person. The host is normally served last
Serve women first	Often done if it does not slow the service. Particular care needs to be taken so as not to confuse things when the host is a woman. A host of either gender is still the host and should always be served last
Silver serve food from the left-hand side of a customer	Ensures that the service dish is nearer the plate for ease of service and to prevent food being spilt on to the person. Customers can more easily see the food being served and make choices if necessary, and members of the service staff are also able to see and control what they are doing
Use separate service gear for different food items	This should be standard. It avoids different food items or sauces being transferred from one dish or plate to another and avoids messy presentation of food on the customers' plates
Serve foods on to plates consistently	For service of the whole main course on to a joint plate, place the main item at the six o'clock position with potatoes served next at the ten past two position and vegetables last at the ten to two position (this also follows the UK Royal National Institute for the Blind (RNIB) recommendations). For main courses with potatoes and vegetables and/or salads served on a separate plate or crescent, the main item is placed in the centre of the main plate with the separate plate or crescent of potatoes and vegetables and/or side salad to the left of this
Serve plated foods from the right-hand side of a customer	Plates can be placed in front of the customer with the right hand; the stack of other plated food is then behind the customer's chair in the left hand. If there is an accident, the plates held in the left hand will go on to the floor rather than over the customer. Plated foods should be placed so that the food items are consistently in the same position for all customers
Serve all beverages from the right-hand side of a customer	Glasses are placed on the right-hand side of a cover and the service of beverages follows from this. For individual drinks and other beverages, the tray is held behind a customer's seat in the server's left hand. Other beverages, such as coffee and tea, are also served from the right. All beverages should also be cleared from the right
Clear from the right-hand side of a customer	Plates can be removed from in front of the customer with the right hand and the stack of plates is then behind the customer's chair, in the server's left hand. If there is an accident, the plates held in the left hand will go on to the floor rather than over the customer. The exception to this is for side plates, which are on the left-hand side of the cover. These are more easily cleared from the left, thus avoiding stretching in front of the customer

Table 14.10 Principles for general working and clearing following service

Principle	Rationale
Use trays	Use trays to bring food and beverage items to the service areas and to clear during and following service. Trays can be brought to, or removed from, sideboards or service tables and also used to serve plated foods from (or to clear plates on to) with service staff working as a pair
Separate the serving at table from food/drink collection and sideboard/ workstation clearing	Ensures that there is always someone in the room to attend to customers and to monitor the overall service, while others are bringing in food and beverage orders or clearing items away from the service station. This approach allows new staff to be trained and ensures that customer contact is primarily through experienced staff
Use checklists for tasks required for clearing after service	In the same way as using checklists for preparatory tasks (see Section 15.6, page 255), using checklists for clearing after service ensures that all members of staff complete all clearing tasks in the same manner

Testing your learning

1 Briefly describe the difference between the service sequence and the customer process.
2 Identify and describe the five main food and beverage service methods.
3 State two reasons why it is essential to develop good technical skills.
4 List four of the basic technical skills used in table service and for each one give an example of how that skill is used in practice.
5 When would you most likely to be serving food using a service spoon in one hand and a service fork in the other?
6 Describe a service salver and give two examples of how it might be used.
7 One of the uses of a service plate is when crumbing down. State one other use of a service plate during service.
8 The wine order should be taken through the:
   (a) eldest lady present
   (b) most senior gentleman present
   (c) the host
   (d) the person with the most knowledge of wine.
9 Briefly describe the main reason for using checklists.
10 Give the main reason why you use a separate service spoon and fork for the service of different food items.
11 Why should you serve cold food before hot food? Why should you serve the wine before the food?
12 You are serving coffee to a party of four customers. From which side of each customer would you set the coffee service on the table and why?

Preparation for service

Units covered

This chapter covers the following units:

Level 1

→ Food and beverage service skills (108)
→ Prepare and clear areas for table/tray service (1FS1, 107)
→ Provide a table/tray service (1FS2, 108)
→ Prepare and clear areas for counter/takeaway service (1FS3, 109)
→ Clean and store crockery and cutlery (1GEN5, 105)

Level 2

→ Food and beverage service skills (209)
→ Provide a counter/takeaway service (1FS4, 110)
→ Serve food at the table (2FS2, 207)
→ Provide a silver service (2FS8, 208)
→ Provide a buffet/carvery service (2FS4, 209)
→ Prepare and clear areas for counter/takeaway service (1FS3, 109)
→ Prepare and clear areas for table service (2FS1, 206)

Learning outcomes

This chapter will help you to:

15.1 Preparation for table service

The term 'mise-en-place' (literally 'put in place' but also meaning preparation for service) is the traditional term used for all the duties carried out in order to prepare the room for service. The supervisor will draw up a duty rota showing the tasks and duties to be completed before service and the members of staff responsible for them.

> **Key term**
>
> **Mis-en-place** – preparation for service

Figure 15.1 Traditional restaurant ready for service (image courtesy of Le Columbier Restaurant, London)

The success of all types of service is determined by the detailed preparation that goes into setting up the service areas prior to the service commencing. It is the success of the preparation duties that helps staff to provide efficient service and to create an ambiance that is attractive and pleasant for the customers.

Order of working

The duties should proceed in a certain order so that they may be carried out effectively and efficiently. For example, dusting should be done before the tables are laid, and vacuuming should be completed before the tables and chairs are put in place. The duties involved in bar preparation may be included within the duty rota depending on the type of establishment

A suggested order of work might be as follows:

1 Dusting
2 Stacking chairs on tables
3 Vacuuming
4 Polishing
5 Arrange tables and chairs according to the table plan
6 Linen
7 Accompaniments
8 Hotplate
9 Stillroom
10 Sideboards/workstations
11 Silver cleaning
12 Other duties such as preparing trolleys.

Some of these duties will be carried out at the same time and the supervisor must ensure they are all completed efficiently.

As the necessary preparatory work is completed the staff report back to the supervisor, who will check that the work has been carried out in a satisfactory manner. The supervisor will then re-allocate the member of staff to other work involved in the setting-up of the service areas.

Using white gloves

In some establishments members of staff wear white cotton gloves when carrying out preparation tasks such as:
- handling linen and paper
- clothing-up tables
- making napkin folds
- handling clean crockery, cutlery and glassware
- laying tables.

The gloves help to prevent soiling of clean service items and finger marks on cleaned and polished service equipment. Clean gloves should be worn for each separate task carried out. They should not be reused for further tasks as this may present a hygiene risk.

15.2 Preparation duties

The duties to be carried out before service begins will vary according to the particular food and beverage service area concerned. A list of the possible tasks and duties is shown below, but not all of these are applicable to every situation and there may be some jobs not listed which are specific to a particular establishment.

Supervisor

Duties might include:

- checking that a full team of staff is present and that all duties on the duty rota are covered
- checking the booking diary for reservations
- making out the seating plan for the meal service to come and allocate customers accordingly
- making out a plan of the various stations and show where each member of staff will be working
- going over the menu with staff immediately before service is due to commence.

Housekeeping duties

Housekeeping duties may also include the reception area and might involve the following:

- vacuuming the carpet and brushing surrounds daily
- cleaning and polishing doors and glass
- emptying waste bins
- performing the daily tasks as indicated on the duty rota, for example:
  - *Monday*: brush and dust tables and chairs
  - *Tuesday*: polish all sideboards, window ledges and cash desk
- each day, on completion of all duties, line up tables and chairs for laying up.

Linen/paper

This applies not only to table, buffet and slip cloths, and glass and waiters' cloths, but also to paper slip cloths and napkins plus dish papers and doilies. Duties might include:

- collecting clean linen from the housekeeping department, checking items against the list and distributing them to the various service points. Spare linen should be folded neatly into the linen basket
- ensuring that stocks are sufficient to meet needs
- laying tablecloths
- folding napkins
- ensuring that glass cloths and waiters' cloths are available
- providing dish papers and doilies as required
- the preparation of the linen basket for return to the linen room.

Hotplate

Duties might include:

- switching on the hotplate and checking that all doors are closed
- placing items in the hotplate according to the menu offered, for example:
  - soup plates
  - consommé cups
  - fish plates
  - joint plates
  - sweet plates
  - coffee cups

- stocking up the hotplate after each service with clean and polished crockery in readiness for the next meal service.

Cutlery

Duties might include:

- collection of cutlery from the storage area (sometimes called a silver room) and polishing and sorting on to trays some or all of the following items, in quantities agreed with the supervisor, in readiness for laying up the tables and setting up the sideboards:

  - service spoons
  - joint/service forks
  - soup spoons
  - fish knives
  - fish forks
  - joint knives

  - side knives
  - sweet spoons
  - sweet forks
  - tea/coffee spoons
  - specialist service equipment as required for the menu

- identifying broken items or those in need of replacing.

Crockery

Duties might include:

- checking and polishing side plates ready for lay-up
- checking and polishing crockery for the hotplate according to the menu and service requirements
- preparation of service plates for sideboards/workstations
- preparation of stocks of crockery for sideboards/workstations, such as fish plates, side plates and saucers.

Glassware

Duties might include:

- collection of the required glassware from the glass pantry (store)
- checking and polishing glassware needed for the general lay-up
- checking and polishing glassware needed for any special events
- checking and polishing glassware required for any special menu dishes, for example goblets for prawn cocktails, tulip glasses for sorbets and also liqueur, port and brandy glasses for the liqueur trolley
- stacking the cleaned and polished glassware on to trays or placing into glass racks in readiness for setting up or movement to the point of service.

Polishing glassware

The following equipment is required to carry out this task:

- a container of near-boiling water (sometimes a little vinegar is added as it helps to remove grease)
- a clean, dry tea cloth
- the required glassware.

The process described here is for single glasses. Larger quantities of glassware may be polished by first placing a glass rack full of inverted glasses over a sink of very hot water in order to steam the glasses. A number of people would then work together to polish the glassware.

Polishing glassware

1 Holding the base of the glass to be cleaned, hold the wine goblet over the steam from the boiling water so that the steam enters the bowl of the glass. Rotate the wine goblet to allow the steam to circulate fully within the bowl of the glass and then hold the base of the glass over the steam. Now hold the base of the wine goblet in the clean, dry teacloth. Place the other hand underneath the tea cloth in readiness to polish the bowl of the glass.

2 Place the thumb of the polishing hand inside the bowl of the glass and the fingers on the outside, holding the bowl of the wine goblet gently but firmly. Rotate the wine goblet with the hand holding the base of the glass. When fully polished, hold the wine goblet up to the light to check that it is clean. Ensure that the base of the glass is also clean.

Cruets, table numbers and butter dishes

Duties might include:

- collection of cruets, table numbers and butter dishes from the silver room
- polishing, checking and filling the cruet sets (salt cellars, peppermills and mustard pots)
- laying on tables of cruet sets, table numbers and butter dishes with butter knives, according to the headwaiter's instructions.

Stillroom

Duties might include:

- the ordering of stores requirements (including bar and accompaniment requirements) to hold over the coming service period
- checking with the supervisor/headwaiter the number of accompaniments and sets of cruets to prepare and the number of sideboards/workstations and tables that will be in use during the service period
- preparation of:
  - beverage service items, for example teapots, coffee pots, cold milk jugs
  - butter scrolls/butter pats and alternatives
  - bread items – brioche, croissants, wholemeal rolls, gristicks
- polishing and refilling oil and vinegar stands, sugar basins and caster sugar dredgers, peppermills and cayenne pepper pots

- preparing all accompaniments such as tomato ketchup, French and English mustard, ground ginger, horseradish sauce, mint sauce, Worcestershire sauce and Parmesan cheese (grated)
- distributing the accompaniments to the sideboards.

Sideboards/workstations

After ensuring that the sideboard/workstation is clean and polished it can be stocked up.

Figure 15.3 gives an example of a sideboard lay-up including:

1	Water jug	11	Service spoons and forks
2	Butter dish	12	Bread basket
3	Check pad on service plate	13	Service salver/plate
4	Assorted condiments	14	Underflats
5	Hotplate	15	Coffee saucers
6	Side knives	16	Side plates
7	Joint knives	17	Sweet/fish plates
8	Fish knives and forks	18	Joint plates
9	Soup spoons, tea and coffee spoons	19	Trays
10	Sweet spoons and forks		

Other items might include:

- specialist cutlery according to the menu, for example soup and sauce ladles
- various crockery according to the menu, such as saucers for consommé cups.

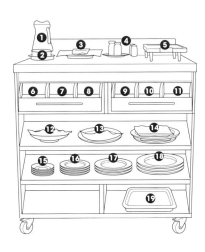

Figure 15.3 Example of a sideboard lay-up

Figure 15.4 Laid sideboard

Display buffet

Duties may include:

- preparation of the buffet table to the supervisor's instructions
- the display of:
  - butter dishes and knives
  - accompaniments
  - cold fish plates
  - special cutlery and tableware as required
  - sauce and soup ladles
  - service spoons and forks
  - spare joint plates for used service gear.

Trolleys

Trolleys, such as those for cheese or for sweets, may need to be set up according to the establishment's requirements. For more information about service from trolleys see Section 18.5, page 309.

Preparing a floral table decoration

A simple centre table display (posy arrangement) can be made in small shallow bowls with oasis in the bowl to hold the flowers. Oasis is a green-coloured sponge-like material that holds moisture and is soft enough for greenery and flower stems to be pushed into it to hold them secure.

Figure 15.5
Centre table posy arrangement

The oasis should be kept moist to maximise the life of the flowers. Moisture content can be checked by lightly pressing the oasis – it should feel wet. The flowers may also be kept moist by lightly spraying them from time to time with a water gun.

Many establishments, as an alternative to the posy arrangement, purchase blooms, often single stem, on a daily basis or as required. These are presented in a single stem vase on the table. This approach is cheaper, less time consuming and equally effective in providing floral décor for tables.

15.3 Clothing-up and napkin folding

The tablecloth and napkins should be handled as little as possible, which will be ensured by laying the tablecloth quickly and properly first time and folding napkins simply on a clean surface, and with clean hands.

Laying a tablecloth

Before laying the tablecloth the table and chairs should be in their correct position. The tabletop should be clean and the table level, with care being taken to ensure that it does not wobble. If the table wobbles slightly, a disc sliced from a cork, a small wedge or an old menu folded neatly can be used to correct the problem. Next, the correct size of tablecloth should be collected. Most tablecloths are folded in what is known as a screen fold.

The waiter should stand between the legs of the table while the tablecloth is being laid, as this ensures that the corners of the cloth cover the legs of the table once the clothing-up has been completed.

The screen fold should be opened out across the table in front of the waiter with the inverted and two single folds facing them, ensuring that the inverted fold is on top.

The tablecloth should then be laid in the following manner.

Laying a tablecloth

1 Place the thumb on top of the inverted fold with the index and third fingers either side of the middle fold.

2 Spread out your arms as close to the width of the table as is possible and lift the tablecloth so that the bottom fold falls free. This should be positioned over the edge of the opposite side of the table from where you are standing.

3 Now let go of the middle fold and open the tablecloth out, by drawing it towards you until the table is covered with the tablecloth. Check that the fall of the cloth is even on all sides.

4 Adjustments may be made by pulling from the edge of the cloth.

If the tablecloth is laid correctly the following should be apparent:
- the corners of the tablecloth should be over (cover) the legs of the table
- the overlap should be even all round the table: 30–45 cm (12–18 in)
- the creases of all tablecloths laid should run the same way in the room.

If two tablecloths are necessary to cover a table for a larger party, then the overlap of the two tablecloths should face away from the entrance to the room. This is for presentation purposes of both the room and the table.

Napkin folds

There are many forms of napkin (or serviette) fold to be found in use in the food and beverage service area. Some are intricate in their detail while others are simpler. The simpler folds are used in everyday service; some of the more complex and difficult folds may only be used on special occasions, such as luncheons, dinners and weddings.

There are three main reasons why the simple folds are better than the more complex ones.
1 The napkin, if folded correctly, can look good and add to the general appearance of the room, whether it is a simple or complex fold.

2   A simpler fold is perhaps more hygienic as the more complex fold involves greater handling to complete. In addition, its appearance, when unfolded to spread over the customer's lap, is poor as it often has many creases.

3   The complex fold takes much more time to complete properly than a very simple fold.

Many of the napkin folds have special names, for example:

- cone
- bishop's mitre
- rose
- cockscomb
- triple wave
- fan
- candle.

The four napkin folds shown in Figures 15.7 (a) to (d) are some of the more common folds used every day in the food and beverage service area and for special occasions. These are simpler folds that may be completed more quickly, requiring less handling by the operator and are therefore more hygienic.

The rose fold of a napkin is one in which rolls or fruit may be presented for the table. It is not often used for a place setting. The triple wave is an attractive fold that may also be used to hold the menu and a name card.

Figure 15.7 (a) Bishop's mitre

Figure 15.7 (b) Rose

Figure 15.7 (c) Cockscomb

Figure 15.7 (d) Triple wave (French fold)

Shown on the following pages are the methods for folding the four napkin folds shown above. Once you become competent at these, you should learn the art of folding others to extend your repertoire.

When folding napkins they must be clean and well starched. As you commence folding the napkin, run the back of your hand over every fold to make the creases firm and sharp.

Preparation for service

Bishop's mitre

1 Lay the napkin out flat in front of you.

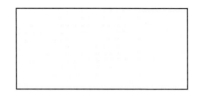

2 Fold it in half, straight side to straight side.

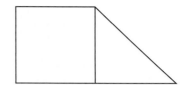

3 Take the top right corner and fold it down to the centre of the bottom line.

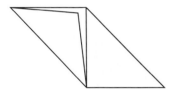

4 Take the bottom left corner and fold it up to meet the centre of the top line.

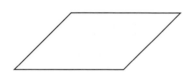

5 Turn the napkin over so that the folds are now facing down.

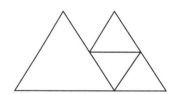

6 Take the top line (edge) and fold it down to meet the base line (bottom edge), leaving the two peaks pointing away from you.

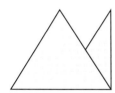

7 Take the bottom right-hand side and fold it under the flap on the left side. Make sure it tucks right under the flap for a snug fit.

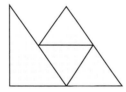

8 Turn it completely over.

9 Again take the bottom right hand-side and fold it under the flap on the left side. Now stand the napkin up by pulling the sides of the base out until it is circular in shape.

Rose

1 Unfold the napkin and lay it out in a square.

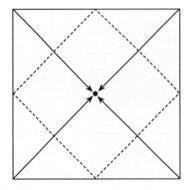

2 Fold the corners into the centre of the napkin.

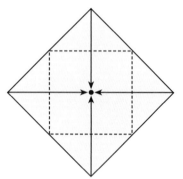

3 Fold the corners into the centre of the napkin for a second time.

4 Turn the whole napkin over so that all the corners folded into the centre are underneath.

5 Fold the corners into the centre once more.

6 Hold the four centre points down by means of an upturned wine goblet.

7 Holding the wine goblet steady, place your hand under each corner and pull up a folded corner of the napkin (petal) on to the bowl of the glass. You now have four petals showing. Now place your hand under the napkin, but between each of the petals, and raise a further four petals. Place on an underplate.

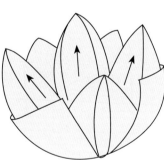

Cockscomb

1 Open the napkin into a square shape.

2 Fold it in half.

3 Fold it in half again to make a square.

4 Rotate the square so that it now forms a diamond shape in front of you. Make sure the four single folds are at the bottom of the diamond.

5 Fold the bottom corner of the diamond to the top corner. You will then have a triangular shape in front of you, with the four single folds on top.

6 Take the right side of the triangle and fold it over on to the centre line.

7 Do the same with the left-hand side.

8 Tuck the two lower triangles (A and B) under the main triangle.

9 Fold the two triangles (C and D) down from the centre line and hold it together. The four single folds should now be on top and at the peak of this fold.

10 Hold this narrow fold firmly, ensuring the four single folds are away from you. In turn, pull each single fold up and towards you.

Triple wave (French fold)

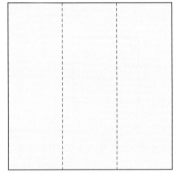 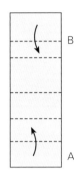 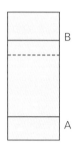

1 Unfold the napkin and lay it out in a square.
Fold the napkin in three along the dotted lines to form a rectangle. NB. For napkins that are already folded in three and then three again, just open the napkin out so that it is in the rectangle shape.

2 Turn the napkin so the narrow side is towards you.
Fold each end of the rectangle, A and B, towards the centre of the napkin, but only one-third of the length of the longer side of the rectangle, i.e. along the dotted lines as shown above.

3 Fold B over once more.

 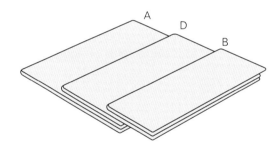

4 Turn edge C under so that A is now the top.

5 The triple wave fold is laid with the steps of the folds away from the customer. A name card or menu, or both, may be placed in between the steps of the fold.

15.4 Laying covers for table service and assisted service

One of the technical terms often used in the foodservice industry is a 'cover' (couvert). The term originates from the custom, up to the fifteenth century, of serving 'under cover' (couvert). This meant to cover the courses and dishes with a large white napkin in order to indicate that all precautions had been taken to avoid the poisoning of guests. In modern foodservice operation the term cover has two definitions, according to the context in which it is being used:

- When discussing how many customers a restaurant or dining room will seat, or how many customers will be attending a cocktail party, we refer to the total number of customers concerned as so many **covers**. For example, a restaurant or dining room will seat a maximum of 85 covers (customers); there will be 250 covers (customers) at a cocktail party; this table will seat a party of six covers (customers).
- When laying a table in readiness for service there are a variety of place settings that may be laid according to the type of meal and service being offered. We refer to this place setting as a certain type of cover being laid. In other words, a **cover** refers to all the necessary cutlery, crockery, glassware and linen required to lay a certain type of place setting for a specific dish or meal.

When deciding on the laying of covers there are two basic service considerations. The first is when cutlery for the meal is to be laid before each course is served. The second is when the cutlery for the meal is to be laid prior to the start of that meal and for all the courses that are to be served. The first approach is known as the à la carte cover, and the second is known as the table d'hôte cover.

> **Key term**
>
> **Covers** – number of people to be served
>
> **Cover** – place setting

À la carte cover

The **à la carte cover** follows the principle that the cutlery for each course will be laid just before each course is served. The traditional cover, given below (and shown in Figure 15.12, therefore represents the cover for hors d'oeuvre, which is the first course in the classic menu sequence. The traditional cover is made up as follows:

- fish plate (centre of cover)
- fish knife
- fish fork
- side plate

- side knife
- napkin
- water glass
- wine glass.

> **Key term**
>
> **À la carte cover** – a type of cover in which the cutlery for each course is laid just before each course is served

Figure 15.12 À la carte cover

Where an à la carte cover has been laid, the cutlery required by the customer for the dishes he or she has chosen will be laid course by course. In other words, there should not, at any time during the meal, be more cutlery on the table than is required by the customer at that given moment in time.

Classic or basic lay-up

There is now a variety of approaches to what is laid for the à la carte form of service. This can include using large decorative cover plates and a side plate and side knife only, or replacing the fish knife and fork with a joint knife and fork. This is sometimes known as a classic or basic lay-up. An example of this type of lay-up is shown in Figure 15.13.

Figure 15.13 Classic or basic cover

If decorative cover plates are used for an à la carte cover, it is common for the first-course plates to be placed on this plate. The first course and the cover plate are then removed when the first course is cleared.

Table d'hôte cover

The **table d'hôte cover** follows the principle that the cutlery for the whole meal will be laid before the first course is served. The traditional cover is made up as follows:

- joint knife
- fish knife
- soup spoon
- joint fork
- fish fork
- sweet fork
- sweet spoon
- side plate
- side knife
- napkin
- water glass
- wine glass.

Key term

Table d'hôte cover – a type of cover in which the cutlery for the whole meal is laid before the first course is served

Again, there are some possible variations to this approach. The sweet spoon and fork may be omitted, for example, or the fish knife and fork replaced with a side knife and small/sweet fork.

Figure 15.14 Table d'hôte cover

Where a table d'hôte cover has been laid the waiter should remove, after the order has been taken, any unnecessary cutlery and relay any extra items that may be required. This means that before the customer commences the meal he or she should have the entire cutlery required for the dishes chosen, set out as their place setting or cover.

Breakfast served in the restaurant

The basic mise-en-place (preparation) for the service of breakfast is normally carried out the evening before, after the service of dinners has finished. To ensure protection against dust until the breakfast staff arrive for duty, the corners of the cloths may be lifted up and over the basic mise-en-place on the tables.

The preparation for service is completed the following morning before the actual service of breakfast commences. This will include turning breakfast cups the right way up and laying the breakfast buffet with items usually served for the first course, such as chilled fruit juices, cereals and fruit compôte, together with all the necessary glasses, plates and tableware required for the service.

The breakfast buffet may also contain preserves and butter and alternatives. Jugs of iced water and glasses should be ready on the buffet throughout the meal, especially if the establishment is catering for American visitors. Preserves are usually now served in individual pots.

Breakfast covers

The breakfast cover may be divided into two types:
- continental breakfast cover
- full breakfast cover.

Cover for a continental breakfast

For a continental breakfast consisting of hot croissants/brioches or hot toast, butter or alternatives, preserves and coffee or tea, the cover would be made up as follows:

- napkin
- side plate and side knife
- sugar basin and tongs or a variety of individual sugar packets in a bowl
- table number
- tea or breakfast cup and saucer with a teaspoon
- stands or under plates for teapot/coffee pot and hot milk/hot water jug.

If the beverage is tea and loose leaves are used then the following additional items will be needed:
- slop basin
- tea strainer.

Figure 15.15 Example of continental breakfast (image courtesy of Six Continents Hotels, London)

Cover for a full breakfast

The full breakfast consists of a number of courses, usually three or four, with a choice of dishes within each course. The cover will therefore include some or all of the following. An example lay-up is given in Figure 15.16.

- napkin
- side plate and side knife
- fish knife and fork
- joint knife and fork
- sweet spoon and fork
- tea or breakfast cup, saucer and teaspoon
- sugar basin and tongs or individual sugar packets (and alternatives) in a bowl
- slop basin
- tea strainer
- stands or under plates for teapot/coffee pot and hot water/hot milk jug
- salt and pepper
- caster sugar in shaker
- table number.

Figure 15.16 Example of a full breakfast cover

Many of the items listed above, for the two types of breakfast, are placed on the table as part of the mise-en-place and before the customer is seated. A number of items are then placed on the table once the customer is seated and has ordered. These include:

- butter dish with butter/alternatives and a butter knife
- preserve dish with preserve and preserve spoon
- jug of cold milk
- other items according to the customer's choice, e.g. mustards
- teapot/coffee pot and hot water/hot milk jug
- toast rack with toast and/or bread basket with hot rolls.

Afternoon tea covers

Two forms of afternoon tea may be available to the customer: afternoon tea and high tea. The latter comprises the afternoon tea menu plus a choice from a limited and modified à la carte menu, generally in the form of a hot snack.

Cover for afternoon tea

The following cover will normally be laid for afternoon tea:

- napkin
- side plate with side or tea knife
- pastry fork
- teacup and saucer and a teaspoon
- jug of cold milk and/or side plate with lemon slices (depending on the tea taken)
- teapot and hot water jug stands or underplates

- sugar basin and tongs or individual packets of sugar (and alternatives)
- slop basin and tea strainer
- butter dish with butter and alternatives, together with a butter knife
- preserve dish on an underplate with a preserve spoon, or side plate with small individual preserve pots
- table number.

The beverage, jug of cold milk, preserve dish and butter dish are only brought to the table when the customers are seated and are not part of the mise-en-place.

Figure 15.17 Example of cover for afternoon tea after the order has been taken

Cover for high tea

The cover for high tea may include:

- napkin
- joint knife and fork
- side plate and side knife
- cruet: salt, pepper, mustard with a mustard spoon
- teacup, saucer and teaspoon
- jug of cold milk and/or side plate with lemon slices (depending on the tea taken)
- teapot and hot water jug stands or underplates

- slop basin and tea strainer
- sugar basin and tongs or individual packets of sugar (and alternatives)
- butter dish with butter and alternatives, together with a butter knife
- preserve dish on an underplate with a preserve spoon or a side plate with small individual preserve pots
- table number.

As with the afternoon tea cover, the beverage, jug of cold milk, preserve dish and butter dish are not part of the mise-en-place and should only be brought to the table when the customers are seated. Any other items of tableware that may be required are brought to the table as for the à la carte service.

Figure 15.18 Example of cover for high tea

Laying the table

Great care should be taken here to ensure uniformity throughout the food and beverage service area. This is one of the many factors which help to determine the ambiance of the room, thus creating a lasting impression upon the customer on his or her arrival.

Laying up

Once the table is clothed-up it should be laid in readiness for service. Cutlery must be laid consistently:

- This is often at 1.25 cm (½ in) from the edge of the table. An alternative to this is to line up the tops of all cutlery.
- Crockery that has a badge or crest is laid so that the badge or crest is at the head or top of the cover.
- After polishing the glasses should be placed at the top right-hand corner of the cover.
- Napkins would now be folded and placed in the centre of the cover.
- Table accompaniments should now be placed on the table according to the custom of the establishment.

Cutlery should be laid from a service salver or service plate. When handling cutlery it is most often held between the thumb and forefinger in the centre at the sides to reduce the risk of finger marks. An alternative to this is to use a service cloth and to hold the items being laid in the service cloth, giving a final polish before setting the items on the table. In some establishments the service staff wear white gloves when laying cleaned and pre-polished tableware on to the tables in order to avoid finger marks.

When laying a cover:

- The cutlery should be laid from the inside to the outside of the cover. This ensures even spacing of the cover and lessens the need to handle the items laid more than is necessary.
- If an à la carte cover is being laid then the first item set on the table should be the fish plate in the centre of each cover.
- If a table d'hôte cover is being laid then the first item to be set on the table should be the napkin or side plate in the centre of each cover. If the side plate is laid in the centre

Preparation for service

of each cover, it will be moved to the left-hand side of the cover when all of the cutlery has been laid.

- The purpose of initially placing something in the centre of the cover is to ensure that the covers are exactly opposite one another and that the cutlery of each cover is the same distance apart.

Examples of the order of laying covers are as follows:

À la carte:
- fish plate at the centre of the cover
- fish knife
- fish fork
- side plate
- side knife
- napkin
- water glass
- wine glass.

Table d'hôte:
- side plate at centre of cover
- joint knife
- fish knife
- soup spoon
- joint fork
- fish fork
- sweet fork
- sweet spoon
- move side plate to the left of cover
- side knife
- napkin
- water glass
- wine glass.

In some operations a trolley is used for storing cutlery. When laying-up, without customers in the restaurant, this trolley is pushed around the tables and the cutlery items are laid after a final polish with a clean, dry tea cloth or waiter's cloth.

Table accompaniments

The table accompaniments required to complete the table lay-up are the same whether an à la carte or table d'hôte cover has been laid:
- cruet: salt, pepper, mustard and mustard spoon
- table number
- floral table centre.

These are the basic items usually required to complete the table lay-up. In some establishments certain extra items will be placed on the table, immediately prior to the service, to complete its lay-up. These may include:
- roll basket
- Melba toast
- peppermill
- butter and alternatives.

15.5 Preparation for self-service, assisted service and single-point service

This section covers self-service (cafeteria and counter) and assisted service (carvery type operations). Preparation for bar service is covered in Section 17.1, page 269.

In order to achieve success in this area, duty rotas and check lists should be drawn up by the supervisor to ensure all tasks are covered and indicating who is responsible for specific tasks. This approach also helps to ensure that staff rotate their duties and are therefore not bored or complacent because they are doing the same job every day.

Cafeteria/counter service

Layout

Within the seating area an allowance of about 0.5–1 m² (3–10 sq ft) per person is sufficient to take account of table space, gangways and access to counters.

- A tray stand is placed at the beginning of the service counter or at the entrance to the service area, so that each customer can collect a tray before proceeding along the counter.
- The layout of the dishes on the counter generally follows the order in which they appear on the menu. This could be as follows: starters, cold meats and salads, bread items, soups, hot fish dishes, hot meat dishes, hot vegetables, hot sweets, cold sweets, ice cream, assorted sandwiches, cakes and pastries, beverages and cold drinks.
- The length of the counter will generally be determined by the size of the menu offered, but should not be too long as this will restrict the speed of service.
- Payment points are sited at the end of the service counter or at the exit to the service area so that customers may pay for their meal before they pass to the seating area.
- Cutlery stands should be placed after the cashiers, together with any ancillary items that may be required, such as napkins and accompaniments.

This helps to ensure that the movement of customers along the service counter remains continuous. Cutlery stands are placed here to allow customers to choose the items they need after making their food and beverage choices. Another advantage of placing the cutlery and ancillary items here is that the customer can return to collect these items, should they initially forget to do so, without interrupting the flow of customers at the service counter.

Figure 15.19 Free-flow cafeteria area (image courtesy of FCSI UK)

Portion and cost control

Great care needs to be taken here and all staff should be made aware of the necessity for good portion control in relation to serving equipment and pre-portioned foods as this ultimately affects profit.

With this form of service, portion control equipment is used to ensure standardisation of the portion size served. Such equipment includes:

- scoops
- ladles
- bowls
- milk dispensers
- cold beverage dispensers.

Pre-portioned foods may also be used, such as:

- butter
- sugars
- jams
- cream
- cheeses
- biscuits.

Carvery-type operations

This is a style of operation that demands good liaison and understanding between both the food service and food preparation staff. This is essential to ensure the guest receives the best possible service. The preparation for service must therefore be adequate both in the room and at the carvery point, and the equipment sufficient in relation to the number of covers it is anticipated will be served. The setting up of the room follows the principles and methods set out for table service.

The carvery

On the carvery point itself the servers and carvers must ensure there is sufficient crockery (main-course plates) for the service and as back-up stock. These will be kept in the hot cupboard or plate lowerators. Small paper napkins should be at hand for the customers to be able to hold the hot main-course plates.

To avoid delays and congestion around the carvery point, it is important to ensure there is sufficient back-up of both equipment and food. The carvers should have available suitable carving equipment for the joints to be carved, together with service and portion control equipment such as slices, ladles, scoops and draining spoons, all in readiness for the food items to be served.

Buffet preparation

The main types of buffet are knife-and-fork, fork and finger buffets. The requirements of a particular occasion and the host's wishes will determine the exact format in setting up the room. Whatever the nature of the occasion there are certain basic principles to follow.

Factors to consider

- The buffet should be set up in a prominent position in the room – the buffet may be one complete display or split into several separate displays around a room. For example: starters and main courses, desserts, hot beverages and bar service.
- There should be ample space on the buffet for display and presentation.
- The buffet should be within easy access of the stillroom and wash-up so that replenishment of the buffet and the clearing of dirty items may be carried out without disturbing the customers.
- There must be enough space for customer circulation – buffets can be positioned and set up so that customers can access one or both sides of the buffet at once.
- Provision should be made for sufficient occasional tables and chairs within the room.
- The total presentation of the room should be attractive and promote a good atmosphere that is appropriate for the occasion.

Setting up the buffet

The exact equipment required when setting up the room will be determined by the occasion, such as a finger buffet for a prize giving, a fork buffet for a retirement party or a knife-and-fork buffet for a wedding party.

The buffet should be covered with suitable cloths (buffet), making sure that:

- the drop of the cloth is within 1.25 cm (approx ½ in) from the ground, all the way around the front and sides of the buffet
- if more than one cloth is used, the creases should be lined up
- where the cloths overlap one another the overlap should be facing away from the entrance to the room
- the ends of the buffet should be box pleated, thereby giving a better overall presentation of the buffet.

Boxing a buffet table

To achieve a neat, crisp finish, the following procedure needs to be carried out with as little handling as possible. This may be achieved by taking the following steps.

1 With assistance, open the screen folded buffet cloth along the length of the buffet table.

2 Stand in front of the table and from the edge place your thumb on the front corner and take the far side of the cloth, lift and bring it back towards you in a semi-circle motion. This will bring the side of the cloth horizontal with the ground.

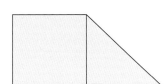

3 The fold on top of the table will now resemble a triangle.

4 Fold this back towards the side of the table, ensuring that the folded edge is in line with the side of the table. Use the back of your hand to flatten the fold. Repeat the procedure at the other end of the table.

The front and sides of the buffet table should be covered and the cloth should be no more than 1.25 cm from the ground.

Should more than one buffet cloth be used to cloth-up the length of the buffet the clothing-up procedure should be repeated. All creases should be in line and slip cloths (white or coloured) may be used to enhance and finish the top of the buffet table.

Buffet displays may be further enhanced by the introduction of a box that has been box-clothed. This can be placed on the buffet table to give extra height and to provide display space for special features.

Table skirting

Figure 15.21 (a) Attaching table skirting to a table edge

Alternative methods of dressing a buffet table may include the use of table skirting (see Figures 15.21 (a) and (b)). Although the initial outlay for such skirting may be high, the ease and simplicity of use makes it very popular for buffet and table decoration. One other feature of skirting is that it is made up of separate panels so that it is comfortable when customers are seated at a table.

Figure 15.21 (b) A buffet table with table skirting attached (images courtesy of Snap-Drape Europe Limited)

Figure 15.22 Example of a stretch cover for a buffet table (image courtesy of Snap-Drape Europe Limited)

A table will be clothed up and then the skirting is attached to the edge of the table by a plastic clip (see Figure 15.21 (a)) which is fitted to the top of the skirting. The skirting is attached to the table by sliding the clip into place over the lip of the table. The plastic clips are removable to allow the fabric to be cleaned.

Alternative methods of covering buffet tables are stretch covers (see Figure 15.22) and custom-fitted covers (see Figure 15.23).

Figure 15.23 Example of custom-fitted buffet table covers (image courtesy of Snap-Drape Europe Limited)

Buffet napkin fold

For buffets, a commonly used napkin fold is the buffet napkin fold (see Figure 15.24). This can be made with paper or linen napkins (see Figure 15.25). It is especially useful as it can be used to hold cutlery so that customers can either help themselves to this at the buffet or it can be given out by staff as customers collect their food from the buffet.

Buffet napkin fold

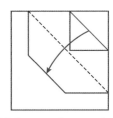

1 Open out the napkin and fold into four, ensuring the four loose edges are at A.

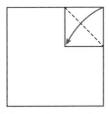

2 Fold down the top flap as indicated.

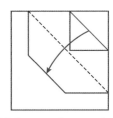

3 Fold the top flap again along the dotted line.

4 Fold down second flap.

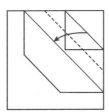

5 Fold second flap again along the dotted line.

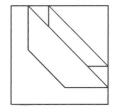

6 Tuck second fold under first fold.

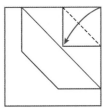

7 Fold napkin along the dotted line, putting the folded part underneath.

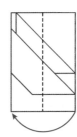

8 Fold napkin along the dotted line.

9 Finished fold.

Setting up the buffet for a reception or buffet tea

When setting up the buffet it is necessary to ensure there is ample space for customer circulation and that a number of occasional tables and chairs are placed around the room. These occasional tables may be covered with clean, well-starched linen cloths and have a small vase of flowers on them.

A raised floral centrepiece on the buffet display can be the focal point around which the dishes of food are placed. Cake stands may also be used for presentation and display purposes.

The afternoon tea tableware, crockery and napkins should be laid along the front of the buffet in groups, with the teacups, saucers and teaspoons concentrated in one or more tea service points as required. Sugar bowls and alternatives may be placed on the buffet or on the occasional tables that are spread around the room.

The tea may be served from urns, which should be kept hot, or pump-dispense insulated jugs, at the separate tea service points along the buffet. Fresh milk should be available in milk jugs. Non-dairy creamers and a range of sugars, sometimes in packets, may also be offered. Tisanes in individual packets together with hot water and slices of lemon might also be available.

15.6 Checklists for preparatory tasks

Checklists are essential to ensure continuity in work methods and to maintain standards. This ensures that whichever member of staff completes a particular task the outcome should always be the same.

Typical checklists for the preparation of a hot food counter, salad bar, dining area, takeaway service and buffet display may be as follows:

Hot food counter preparation

1   Turn on hot counter, allowing enough time for it to heat up to the correct temperature.
2   Ensure that an adequate number of plates for the day's service are available on the hot food service counter or in plate lowerators, and also in an accessible place near the hot food counter as back-up stock.
3   Transfer regenerated hot food from the oven to the hot food counter:
    - use oven cloths when handling hot food to avoid accidents and spillages
    - if appropriate, use a tray when transferring hot food to avoid accidents and spillages.
4   Check hot food menu items for the day and ensure that before service begins there is one dish of each menu item on the hot food counter.
5   Ensure that all hot food is properly covered to prevent any heat loss and deterioration in quality.
6   Have cleaning materials available to wipe any spills.
7   Ensure that for each dish on the hot food counter there is an appropriate service implement. The implements will depend on the dish but are likely to include:
    - large spoons for dishes such as vegetarian lasagne
    - perforated large spoons for dishes such as boiled vegetables (to drain off excess water)
    - ladles for dishes such as seafood mornay, soups and sauces
    - food tongs for dishes such as fried plantain and Caribbean chicken
    - fish slices for dishes such as pizza.

8   When service implements are not in use, remember to return each one to its designated position on the hot food service counter. This prevents any confusion during a busy service period, which may otherwise arise if service implements have been misplaced.

Salad bar counter preparation

1   Turn on the salad bar, allowing enough time for it to chill to the correct temperature.
2   Ensure an adequate number of required salad bowls and plates are available for the day's service of salads, pâtés, cold meats, cold quiches and flans, cold pies, cheeses and items such as taramasalata, humous and tsatsiki. Remember:
    ● bowls are for salads only
    ● plates should be used for the other cold items detailed above.
3   At any one time there should be enough salad bowls and plates on the cold counter for customer service, plus a back-up stock beneath the salad bar.
4   Ensure that service utensils are ready and situated in their designated places for service, including:
    ● salad tongs for dry salads such as freshly prepared green salad
    ● large spoons for wet salads such as champignons à la grecque
    ● fish slices for pâté, cold meats, cold quiches or flans and cold pies
    ● large spoons for taramasalata, humous and tsatsiki
    ● tongs for sliced French sticks and granary rolls.
5   Transfer prepared salad items from the kitchen to the chilled salad bar.
6   Cover all food prior to service.
7   Have cleaning materials ready to maintain appearance and cleanliness.

Preparing dining area for cafeteria/counter service

1   Arrange tables and chairs, making sure they are all clean.
2   Wipe each table.
3   Ensure adequate and clean cutlery provisions for the day's service are in place.
4   Ensure trays are clean and there is an adequate supply in the tray stack, ready for the customers' use.
5   Ensure all salt and pepper cruets are filled and that there is one pair on each table. If using sachets of salt and pepper ensure that there are two bowls containing salt and pepper, respectively, at the counter near the payment point. Other sauces should be immediately available, for example sachets of tomato sauce, brown sauce, mayonnaise and tartare sauce. Sachets of white and brown sugars and alternatives must also be on hand to accompany hot beverages.
6   Fill drinking water jugs and place them in their designated place or make sure the water dispenser is in working order.
7   Ensure the napkin dispenser is filled up.
8   Ensure the clearing-up trolley and lined bins for different kinds of waste are in position.
9   Have cleaning materials ready to wipe clean tables and used trays during service.

Takeaway service preparation

Below is an example checklist for the setting up of a takeaway area prior to service.
1   Ensure all equipment is functioning correctly and switched on.
2   Check all temperature-controlled equipment is at the correct temperature.
3   Make sure adequate supplies of packaging, napkins and plates are available.
4   Ensure that the takeaway menu and prices are clearly displayed.

5 Ensure that sufficient supplies of ready-prepared food items and beverages are to hand to ensure minimum delay on receipt of orders.

6 Prepare foods using the 'batch cooking' approach to ensure the quality and freshness of the product at all times.

7 Ensure that the necessary uniforms, such as hats, overalls and aprons, are worn in all preparation areas.

8 For safety reasons, have available such items as oven cloths, tea towels and trays.

9 Have available and on show sales literature to assist in projecting the image of the establishment.

10 Make sure all serving utensils are available and to hand.

11 Ensure that everything is in its place and therefore easily found as required. This will assist in an efficient work method.

12 Check that waste bins for the different types of waste are available with clean plastic sacks in them.

13 Ensure that all working/serving surfaces are clean and have been wiped down prior to service with the appropriate cleaning materials.

14 Have cleaning materials available for wiping down and in case of spillages.

15 In a takeaway service, care must be taken to ensure the quality of the product, hygiene, packaging and labelling, and temperature control.

Buffet preparation

Duties may include:

- preparation of the buffet table to the supervisor's instructions
- the display of:
  - accompaniments
  - food items
  - underplates for large dishes
  - service spoons and forks and other serving utensils, including carving knives if required
  - hot water jugs for joint knives for pâtés or mousses
  - crockery, glassware and cutlery as required
  - beverage items as required
  - floral decorations
  - placement of chaffing dishes (see Figure 15.26).

Figure 15.26 Chaffing dishes used for buffets (image courtesy of Steelite International)

Testing your learning

1. List five items that would normally be used when setting a table in the restaurant.
2. State one reason why it is important to set up the food and beverage service areas correctly.
3. When clearing the table at the end of the main course, what is the main reason for clearing as much as possible in one visit to the table?
4. How should clean glassware be held when placing it on the table?
5. List three items of service equipment that the server should have available prior to silver serving a main course, that has already been brought into the restaurant.
6. In some establishments members of staff wear white cotton gloves when carrying out preparation tasks. What is the purpose of this?
7. You are responsible for the preparation of the service hotplate. Describe what your duties might be.
8. You are required to 'steam' clean ten wine goblets in readiness for setting the table for a special party. List the equipment required to carry out this task and state how you would convey these wine goblets to the table.
9. Where should the waiter stand when laying a tablecloth?
10. What type of linen is folded into a 'screen' fold?
11. Name two factors you would look for to ensure that a tablecloth had been laid correctly.
12. List three of the more common napkin folds.
13. There are two definitions of the word 'cover'. Describe one of these.
14. List the equipment required to lay a traditional à la carte cover.
15. What would be the first item of equipment set on the table when laying a traditional table d'hôte cover?
16. When laying a cover the cutlery should be laid from the inside to the outside of the place setting – true or false?
17. How would you define 'table accompaniments' in relation to laying a table?
18. In a self-service operation, where would you expect to find the cutlery stands positioned?
19. Identify three of the key factors to consider when setting up for a buffet-style function.
20. What are the main types of buffet? Give an example of when each might be used.

Taking customer orders

16

Units covered

This chapter covers the following units:

Level 1

→ Food and beverage service skills (108)
→ Bar service skills (109)
→ Prepare and clear areas for table/tray service (1FS1, 107)
→ Provide a table/tray service (1FS2, 108)

Level 2

→ Food and beverage service skills (209)
→ Principles of customer service in hospitality, leisure, travel and tourism (211)
→ Provide a counter/takeaway service (1FS4, 110)
→ Serve food at the table (2FS2, 207)
→ Provide a silver service (2FS8, 208)
→ Provide a buffet/carvery service (2FS4, 209)
→ Serve alcoholic and soft drinks (2BS2, 212)
→ Prepare and serve cocktails (2BS3, 213)
→ Prepare and serve wines (2BS4, 214)
→ Prepare and serve hot drinks using specialist equipment (2BS8, 218)

16.1 Personal (or positive) selling

Service staff contribute to the customers' perception of value for money, hygiene and cleanliness, the level of service and the atmosphere that the customer experiences – their contribution to the meal experience is therefore vital.

Good food and beverage service staff must have a detailed knowledge of the food and beverages on offer, be technically competent, have well-developed interpersonal skills and be able to work as part of a team.

Personal selling abilities are essential for all aspects of successful food and beverage service and so all service staff should have good personal selling techniques. Personal selling refers specifically to the ability of the staff in a food and beverage operation to

> **Key term**
>
> **Personal selling** – when food and beverage service staff contribute to the promotion of sales

contribute to the promotion of sales. Sometimes this is also referred to as 'up selling' but more usually 'using positive selling techniques'.

Key term

Up selling – another name for personal selling

For successful personal selling, service staff should be able to:

- describe the food, wines and drinks on offer in an informative and appealing way, that makes the product sound interesting and desirable
- use the opportunity to promote specific items or deals when seeking orders from the customer
- apply positive selling techniques to seek information from the customer in a way that promotes sales, for example rather than asking *if* a sweet is required, ask *which* sweet is required
- use opportunities for the use of positive selling techniques to promote the sale of additional items such as extra garnishes, special sauces or accompanying drinks, such as a dessert wine with a sweet course
- provide a competent service of the items for sale and seek customers' views on the acceptability of the food, drinks and the service.

Positive selling is especially important where there are specific promotions. The promise of a particular type of menu or drink, a special deal or the availability of a particular service can often be devalued by the inability of the staff to fulfil the requirements as promised. It is therefore important to involve service staff when creating particular offers and to ensure that briefing and training are given so that the customer can actually experience what has been promised.

What the server needs to know

Members of staff will feel more confident about selling if they have information about the products on offer – if staff can 'tell well' they can then 'sell well'. Examples of the type of information staff will need to know include:

- a description of what the item is (food, wine or other drink) and an explanation of how it is prepared and served
- where the produce comes from
- what the local animals are fed on
- where the fish are caught
- where the local fruit and vegetables are grown
- how the produce is delivered
- where and how the local drinks are made
- what the specialities of the establishment are and their origin.

There are various ways of enhancing the product knowledge of staff, such as:

- arranging for staff visits to suppliers
- arranging visits to other establishments that use local produce
- seeking out supplier information
- allowing staff to taste products
- arranging for staff to visit local trade fairs
- organising training and briefing sessions for staff.

16.2 Methods of taking food and beverage orders

There are four main methods of taking food and beverage orders from customers. These are summarised in Table 16.1.

Table 16.1 Main methods of taking food and beverage orders

Method	Description
Triplicate	Order is taken; top copy goes to the supply point; second copy is sent to the cashier for billing; third copy is retained by the server as a means of reference during service
Duplicate	Order is taken; top copy goes to the supply point; second copy is retained for service and billing purposes
Service with order	Order is taken; customer is served and payment received according to that order, for example bar service or takeaway methods
Pre-ordered	a) Individually, for example room service breakfast b) Hospital tray system c) Events

All order-taking methods are based on these four basic concepts. Even the most sophisticated electronic system is based on either the triplicate or duplicate method. Orders can be written by staff on check pads or keyed in on handheld terminals.

Customers can also handwrite orders (as in some bar operations) or use electronic systems such as iPads and tablets. There are systems where the menu is projected on to tabletops enabling the seated customers to select their order from these interactive displays.

The written order is then either communicated by hand to the food production or beverage provision areas or, for computer-based systems, electronically to visual display units (VDUs) or printout terminals in those areas. The main billing systems used are described in Section 19.6, page 338.

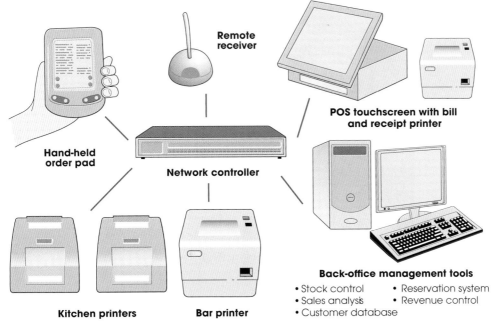

Figure 16.1 Electronic system for order taking and communication to food production and bar areas

Triplicate checking method

As the name implies, this order-taking method is where the food check consists of three copies. To ensure efficient control the server must fill in the following information in the four corners of the check:

- table number or room number
- number of covers
- date
- signature of server taking the order.

Writing the order

When taking the food order from the table d'hôte menu, it is written from top to bottom of the food check.

- Most often the customers initially only order their first and main courses.
- A second new food check is written out for the sweet course, this order being taken after the main course is finished.
- A third new check will then be completed if any beverages such as coffee, tea or tisanes are required.
- Should the food order be taken from the á la carte menu similar procedures are followed except that customers may order course by course according to their needs.

All checks should be written clearly. Abbreviations may be used when taking the order as long as everyone understands them, so that the correct order is completed.

When taking orders a note should be taken of who is having what order. This ensures that specific orders are identified and that they are served to the correct customer. A system for ensuring that the right customer receives the correct food is to identify on the order which customer is having which dish. A check pad design that might be used for this is shown in Figure 16.2. An electronic handheld order-taking system is show in Figure 16.3.

Figure 16.2 Check pad design enabling the waiter to identify specific orders (image courtesy of National Checking Co)

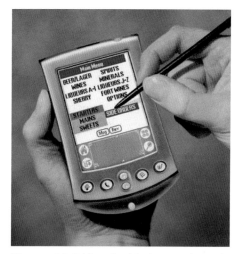

Figure 16.3 Handheld electronic pad for order taking (image courtesy of Uniwell Systems (UK) Ltd/Palm TEQ UK)

Triplicate food check

- The top copy of the food order goes to the kitchen and is handed to the aboyeur at the hotplate (pass).
- The duplicate goes to the cashier who makes out the customer's bill.
- The flimsy, or third copy, is kept by the waiter at his or her workstation for reference.
- Any checks or bills that have to be cancelled should have the signature of either the headwaiter or supervisor on them, as should checks and bills that have alterations made on them.

Duplicate checking method

This is more likely to be found in casual dining establishments where food is being ordered. It is also used for beverage orders.

As the name implies, there are two copies of each of these food checks, each set being serial numbered. The top copy of the food check is usually carbon-backed but, if not, a sheet of carbon must be placed between the top and duplicate copy every time a fresh order is taken.

For control purposes the top copy may have printed on it a server's number or letter. This should be the number or letter given to a waiter on joining the staff. The control and accounts department should be informed of the person to whom the number/letter applies, and he or she retains it throughout their employment.

Perforated checks

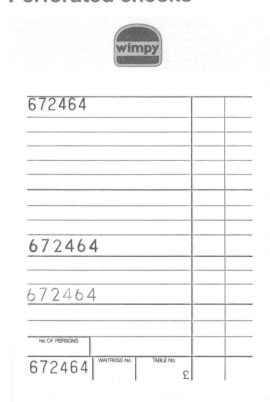

Sometimes the top copy of the set of food and drink checks is made up of a number of perforated slips, usually four to five in number. There is a section at the bottom of the food and drink check for the table number to be entered. The top copy sometimes has a cash column for entering the price of a meal or the dishes ordered but, if this is not the case, the waiter must enter the prices independently on the duplicate copy against the particular dishes ordered.

When writing out a customer's order a different perforated slip should be used for each course or beverage. The server must remember to write out the number of covers and the order on each slip. Before sending each slip to the hotplate, check that the details are entered correctly on the duplicate copy.

Figure 16.4 Example of a duplicated order pad with perforated sections

As soon as the first course is served, and allowing time for this course to be consumed, the second perforated slip showing the next course or beverage order is taken to the hotplate or bar area by the waiter. Similar procedures as with the first course are followed and this dish will then be collected when required. This same procedure is carried on throughout the meal. When there are insufficient perforated slips, a supplementary check pad is used.

Beverage orders

For beverage orders an efficient system must operate to ensure that:

- the correct wine and other drinks are served at the right table
- the service provided is charged to the correct bill
- a record is kept of all wine and other drinks issued from the bar
- management is able to assess sales over a financial period and make comparisons.

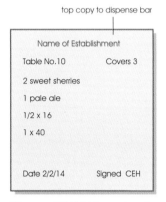

top copy to dispense bar

Name of Establishment

Table No.10   Covers 3

2 sweet sherries

1 pale ale

1/2 x 16

1 x 40

Date 2/2/14   Signed CEH

Figure 16.5 Wine check

The usual system of control is a duplicate check pad. The colour of the check pad may be pink or white, but it is generally pink or some other colour to distinguish it from a food check. This acts as an aid to the cashier and the accounts department in differentiating quickly between food (white) and drink (pink) checks (see Figure 16.5).

When the beverage order is taken service staff must remember to fill in the four items of information required, one in each corner of the check. These are as follows:

- table number or room number
- number of covers
- date
- signature.

Abbreviations are allowed when writing the order as long as they are understood by the bar staff and the cashier. When wines are ordered only the bin number, together with the number of bottles required, should be written down. The bin number is an aid to the bar staff and cellar staff in finding the wine quickly. Each wine in the wine list will have a bin number printed against it.

On taking the order the staff should hand both copies to the bar staff, who retain the top copy, put up the order and leave the duplicate copy with the order. This enables the staff to see which order is which when they come to collect their wines and drinks. After serving the wines and drinks the duplicate copy is handed to the cashier.

16.3 Special checks

In certain instances it is necessary to write out special checks. These are described below.

To follow/suivant

```
Name of Establishment

Table No.4        No of covers 2


           Follow on
         2 Peach flambé




Date 2/2/14        Signed  CEH
```

Figure 16.6 Food check: to follow/suivant

This is used when it is necessary to write out more than one food check for a meal. For instance, where a sweet check is written out after the first and main course have been cleared. At the head of this check should be written the words 'to follow' (suivant), which indicates that one check has already been written out for that particular table (see Figure 16.6).

Supplement

```
Name of Establishment

Table No.4        No of covers 2


          Supplement
           1 Peas N/C




Date 2/2/14        Signed  CEH
```

Figure 16.7 Food check: supplement

When an extra portion of food is required because insufficient has been sent from the kitchen, a special check must be written out headed 'supplement' (see Figure 16.7). This means the food is a supplement to what has already been previously sent and this check should be signed by the headwaiter or supervisor. Normally there is no charge (n/c), but this depends on the policy of the establishment concerned.

Return and in its place/retour and en place

```
Name of Establishment

Table No.4        No of covers 2


            Return
        1 Roast chicken


           In place
        1 Poached Chicken


Date 2/2/14        Signed  CEH
```

Figure 16.8 Food check: return/in its place

Where a wrong dish has been ordered and has to be sent back to the kitchen and replaced, a special check must again be made out (see Figure 16.8). Two main headings are used on this special check, 'retour' (or 'return') and the name of the dish going back to the kitchen, and 'en place' (or 'in its place') and the name of the new dish to be served. If the service being carried out is from an à la carte menu then the prices of the two dishes must be shown.

Accident

Name of Establishment

Table No.4   No of covers 2

Accident
2 vegetables N/C

Date 2/2/14   Signed CEH

Figure 16.9 Food check: accident

It occasionally happens that the waiter may have an accident in the room and perhaps some vegetables are dropped. These must be replaced without any extra charge to the customer. Here a check must be completed headed 'accident' (see Figure 16.9). It will show the number of portions of vegetables required and should be signed by the headwaiter or supervisor in charge. 'No charge' (n/c) is stated on the check to ensure that no charge is made to the customer.

16.4 Variations in order-taking methods

Menu order and customer bill

This shows the menu order and customer's bill combined on one sheet and would be allocated to each party of customers. When the order is taken each customer's requirements would be written down in the column next to the price column. For example, if a party of two customers requested two cream soups, one mushroom omelette and chips, and one fried cod and chips, it would be noted down as shown in Figure 16.10.

Soup		
Cream soup	2.60	2
Hot dishes		
Omelette served with chips and salad		
Plain		
Cheese		
Ham		
Mushroom	4.50	1
Tomato		
Fried cod and chips	4.75	1

Figure 16.10 Quick service menu order and customer bill

Single order sheet

A further simple form of checking is used in cafés, quick-turnover restaurants and department stores. It is a simple form of ordering that may be used, or adapted for use, in various forms of operation.

The menu is normally very limited. The server takes the order and marks down the customer's requirements, calls for the order verbally over the hotplate and, when the customer requests the bill, prices the order sheet and hands it to him/her. The customer then hands it to the cashier on leaving and pays the required amount. There is only one copy of this order and bill combined, and the cashier retains this for control purposes after the customer has made the necessary payment. A hand-written receipt may be given to the customer upon request.

Customer self-complete order

A more modern trend is to ask customers to take their own food and drink order. This method is often found in bar operations and it allows staff to concentrate on the service of food (plate service) and beverages, and to accept payments. The customer order form may take the format shown in Figure 16.11.

Please note down your table number and choice of meals on this slip. Take it with you and place your order and pay at the food till	TABLE NUMBER	Main meals
Starters		
Children's meals	Side orders	Drinks
	Desserts, coffees and teas may be ordered at the food till at the end of your meal	

Figure 16.11 Example of customer self-complete order sheet

The order for the food and drink requirements, once complete, is taken by the customer to the food till and sent electronically by a member of staff to the kitchen where a printed copy is processed for the kitchen staff to produce the dishes required.

After submitting the initial food and beverage order at the food till, an account will be opened using the table number and by processing the customer's credit card. This is so that any additional items such as sweets, coffee or alcoholic beverages may be added to the bill. The customer may then pay the total bill at the conclusion of their meal. These additional items required may be ordered at the food till or at the customer's table.

16.5 Additional considerations when taking food and beverage orders

Taking children's orders

Staff should pay special attention when taking orders for children. Staff need to be aware of:
- the availability and choice of children's meals
- what the children's meals consist of
- portion size, for example the number of sausages
- the cost per head
- the need to make a special note of any specific requests, such as no baked beans
- the need to serve young/small children first as they often become agitated when everyone else has been served and their meal is still to come
- the importance of not overfilling cups, bowls or glasses
- the need to ensure that children's plates are warm rather than hot to avoid mishaps
- providing children with the establishment's 'give aways' in order to keep them occupied, for example a place mat to be coloured in. This can also encourage sales.

Customers with additional needs

Customers with additional needs may require particular attention. These are customers who may be hearing impaired, blind or partially sighted. In these instances consider the following:

- Where applicable, when taking the order, face the customer so they see you full face.
- Speak normally but distinctly.
- Keep descriptions to a minimum.
- Indicate clearly any particular choices that are available with a specific dish, for example a choice of dips being available with a starter, or the different degrees of cooking available for a grilled steak.
- Read back the order given for confirmation.

Other additional needs may relate to vegetarians, those with particular religious or cultural restrictions and those with special dietary needs (see Section 8.2, page 126).

Testing your learning

1 List four of the essential pieces of information that must be written on to the triplicate food check when taking an order.
2 When taking food and beverage orders all service staff should have good personal selling techniques. Explain what is meant by the term 'personal selling'.
3 Identify the four main methods of taking food and beverage orders from customers. Describe one of these methods in detail.
4 When taking food orders, orders are written on the food check from top to bottom – true or false?
5 A customer has ordered a starter, main course, sweet and tisane. How many checks will need to be written out if using the triplicate checking system?
6 Give one reason why great care should be taken when using abbreviations in writing down a food order.
7 A food order has been taken using the triplicate system. Who receives each of the three copies?
8 Briefly describe the duplicate checking method.
9 If the customer is a hotel resident what additional piece of information might be included on the check?
10 Within the context of personal selling, describe two ways in which staff should be able to increase sales.
11 As the supervisor, list three ways by which you may enhance the product knowledge of your staff.
12 What is the term written at the head of a sweet check when using the triplicate checking system?
13 You see the term 'n/c' on a food check, what does this indicate?
14 A wrong dish has been ordered and needs to be sent back to the kitchen and replaced. A special food check must be written out to replace this dish. What are the two main headings you would expect to see on a food check of this nature?
15 List two things that members of staff need to be aware of when taking an order from and serving food to children.

Bar service skills

Units covered

This chapter covers the following units:

Level 1

→ Bar service skills (109)
→ Prepare and clear areas for drink service (1BS2, 113)
→ Serve drinks (1BS2)

Level 2

→ Food and beverage service skills (209)
→ Serve alcoholic and soft drinks (2BS2, 212)
→ Prepare and serve cocktails (2BS3, 213)
→ Prepare and serve wines (2BS4, 214)
→ Prepare and clear the bar area (2BS1, 211)
→ Maintain cellar and kegs (2BS5, 215)
→ Clear dispense lines (2BS6, 216)
→ Receive, store and issue drinks stock (2BS9, 219)

Learning outcomes

This chapter will help you to:

17.1 Preparation for bar service

When carried out well, beverage service indicates that the standards of the establishment are set high and that members of the service staff are well trained. This contributes to sales and return visits to the establishment. Each establishment will have its own service standards and thorough training should be carried out to ensure that these standards are met.

Figure 17.1 Bar and seating area (image courtesy of Gleneagles Hotel, Scotland)

Chapters 10 to 13 provide information on wine and drink lists and various other beverages. Refer to these chapters for information as required. The essential technical service skills used in food and beverage service are described in Chapter 14, page 214, while this chapter explains how these service skills are applied to bar and beverage service. Chapter 15 gives information on preparation for service and Chapter 16 describes the different ways customers' orders can be taken. Refer to these chapters alongside the beverage service information in this chapter.

Generally bar areas are on show to the customer and therefore their overall presentation helps add to the ambiance of an establishment. Three key factors that help to ensure efficient and successful service from the bar are safety, hygiene and attention to detail in the preparation of the bar.

Duties may include:
- Opening the bar.
- Taking bar silver requiring cleaning to the silver person.
- Clearing any debris left from the previous day.
- Wiping down bar tops.
- Cleaning shelves and swabbing the bar floor.
- Checking optics.
- Restocking the bar with beverage items as required.
- Preparing ice buckets, wine coolers, service trays and water jugs.
- Organising check pads and wine lists.
- Cleaning and polishing apéritif and wine glasses.
- Preparing and checking the liqueur trolley for glasses, stock and bottle presentation.
- Preparing the bar service top according to the standards of the establishment. This may include some or all of the following items:

  - cutting board
  - fruit knife
  - fruit: lemons, oranges, apples
  - cucumber
  - fresh eggs (for cocktails)
  - mixing glass and bar mixing spoon
  - Hawthorne strainer
  - wine funnel
  - olives, cocktail cherries
  - cocktail shaker/strainer
  - nuts and crisps
  - coloured sugar

  - Angostura bitters
  - peach bitters
  - Worcestershire sauce
  - cocktail sticks
  - cherries in glass
  - straws in sherry glass
  - tea strainer
  - wine coasters
  - spirit measures
  - soda siphon
  - ice bucket and tongs.

For further information on the bar and bar equipment see Section 3.5, page 54.

Bar service skills

17.2 Glassware

Each establishment will have its own range of glassware for the service of drinks. Examples of glasses for the service of drinks are shown in Figure 17.2. It is also common to use branded glassware for branded products as a company standard.

Cocktail glasses: for cocktails generally and smaller: for Pink Lady and White Lady

The saucer: for Champagne cocktails and Daisies. Not really used much now

The tulip: all Champagne and sparkling wines and also for Buck's Fizz and the Grasshopper

The flute: for sparkling wines generally and also for Brandy Alexander and Kir Royale

Paris goblet: in various sizes and used for wines, waters and beers. Also used for Cobblers, Pina Colada and Green Blazer

Worthington: for bottled beers, soft drinks and for Pimms, Coolers and long drinks such as Fruit Cups

Rocks/Old Fashioned glass: also known as whisky glass, often used for any spirits and mixers. Also used for drinks such as Old Fashioned and Negroni

Highball/Collins glass: used for spirits and mixers and for Highballs, John Collins, Tom Collins, Mint Julep, Tequila Sunrise and Spritzers

Brandy balloon: small for brandies and for B & B and brandy and liqueur-based cocktails, for frappés and for liqueurs. Larger for long drinks such as Pimms

Sour glass: for spirits and mixers and for sours and as an alternative to rocks glass

Martini Cocktail glass: for Dry, Medium and Sweet Martinis and Manhattans but also used for other cocktails

Slim Jim: for spirits and mixers and for sours and as an alternative to highball glass

Copita (sherry): mainly for sherry but also used for sweet wines

Elgin: traditional glass used for sherry in single and double measure (Schooner) sizes. Also in smaller version used for liqueurs

Port or sherry (dock) glass: used for both ports and sherries and also for sweet wines

Lager/pilsner: different sizes used for bottled and draught lager beers

Beer (straight): traditional beer glass in different sizes for half and full measures of any beers and also beer based mixed drinks

Beer (dimple): traditional beer glass in different sizes for half and full measures of any beers and also beer based mixed drinks, including Black Velvet and also Pimms

Figure 17.2 Examples of drinking glasses and their uses

Many establishments serve bar drinks on to a glass coaster (often paper) which may also be branded; stirrers and straws may also be added to drinks at the point of sale. When serving in a lounge or restaurant, drinks should always be carried to the customer on a service salver.

Carrying glasses

There are two basic methods of carrying glasses in food and beverage service areas: by hand or on a service salver (see Section 14.7, page 223).

Glasses may also be carried in glass racks made of plastic. These are often used to carry glasses during the setting up of the restaurant and for functions. These racks allow glasses to be carried in bulk once they have been washed and polished at a central point (see Figure 17.3). Glass racks are also used for dirty glasses (see Figure 17.4) and many can be put through a glass-washing machine.

Figure 17.3 Carrying clean glasses in a rack

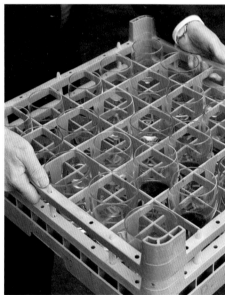

Figure 17.4 Carrying dirty glasses in a rack

17.3 Popular bar drinks

Details of how to serve popular bar drinks are shown in Table 17.1 below.

Table 17.1 Service of bar drinks

Baileys	Either chilled or with crushed ice as frappé
Brandy	No additions to good brandies. Popular mixers for lesser brandies are lemonade or peppermint, together with ice
Campari	Soda water or lemonade together with ice and a slice of orange
Dark rum	Lemonade or cola with ice and slice of lemon/lime or with blackcurrant and no ice
Sherries	Served chilled
Fruit juices	Served chilled or with lemonade, tonic water or sparkling mineral water. Also served with ice and a slice of lemon, orange or other fruit
Gin	Angostura bitters and ice (Pink Gin) or with tonic water or bitter lemon together with ice and a slice of lemon/lime
Liqueurs	May be served alone or on crushed ice as frappé

Bar service skills

Mineral water	Properly served chilled only, but can be with ice and lemon/lime at the request of the guest. Sometimes served with cordials or fruit juices
Aerated waters	Served chilled or with ice and a slice of lemon/lime or orange. Sometimes served with cordials
Pernod	Water and with ice offered and sometimes with cordials or lemonade
Pimm's	Lemonade, ice and slices of lemon, cucumber, apple, orange and a sprig of mint. Sometimes also topped up with ginger ale, soda or tonic water
Port (white)	Serve chilled, sometimes with ice and a slice of lemon/lime
Port (ruby)	Good port served alone. Lesser port either by itself or with lemonade and ice
Sambuca	Coffee bean and set alight (for safety reasons this should be done at the table and the flame extinguished as soon as the oil from the bean is released into the drink)
Vermouths	With ice and a slice of lemon/lime or sometimes with lemonade. Dry vermouths may be served with an olive; sweeter vermouths with a cocktail cherry
Vodka	Tonic water, lemonade, ice and a slice of lemon/lime; orange cordial, ice and a slice of orange; lime cordial, ice and a slice of lemon/lime; a range of fresh juices with ice and slice of lemon/lime
Whisk(e)y	Natural or with water (often still mineral water), with ice offered, or with dry ginger, Canada Dry or soda water and with ice offered
Wine	By the glass and sometimes for white wine, with soda water, or sparkling mineral water or lemonade as a spritzer
White rum	Natural with ice or with cola, ice and a slice of lemon/lime

17.4 Non-alcoholic bar beverages – cold

Aerated waters

Aerated waters may be served on their own, chilled, in either Slim Jim tumblers, wine goblets, Highball glasses or 34.08 cl (12 fl oz) short-stemmed beer glasses, depending on the requirements of the customer and the policy of the establishment. They may also accompany other drinks as mixers, for example:

- whisky and dry ginger
- gin and tonic
- vodka and bitter lemon
- rum and cola.

Natural spring waters/mineral waters

Natural spring or mineral waters are normally drunk on their own for medicinal purposes or where the tap water quality cannot be guaranteed. Some mineral waters may be mixed with alcoholic beverages to form an appetising drink. In all cases they should be drunk well chilled, at approximately 7–10°C (42–48°F). If drunk on their own, they should be served in an 18.93 cl (6⅔ fl oz) Paris goblet or a Slim Jim tumbler. Examples include Apollinaris, Buxton, Malvern, Perrier and Badoit.

Squashes

A squash may be served on its own diluted by water or lemonade. Squashes are also used as mixers for spirits and in cocktails, or used as the base for drinks such as fruit cups.

- **Service from the bar**: a measure of squash should be poured into a tumbler or 34.08 cl (12 fl oz) short-stemmed beer glass containing ice. This is topped up with iced water or the soda syphon. The edge of the glass should be decorated with a slice of fruit where applicable and drinking straws added.

- **Service from the lounge or restaurant**: the wine butler or lounge waiter must take all the items required to give efficient service on a service salver to the customer. These items will include:
  - a measure of squash in a tumbler or 34.08 cl (12 fl oz) short-stemmed beer glass
  - straws
  - jug of iced water (on an underplate to prevent the condensation running on to the table)
  - small ice bucket and tongs (on an underplate because of condensation)
  - soda syphon
  - a coaster on which to place the glass in the lounge.

The coaster should be placed on the side table in the lounge and the glass containing the measure of squash placed on the coaster. The waiter should then add the ice and ask whether the customer would like iced water or soda to be added. Drinking straws should be placed in the glass at the last moment if required. It may be necessary to leave the iced water and ice bucket on the side table for the customer. If this is the case they should be left on underplates.

Juices

Juices are held in stock in the bar as either bottled/canned/carton or freshly squeezed.

All juices should be served chilled in a 14.20 cl (5 fl oz) goblet or alternative glass.
- **Tomato juice**: should be served chilled in a 14.20 cl (5 fl oz) goblet or other glass, on a doily on an underplate with a teaspoon. The Worcestershire sauce should be shaken, the top removed, placed on an underplate and offered as an accompaniment. The goblet may have a slice of lemon placed over the edge as additional presentation.
- **Fresh fruit juice**: if fresh fruit juice is to be served in the lounge, then the service should be similar to the service of squash described above, except that a small bowl of caster sugar on an underplate with a teaspoon should be taken to the table.

Syrups

Syrups are never served as drinks in their own right. They are concentrated, sweet, fruit flavourings used as a base for cocktails, fruit cups and milkshakes or mixed with soda water as a long drink.

17.5 Cocktails

There are four main methods of making cocktails:
- shaken, for example a Whisky Sour
- stirred, for example a Dry Martini
- built (sometimes referred to as 'muddled'), for example a Mojito
- layered (sometimes referred to as 'poured'), for example a B52.

Bar service skills

Figure 17.5 (a) Whisky Sour   **Figure 17.5 (b)** Dry Martini

Figure 17.5 (c) Mojito   **Figure 17.5 (d)** B52

A list of cocktail and mixed-drink ingredients and methods is given in Annex A, page 346. Examples of bar equipment are shown in Section 3.5, page 53.

Cocktails should always be served well chilled in an appropriately sized glass with the correct garnish, straw and umbrella, according to the policy of the establishment. Many cocktails are served in a traditional V-shaped cocktail glass (often called a Martini glass) but, if the cocktail is a long drink, then a larger glass such as a Slim Jim or Highball will be better suited. The key consideration here should be the presentation of the cocktail as seen by the customer.

Points to note when making cocktails

- Ice should always be clear and clean.
- Do not overfill the cocktail shaker.
- Effervescent drinks should never be shaken.
- To avoid spillage, do not fill glasses to the brim.
- When egg white or yolk is an ingredient, first break the egg into separate containers before use.
- Serve cocktails in chilled glasses.
- To shake, use short and snappy actions.
- Always place ice in the shaker or mixing glass first, followed by non-alcoholic and then alcoholic beverages.
- To stir, stir briskly until the blend is cold.
- As a general rule a mixing glass is used for those cocktails based on liqueurs or wines (clear liquids).

- Shakers are used for cocktails that might include fruit juices, cream, sugar and similar ingredients.
- When egg white or yolk is an ingredient then a Boston shaker should normally be used.
- Always add the garnish after the cocktail has been made and to the glass in which the cocktail is to be served.
- Always measure out ingredients; inaccurate amounts spoil the balance of the blend and taste.
- Never use the same ice twice.

17.6 Service of wines

The sommelier, wine waiter or bar staff must be able to advise and suggest wines to the customer as required. This means that the wine waiter must have a good knowledge of the wines on the wine list and be able to identify examples of wines that will match well with the menu dishes. Immediately after the food order has been taken the wine list should again be presented to the host so that he or she may order wine to accompany the meals that the guests have ordered.

There are seven key aspects of serving wines.

1   The wine waiter must be able to describe the wines and their characteristics honestly – bluffing should be avoided.
2   Always serve the wine before the food. Avoid any delay in serving the food once the wine has been served.
3   Serve wine at the correct temperature – it is better to tell the customer that the wine is not at the right temperature for service rather than resorting to quick heating or cooling methods as these can damage the wine.
4   Treat wine with respect and demonstrate a high level of technical skill, supported by the use of high-quality service equipment. As the customer is paying for the wine and the service, they have the right to expect their chosen wine to be treated with care.
5   When pouring wine, the neck of the bottle should be over the glass but not resting on the rim in case of an accident. Care should be taken to avoid splashing the wine and, when pouring is complete, the bottle should be twisted and raised as it is taken away. This prevents drops of wine falling on the tablecloth or on the customer's clothes. Any drops on the rim of the bottle should be wiped away with a clean service cloth or napkin.
6   Do not overfill glasses. Fill glasses to the right level, usually to the widest part of the bowl or two-thirds full, whichever is the lesser. Sparkling wine served in a flute is usually filled to about two-thirds to three-quarters of the glass. Doing so helps the wine to be better appreciated and looks better too.
7   Avoid unnecessary topping up – it does not sell more wine and it often irritates customers. Another reason for being cautious about topping up wine glasses is that the customer may be driving. If wine is constantly topped up the customer may not notice how much they are consuming. In general, it is preferable to ask the customer about topping up their wine.

Serving temperatures for wines

- **Red wines**: 15.5–18°C (60–65°F). Some young red wines may also be drunk cool at about 12.5–15.5°C (55–60°F).
- **White wines**: 10–12.5°C (50–55°F).
- **Dessert wines, Champagne and other sparkling white wines**: 4.5–10°C (40–50°F).

Wine glasses

Wines may be served in the types of glasses indicated below:

● Champagne and other sparkling wines: flute or tulip-shaped glass
● German and Alsace wines: traditionally long-stemmed German wine glasses but nowadays a medium-size wine glass
● White wines: medium-size wine glass
● Rosé wines: flute or medium-size wine glass
● Red wines: large wine glass

Examples of wine bottle types and glasses for wine are shown in Figure 17.6.

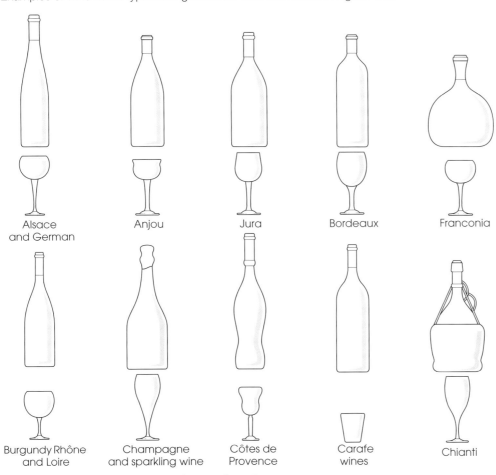

Figure 17.6 Bottle types and glasses for wine

Service of white wine

Obtain the wine from the bar or storage area. Check that the order is correct and that the wine is clear and at the correct service temperature. Take it to the table in an ice bucket and place the ice bucket in a stand.

1 Present the bottle to the host with the label showing – this allows him or her to check that the correct wine is to be served. Ensure the correct glasses are placed on the table for the wine to be served. Make sure a clean napkin is tied to the handle of the ice bucket – this is used to wipe away condensation and water from the outside of the bottle before pouring the wine.

2 Using a wine knife, cut the foil all the way round, below or above the bottle rim, at the top of the bottle (some bottles have small caps rather than foils). The top of the foil only is then removed and the top of the cork is wiped with the napkin.

3 Remove the cork using a wine knife. Smell the cork in case the wine is 'corked'. Place the cork in the ice bucket. If the wine is a high-quality vintage wine then the cork would generally be placed on a side plate at the head of the host's cover. This cork should have the name and year of the wine printed on it. Wipe the inside of the neck of the bottle with the napkin. Wipe the bottle dry.

4 Hold the bottle for pouring so that the label may be seen. Use the waiter's cloth in the other hand, folded, to catch any drips from the neck of the bottle. Give a taste of the wine to the host, pouring from the right-hand side. He or she should acknowledge that the wine is suitable, i.e. that it has the correct taste, bouquet and temperature.

5 Serve ladies first, then gentlemen and the host last, always commencing from the host's right. However, nowadays service often follows from one customer to the next, anti-clockwise.

6 Fill each glass two-thirds full or to the widest part of the bowl – whichever is the lower. This leaves room for an appreciation of the bouquet.

7   Replace the remaining wine in the wine bucket and refill the glasses when necessary.

8   If a fresh bottle is required, then fresh glasses should be placed upon the table, and the host asked to taste the new wine before it is served.

9   On finishing pouring a glass of wine, twist the neck of the bottle and raise it at the same time to prevents drops from falling on the tablecloth.

Note

For bottles with screw caps, the opening procedure is to hold the whole length of the seal in the opening hand and to hold the base of the bottle in the other hand. The closure is held firmly in the opening hand with more pressure from the thumb and first finger around the cap itself. The bottle is then sharply twisted using the hand holding the base. There will be a click and then the upper part of the screw top can be removed.

Service of red wine

The basic procedure for the opening and serving of red wines is the same as for white wines described above. If the red wine to be opened is young the bottle may stand on an underplate or coaster on the table and be opened from this position. This adds to the overall presentation of the bottle and may prevent drips of red wine from staining the tablecloth. Although there is no technical reason why red wine should be served with the bottle in a wine basket or wine cradle, these are used in a number of establishments for display/presentation purposes. They also assist in retaining the sediment, found in some older red wines, in the base of the bottle.

The cork should be removed from the bottle of red wine as early as possible so that the wine may attain room temperature naturally. If the wine is of age and/or is likely to have heavy sediment, then the wine should be **decanted**. It should be placed in a wine basket when first presented to the customer. Placing the bottle in a wine basket helps to keep the bottle as horizontal as possible, comparable to its storage position in the cellar, in order to prevent the sediment from being shaken up. The wine should then be opened and decanted. Alternatively, if the wine is ordered in advance, it can be left standing (unopened) for a few days before opening to allow any sediment to drop to the bottom of the bottle.

> **Key term**
>
> **Decanting** – the movement of wine from its original container to a fresh glass receptacle, leaving the sediment behind

Decanting wine

Decanting is the movement of wine from its original container to a fresh glass receptacle, leaving the sediment behind.

There is a trend nowadays to decant younger red wines, simply because exposure to air improves the bouquet and softens and mellows the wine. Decanting also enhances the appearance of the wine, especially when presented in a fine wine decanter. However, the permission of the host should always be sought before decanting a wine in the restaurant.

Decanting wine

1 Extract the cork carefully. The cork may disintegrate because of long contact with alcohol, so be careful. Place a single point light behind the shoulder of the bottle, a candle if you are decanting in front of customers, but a torch, light bulb or any light source will do.

2 Carefully pour the wine into an absolutely clean decanter. The light will reveal the first sign of sediment entering the neck of the bottle.

3 As soon as sediment is seen, stop pouring into the decanter but continue pouring into a glass. The latter wine, when it settles, can be used as a taster or for sauces in the kitchen.

4 The wine should always be checked to make sure that it is clear before being presented at the table for service.

5 If the wine is not clear after decanting then it should be decanted again into a fresh decanter, but this time using a wine funnel that has a piece of fine muslin in the mouth of the funnel. If the wine is still not clear it should not be served and a new bottle of the wine selected. It is also more common now for a wine funnel to be used as part of the decanting process generally.

Very old red wine can break up with too much exposure to air. These wines can be left to stand for a few days to allow the sediment to settle in the bottom of the bottle. The bottle is then opened before the meal is served and the wine is poured very carefully straight into the glass, with the bottle held in the pouring position as each glass is approached. This prevents the wine slopping back to disturb the sediment. Sufficient glasses should be available to finish the bottle, thereby ensuring that the wine does not re-mingle with its sediment during the pouring process.

Service of Champagne and sparkling wine

The same method is used for opening all sparkling wines. The wine should be served well chilled in order to obtain the full effect of the secondary fermentation in the bottle – effervescence and bouquet. The pressure in a Champagne bottle, due to its maturing and secondary fermentation, is about 5 kg per cm² (about 70 lb per sq in). Great care must therefore be taken not to shake the bottle otherwise the pressure will build up and could cause an accident.

Service of Champagne and sparkling wine

1 After presenting the bottle to the host, the wine is ready for opening.

2 The neck of the bottle should be kept pointed towards a safe area in the restaurant during the opening process to avoid any accidents to customers should the cork be released suddenly.

3 The thumb should be held over the cork with the remainder of the hand holding the neck of the bottle.

4 The foil around the top of the cork is separated from the foil around the neck of the bottle by pulling on the tab on the foil, or by using a wine knife to cut it. The foil is not removed.

5 The wine cage is untwisted and is carefully loosened, but not removed.

6 Then, holding the cork and the cage in one hand, the bottom of the bottle should be twisted with the other hand to slowly release the cork.

7 The cork is removed.

Sparkling wine should be served in a flute or tulip-shaped glass, from the right-hand side of each customer. It is also worth considering lifting and holding the glass by the stem so as to pour the wine more easily and quickly, and to reduce the frothing of the wine.

Serving wine by the glass

Many establishments offer a range of wines for sale by the glass. Wines are mostly offered in 125 ml or 175 ml measures. With the exception of sparkling wines, it is often better to serve the wine in a glass larger than the measure. This allows the aroma to develop in the glass and the wine to be better appreciated. Many establishments now also pour a measure of wine into a small carafe or pichet for the service of wine by the glass. This then allows the customer to pour the wine into their glass as required.

Storage of open wine

Once a bottle is opened the wine can deteriorate quite quickly as it reacts with the air and oxidises. There are various methods of keeping wines once they have been opened. Some work by creating a vacuum within the bottle and then sealing the bottle with a removable closure, either manually or mechanically. Another system involves putting a layer of carbon dioxide gas (CO_2) on the surface of the wine, which prevents air getting to it.

17.7 Service of beers and ciders

Beer and ciders should be served at a temperature of 12.5–15.5°C (55–60°F), with lagers generally cooler than other beers at 8.0–10.5°C (48–51°F). Many different varieties of bottled beers are also served chilled. Draught beer and cider, on its route from the keg/cask to the pump, often passes through a chilling unit.

Types of beer and cider glasses

All glasses used should be spotlessly clean with no finger marks, grease or lipstick on them. Pouring beer into a dirty glass will cause it to go flat very quickly. The main types of beer and cider glasses are:

- half pint/pint tankards for draught beer
- pint tumblers for draught beer
- tumblers for any bottled beer
- short-stemmed 34.08 cl (12 fl oz) beer glass for stouts
- lager glass for lager
- wine goblets in various sizes including 22.72, 28.40 and 34.08 cl (8, 10 and 12 fl oz) for brown/pale/strong ales.

Increasing sales of beers to be consumed with restaurant meals has encouraged changes in styles of glassware used. Generally these beer glasses, although often based on the listing above, are more elegant in style and made of higher-quality glass; they may also be branded to match the product.

Pouring beers and ciders

Draught or bottled beer and cider should be poured slowly down the inside of the glass, with the glass held at a slight angle (see Figure 17.10). This is especially important where a beer may produce a large head if it is not poured slowly and carefully, for example, Guinness or stouts.

Pouring bottled beers

1 Hold the bottle and the glass at an angle to each other. The neck of the bottle should not be placed in the beer when pouring.

2 Pour the beer slowly so as not to form too much of a head.

3 As the bottle is emptied the glass should be upright in the hand.

- If a bottled beer has a sediment, a little beer must be left in the base of the bottle to ensure that the sediment does not go into the poured beer.

Draught beers should have a small head on them. The bar person should ensure that he or she serves the correct quantity of beer with a small head and not a large head to make up the quantity required. A beer in good condition will have a head, or froth of the beer, clinging to the inside of the glass as the beer is drunk. This is sometimes called lace on the glass. Some establishments will also train staff to create a pattern in with the froth to tie in the brand such as a shamrock for Guinness.

Service of draught beer

1 Hold the glass at an angle when the pouring begins as the tap of the beer engine is pulled.

2 Ensure the beer is poured slowly so as not to form too much of a head, and bring the glass upright as the glass fills up with beer

17.8 Service of liqueurs

Liqueurs (sweetened and flavoured spirits) may be served by the glass or, in a restaurant, they may also be served from a liqueur trolley at the table.

If a customer asks for a liqueur to be served **frappé**, for example crème de menthe frappé, it is served on crushed ice and a larger glass will be needed. The glass should be two-thirds filled with crushed ice and then the measure of liqueur poured over the ice. Two short drinking straws should be placed into the glass before the liqueur is served.

If a liqueur is requested with cream, for example Tia Maria with cream, then the cream is slowly poured over the back of a teaspoon to settle on the top of the selected liqueur.

Key term

Frappé – served on crushed ice

Basic equipment required on a liqueur trolley:

- assorted liqueurs
- assorted glasses – liqueur/brandy/port
- draining stand
- 25 and 50 ml measures
- service salver
- drinking straws (short stemmed)
- jug of double cream (for topping drinks such as Tia Maria)
- teaspoons
- ice
- wine list and check pad.

Other beverages served from the liqueur trolley include brandies and fortified (liqueur) wines such as port or Madeira.

Figure 17.12 Bar trolley for the service of liqueurs (image courtesy of Euroservice UK)

17.9 Beverage stock control

Determining stock levels

For the establishment as a whole, the central stock levels needed to meet expected sales demand may be determined by using past sales data. As well as ensuring stock levels meet expected demand, using this historic data can also minimise the amount of money tied up in the stock being held. Good stock control can be supported by the application of a '**just in time**' (**JIT**) approach to purchasing. JIT involves only ordering stock as required in order to meet forecasted demand, rather than holding unnecessarily high stock levels, just in case.

Key term

Just in time (JIT) – only ordering stock when it is needed

All the individual outlets within an establishment, such as the lounge, lounge bar, cocktail bar, saloon bar, brasserie, dispense bars and floor service, should draw their stock on a daily or weekly basis from the cellar. Each outlet will hold a set level of stock or liquor called '**par stock**' that is sufficient for a service period – this can be a session or a day, or up to a week. The level of the par stock will be determined by:

- the amount of storage space available in the service areas
- expected sales demand
- time it take for deliveries.

At the end of each service period, each individual outlet will **requisition** for the amount of drink consumed in that one service period to ensure that the stock level is brought back up to par.

Key terms

Par stock – set level of stock

Requisition – complete an order for stock from the stores

Receiving stock

When receiving stock it is important that the quantity, quality and use by dates are checked. Use the delivery note to check against the order form because, once the delivered stock is signed for, it then becomes the responsibility of the establishment. Items that are damaged during transportation and delivery must be identified and the supplier will issue a credit note so the establishment does not get charged for these products. Prior to the delivery it is advisable to get the empty kegs, casks, crates and gas cylinders ready for collection. These are chargeable containers and should be returned to the supplier once they are empty. This also prevents a build-up of empty stock in your cellar.

Beverage control procedures

In any foodservice establishment where income is received from the sale of wine and drink, a system of control and costing must be put into operation. The system used will depend entirely on the policy of the establishment. Some or all of the record books listed in Table 17.2 may be necessary, depending on the requirements of the foodservice operation.

Table 17.2 Record books used in beverage control

Book	Used to record
Order book	Orders made to suppliers
Goods inwards/goods received book	Goods received from suppliers
Goods returned book	Goods that are sent back to suppliers
Returnable containers book	Returnable containers sent back to suppliers
Cellar ledger	Stock movement in and out of the cellar
Bin cards	Stock of individual lines in the cellar
Requisition book	Restocking orders for individual service areas
Daily consumption sheets	Usage of stock in individual service areas
Ullage book	Breakage, spillage and wastage
Off-sales book	Items sold at off-sale prices
Transfers book	Movement of stock between different service areas

Although referred to as books here, most modern systems are computer-based. However, the basic processes are the same whatever the method being used to record the data. A summary of the basic steps in bar and cellar control is given in Figure 17.13.

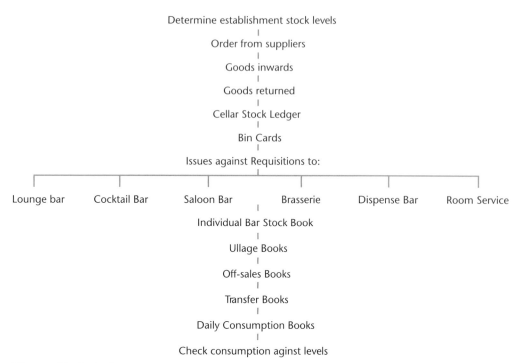

Determine establishment stock levels
|
Order from suppliers
|
Goods inwards
|
Goods returned
|
Cellar Stock Ledger
|
Bin Cards
|
Issues against Requisitions to:

| Lounge bar | Cocktail Bar | Saloon Bar | Brasserie | Dispense Bar | Room Service |

Individual Bar Stock Book
|
Ullage Books
|
Off-sales Books
|
Transfer Books
|
Daily Consumption Books
|
Check consumption aginst levels

Figure 17.13 Basic steps in bar and cellar control

Stock taking

All drinks are valuable commodities and have a limited shelf life. Use by dates must be carefully observed and managed to avoid unnecessary waste that is costly to the business. Regular stock takes will ensure the correct level of stock for the business is maintained and will provide a check against inaccuracies and theft. Businesses will conduct stock takes on a weekly or monthly basis depending on their policy. Spot checks can also take place at other times. If you are responsible for completing a stock take, any discrepancies must be reported to your manager.

17.10 Maintain safety and security of cellars

Safety procedures

- Cellars can be dangerous places to work in because of the many hazards present. Correct working practice should be respected and followed at all times to ensure the safety of the employees and customers.
- Appropriate protective clothing to be worn when working in the cellar. Safety goggles, steal toe-capped shoes, aprons and heavy-duty gloves should be available for employees to use.
- Gas cylinders should be secured to the cellar wall with a chain, safety strap or clamp when in use. Empty or unused cylinders should be laid down on the cellar floor to prevent them falling over.
- Carbon dioxide and nitrogen gases can leak from damaged casks, joints and connections. Both these gases are odourless and, if inhaled, can cause a person to become unconscious. If a leak is suspected then the gas supply must be turned off immediately.

- Cylinders are high-pressure containers that are charged to 660 psi (pounds per square inch) and can be lethal if damaged. If a cylinder is damaged do not use it and inform your manager or supplier.
- Always use correct manual handling of casks, kegs and gas bottles. To prevent back injury kegs and barrels should be moved around the cellar by rolling them across the floor. These are heavy items that may require two people to lift them safely.
- Casks remaining on the floor should be bung uppermost to better withstand the pressure.
- The cellar floor should be washed down weekly with a weak solution of chloride and lime (mild bleach).
- All cellar equipment should be kept scrupulously clean.
- Drink crates should be stored correctly so they do not topple over. Full crates should not be stacked on empty crates as they will be top heavy and become unstable.
- Do not tamper with a cask or barrel. These are pressurised containers whether they are empty or full. If a cask or barrel is damaged do not use it and inform your manager or supplier.

Figure 17.14 Cellar equipment

A cellar should only be used for the storage of cellar equipment and drinks. Equipment that you would expect to find in a cellar is listed in Table 17.3.

Table 17.3 Cellar equipment

Recommended equipment	Use
Thermometers	Used to check cellar and beer temperatures
Humidity gauges	Used to check the humidity of the cellar
Stainless steel buckets	Collecting **ullage** and to clean equipment
Brushes	Different sizes to clean beer lines and equipment
Mallet	Used to punch the **shive** on a cask ales so a **spile** can be fitted to let the beer vent
Dipstick	To check the levels of beer
Mop and bucket	To clean the cellar floor
Cask taps, spiles, corks, bungs	To maintain the dispensing of beer

Key terms

Ullage – unable to be sold. Collected from drip trays or left in the bottom of kegs or casks

Shive – wooden disc placed within opening of a beer cast

Spile – peg that fits the air hole of the shive

Security procedures

A cellar should always be locked when left unattended. Access maybe restricted to key personnel to make the control of stock easier to enforce. Remember that the contents of a cellar are valuable and are susceptible to pilfering.

17.11 Prepare kegs, casks and gas for use

Cellar storage of beer

Keg beers

Keg beers have a typical maximum shelf life of 12 weeks. Keg beer should be consumed within three days after the container has been opened, but this can be extended to up to seven days with correct temperature control and good hygiene practices.

- It is good practice to turn off the supply of carbon dioxide to the keg between sessions, because the beer can absorb the carbon dioxide making it difficult to dispense. To alleviate this problem, a mixed-gas system of carbon dioxide and nitrogen can be used.
- Before using the keg check the best before date, that the new keg is full and that the gyle label is attached to the spear head.
- Turn off the gas supply to the keg.

Figure 17.15 Keg beers stored in a cellar

- Release the **broaching head** correctly (there are two main types: lever operated and pushdown, twist and lock).
- Remove the used keg and replace with the new keg.
- Remove the plastic **gyle cap** from the **spear head** and connect the broaching head to the keg.
- Turn on the gas supply and ensure the beer is flowing at the beer tap.

Cask conditioned beer

Figure 17.16 Cask beers stored on a stillage rack with shive and spile in place

Cask conditioned beers have a typical maximum shelf life of five weeks. Once the cask has been delivered to the cellar it needs to be stillaged by being placed on a **stillage rack** and secured in place using scotches. It can take between 12 and 36 hours for the yeast to settle and the beer to become clear and bright and ready for dispensing. The cask beer should be consumed within three days after the container has been broached.

To prepare the cask for use a wooden peg is tapped into the cask closure to release the excess carbon dioxide. There are two types of pegs:

- Soft pegs made of porous wood that allow the gas to vent naturally.

- Hard pegs made of hard wood or plastic that are impervious to gas and keep the natural condition of the cask when it is not being dispensed.

Finally, a tap is driven through the **keystone** of the cask so the **beer line** can be connected.

Factors that determine good beer cellar management

- Good ventilation to maintain the air quality, prevent dampness and the growth of mould.
- Effective lighting so stock and equipment can easily be located and to maintain a safe environment.
- Walls and ceiling must be kept clean and maintained.
- The floor should be kept clean, dry and free of rubbish.
- Even temperatures of 13–15°C (55–58°F) to prevent the spoilage of stock.
- Avoidance of strong draughts and wide ranges of temperature.
- Beer left in pipes after closing time should be drawn off.
- Care should be taken that the cellar is not overstocked as stock takes up space and costs money.
- All spiles removed during service should be replaced after closing time.
- Any ullage should be returned to the brewery as soon as possible.
- Reordering should be carried out on one set day every week after checking the stock of beers, wines, minerals, etc.
- Strict rotation of stock must be exercised, with new bottle crates or cases being placed at the rear and old stock pulled to the front for first issue.

By following these points you should be able to maintain a consistent, quality product, but sometimes unexpected problems do occur – see Table 17.4 for common faults and cures.

Table 17.4 Fault diagnosis of beer

Fault	Cause	Cure
Cloudy beer	Dirty beer lines	Clean beer lines
	Low cellar temperature	Check cellar temperature
Fobbing	Dirty beer lines	Clean beer lines
	High cellar temperature	Check cellar temperature
Flat beer	Dirty glass	Check glass washing procedures
Sour beer	Out-of-date or infected beer	Change beer keg or cask Return to supplier
Warm beer	Failure of in-line cooling system	Check that the cooling system is working. If not call an approved engineer
Low gas pressure	Empty gas cylinder	Check gas cylinder
	Gas leak in the system	Check pipes and connections for leaks by using a detergent around the joints. If bubbles appear then gas is escaping

> **Key terms**
>
> **Keystone** – disc in the base of a beer cask in which the beer tap is installed
>
> **Beer line** – plastic hose connecting the keg or cask (barrel) to the beer engine or dispensing unit

> **Key term**
>
> **Fobbing** – excess foaming of beer

Cellar storage of wine

Wines should ideally be stored in an underground cellar with a northerly aspect and is free from vibrations, excessive dampness, draughts and odours. The cellar should be absolutely clean and well ventilated, with only subdued lighting and a constant cool temperature of 12.5°C (55°F) to help the wine develop gradually. Humidity should be kept between 45 per cent and 65 per cent to prevent dampness and the wine corks from drying out.

Wines should be stored on their sides in bins so that the wine remains in contact with the cork. This keeps the cork expanded and prevents air from entering the wine – a process that quickly turns wine to vinegar. Wines should also be stored with labels uppermost. This ensures that the wines can be easily identified and it protects the label by keeping it away from the base surface of the bin. It also ensures that any sediment is always located on the side of the bottle away from the label. This approach is also used for wines with alternative stoppers such as screw tops.

White, sparkling and rosé wines are kept in the coolest part of the cellar and in bins nearest the ground (because warm air rises). Red wines are best stored in the upper bins. Commercial establishments usually have special refrigerators or cooling cabinets to keep sparkling, white and rosé wines at serving temperature.

Other drinks

Spirits, liqueurs, squashes, juices and mineral waters are stored upright in their containers, as are fortified wines. The exceptions are port-style wines, which are destined for lying down, and these are treated as for wines above.

17.12 Clean drink dispense lines

Keg beer lines should be cleaned once a week on average. This will prevent the build-up of yeast deposits that will eventually restrict the flow of the beer. Clean beer lines will keep the beer clear and bright. All cleaning chemicals should be kept in a separate locked cupboard. Before using a cleaning agent always check the manufacturer's instructions.

Before handling cleaning fluid you should wear the appropriate protective clothing: PVC gloves, goggles and an apron.

- Turn off the gas supply to the keg.
- Remove the keg couplers and clean them in a bucket of warm water with a cleaning fluid solution mix and rinse with clean water.
- Clean the cleaning socket that the keg coupler connects with, with a cleaning fluid solution mix and rinse with clean water.
- Connect each keg coupler to its correct cleaning socket and turn on the gas supply.
- Turn off the beer coolers to prevent the cleaning solution freezing in the beer lines.
- Fill the cleaning container with clean, cold water.
- Place buckets under the beer taps, remove the diffusers and draw the water through the beer lines until all traces of beer have been removed.
- Carefully follow the manufacturer's instructions, mixing the right amount of cleaning fluid for the size of your cleaning container.
- Draw the cleaning solution through the beer line.
- After about 15 minutes draw fresh cleaning solution through the beer line.
- If the system is heavily soiled you may want to repeat this process a couple more times, but do not leave in longer than recommended by the manufacturer's instructions on the cleaning fluid container.
- Thoroughly rinse the cleaning container and refill with clean, cold water.

- Draw the water through the beer lines until all traces of the cleaning solution have been flushed through.
- Reconnect the beer couplers, switch the gas back on, replace the diffusers and draw the beer through the beer line.

Cask conditioned beer lines need to be cleaned more frequently than keg beer lines because live yeasts exist in the beer so the beer lines will become contaminated.
- Turn off the flow of beer at the cask tap.
- Unscrew the line fitting from the cask tap and allow any beer in the line to flow into a clean stainless steel bucket. This can be returned once cleaning has been completed.
- Place the end of the beer line in cleaning solution.
- Draw the cleaning solution through the beer line using the hand pump on the bar. Leave for the recommended time.
- Place the end of the beer line in a container of fresh water and pull the water through the line until all the cleaning fluid has been removed from the beer line.
- Remove the beer line from the fresh water and draw through the water in the line.
- Reconnect the beer line to the cask and draw the beer through the line until it appears at the beer pump.

Note

Before dispensing beer from a recently cleaned beer line check that there is no trace of the cleaning agent. This can be achieved by sight, smell and taste. Serving beer with a cleaning agent present can cause sickness, diarrhoea and allergic reactions.

Testing your learning

1   List five duties that should be completed before opening a bar for service.
2   Why is it important to treat wine with respect and demonstrate a high level of technical skill, supported by the use of high-quality service equipment?
3   When serving wine at the table, state one of the main reasons why it is important to avoid unnecessary topping up.
4   List the four main pieces of equipment that would be used to serve a bottle of white wine at the table in a restaurant.
5   Explain why wine served in the restaurant may be decanted.
6   Identify one possible cause of the following faults found in beers:
    (a) cloudy beer, (b) flat beer, (c) sour beer.
7   What is the correct temperature that a cellar should be maintained at?
8   Briefly describe the difference between a hard and soft peg.
9   What is the shelf life of cask conditioned beer?
10 List four books that are used in beverage control and describe their uses.
11 Explain the term 'par stock'.
12 You notice a bottle has been broken in a delivery. Who should you notify?
13 Explain why an unattended cellar should be locked.
14 Give two methods of safely attaching a full gas cylinder to the cellar wall.
15 Describe the correct lifting procedure when lifting a cask.
16 If you suspect a gas leak in the cellar, what should you do?
17 Why is it important to check use by dates on all stock items?
18 How often should a stock take be completed?

Food and beverage service skills

Units covered

This chapter covers the following units:

Level 1

→ Food and beverage service skills (108)
→ Prepare and clear areas for drink service (1BS2, 113)
→ Prepare and clear areas for table/tray service (1FS1, 107)
→ Provide a table/tray service (1FS2, 108)
→ Prepare and clear areas for counter/takeaway service (1FS3, 109)
→ Clean and store crockery and cutlery (1GEN5, 105)

Level 2

→ Food and beverage service skills (209)
→ Provide a counter/takeaway service (1FS4, 110)
→ Serve food at the table (2FS2, 207)
→ Provide a silver service (2FS8, 208)
→ Provide a buffet/carvery service (2FS4, 209)
→ Prepare and serve hot drinks using specialist equipment (2BS8, 218)
→ Prepare and clear areas for counter/takeaway service (1FS3, 109)
→ Prepare and clear areas for table service (2FS1, 206)

Learning outcomes

This chapter will help you to:

18.1 Table service

Menu knowledge is covered in Chapters 8 and 9. The essential technical service skills used in food and beverage service are described in Chapter 14. This chapter now explains the application of those essential technical service skills. Chapter 15 gives information on preparation for service and Chapter 16 describes the different ways that customers' orders can be taken. Refer to the above chapters before considering the service information in this chapter.

> **Key term**
>
> **Table service** – the customer is served at a laid table. This type of service, which includes plated service and silver service, is found in many types of restaurants and cafés, and in banqueting

Pre-service tasks

Food and beverage service staff should be on duty with sufficient time before the service is due to commence to:

- check the sideboards/workstations have all the equipment necessary for service
- check that tables are laid correctly
- check the menu and ensure they have a full understanding of the dishes, methods of cooking, garnishes, the correct covers, accompaniments and mode of service
- ascertain the allocation of stations/workareas and other duties, if these are not already known
- allow the headwaiter/supervisor to check that all staff are dressed correctly in a clean and well-presented uniform of the establishment.

Order of service of a meal

In the example for the order of service given below, customers are having a starter, main course and sweet, to be accompanied by apéritifs (a pre-meal drink, for example gin and tonic), wine with the meal and liqueurs.

1 Greet customers and check to see if they have a reservation.
2 Assist with the customers' coats as required.
3 Offer an apéritif in the lounge or reception area or, if preferred, to have one at their table.
4 If they are to have the apéritif at their table, lead the customers to their table.

Figure 18.1 (a) Laid table with napkins being placed on to customer's laps and menus being presented

5 Assist customers with their seats and place their napkins over their laps – see Figure 18.1 (a).
6 The order for any apéritifs is taken and the order is then served.
7 Present open menus to each customer, host last. Bread is offered, butter and alternatives are placed on the table, and any chilled water ordered is poured.

Note

At this point all the customers at the table will have something to read, drink and eat, so they can be left for a while to allow them time to make their selection.

8 If required explain the menu items and take the food order, usually from the host but each guest may be asked separately. Confirm all the items ordered together with degrees of cooking and sauces ordered.

9 Immediately after the food order has been taken, check with the host to see if wine is required to accompany the meal. Adjust the glassware for the wine to be served.

10 Adjust the cover for the first course. In more casual establishments the covers are laid for the first and main course at the beginning of the meal.

11 The wine ordered will be presented to the host to confirm that the correct bottle of wine is about to be opened.

12 The wine or other beverages are always served before the food. Offer the host (or whoever ordered the wine) to taste the wine to assess the quality of the contents and that the serving temperature is correct. The person tasting the wine always has their glass topped up last.

13 Serve the plated first course(s) now, cold before hot, and the accompaniments are then offered – see Figure 18.1 (b). Once all plates are on the table, explanations of the dishes are given to the customers.

Figure 18.1 (b) Plated first course being served

14 The server will now check the table to ensure everything is satisfactory and the customers have all they require.

15 Wine and water glasses will be topped up as necessary – see Figure 18.1 (c). Remove used or empty glasses.

Figure 18.1 (c) Wine glasses being topped up

16 When all the customers have finished their first courses, clear the first-course plates using the correct stacking techniques and remove any accompaniments – see Figure 18.1 (d).

Figure 18.1 (d) Plated first course being removed

17 If necessary the covers should be laid or adjusted for the main course.

18 If a different wine is to be served with the main course, the correct glasses should be placed on the table and the wine then served before the food in the same way as the previous wine. If a bottle of the same wine is to be served then this is normally offered with a clean glass for tasting the new wine.

19 The plated main course(s) are served from the right-hand side of the customer, cold before hot, and accompaniments offered – see Figure 18.1 (e). When all plates are on the table, explain the dishes to the customers.

Figure 18.1 (e) Plated main course being served from the right

20 The server will now check to ensure everything is satisfactory and the customers have all they require.

21 Wine and water glasses will be topped up as necessary.

22 When customers have finished eating their main courses, clear the main-course plates and cutlery, side plates and knives, all accompaniments, butter dish and the cruet set using the correct clearing techniques – see Figure 18.1 (f) and Figure 18.1 (g).

Figure 18.1 (f) Plated main course being cleared

Figure 18.1 (g) Side plates being cleared

23 The table is then crumbed down – see Figure 18.1 (h) – for an explanation of this process see page 306.

Figure 18.1 (h) Crumbing down with a 'crumber'

24 Present the sweet menu. Advise customers on the dishes as necessary. Take the order and confirm the order back to check it is correct.
25 Covers for the sweet course are laid – see Figure 18.1 (i).

Figure 18.1 (i) Sweet cutlery being put into position

26 Empty or used wine glasses and bottles are cleared away.

27 If wine is to be served with the sweet course, the correct glasses should be placed on the table and then served before the food.

28 The plated sweet course(s) will now be served from the right-hand side of the customer, cold before hot, and accompaniments offered – see Figure 18.1 (j). Once all plates are on the table, explain the dishes to the customers.

Figure 18.1 (j) Plated sweet course being served from the right.

29 Offer any appropriate accompaniments such as caster sugar, custard or cream with the sweet course.

30 Clear the sweet course and remove accompaniments.

31 The server will now take the hot beverage order for tea, coffee or other beverages if not taken with the sweet order.

32 While the hot beverages are being prepared, a drink order for digestifs, such as liqueurs, brandy or port, will be taken.

33 Tea and coffee or other beverages will be served – see Figure 18.1(k) – for further information on the service of tea, coffee and other hot beverages, see page 307.)

Figure 18.1(k) Service of coffee

34 If petits fours/*friandises* are to be served then these are offered to the customers or placed on the table.

35 When required the bill will be presented to the host. The server will receive payment from the host. (For billing see Section 19.8, page 339.)

36 The server will see the customers out, assisting with their coats if required.

37 The table is cleared down and then re-laid if required.

Removal of spare covers

In many instances the number of customers in a party is fewer than the table is laid for. The waiter must then remove the spare cover(s) laid on the table. General considerations are that customers, where possible, should face into the room. The cover should be removed using a service plate or a service salver. When this has been done the position of the other covers should be adjusted if necessary and the table accompaniments repositioned. The spare chair should also be removed.

Where there is an uneven number of customers each side of a table, the covers should be positioned so that the full length of the table is used for both sides, by spacing the covers out on each side. This ensures that one customer is not left facing a space on the other side of the table.

18.2 Silver service

Silver service (or English service) is a higher technical level of service which is not as widely used as it once was but is still used in a wide variety of establishments. Expertise in this technique can only be achieved with practise.

The order of service for silver service is similar to the one given above (pages 293–298). The key difference is in the way the food is served at the table.

Silver service of first courses

For silver service of the first course the plates will be laid in front of each customer, the dishes to be served will be presented to the table and an explanation of the dishes given. The first course(s) will then be silver served to the customers from their left-hand side and any accompaniments will be offered. Plated foods will be offered from the right-hand side.

> **Key term**
>
> **Silver service –** presentation and service of food by waiting staff onto customers' plates from food flats or dishes, using a spoon and fork

Service of soup

Soup may be served pre-plated, from a tureen at the sideboard or on the guéridon, or silver served from an individual tureen as shown in Figure 18.2. The waiter ensures that the soup is poured away from the customer to avoid splashes on to the customer's clothing. The underflat acts as a drip plate to prevent any spillage from going on the tablecloth.

Figure 18.2 Silver service of soup from an individual tureen

Consommé is traditionally served in a consommé cup on a consommé saucer with a fishplate underneath. It is traditional for this type of soup to be eaten with a sweet spoon. This is because consommé was originally taken before going home, after a function, as a warming beverage. It was originally drunk from this large cup. The garnish was eaten with the sweet spoon. The tradition of the sweet spoon has continued, but a soup spoon is also acceptable.

Figure 18.3 Service of soup from a multiportion tureen

Silver service of main courses

The main course(s) will be silver served to the customer from their left-hand side and accompaniments will also be offered from the left (see Figure 18.4).

- The correct cover is laid prior to the food item ordered being served.
- Dishes to be served will be presented to the table and explanations given.
- The service cloth is folded neatly and placed on the palm of the hand as protection against heat from the serving dish.

- The fold of the cloth should be on the tips of the fingers.
- The dish is presented to the customer so they may see the complete dish as it has come from the kitchen. This is to show off the chef's artistry in presentation.
- The serving dish should be held a little above the hot joint plate with the front edge slightly overlapping the rim of the hot joint plate.
- The portion of food is placed in the six o'clock position (i.e. nearest to the customer) on the hot joint plate (see Figure 18.4b).
- When moving to serve the second portion, the flat should be rotated on the service cloth so the next portion to be served will be nearest the hot main-course plate.
- Note that the portion of food served, on the plate nearest to the customer, allows ample room on the plate to serve and present the potatoes and other vegetables attractively.
- If vegetables are being served on to separate plates, then the main food item (meat or fish) is placed in the middle of the hot main-course plate.

Figure 18.4 (a) Silver service of main course

Figure 18.4 (b) Service of food nearest the customer

Silver service of potatoes and vegetables

- The general rule is for potatoes to be served before vegetables.
- When serving either potatoes or vegetables, the vegetable dish itself should always be placed on an underflat with a napkin on it. This is for presentation purposes.
- The purpose of the napkin is also to prevent the vegetable dish slipping about on the underflat while the service is being carried out.
- A separate service spoon and fork should be used for each different type of potato and vegetable dish to be served.
- Note again the use of the service cloth as protection against heat and to allow the easier rotation of the vegetable dish on its underflat. This ensures the items to be served are nearest the hot main-course plate.
- With the serving dish in its correct position, the potato dish nearest the hot joint plate should be served.
- The potato dish served is placed on the hot joint plate on the far side, in the two o'clock position, allowing the server to work towards themself as they serve the remaining food items ordered and making it easier to present the food attractively (see Figure 18.5(a)). Any vegetables to be served are therefore placed on the hot joint plate nearer to the server and in the ten o'clock position (see Figure 18.5(b)).

- Creamed potato is served by placing the service fork into the service spoon and then taking a scoop of the creamed potato from the vegetable dish. This is then carried to the hot main-course plate and the fork moved slightly. The potato should then fall off on to the plate.

Figure 18.5 (a) and **(b)** Silver service of potatoes and vegetables

Figure 18.5 shows the use of an underflat under the potato and vegetable dishes. It also indicates:

- how a variety of potatoes and vegetables can be served at one time by using a large underflat
- the use of a service cloth for protection from heat and to prevent the underflat from slipping
- the correct handling of the service spoon and fork
- the separate service spoon and fork for each different potato and vegetable dish to be served
- service from the left-hand side of the customer.

Silver service of accompanying sauces

- The sauce should be presented in a sauceboat on an underplate, with a sauce ladle.
- A ladleful of sauce should be lifted clear of the sauceboat.
- The underside of the sauce ladle should then be run over the edge of the sauceboat to avoid any drips falling on the tablecloth or over the edge of the customer's plate.
- The sauce should be napped over the portion of meat already served or at the side of the meat, depending on the customer's preference.

Figure 18.5 (c)

18.3 Clearing during service

The main method of clearing in a plated and table service operation, and with customers in the room, is described below.

Clearing techniques

Developing good clearing techniques helps to:
- enhance speed and efficiency
- avoid the possibility of accidents
- create minimum inconvenience to customers
- allow more to be cleared, in less time and in fewer journeys
- provide the opportunity for plates, cutlery, glassware, and linen, paper and food waste items to be separated according to the needs of the establishment
- allow for dirties to be collected and stacked neatly and correctly on the sideboard/ workstation or trolley.

The main method of clearing in a plated and table service operation, and with customers in the room, is described below.

All clearing techniques stem from the two main hand positions shown in Section 14.4, Figures 14.3 (a) and (b), page 220.

Expertise comes with regular practice.
- Dirty plates should always be cleared from the right-hand side of the customer.
- The server should position himself or herself, taking up a sideways stance at the table.

Clearing soup plates

1 The server, having positioned himself or herself correctly, will pick up the first dirty soup plate on its underplate. This stance allows the waiter to pass the dirty soup service from the clearing hand to the holding hand. Using this procedure ensures the dirty plates are held away from the table and customers, reducing the likelihood of accidents. The first dirty soup plate should be held firmly on its underplate with the latter pushed up firmly between the thumb and the first and second fingers. It is important that this first dirty soup plate is held firmly as succeeding dirties are built up on this one, meaning there is a considerable weight to be held.

2 The second dirty soup plate on its underplate cleared and positioned on the holding hand.

3 The position of the second dirty soup plate on the holding hand. The soup spoon is taken from the lower soup plate and placed in the upper soup plate.

4 The upper soup plate with its two soup spoons now placed in the lower soup plate, leaving the upper underplate behind. The third dirty soup plate with its underplate is now cleared from the right and placed on the upper underplate on the holding hand. The above procedure is then repeated each time a dirty soup plate on its underplate is cleared.

Clearing starter and joint plates

1 One of the two main hand positions previously shown in Section 14.4 (page 220) and the first dirty joint plate cleared. The dirty plate should be held firmly pushed up to the joint between the thumb and the first and second finger. Note the position of the cutlery: the fork held firmly with the thumb over the end of its handle and the blade of the joint knife placed under the arch in the handle of the fork. Any debris or crumbs will be pushed into the triangle formed by the handles of the joint knife and joint fork and the rim of the plate. This is nearest the holding hand.

2 The second dirty joint plate cleared and positioned on the holding hand.

3 The second dirty joint knife positioned correctly and debris is cleared from the upper joint plate on to the lower joint plate using the second dirty joint fork cleared. This procedure is carried out as the waiter moves on to their next position in readiness to clear the third dirty joint plate.

4 The holding hand with the already-cleared items held correctly and ready to receive the next dirty joint plate to be cleared.

Clearing side plates

This method generally allows the waiter to clear more dirty side plates and side knives in one journey between sideboard/workstation and table, and is especially useful when working in a banqueting situation.

1 Debris is cleared from the upper dirty side plate and on to the service salver/plate. Side plates are cleared using a service salver or service plate to allow a larger working surface on which to clear the dirty side knives and any debris remaining.

2 The holding hand having cleared four place settings with the dirty items and debris stacked correctly and safely.

Clearing joint plates and side plates in one journey to the table

Figure 18.9 shows the dirty joint plates and cutlery correctly stacked and with the side plates and side knives also being cleared in one journey to the table. This is an alternative to clearing the joint plates and then the side plates in two phases.

Figure 18.9 Clearing joint and side plates in one journey

Clearing accompaniments

The service plate is also used to clear such items as the cruet, peppermill or other accompaniments, which may not already be set on an underplate.

Crumbing down

The process of crumbing down usually takes place after the main course has been cleared and before the sweet order is taken and served. The purpose is to remove any crumbs or debris left on the tablecloth at this stage of the meal.

The items of equipment used to crumb down are:
- a service plate (a joint plate with a napkin on it)
- a waiter's cloth or service cloth, or a metal crumber or a crumber brush and pan.

If a table d'hôte cover has previously been laid, the sweet spoon and fork, prior to crumbing down, should normally be positioned at the head of the cover. However, if an à la carte cover has initially been laid, then after the main course has been cleared there should be no tableware on the table prior to crumbing down.

1 Crumbing down commences from the left-hand side of the first customer. The service plate is placed just beneath the lip (edge) of the table. Crumbs are brushed towards the plate using a folded napkin, a specialist crumber brush or a metal crumber.
2 This having been completed, the sweet fork is moved from the head of the place setting to the left-hand side of the cover.
3 The waiter now moves to the right-hand side of the same customer and completes the crumbing down of this place setting.
4 The sweet spoon is then moved from the head of the place setting to the right-hand side of the cover.
5 While the sweet spoon and sweet fork are being moved to their correct positions, the service cloth is held under the service plate by the fingers of the holding-hand.
6 Having completed the crumbing down procedure for one place setting, the waiter is now correctly positioned to commence again the crumbing down of the next place setting, i.e. to the left of the next customer.

Figure 18.10 Crumbing down: note the neatly folded service cloth

Figure 18.11 Crumbing down using a crumber

Figure 18.12 Sweet cutlery in place after crumbing down

18.4 Service of hot beverages

Tea and coffee

Tray service

The following equipment is required for the tray service of coffee or tea:

Coffee tray:
- tray or salver
- tray cloth/napkin
- teacup and saucer
- teaspoon
- sugar basin and tongs or a teaspoon according to the type of sugar offered
- coffee pot
- jug of cream or hot milk
- stands for the coffee pot and hot milk jug.

Tea tray:
- tray or salver
- tray cloth/napkin
- teapot
- hot water jug
- jug of cold milk
- slop basin
- tea strainer
- stands for teapot and hot water jug
- sugar basin and tongs
- teacup and saucer
- teaspoon.

Variations of this basic equipment will depend on the type of coffee or tea that is being served. General points to note in laying up a coffee or tea tray are given below.
- Position the items to ensure an evenly balanced tray for carrying.
- Position the items for the convenience of the customer: beverage on the right with spouts facing inwards, and handles outwards and towards the customer for ease of access.
- Ensure the beverage is placed on the tray at the last moment so that it is served hot.

For the various types of tea and their service see Section 12.1, page 172.

For a list of modern by-the-cup coffee styles see Section 12.2, page 176.

Serving tea and coffee for table and assisted service

Tea is not usually served but the teapot is placed on the table on a stand and to the right-hand side of the person who ordered. The customers will then help themselves. The cold milk and sugars (and alternatives) are also placed on to the table.

Coffee may be silver served at the table from a service salver. However, this traditional method of serving coffee is not so common today. Generally other speedier methods are used, such as placing the cafètiere on the table together with milk and sugars (and alternatives) for customers to help themselves.

Other methods of serving tea and coffee are:
- Service from a pot of tea or a pot of hot black coffee held on the sideboard on a hotplate. Cold milk, hot milk or cream and sugars are placed on the table.
- Service of both cold milk and hot milk or cream together with the tea and coffee from pots, one held in each of the waiter's hands. Sugars are placed on the table for customers to help themselves.
- In event catering, where larger numbers often have to be served, the cold milk, hot milk or cream and sugars are often placed on the table for customers to help themselves. The tea and coffee is then served from a 1 litre capacity vacuum flask, which may be kept on the waiters' sideboard in readiness for replenishment should the customers require it. This method of holding and serving tea and coffee ensures that it remains hot at all times. (For examples of vacuum jugs for tea or coffee see Figure 12.7, page 183.)

When serving tea and coffee from multi-portion pots/urns it is usual to remove the tea leaves, coffee grounds or tea/coffee bags once the beverage has brewed, so that the tea and coffee does not become stewed.

Placement of tea and coffee cups from a tray

- Figure 18.13 (a) shows the beverage equipment required, positioned on the service salver, assuming a table of four customers is to be served. Using this method the server only has to make one journey from the sideboard/workstation to the restaurant or lounge table.
- Note the beverage service for each customer is made up of a teacup on its saucer, with a teaspoon resting in the saucer and at right angles under the handle of the cup.
- The beverage service is placed on the table from the customer's right-hand side, as the beverage ordered will be served from the right.
- The beverage service is positioned on the right-hand side of the customer with the handle to the right and the teaspoon set at right angles under the handle of the cup.
- While moving to the right-hand side of the second customer, the server will place a teacup on a tea saucer and a teaspoon in the saucer and at right angles under the handle of the cup. This beverage service is then ready to place on the right-hand side of the second customer – see Figure 18.13 (b).
- This procedure is then repeated until all the beverage services have been placed on the table for those customers requiring tea or coffee.

Figure 18.13 (a) Service salver before service of the first cup and saucer

Figure 18.13 (b) Service salver by the time the second customer is reached

Food and beverage service skills

When coffee is served after lunch or dinner, teacups are now more commonly used. The use of small coffee cups (demi-tasse) has declined for conventional coffee service although they are still sometimes used in event catering. These cups are also used for espresso.

Serving hot chocolate

Figure 18.14 Service of hot chocolate in a glass with additional toppings

Hot chocolate is most often served individually in special heat-resistant glasses that fit into a special holder with a handle. It can also be served in a mug. Hot chocolate may also be presented in a pot or jug for the customer to pour into a teacup. Usually white sugar and sweeteners are offered for the customer to add, so the glasses or mugs are usually presented on side plates or saucers together with a teaspoon. Teacups are presented on saucers together with a teaspoon.

Other hot beverages

Other hot drinks, including malted drinks such as Horlicks and Ovaltine, are served in the same way as hot chocolate but without any additional cream or toppings. However, mocha would be treated the same as hot chocolate.

Tisanes (fruit or herbal teas) are becoming popular; they contain no caffeine or tannin and are consumed either hot or cold, without the addition of milk. Service is the same as for normal tea as above or in a tea glass.

Alcoholic hot drinks such as mulled wine, glühwein, wassail (mulled cider) and hot buttered rum are usually served during the winter and regional recipes are often favoured. They can be served in mugs or latte glasses.

18.5 Service enhancements ('table theatre')

Service enhancements (sometimes referred to as '**table theatre**') include service from trolleys. These can include cheese, sweet carving or drinks trolleys and also **guéridon service**. The various trolleys provide opportunities to use them as selling aids as they display the items on offer to the customers. These service enhancements are, however, more costly to provide as they:

- take longer than plated or silver service
- require a higher level of service skills
- require the use of more expensive and elaborate equipment
- require larger service areas to allow for the movement of the trolleys.

When serving from a trolley, the trolley should always be positioned between the staff and customer as if it were in a shop. Sweet, cheese and drinks trolleys should be attractively presented from the customer's point of view and well laid out from behind for the server. Plates for dirty service equipment should therefore be to the back of the trolley. Staff should explain food or beverage items to customers, either from behind the trolley, to the

Key terms

Table theatre – a service enhancement in which food and beverages are served from trolleys. These can include cheese, sweet carving or drinks trolleys and also guéridon service

Guéridon service – service using a movable service table or trolley from which food may be served

side of the trolley or standing by the table, but not in front of the trolley. For larger parties the server can go to the customers at the table and then explain the items from there, ensuring that the customers can see the trolley.

When working at a trolley, food is not usually served by the spoon-and-fork technique. Instead, service is with one implement in one hand and another in the other hand with the service on to plates on the trolley. This is more accurate and quicker.

Sweet and cheese trolleys

When the customer makes a selection from the sweet or cheese trolley, a plate should be positioned near the item to be served. Then, using the service equipment (one in each hand) the food should be portioned and transferred neatly to the plate. The plate should then be placed in front of the customer from the right. For larger parties, two people will be required – one to take the orders and place the plate with food in front of the customer, the other to stand at the trolley and portion and plate the foods.

Some sweet and cheese trolleys have a plate-holding ring within their design. In this instance the dish holding the food item ordered must be placed next to this holding ring. When the food item is portioned it may then be transferred easily and safely on to the customer's plate, there being minimum distance between the dish holding the food item ordered and the customer's plate. For temperature-control purposes many sweet trolleys now come with ice pack compartments, which should be replenished before each service.

Serving cheese

Figure 18.15 A cheese trolley (image courtesy of Euroservice UK)

On a traditional menu the cheese course is served before the sweet/dessert course, but cheese may also be chosen instead of a sweet/dessert course. Cheese is often served plated. The cover is a side knife and small/sweet fork. Cheese may also be served from a selection presented on a cheese board or a cheese trolley.

For service of cheese from a selection the procedure would be as follows:

Equipment
- Cheese board or cheese trolley
- Sufficient cheese knives for cutting and portioning the different cheeses
- Plates for the service of cheese – often a fish or sweet plate.

Cover
- Fish or sweet-size plate
- Side knife and sometimes a small/sweet fork.

Accompaniments
Accompaniments set on the table may include:
- cruet (salt, pepper and mustard)
- butter or alternative

- celery served in a celery glass part filled with crushed ice, on an underplate
- radishes (when in season) placed in a glass bowl on an underplate with teaspoon
- caster sugar for cream cheeses
- assorted cheese biscuits (cream crackers, Ryvita, sweet digestives, water biscuits, etc.) or various breads.

Method

- Ensure the entire 'mise-en-place' (term meaning literally 'put in place' but also meaning preparation for service) is complete before commencing.
- Check that all the cheeses on the trolley are known in order to be able to explain them to the customer.
- Check cheeses are properly presented (if cheese is wrapped in foil this must be removed by the waiter before serving). The waiter should remove the cheese rind if it is not palatable (edible). This is not necessary in the case of Camembert and Brie as the rind of these two French cheeses is palatable.

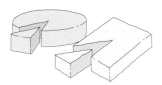

Round and square cheeses can be presented whole and then portioned by being cut into triangular pieces. Note that with square or oblong cheeses one of the cuts is at an angle.

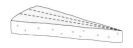

Brie or similar type cheeses may be either presented whole or cut into triangular slices and then portioned by being sliced (much like a cake) as required.

Small soft cheeses such as goat's cheeses may be presented whole and then portioned by being cut in half or quarter as the customer requests.

Flattened or pyramid shaped cheeses may be presented whole and then portioned by being cut into small triangles by keeping one side of each cut at an angle.

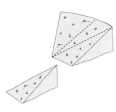

Largish wedges of blue cheeses can be cut from a cylinder or half cylinder of cheese for presentation, and these wedges are then cut into smaller wedges for service. Other cheeses bought in cylinders or half cylinders can be cut and presented for service and then portioned in the same way.

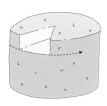

A cylinder (truckle) or half cylinder of cheese may also be presented whole and then portioned by individual wedges being cut from it. In order to do this the cheese is first cut around at about 25 to 30 cm. This is also an alternative to the tradition of Stilton being portioned by scooping the cheese out from the top of the cylinder after removing the top rind.

Figure 18.16 Examples of methods for cutting, portioning and presenting cheeses

- Present the cheese board or trolley at the table.
- Explain the cheeses available to the customer.
- Cut or portion the cheeses and present on plates as required. Figure 18.16 gives examples of the methods for cutting, portioning and presenting cheeses.
- Present in front of the customer and offer further accompaniments at the table as required (see Section 9.10, page 154).

Serving sweets

Sweets are often served plated or presented in a sweet dish such as a sundae glass. If served from a trolley then they are plated at the trolley (see Figure 18.17). Cut portions of cakes or pies are normally put on the table so that the point is towards the customer (see Figure 18.18). Examples of the types of sweet are given in Section 9.11, Table 9.16, page 156.

There are no particular accompaniments to sweets. The customer may require a sugar sifter or, depending on the nature of the sweet selected, sauces such as custard or sauce à l'Anglaise may be offered. Alternatives to this might be single cream or whipped cream.

Figure 18.18 Placing a plated sweet course – a cake showing the point towards the customer

Figure 18.17 Service from sweet trolley (image courtesy of Euroservice UK)

Serving savouries

On the lunch and dinner menu a savoury may generally be served as an alternative to a sweet. In a banquet it may be a separate course served in addition to either a sweet or cheese course. Examples of savouries are given in Section 9.12, Table 9.17, page 157.

Savouries are usually pre-portioned by the kitchen and are served to the customer plated after the cover has been laid and the accompaniments placed on the table. The cover for a savoury is usually a side knife and a sweet fork.

Accompaniments

The accompaniments are:
- salt and pepper
- cayenne pepper
- peppermill
- Worcestershire sauce (usually only with meat savouries).

Serving dessert (fresh fruit and nuts)

Dessert may include all types of fresh fruit and nuts according to season, although the majority of the more popular items are now available all year round. Some of the more popular items are dessert apples, pears, bananas, oranges, mandarins, tangerines, black and white grapes, pineapple and assorted nuts such as Brazils. Sometimes a box of dates may appear in the fruit basket.

Accompaniments

The following accompaniments should be set on the table:
- caster sugar holder on a sideplate
- salt for nuts.

Note

Always remember to push trolleys and not to pull them. This enables a trolley to be controlled when steering and to ensure it is moved safely to avoid accidents.

Service using a guéridon

Service using a guéridon is an enhanced form of table service. It is normally found in establishments with an à la carte menu and higher levels of service. The definition of the term guéridon is a movable service table or trolley from which food may be served. In effect the guéridon is a movable sideboard or service station carrying sufficient equipment for the service requirements, together with any spare equipment that may be necessary.

Guéridon service usually indicates serving foods on to the customers' plates at the guéridon. Guéridon service is also often used to refer to other enhanced service techniques such as service using a drinks trolley, carving trolley, cheese trolley or a sweet trolley.

Further enhancements to the basic guéridon service include:
- preparing and serving foods in the service area such as salads and dressings
- carving, jointing or filleting foods in a service area
- flambage (the preparation and finishing, or cooking, of foods in the restaurant, which are also flambéed).

Approaches to guéridon service

For guéridon service the taking of food orders is similar to that described in Chapter 16, page 259). When guéridon service is being undertaken all dishes must be presented to the customers at the table before the actual service of the food and especially before the portioning, filleting, jointing, carving or service of any dish. This is so that the customers can see the dishes as the kitchen has presented them before the dishes are served. Customers can also confirm that the orders are correct.

Mise-en-place for guéridon service

In many establishments where guéridon service is carried out, the basic layout is standardised. This is to ensure that the required standards of service are met and that safety is a prime consideration of all the service staff. There are many designs of guéridon available on the market today, but the basic format for the lay-up of the top of the guéridon may be as shown in Figure 18.19.

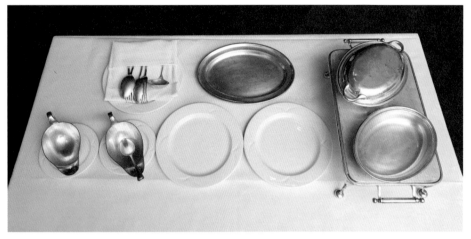

Figure 18.19 Example of basic guéridon lay-up

If hotplates or food warmers are used then these are placed on the left-hand side on the top of the guéridon. These heaters may be gas, electric or methylated spirit.

Procedure for guéridon service

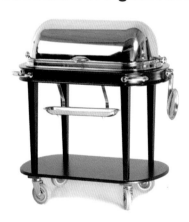

Figure 18.20 Carving trolley (image courtesy of Euroservice UK)

- Guéridon service is essentially a chef and commis service. There must therefore be complete liaison and teamwork between them and the other members of the team.
- Always push the guéridon, never pull it. This helps to control and steer the guéridon in the right direction and avoid accidents.
- The guéridon should be kept in one position for the service of a complete course and not moved from customer to customer.
- Unlike silver service, where the spoon and fork are used together in one hand, guéridon service requires that the spoon and fork are used one in each hand. This gives more control and makes the service quicker.
- The dish is first presented to the customer and the name of the dish is stated, for example: 'Your Dover sole, madam'. The dish is then returned to the guéridon.
- Hot serving plates are placed on the side of the trolley, with the dish for the food to be served placed on to the hotplate.
- The food dishes are then served on to the customers' plates. This may also include portioning, carving, jointing or filleting if necessary.
- When transferring foods and liquids from the service flats and dishes to the plate, always run the fork along the underside of the spoon to avoid drips marking the plate.
- The waiter may then serve the potatoes and vegetables on to the plate while the plates are still on the guéridon. The waiter also serves the sauces on to the plates. The plates are then placed in front of the customers.
- Alternatively, where more than two covers are being served from the guéridon, only the main dish of each customer would be served from the guéridon, with potatoes and vegetables, sauces and accompaniments being served to the customer once the main food items have been served on to the customers' plates and put in front of the customers.

Food and beverage service skills

- The commis must always keep the guéridon clear of dirties.
- When the service is finished at one table, wipe down the guéridon and move on to the next table immediately. It will then be ready for the commis coming from the kitchen with a loaded tray.

Note

Never carve on silver or stainless steel flats or dishes as a knife can ruin them. Use either a carving board or a hot joint plate.

Service considerations for a variety of different foods are shown in Table 18.1.

Table 18.1 Service considerations for different foods

Hors d'oeuvres or other appetisers	These are served in the usual way except for various speciality dishes (see also Section 9.3, page 144)
Soups	Always served from the guéridon, whether in individual soup tureens or in larger soup tureens requiring a ladle
Egg dishes	Unless there is any special treatment required these are served straight to the table
Pasta and rice dishes	Served on to the customers' plates at the guéridon. Pasta is served by lifting the pasta high from the serving dish using a service spoon and fork, and then moving this over to the customer's plate and lowering the pasta on to the plate. Accompaniments are offered at the table
Fish dishes	Served from the presentation dishes or flats on to the customers' plates. Some fish dishes may be presented for filleting or carving at the guéridon and this is carried out, served and presented on to the customer's plate at the guéridon
Meats	Served from the presentation dishes or flats on to the customer's plates. Some meat dishes may be presented for carving or jointing at the guéridon and this is then carried out but always on a carving board. The dish is then served directly on to the customer's plate at the guéridon
Potatoes and vegetables	Either served on to the customer's plate at the guéridon, or served as in silver service, after the main courses have been put on to the customer's plate and placed in front of them. Sauces and accompaniments are served at the table
Cheese	May be served plated or often served from a cheese trolley, but may also be served from a cheese presentation (such as a cheese board), which is presented on a guéridon
Sweet	Unless pre-plated or served from a cold sweet trolley, sweet dishes are served from the presentation dishes or flats on to the customer's plate at the guéridon. Some sweet dishes may be presented for portioning at the guéridon and this is then carried out and then served directly on to the customer's plate at the guéridon
Savoury	Unless pre-plated these are served on to the customer's plate at the guéridon
Coffee and tea	Usual service is at the table unless speciality coffees are required

Cleanliness and hygiene

The standard of cleanliness of the carver and their equipment during the practical application of the craft are of the utmost importance. Good service practices are listed below.

- Always wear spotlessly clean protective clothing. Remember customers are watching a demonstration of the craft.
- Ensure that personal cleanliness is given priority as you are working in the vicinity of your customers as well as handling food.
- Always pre-check work areas and equipment to ensure good hygiene practices.
- Do not move meat, poultry or game excessively when on a board for carving or jointing.

- Carve as required and do not pre-carve too much or too early.
- Keep all meat, poultry or game under cover, be it hot or cold, and at the correct serving temperature.
- Be constantly vigilant for any sign of deterioration in the food being offered.
- At the conclusion of each service ensure all equipment is thoroughly cleaned and well rinsed.

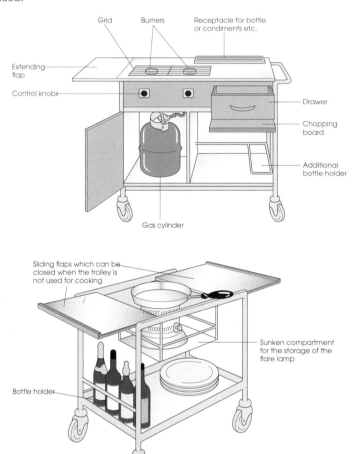

Figure 18.21 Examples of flambé trolleys (a) Gas-fuelled flambé trolley; (b) Flambé trolley with flare lamp]

Introduction to carving, jointing and filleting

Carving techniques are craft skills of real value to the foodservice trade. They are required in restaurants using a carving trolley, in **carvery**-type operations, for serving at a **buffet** and for special occasions. In some establishments these tasks are carried out by service staff as part of their usual service duties, especially for guéridon service. In other establishments there may be a specialist carver (**trancheur**). Carving, filleting and jointing skills are also necessary for counter or buffet assistants.

All customers have their likes and dislikes – the meat to be medium or well done, some with fat or very little fat, a portion carved from the end of the joint, sliced thinly or thickly, white meat only, a mix of white and brown meat and so on. The service staff must acknowledge all of these requests while remaining organised and efficient. They must have all the correct equipment to hand for the foods to be served, together with the appropriate accompaniments and sauces.

Carving, jointing and filleting skills

Carving, jointing and filleting are skilled arts only perfected by continual practice. General considerations are as follows:

- Always use a very sharp knife, making sure it is sharpened beforehand and not in front of the customer. Remember you are going to carve a joint, not cut it to pieces.
- Carving is best achieved by pulling the knife back towards you and not by pushing the knife forwards.
- Use the whole length of the knife in order to let the knife cut the food properly.
- Cut economically and correctly to maximise the portions obtained and to keep wastage to a minimum.
- Work quickly and efficiently to avoid hold ups in the room.
- Meat is carved across the grain, with the exception of saddle of mutton or lamb, which is sometimes cut at right angles to the ribs.
- The carving fork must hold the joint firmly to prevent accidents. For smaller joints use the fork with the prongs pointed down to hold the food. For larger joints use the fork to pierce the meat to hold it steady while carving.
- Practise as much as possible to acquire expertise in the art of carving and to develop confidence in front of the customer.

Methods of carving, jointing and filleting

The carving of all hot food must be performed quickly so that there is minimum heat loss. General guidance on carving, jointing and filleting is given in Table 18.2.

Table 18.2 General guidance on carving, filleting and jointing

Beef and ham	Always cut very thinly
Rib of beef	May either be carved on the bone or by being first removed from the bone and then sliced
Steaks	Chateaubriand or entrecôte double are sliced at angles, either in half or into more slices, depending on the customer's preference
Lamb, mutton, pork, tongue and veal	Carved at double the thickness of beef and ham
Saddle of lamb	Carved along the loin in long, fairly thick slices
Shoulder of lamb	This has an awkward bone formation. Starting from the top, cut down to the bone, then work from top to bottom, then turn the piece over and work gradually round
Lamb best ends	These are sliced into individual cutlets by carving between the cutlet bones; best ends can also be double cut by cutting close to each side of the bone
Boiled beef and pressed meats	Generally carved slightly thicker than roast meats and each portion will include some fat. Boiled beef should be carved with the grain to avoid the meat shredding
Cold ham	Carved on to the bone from top to bottom in very thin slices
Whole chicken	A medium-sized bird is often dissected into eight pieces, making up four portions
Poussin and small feathered game	May be offered whole or split into two portions
Duckling	May be carved into four/six portions: two legs, two wings and the breast cut into long strips
Turkey and other large birds	Often portioned into legs, wings and breast, and then carved into slices separately. Make up portions with white meat from the wings or breast together with a slice of brown meat off the leg and a share of the stuffing. Alternatively, the bird may be left whole with the joints separated from the main carcass so as to allow for carving without jointing first

Poached salmon	This is first skinned whether it is hot or cold. It is then served in fillets, one from each side of the bone. Cut slices up to 10 cm (4 in) long and 2.5 cm (1 in) thick
Lobster and crayfish	Hold firmly. Pierce vertically with a strong knife and cut with a levering motion towards tail and head. Hold shell down with a spoon on a dish, slowly lifting out the meat with a fork. Slice the meat diagonally
Sole	First remove the bones along either edge. Then draw the fillets apart with the aid of two large forks. Serve a top and bottom fillet per portion

Selection of tools

- For most joints a knife with a blade of 25–30 cm (10–12 in) long and about 2.5 cm (1 in) wide is required.
- For poultry or game a knife with a blade of 20 cm (8 in) long is more suitable.
- For ham a carving knife with a long flexible blade is preferred. This is often referred to as a ham knife.
- Serrated knives do not always cut better than a plain bladed knife, with the latter giving a cleaner cut.
- A carving fork is needed to hold the joint firmly in position when carving.
- Carve on a board, either wooden or plastic. Avoid carving on china plates or metal. Apart from the damage this can cause (especially with silver) small splinters of metal can become attached to the meat slices.

During service staff must act as salespeople and be able to sell the dishes on the menu by giving a brief and accurate description. The carving trolley supplements this by being a visual aid to selling and should be at the table as the waiter takes the orders so that they may suggest and show particular items to the customer.

Presentation of the trolley

- The carver must always ensure that the carving trolley is correctly laid up before it is taken to the table.
- The plate rest for the hot joint plates should be extended and the two containers for gravy and sauces should be already filled. These two containers should always be placed at the end nearest the plate rest. This is for ease of service and also provides the shortest space between the containers and the plates.
- When being used the carving trolley should be placed next to the customer's table, in between the customer and the carver. This ensures that the customer can see every operation performed by the carver and appreciate the skills involved.
- The trolley should be positioned to ensure that the safety valve is on the side away from the carver. This is to ensure that the carver will not be scalded when using the trolley.
- The trolley should be positioned in such a way that the lid is drawn back from the trolley towards the carver so as to reveal the food to the customer.

Care and maintenance of equipment

It is the visual display of preparing food at the table that is attractive to many customers. All actions must therefore meet the highest hygiene and safety standards, and good planning and organisation can achieve this. The hygiene and safety factors relating to guéridon service are described below.

- Hygiene and appearance of staff should be of the highest standard (see Section 6.4, page 100).

- All equipment should be spotlessly clean and polished daily.
- Food should not be handled with bare hands.
- Trolleys should be wiped down between each use.
- The hotplate or lamp should never be placed outside of the trolley legs.
- The trolley should not be positioned for use close to curtains or soft furnishings.
- Spirits and other alcoholic liquors should never be left near heated trolleys or naked flames.
- Spirits and other alcoholic liquors should be handled carefully when flaming dishes.
- The trolley should not be moved around the restaurant with food or equipment on it.
- Lamps should be checked on a daily basis to ensure they are in good working order.

A daily safety inspection and cleaning programme should be enforced through the use of a cleaning rota or schedule. The food service personnel should carry out this work as part of the normal mise-en-place period and under the supervision of a senior member of the team.

18.6 Counter self-service and single-point service

The three groups of service methods discussed in this section are:
1   **Self-service**: where the customer is required to help him or herself from a counter or buffet.
2   **Assisted service**: where the customer is served part of the meal at a table and is required to obtain part through self-service from some form of display or buffet.
3   **Single-point service**: where the customer orders, pays and receives the food and beverages at one point.

For these three groups of service methods the customer comes to where the food and beverage service is offered, and the service is provided in areas primarily designed for that purpose. In these groups of service methods, the customers can be involved in:
- viewing the menu and beverages on offer
- making a selection
- being served with the food and beverage items selected/ordered
- paying for the items
- collecting ancillary items (cutlery, seasonings, sauces, napkins) as required
- selecting a table where their food and beverage order may be consumed, or leaving the establishment if the order is for takeaway
- disposing of dirties as appropriate.

The customer processes for these three groups of service methods are summarised, together with the other two groups of service methods, in Section 14.1 (page 214). For the full identification of the five groups of service methods, see Table 14.3 (page 217).

Pre-service tasks

Members of staff must be on duty in sufficient time before the service is due to commence to allow them to:
- check that all work areas have the required equipment in readiness for the service to commence
- check that the dining area is set up correctly

> **Key terms**
>
> **Self-service** – the customer is required to help him or herself from a counter or buffet
>
> **Assisted service** – the customer is served part of the meal at a table and obtains the other part through self-service from some form of display or buffet
>
> **Single-point service** – the customer orders, pays and receives the food and beverages at one point

- ensure that they have a complete knowledge of all beverages and food dishes being offered, including ingredients, accompaniments, vegetarian dishes and those dishes not suitable for allergy sufferers
- determine the availability of back-up food and in what quantities
- determine the amount of back-up crockery on hand, should it be required
- check all temperature-controlled equipment is functioning at the required temperatures
- ensure that they themselves are presented correctly, with the recognised uniforms and service cloths for use with the hot equipment and crockery.

Self-service

The main form of self-service is found in cafeterias. In this form of service customers collect a tray from the beginning of the service counter, move along the counter to select their meal, pay and then collect the required cutlery for their meal, together with any ancillary items. Some 'call order' (cooked to order) food production may be included in cafeterias.

Menus should be prominently displayed at the entrance to the cafeteria or foodservice area so that customers may decide as far as possible what meal they will purchase before arriving at the service points. This saves time later and ensures that customer turnover is as quick as possible.

Cafeterias often have a straight-line counter where customers queue in line formation past a service counter and choose their menu requirements in stages before loading them on to a tray and proceeding to a payment point at the end of the counter. The layout of the counter may include a carousel – a revolving stacked counter – in order to save display space.

Where customer turnover is particularly high in a very narrow period of time, and when space is limited, then a variation on the cafeteria **straight-line counter**-type service may operate. Examples of these are:
- **Free-flow**: selection as in counter (above) but in a foodservice area where customers move at will to random service points; customers usually exit area via a payment point.
- **Echelon**: series of counters at angles to the customer flow within a free-flow area, thus saving space.
- **Supermarket/shopping mall**: island service points within a free-flow area.

Each of the service points may offer a different main-course dish, together with the potatoes, vegetable dishes, sauces and accompaniments as appropriate. Other service points offer hot and cold sweets, beverages, sandwiches, pastries, confectionery items and miscellaneous foods. On entering the foodservice area the customer can check the menu to see what they require and then go immediately to the appropriate service point. The advantage of this system is that those selecting a full meal do not hold up a customer who requires just a sandwich and a hot drink.

> ## Key term
>
> **Straight-line counter** – all foods are displayed on one long counter and customers move along the counter in order

Figure 18.22 Service counter

Order of service

The customer's progress from their entry into the eating area through to the conclusion of the meal is as follows:

- The customer enters the eating area.
- Views the menus and dishes available.
- Collects a tray from the tray stack, which may be sited at the entrance to the service area or at the beginning of the service counter, or at each separate service point.
- Proceeds to the service counter (straight line), or single/staggered service point (echelon), or island service point (shopping mall) to view the display of food and drink available and to make their choices and place them on their tray.
- Completes the payment required at the end of the counter.
- Proceeds to the cutlery stand and select their requirements.
- Also selects napkins, seasonings and sauces.
- Chooses a table and consumes the meal.
- At the conclusion of the meal takes the tray of dirties to the nearest tray stand. Disposable items are placed in the correct waste bins provided (according to type of waste for recycling).
- Table cleaners/clearers clear anything remaining and wipe down tabletops in readiness for the next customer.

Assisted service

The main form of assisted service is found in carvery-type operations. The customer is served part of the meal at a table and is required to obtain part through self-service from some form of display or buffet. Customers are able to help themselves to joints and other dishes but usually with the assistance of a carver or server at the buffet.

This form of service is also used for breakfast service, afternoon tea service and for events.

Assisted service involves the customer in two methods of food service, namely table service and self-service. Here the server is also usually responsible for the service of both food (starters, desserts and hot beverages) and alcoholic beverages on their allocated tables. They will be assisted by chefs/carvers at the carvery for the service of the main course.

The order of service for a meal in a carvery-type operation will proceed in almost exactly the same way as for table service (see Section 18.1, page 292). The difference here is that the main course is not served at the table; instead the customer approaches the carvery point to receive this course. This is now the assisted/self-service part of the carvery service. Customers may also, should they wish, return to the carvery point to replenish their plates.

Service of food at the carvery display

- All food items served on to plates should be attractively presented and arranged.
- If food has not already been pre-plated, it should be served on to plates using a service spoon in one hand and a service fork in the other, and should be placed neatly on to the customer's plate.
- Alternative service equipment might be used and this will be determined by the nature of the dishes displayed on the buffet (carvery), for example scoops, sauce ladles, soup ladles, slices, serving spoons and knives.
- Care must be taken to ensure stocks of crockery and food on the buffet have adequate back-up stock; food items should be reordered before they run out.

Note

For food safety reasons prepared foods must be held at specific temperatures. Chilled foods must be kept at or below 8°C (26.4°F). Foods being kept hot should remain at or above 63°C (145. 4°F). Food may be left at room temperature for limited periods during service or when on display. However, these flexibilities can be used only once for each batch of food. The temperature of chilled foods can only exceed 8°C for a maximum of four hours. The temperature of hot foods can only fall below 63°C for a maximum of two hours.

Service from buffets

Depending on the nature of the occasion and the style of buffet on offer, the customers may queue at the buffet to receive their food or they may be called up to the buffet, table by table. The customers will take a tray or be given a plate and then proceed along the buffet to make their selection. The main principles for service here follow those for counter/cafeteria service and carvery service.

- **Buffet or American breakfast**: the buffet can be used for any type of breakfast, with the most extensive often called an American Buffet Breakfast. For the service of this style of breakfast customers are presented with the breakfast menu when they sit down and from that they make their choice of either the full breakfast or other types of breakfast. With a buffet breakfast all items are self-served from the buffet, with perhaps the exception of any egg dishes or other cooked-to-order items and also the beverages required.
- **Buffet reception**: a buffet reception is offered for special functions and private parties only and, as the name implies, the food and beverages are served from a buffet table. Usually there is no seating but a range of individual tables spaced around the reception area.

During the reception some of the staff must be positioned behind the buffet for the service and replenishment of the dishes of food and beverages. Other members of staff should circulate the room with the food and to clear away any dirty items. As the dishes on the buffet become depleted, they should be quickly replenished or cleared away so that the buffet continues to look clean and tidy.

Example checklists

Typical checklists for staff to follow in performance of service standards related to a buffet or counter, salad bar and dining areas are given below.

Hot and cold counters

- Do not leave the hot food service counter unattended once service begins, as this will cause congestion in the flow of service.
- Arrange for someone to take your place if you have to leave the service area for any reason.
- Wipe up any spillages immediately. Spillages left on a hot counter for too long will harden and create problems later with cleaning.
- When serving, it is important to adhere to portion-control specifications.
- When a dish of hot food is only one-third full inform the kitchen that more will be needed. Do not allow food items to run out during service. If the end of service time is approaching, check with the supervisor before requesting more.
- Ensure plates are kept well stocked. If running low on plates on the service counter, replenish immediately from back-up stock.
- Hot food items left too long in the hot food service counter prior to service may deteriorate. The time factor here is important. Allow minimum time between placing in/on the hot food service counter and serving. This will help to ensure that the food item, when requested, is served in prime condition.
- Ensure the correct holding temperature is set for both hot and cold counters. This will mean all foods are served at the correct temperatures and will retain their quality as menu items.

Salad bar

- Keep a constant eye on food levels in the salad bar.
- Never refill bowls or replenish plates at the counter. Take a bowl or plate to the kitchen and fill or replenish it there.
- Replace service spoons, slices, etc., to their respective bowls, dishes and plates, if misplaced by customers.
- Wipe up any spillages immediately.
- Keep the salad bar tidy, well arranged and well presented at all times.
- Keep a constant eye on the supply of bowls and plates for the salad counter service.
- Remember: do not wait for a supply of salad bowls and plates to run out before replenishing from the back-up supply (beneath the cold counter). During a busy service period this will inevitably hinder the flow of service.

Dining areas

- Ensure the clearing station is ready and in place, and that the following items are available:
  - lined bin
  - bin liners
  - clearing trolley
  - wiping cloth
  - recommended cleaning materials.
- Keep a constant eye on tables and make sure they are clean and tidy at all times. Change table covers regularly, as and when required. An untidy and messy table is not pleasant for the customer.

- The dining area should be self-clearing, i.e. customers are requested to return their trays containing used plates and cutlery to the clearing station. Failing this, promptly clear tables of any trays.
- At the clearing station:
  - empty the tray of used plates and cutlery etc., and stack ready for the dishwasher
  - empty disposable contents of a tray into a lined standing bin
  - wipe the tray clean with recommended cleaning materials.
- Return the stack of cleaned trays to the tray stack, lining each tray with a paper liner (if used) before putting into place.
- Ensure there is always enough water in the drinking water jugs.
- Ensure there are enough napkins in the napkin dispenser.
- Check cutlery containers are adequately stocked.

Note

During service always ensure that, at any one time, there is an adequate supply of trays in the tray rack ready for the customers' use.

Single-point service

The main forms of single-point service are found in the following types of establishments.
- **Takeaways**: where the customer orders and is served from a single point, at a counter, hatch or snack stand; the customer consumes off the premises; some takeaway establishments provide dining areas. This also includes drive-thrus, where the customer drives their vehicle past the order, payment and collection points.
- **Food courts**: series of autonomous counters where customers may either order and eat or buy from a number of counters and eat in a separate eating area, or takeaway.
- **Kiosk**: outstation used to provide service for peak demand or in a specific location; may be open for customers to order and be served, or used for dispensing to staff only.
- **Vending**: provision of food service and beverage service by means of automatic retailing.
- **Bar**: order, service and payment point and consumption area in licensed premises.

Bar food service

The service of food and beverages in bars may be to customers at the bar or alternatively to customers seated at tables. If customers are to be served at tables then the procedures for this are based on table service as described in Section 18.1, page 292. Customers at the bar will have their order taken and served at the bar, with payment usually taken at the same time.

Figure 18.23 Bar and seating area (image courtesy of Gleneagles Hotel, Scotland)

For information on bar preparation refer to bar equipment in Section 3.5, page 54, and bar preparation in Section 17.1, page 269. For information on the service of alcoholic drinks and non-alcoholic drinks refer to Chapter 17.

18.7 Clearing for counter self-service and single-point service

The main methods for clearing in foodservice operations are summarised in Table 18.3.

Table 18.3 Clearing methods (source *Croner's Catering*)

System	Description
Manual	The collection and sorting to trolleys by operators for transportation to the wash-up area
Semi-self-clear	The placing of soiled ware by customers on strategically placed trolleys within the dining area for removal by operators
Self-clear	The placing of soiled ware by customers on a conveyor or conveyor belt tray-collecting system for mechanical transportation to the wash-up area
Self-clear and strip	The placing of soiled ware into conveyor belt baskets by customers for direct entry of the baskets through the dishwashing machines

In all cases food waste and disposable items are usually put directly into the waste bins provided, which are often separated into different recyclable types such as food, paper, plastics and cans.

Clearing tables in the dining areas

As tables are vacated and customers remain in the room, the procedures described below may be followed:
- The basic clearing techniques described in Section 18.3 (page 302) can be employed as appropriate.
- Once plates are cleared from the table, the debris (food wastage) would be scraped from plates into a plastic bowl. These bowls of food wastage must be cleared on a regular basis from the workstations for hygiene reasons and to avoid smells affecting the dining area.

- Used cutlery is often initially placed into a plastic bowl containing hot water and a liquid soap detergent. This loosens grease and oil from the cutlery prior to it being placed into the dishwasher for washing, rinsing and sterilisation. Alternatively, dirty cutlery may be placed into cutlery stands at the workstation or on the clearing trolley in readiness for transportation to the wash-up area, where they would be placed into the dishwasher.
- Stack same-sized plates together on a tray; never mix sizes as this can cause a safety hazard resulting in accidents to staff or customers. Spread the weight load on a tray evenly to make it easier to carry. Further information on carrying trays may be found in Section 14.8 (page 225).
- Glassware should be cleared on to separate trays from crockery and cutlery. This way it is less likely for accidents to occur. Dirty glassware will be taken to the workstation and can be put into glass racks for transportation to the wash-up area.
- Immediately customers vacate their tables the dining area staff should clear any remaining items from the table on to trays and return them to the workstation. The tables should be wiped down with anti-bacterial cleaning agents and any table accompaniments normally set on the table as part of the lay-up should be replenished.

18.8 Function/banquet service

Traditional service

- For formal events it is normal practice that the top-table service staff always commence serving/clearing first.
- The banqueting/events headwaiter will organise their staff so that, at a given signal, the top-table service staff can begin to serve, immediately followed by all the other service staff.
- The banqueting/events headwaiter will not give any signal to clear a course until all guests have finished eating.
- All staff should leave and enter the room led by the top-table staff and followed by the other service staff in a predetermined order.
- This predetermined order generally means that those staff with stations furthest from the service doors should be nearer the top-table service staff in the line-up.
- Theoretically this means that, when entering the room, all service staff reach their stations at more or less the same time.

Figure 18.24 A function room ready for an event

- Each member of staff then serves their own table using the predetermined service method – either full silver service or a combination of plated and silver service.
- When deciding on the predetermined order, another factor that should influence the final decision is that of safety. As far as it is possible, any cross-flow of staff and bottlenecks in their movement to and from the room should be avoided.

Food and beverage service skills

Wave service

Wave service can be used mainly when meals are plated, although some establishments also use this style of service organisation for silver service and other forms of service. It is a way of saving on staffing for conventional service and/or speeding up service for plated systems.

The term 'wave' comes from the approach where tables are not served altogether but are served over a period of time, with individual guests on some tables being served quickly at one time before the service on other tables is started. There are two basic approaches to this:

1 For both plated service and traditional silver service, the staff from two tables next to each other will work together as a team. This happens throughout the room. The pair work together to serve one of the tables completely and then will assist each other to completely serve the other table.

2 The alternative is for a larger group of staff to work as a team, serving one table completely at a time before going on to the next. This is especially useful when plated service is being used for the food.

The resulting effect of adopting these approaches is that tables are served throughout the room, over a period, but with each individual table's service being completed quickly.

Wave service may also be used for events where guests are seated on a top table and sprigs. In this case, sections of the banquet tables are served before moving to another section of the table layout.

For plated service, one of the difficulties is ensuring that the food is hot when being served. For table service the speed of the transfer of the plate from the kitchen can ensure that the food is hot when reaching the table, assuming of course that the food has also been presented on to hot plates.

Key term

Wave service – service of whole tables, one at a time and proceeding across the room

18.9 Room service

Depending on the type of establishment, the service offered here may vary from only a tray service for continental breakfast to the service of all meals and beverages (table service) in the room over a 24-hour period. Staff should have a wide and varied knowledge of the service of all types of meals and beverages and the technical skills involved.

Tray service

The laying up of a tray involves the same procedure, with a few exceptions, as laying up a table in the restaurant. As most orders for room service are known in advance the tray may be laid according to the order. The main differences between laying a tray and a table for service in a restaurant are:

- a tray cloth replaces the tablecloth
- underplates are usually left out because of lack of space and to reduce the weight of the tray.

With standard orders for service in the rooms, the trays are often laid up in advance and kept in the pantry covered with a clean cloth.

The positioning of the items on the tray is important:

- Items should be placed so that everything is to hand for the guest. For example, a beverage and the cup, saucer and teaspoon should be placed to the top centre-right of the tray, as this is in the correct position for pouring and helps balance the tray.

- Any bottled proprietary sauce required should be laid flat to avoid accidents when carrying the tray.
- The spouts of hot beverage pots or jugs should face inwards, to avoid spillages, which may cause scalding to the server or slippages on wet floors.

The service procedure:

- On arriving at the door of the room, the member of staff should knock loudly, wait for a reply, and then enter, placing the tray on a table and then adjusting the items on the tray as appropriate.
- If there are two or more people taking a meal into the guest's room, it may be necessary to lay up a table or trolley – see Figure 18.25 (a)–(c) and to serve the meal in the same way as in the restaurant. After approximately 45 minutes the floor service staff should return to the room, knock and wait for a reply, enter and ask if it is convenient to clear the tray away.

 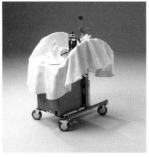 

Figure 18.25 Room service tables (a) Opened (b) Laid and folded for transportation (c) Laid and opened for service, with hot cupboard fitted (images courtesy of Burgess Furniture Ltd, London)

18.10 Lounge service

The lounge is very often the front window of the establishment, so the standards of service should be high to reflect overall standards. This responsibility rests with the lounge staff and they must therefore be of smart appearance, efficient and attentive to hotel guests and other customers.

Lounge staff should have a good knowledge of food and beverage service, especially the licensing laws, and of the technical skills required to provide a competent service. Throughout the day the lounge staff must ensure that the areas are presentable at all times.

The lounge staff must be prepared for the following types of service in the lounge:

- various breakfast foods
- morning coffee
- apéritifs and cocktails before lunch
- coffee, liqueurs and brandy after lunch and dinner services
- afternoon tea
- apéritifs and cocktails before dinner
- service of late-night beverages, both alcoholic and non-alcoholic
- other snacks throughout the day, depending on the type of establishment.

Chance customers usually pay for the service at the time. Resident hotel guests may not wish to pay in the lounge and staff must then ensure that the hotel guest signs the check to confirm the services received. The check must show the correct room number. The amount should then be charged to the guest's hotel account.

18.11 After-service duties

At the end of service a range of duties need to be completed. These duties are carried out with or without customers in the service/dining areas. Depending on the type of establishment these duties may be carried out at the conclusion of a meal period or towards the end of the working day or continue throughout the day.

The general duties that may be carried out at the end of service, and without customers in the service areas, are:

- Clear the cold buffet to the larder. Collect and wash all carving knives and assist generally in clearing the foodservice areas.
- Collect all linen, both clean and dirty, and check that the correct quantities of each item of linen are returned. Used napkins should be tied in bundles of ten. All linen should be placed in the linen basket and returned with the linen list to the linen room or according to the establishment policy.
- Switch off the hotplate. Clear away any service silver or other service dishes remaining and restock the hotplate with clean crockery.
- Return cutlery, glassware, crockery, tableware and trolleys to their designated storage areas.
- Collect all cruets and accompaniments and return them to their correct storage place. Where appropriate, return sauces, etc., to their original containers.
- Check all the sideboards/workstations are completely empty.
- Clear down the bar top, put all the equipment away and wash and polish used glasses. These should be put away in their correct storage place. Remove all empty bottles, etc. Complete consumption and stock sheets. Bar shutters and doors should be made secure.
- Restock the bar from the cellar.
- Empty all beverage service equipment, wash and put away. All perishable materials should be put away in their correct storage places. Still-sets and milk urns should be emptied, washed out and then left standing with cold water in them. Other beverage-making equipment should be cleaned according to the manufacturer's instructions.
- Empty and clean all trolleys and return them to their storage places. Any unused food items from the trolleys should be returned to the appropriate department. Any service equipment used on the trolleys should be cleaned and returned to storage areas.
- Reset duties should be completed in readiness for the next service period. This might include both table lay-ups and sideboard/workstation lay-ups.
- As appropriate all dining area tables and chairs should be wiped down with anti-bacterial cleaning agent.
- Replenish napkin holders, sugar sachets, sauce sachets, cutlery trays and tray stacks as appropriate.

At all times consideration should be given to sustainability issues, including the recycling of used items, the management of waste and the control of energy.

Specific after-service duties

Certain after-service duties will need to be carried out by food and beverage service staff. Allocation of specific responsibilities helps to ensure that all areas are left safe, clean and restocked in readiness for the next service. Examples of these specific duties are shown below.

Headwaiter/supervisor

1 Ensure gas and electrical appliances are switched off and plugs removed from sockets.
2 Return any special equipment to the appropriate work/storage area.
3 Secure all windows and check fire exits.
4 Check that all tasks are completed in a satisfactory manner prior to staff completing their shift.

Station waiter/server/dining area attendant

1 Replace all equipment in the sideboard/workstations according to the equipment listing checklists.
2 Wipe down the sideboard and trolleys, clearing all dirty equipment to the wash-up area.
3 Clear down tables and crumb down. Relay tablecloths and slip cloths as appropriate.
4 Reset tables and sideboards/workstation if required.
5 Switch off and clean sideboard hotplates.
6 Return special equipment to work/storage areas.
7 Return to store cupboards any surplus crockery and silver.
8 Remove plugs, having switched off all electrical sockets.
9 Mop, vacuum and sweep floors as appropriate.

Stillroom staff

1 Ensure the correct storage of such food items as bread, butter, milk, teabags and ground coffee.
2 Wipe down all working surfaces.
3 Clean and tidy the stillroom fridge and check its working temperature.
4 Check that all equipment is left clean and stored in its correct place.
5 Leftover foods to be placed into clean containers and stored correctly.
6 All surplus accompaniments to be stored correctly in proprietary jars and their lids to be wiped down.
7 Switch off applicable electrical appliances.
8 Make sure all carrying trays are wiped down and stacked correctly.
9 All surplus teapots/coffee pots, etc., to be stored in the appropriate storage area.
10 Check area of responsibility with the headwaiter/supervisor, or the person taking over the area, prior to leaving.

Figure 18.26 Stillroom area cleared at the end of service

Buffet/counter staff

1 Turn off the electricity supply to the hot- and cold-food counters.
2 Clear the hot- and cold-food counters and return all leftover food to the kitchen.
3 Turn off the power supply to the oven at the wall.
4 Clear the oven of any remaining food.
5 Important: write down on the day sheet the number of portions of each type of regenerated meal that is left over as waste. This exercise is essential for portion control monitoring and gives an indication of the popularity or otherwise of any one particular dish. Hand in the daily sheet to the supervisor who will then prepare a consumption sheet to show what was taken out and what is now left. This will then be entered into the sales analysis book.
6 Clean all service utensils, such as serving spoons, ladles, fish slices, knives and trays that have been used during the course of the day in hot-food preparation and service. Wipe them dry.
7 Return all cleaned and dried service utensils to the appropriate storage places ready for the next day's use.
8 Check the stock of plates needed for the next day's service of food.
9 Check area of responsibility with supervisor.

Figure 18.27 Counter service unit cleaned and ready for the next service

1   List three of the six basic technical skills that are necessary in food and beverage service.

2   Why is it important that all members of staff follow the same service principles?

3   When preparing for service what is the main reason checklists are used?

4   List five items that would normally be used when setting a table in a restaurant.

5   List three items of service equipment that the server should have available prior to silver serving a main course, which has already been brought into the restaurant.

6   From which side of the customer are plated foods served?

7   From which side of the customer are dirty plates removed?

8   From which side of the customer are foods silver served on to plates?

9   Two customers have ordered a hot main meat course together with one potato and one vegetable dish each. Describe the standard positioning of foods on the hot joint plate once the food has been silver served.

10 Identify two reasons why service enhancements (sometimes referred to as table theatre) are more costly to provide.

11 Give three reasons why it is important to develop good clearing techniques.

12 In restaurant service what is the main purpose of 'crumbing down'?

In practice

1 Demonstrate the preparation and serving, maintaining and clearing of at least two tables for both food service and the associated beverages within a working environment.

- Carry out preparation activities including setting the tables and organising the workstations.
- Meet, greet and seat the customers.
- Advise customers on food and beverage items.
- Take food and beverage orders and process them.
- Serve a range of plated food items and silver serve at least one item.
- Clear during and after service.
- Clean and store equipment.
- During the table service you are also required to:
  - present, open and serve a bottle of wine
  - serve drinks using a tray.

In all cases you must use specialist equipment and follow the establishment's and health and safety requirements.

2 Keep a record of when you carried out this activity by copying and completing the form below or similar. Ask your tutor/supervisor to initial each skill on the form to show that you have met the required standards for your establishment. Also ask them to comment on your performance to help you improve if necessary.

Record of preparing and serving in a restaurant

Name.. Date..........................

Maintained professional image; worn clean, full, pressed uniform; demonstrated personal hygiene and tidiness throughout	
Followed service conventions as appropriate	
Used the correct forms of address throughout	
Set up tables and workstation stations: • following establishment requirements • accurately and efficiently using correct equipment • confidently within designated timings	
Met, greeted and seated customers and responded to any questions while taking and processing orders	
Used positive selling techniques as appropriate	
Anticipated customers' needs throughout the service and responded to customer requests promptly throughout the service	
Anticipated requirements for extra cutlery and provided additional cutlery at appropriate times	
Served bottle of wine/Champagne and drinks from a tray following establishment's requirements	
Topped up/offered additional beverages using correct procedures	
Served correct dishes to customers	
Identified the dish to the customer on presenting it at the table	
Silver served at least one item	
Efficiently cleared the table (crumb down if appropriate) and stacked plates correctly	
Maintained focus on service until customers departed	
Carried out clearing and other required duties following service and left the section as per establishment requirements	

Bookings, billing and payments

Units covered

This chapter covers the following units:

Level 1

→ Dealing with payments and bookings (107)
→ Maintain and deal with payments (2GEN9, 205)

Level 2

→ Handling payments and maintaining the payment point (210)
→ Maintain and deal with payments (2GEN9, 205)

Learning outcomes		
This chapter will help you to:		
1	Describe the process of taking bookings	334
2	Identify the information required when taking a booking	335
3	Follow the procedure for taking bookings	335
4	Take larger party bookings	336
5	State the purpose of control systems	337
6	Identify order taking and billing method control systems	338
7	Maintain the payment point	338
8	State the different billing methods	339
9	State the different payment methods	340
10	Describe the purpose of sales summary sheets	343
11	Give examples of performance measures	343

19.1 Taking bookings

The procedure for booking a table is often the first contact that a potential customer has with the establishment. It is therefore of the utmost importance that the right impression is given. This will be reflected in your tone of voice, appearance, attitude to the customer and the knowledge you show in asking the right questions in order to gain the correct information to enter on your booking sheet. The right approach will immediately put the customer at ease and allow them to respond more clearly and accurately. They will feel that you wish to assist them in every way you can. It may also encourage future sales due to your pleasant and knowledgeable response.

Bookings may be taken:

- by post
- by email
- by telephone

- via the internet (using online systems)
- by the customer coming to the establishment in person.

19.2 The booking sheet

Most establishments will use some form of booking sheet, either manual or electronic.

The basic information required is the same regardless of how the bookings are taken.

An example of the information that might be required on a booking sheet is given in Figure 19.1. This includes:

- day and date
- name of the customer
- customer's telephone number
- number of covers required
- time of the event – arrival
- any special requirements, for example dietary or disability needs
- signature of the person taking the booking in case of any queries.

This form also shows the maximum number of covers to be booked for a service period and enables a running total of pre-booked covers to be kept. Depending on the policy of the establishment and the total number of covers requested when a booking is being made, written confirmation may be required and/or credit card details taken in order to secure a deposit.

Other information that might be sought includes:

- whether the occasion of the meal is for a special event, such as an anniversary or birthday
- customer preferences about the size, shape and location of a table
- special requests such as requirements for a birthday/anniversary cake and other information, such as customers with allergies.

Should party bookings require special menus, the booking should be referred to the supervisor. Procedures similar to large party bookings (see Section 19.4) will then be adopted.

Restaurant............	Day.............	Date............		Maximum covers............		
Name	Tel. no.	Covers	Arrival time	Running total	Special requirements	Signature

Figure 19.1 Example of a booking sheet

19.3 Procedure for taking bookings

When taking bookings extreme care needs to be taken to ensure all booking details are correct. Should any error be made or if the information is unclear it can result in:

- poor customer and establishment relations
- loss of sales

- tension among the staff resulting in a lowering of standards in the workplace
- problems relating to seating, space available and the provision for those customers with additional needs
- disturbance to other customers.

Bookings by telephone

When taking a booking by telephone the procedure shown below might be used.

- When the telephone rings, lift the receiver and say either: 'Good morning', 'Good afternoon' or 'Good evening', and state the name of the establishment, then 'How may I help you?'
- If the customer is making the booking in person then say either: 'Good morning', 'Good afternoon' or 'Good evening Sir/Madam, how may I help you?'
- When taking the booking the essential information required is as listed previously.
- When you have received this information from the customer and made your notes, the full details of the booking should be repeated back to the customer to check that you have understood the customer's requirements properly and to give the customer the opportunity to confirm the details.
- At the end of a telephone call for a booking you should say: 'Thank you for your booking, we shall look forward to seeing you on …'

Other bookings

The procedure for taking a booking in person are similar to those for taking a booking via the telephone. When dealing with bookings by post or email the information required is the same as that described above.

Confirmation of a booking is normally sent back to the customer by the same method as the booking was received, for example by email or post.

Internet bookings are often automatically confirmed to the customer at the time the booking is made. The details of the booking are then forwarded to the establishment for inclusion on the booking sheet.

Cancellations

When a cancellation is received, the cancellation details are confirmed back to the customer by repeating his/her request over the telephone. It is also good practice to then ask if you can take a booking for any other occasion in place of the cancellation.

19.4 Larger party bookings

There will often be different procedures in an establishment for dealing with bookings for larger parties, for example for parties of six covers or more. When a customer is ready to make a booking a file is opened. This can be handwritten or computerised depending on the establishment. The file will contain the client's details and will be used to hold all the requirements for the particular event, as well as all correspondence sent and received. The basic information that is recorded is as listed previously. There will also be additional specific information required according to the nature of the occasion. This may include:

- date and time of event (including access and clear down times)
- type of event – such as birthday celebration, wedding, conference, cocktail party or exhibition

- food and beverage requirements
- service methods (including wines and drinks being inclusive or requiring a cash payment)
- table plan
- price being charged (for the party as a whole or charged as the price per head) and the inclusion or otherwise of service charges
- additional charges that will be made
- provision for customers with additional needs
- deadline for confirmation of final numbers
- contractual requirements (deposit payments, payment in advance, etc.)
- car parking requirements.

19.5 Purpose of control systems

In order to make maximum profit for an establishment a control system covering the sale of all food and beverages in a foodservice operation is essential. The type of control system used will vary from one operation to another.

In large establishments a control and accounts department will be in overall charge of the efficient running and working of the control systems used. In a smaller establishment this may be managed by an assistant manager, who will personally carry out the necessary daily and weekly checks. To make it easier for food and beverage service staff to operate, control systems should be kept as simple as possible.

- A control system essentially monitors areas where selling takes place.
- There must be efficient control of all food and beverage items issued from the various departments.
- The system should reduce any theft and keep wastage to a minimum.
- Management should be provided with any information they require for costing purposes and so that they may estimate accurately for the coming financial period.
- The cashier should be able to make out the customer's bill correctly so that the customer is neither overcharged nor undercharged.
- The system should show a breakdown of sales and income received in order that adjustments and improvements may be made.

The main control methods in use in foodservice establishments are:
- Order taking methods (see Section 16.2, page 261).
- Billing methods (see Section 19.8, page 339).
- Sales summary sheets (see Section 19.10, page 343).
- Performance measures (see Section 19.11, page 343).

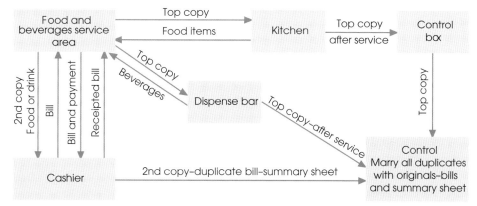

Figure 19.2 Flow chart of food and beverage checking system

The process of food and beverage revenue control is summarised in Figure 19.2. This chart is based on the triplicate method for food and the duplicate method for the dispense bar. The chart indicates that all top copies go to the dispense points (bar, kitchen) and follows the flow of information through until top and second copies are matched up by control.

19.6 Order taking and billing method control systems

The systems that are used to support the various order taking and billing methods are summarised in Table 19.1.

Table 19.1 Order taking and billing method control systems

Method	Description
Manual systems	Handwritten duplicate or triplicate checks for ordering from kitchen and bar, and for informing the cashier. Often used with a cash till or cash register. Found in independent restaurants and cafés
Pre-checking system	Orders entered directly on to a keyboard; each order check is printed with a duplicate and retains a record of all transactions. Keyboard may be pre-set or pre-priced. Found in many full-service restaurants
Electronic cash registers	Allows for a wider range of functions including sales analysis. Installed as stand-alone or linked systems. Found in store restaurants, cafeterias and bars
Electronic point of sale (EPOS) control systems	Separate keyboard terminals in the various service areas, linked to remote printers or visual display units (VDUs) in the kitchen, bar, etc. Terminals can be fixed or set in docking stations for hand-held use. In hotels this equipment may also be linked to the hotel accounting systems. More sophisticated systems (point-of-sale, computerised and satellite) provide for increasingly efficient service at the point of sale, as well as improving the flow and quality of information to management for control purposes. (For an illustration of an electronic hand-held control system, see Figure 19.3, page 338)
Computerised systems	Enables a number of serving terminals, intelligent tills and remote printers to be controlled by a master unit compatible with standard computer hardware. Functions may also include a variety of performance measures, such as planning and costing, sales analysis, gross profit reporting, stock control, reordering and forecasting, VAT returns, payroll, staff scheduling and account information. Often found in hotels, fast-food and chain restaurants
Satellite stations	Remote terminals linked by telephone to a central processor to enable sales performance to be analysed (usually overnight) and reported back. These systems are found in fast-food and chain restaurant operations

19.7 Maintaining the payment point

Before the start of service the cashier should have made all relevant checks and have the required materials to hand. Each establishment will have its own procedure but will generally include the following:

- Check the float: if it is incorrect follow the company procedure.
- Ensure the cash drawer is properly organised with notes and coins in the relevant compartments.
- Ensure there are enough till/printer rolls, promotional items, bill folders, stapler, paper clips, pens and credit/debit card vouchers for the back-up manual system.

The cashier's duties for table and assisted service may be summarised as follows:
- issuing and recording of check books
- maintaining cash floats
- preparation of customer bills
- maintaining copies of the food and wine orders together with the bills in case of server or customer queries
- counter-signing spoilt checks
- receiving payments (which may include cash, credit card and cheque payments as well as luncheon vouchers or other forms of prepaid voucher)
- receiving all unused checks back
- ensuring payments are balanced with manual or electronic sales summaries
- delivering the reports and payment to the control department.

Payments may be processed by the waiting staff or the cashier.

Where services are provided to residents in hotel lounges and in room service, payment might not be taken at the same time. Therefore, all bills must be signed by the resident concerned to show he or she has received a particular service. When a resident signs a bill the waiting staff must ensure the correct room number is obtained so that the charge can be made on the right bill. These bills should then be immediately passed to the control and accounts department. It is their job to ensure that the bills are posted on to the guest's account. In this way all residents' bills are kept up to date and all services provided are charged for.

19.8 Billing methods

The seven basic billing methods are described in Table 19.2.

Table 19.2 Billing methods

Method	Description
Bill as check	Second copy of order used as bill
Separate bill	Bill made up from duplicate check and presented to customer
Bill with order	Service to order and billing at same time, for example bar or takeaway service methods
Pre-paid	Customer purchases ticket or card in advance, either for specific meal or specific value
Voucher	Customer has credit issued by a third party for either a specific meal or specific value, for example a luncheon voucher or tourist agency voucher
No charge	Customer not paying – credit transaction
Deferred	Refers to, for example, event catering where the bill is to be paid by the organiser, or customers who have an account

All billing methods are based on these seven concepts. The main systems used to support these methods and the different payment methods are described in Section 19.9.

Figure 19.3 Electronic point of sale billing and payment system

Figure 19.4 Example of a bill

```
PALM COURT RESTAURANT & LOUNGE
        The Langham, London
          VAT: 672331741
  1014 No11                       1
  115/1       1546         GST 2
          10NOV'13 21:
  ---------------------------------
  1 053 LP NV Half          40.00
  1 Dec. Sp 750ml            5.00
  1 Gravadlax               14.00
  1 Scallops 3 pcs          14.00
  2 Fillet Steak            56.00
  2 Chips                    7.50
    2 SAUV BLNC, 125ML
  2 Open Beverage           16.00
  3 GL Pinot Noir           46.50
  1 Sharing Petit Four      10.00
    SUBTOTAL               209.00
  12.5% SERV CHG             26.13
  21:30 TOTAL DUE     GBP235.13
  39.19  VAT 20.0%         235.13


  Gratuity:_____

  Name:_____

  Room:_____

  Signature:
  A discretionary (2.5% Svc Charge
  has been added to your total.
          VAT: 672331741
```

19.9 Payment methods

There are various ways of making payments for goods or services received. The main methods of payment are described below.

Cash

When accepting cash the amount of cash received by the operator should always be discretely checked in front of the customer and, when change is given, it should be counted back to the customer. Any notes received by the operator should be checked to ensure they are not forgeries. An itemised and receipted bill should always accompany the change.

Cheque

The use of cheques is declining. The acceptance of cheques is now mostly restricted to the payment of invoices, for example, for monthly accounts.   For payments in food and beverage operations, the acceptance of a cheque is dependent on the policy of the establishment and is most often limited to known regular customers. If checks are being accepted then the operator receiving the cheque should make sure:

- it is dated correctly
- it is made payable to the correct firm or company
- the correct amount is filled in
- it is signed by the person indicated on the cheque.

It is also normal practice for some additional form of identification to be required, such as a credit or debit card. In this case the credit or debit card must be in date and the signature on the cheque must be the same as that on the credit or debit card. In the case of a debit card, the bank sort code and account number should also be the same.

Credit cards/debit cards/charge cards

Figure 19.5 Example of a hand-held credit/debit card payment terminal with printer

- **Credit cards**: allow customers to spend up to a predetermined limit. The customer receives a statement of payments at the end of each month, which can then be paid off in full or in part. Interest is charged on any remaining balance.
- **Debit cards**: used in a similar way to a credit card but the amount due is immediately deducted from the customer's bank account. Examples include the Visa Debit, Maestro and Visa Electron.
- **Charge cards**: these work in a similar way to credit cards but the customer is invoiced once a month. The account must then be paid up in full. Examples include American Express and Diners Club cards.

On receipt of a credit, debit or charge card the operator should check that it is still valid by looking at the dates on the card. Most credit/debit/charge cards are now verified using chip and PIN but in some instances they may be signature verified.

Signature verified

This is a manual system in which the validity of the card is checked, often through an online or dial-up connection to the card issuer, by passing it through an electronic card reader. Once verified, the details of the transaction are printed in the form of an itemised bill, which the customer is then asked to sign. A copy of this itemised bill is given as a receipt. Some establishments also make out a sales voucher. The customer is then requested to sign the voucher, after which the operator should check the signature with that on the card. The customer receives a copy of the voucher as a receipt.

Chip and PIN

Chip and PIN means that the customer enters their PIN (personal identification number) into a keypad when they use a credit, debit or charge card for face-to-face transactions in shops, hotels or restaurants.

- The POS (point of sale) terminals provide step-by-step instructions on how to complete a transaction.
- Customers *must* enter their own PIN – it is not secure for a member of staff to do it and customers are required not to reveal their PIN to anyone.
- The prompts on the POS terminal screen are followed and the payment is processed.
- The card is then removed from the card reader.
- The receipt is issued and the receipt and the card are returned to the customer.

There are two ways of dealing with payments in restaurants:

- The customer may be asked to come to the cash desk or workstation to complete the payment transaction there – some customers may prefer this.
- A hand-held self-powered terminal is taken to the customer at their table.

Note

Some establishments may limit how many cards can be used to pay one bill.

If problems are experienced during the operation of the card (PDQ) machine and the operator is unable to process the transaction, then a back-up manual card swipe system can be used.

Locked PIN

If the customer enters the wrong PIN three times in a row, the card will become temporarily unusable. Customers can unlock their PIN by contacting their card issuer. Contact numbers are on the back of most cards and most cash machines have an unlock PIN facility.

People with disabilities

The procedures for taking payment from people with disabilities are generally the same as described above. However, some additional considerations are given below.

1   Offer to assist when needed and, most importantly, exercise patience to ensure that the customer has enough time to complete a stress-free transaction.
2   Make sure all customers, including those who use wheelchairs, can easily reach the desk or table to sign the bill or to access the PIN pad.
3   Follow the terminal prompts – some cardholders may have chip and signature cards instead of chip and PIN cards. Chip and PIN terminals will recognise this type of card and automatically ask for a signature.
4   Encourage or help the customer to pick up the PIN pad from the cradle if appropriate.
5   Suggest that the customer shields the PIN pad from other customers as they enter their PIN.

Declined transactions

Procedures for declined transactions are the same for any credit card/debit card/charge card payments, whether signature verified or chip and PIN. If a card is declined, always ask for an alternative method of payment.

Travellers cheques

These may be issued in sterling, US dollars, Euros and other currencies. The travellers cheque must be signed once when issued and again when used as payment or when exchanging for cash. The rate of exchange will be that at the time of the transaction. All travellers cheques come in different values and this value is guaranteed as long as the two signatures match. When a payment is made by travellers cheque the customer must:
● date the cheque or cheques required
● make them payable to the establishment concerned
● sign the cheque or cheques for a second time in the space indicated.

The cashier will then:
● match the two signatures
● ask for other identification to check the two signatures against, for example, the customer's passport
● give change where needed, most often in the local currency.

Vouchers and tokens

Vouchers, such as Luncheon Vouchers, may be offered in exchange for food in those establishments that accept them. The vouchers have an expiry date. Should food be purchased above the value of the voucher, the difference must be paid for in cash.

Tokens might be exchanged for specific meals or for certain values. If food purchased is more than the value of the token then the difference is again paid in cash. No change can be given for purchases valued at less than the token being exchanged.

Dealing with discrepancies

When dealing with cash, do not allow anyone to interrupt you during the transaction or get involved with the counting of money as this will only lead to confusion.

- Always double check cash received before placing it in the till and any change before giving it out.
- If you make a mistake always apologise and remain polite. If you feel you cannot deal with a situation, ask for assistance from your supervisor or manager.
- Bank notes should be checked for forgeries and, if found to be fake, then they must not be accepted. You should explain why you cannot accept them, advising the customer to take the note to the police station.
- If credit card fraud is suspected the credit card company may request that the card is retained. Suggest to the customer that they contact the company to discuss the matter. You may wish to offer the use of a telephone with some privacy.

19.10 Sales summary sheets

At the end of a service period sales summary sheets are produced. These are also known as restaurant analysis sheets, bill summaries or records of restaurant sales.

The purpose of the sales summary sheet is to provide:

- a way of checking and ensuring the revenue matches the items sold
- the reconciliation of items with different gross profits
- sales mix information
- records of popular/unpopular items
- records for stock control.

They may also include breakdowns of individual staff sales or specific till sales.

There are many different formats for sales summaries and these are often electronically produced. Depending on the needs of the establishment, the information may include:

- date
- address of food and beverage outlet (if more than one exists)
- period of service
- bill numbers
- table numbers
- number of covers per table
- bill totals
- analysis of sales, e.g. food, beverages, or more detailed, such as menu and wine and drink list items
- various performance measures
- cashier's name.

19.11 Performance measures

A range of information is collected during the revenue control phase. This information is often given automatically on the sales summaries and control sheets, and includes the following performance measures:

- **Average spend per customer (or per head)**: this is a calculation of the average amount spent per person during a service period. It is calculated by dividing the total sales by the number of people or covers served.

- **Average check**: this performance measure is useful in bars or takeaway operations where the actual number of customers is not known. This data can also be used to calculate the average number of customers in a group.
- **Sales mix data**: provides information on:
  - popular/unpopular items on the menu/drinks lists
  - records for stock control, for example to help predict future demand
  - changes in customers' interests
  - where profits/losses are being made.
- **Seat turnover**: this is a pointer to efficiency. It shows how many times a seat is being used during a service period. In a snack bar the seat turnover might be four to five times per service period. In an expensive restaurant the seat turnover might be once per service period. In operations where customers do not occupy specific seats (such as in cafeterias or takeaway operations) the customer throughput is calculated by the number of till transactions per service period (e.g. lunch) or time period (e.g. per hour).
- **Sales per square metre or per foot**: an alternative method of comparison between establishments is to calculate the sales per square metre or per foot. This is particularly useful in bars or takeaway operations where earnings per seat cannot be calculated. It is calculated by dividing the total sales by the square meterage of the service area, for a specific service period.

Relationship between revenue, costs and profits

In sales summary sheets there is often a breakdown of costs against the revenue. For a foodservice operation there is a relationship between the **costs** of running the operation, the **revenue** that is received and the **profit** that is made. In foodservice operations there are three elements of cost:

1 **Food or beverage costs**: often called cost of sales.
2 **Labour**: wages, salaries, staff feeding, uniforms.
3 **Overheads**: rent, rates, advertising, fuel.

Food and beverage costs	Cost of sales
Labour costs	Gross profit
Overhead costs	
Net profit	
Total sales £	Revenue 100%

Figure 19.6 Summary of the relationship between revenue, costs and profits in foodservice operations

There are also two types of profit:

1 **Gross profit**: total revenue *less* cost of sales.
2 **Net profit**: gross profit *less* labour costs and overhead costs.

In foodservice operations sales, or revenue, is always equal to 100 per cent. Therefore, the relationship between the elements of costs and profits in foodservice operations may be seen as shown in Figure 19.6.

All elements of cost and profits in a foodservice operation are therefore always calculated as a percentage of the total sales figures. This is different to many retail operations, where the cost of sales figures are taken as 100 per cent, so the gross profit percentage is worked out as a percentage of the cost price.

Note

In kitchen operations gross profit is sometimes called kitchen percentage or kitchen profit.

Testing your learning

1 List five pieces of essential information that should be recorded when taking a booking over the phone.
2 Briefly describe five of the duties performed by a cashier.
3 List three things that must be written on to a triplicate food check when taking an order.
4 Briefly explain three of the seven billing methods.
5 Give one reason why it is important when taking cash payments to ensure there is sufficient change and notes at the payment point.
6 List two ways to maintain the safety of the till.
7 Describe three different methods that you could use to pay a restaurant bill.
8 Briefly describe the process for taking payment using the chip and PIN system for credit/debit/charge cards.
9 What are the possible consequences of not reporting/recording mistakes at the payment point?
10 Who is responsible for the accuracy of the payment point?

In practice

Taking a booking

Taking restaurant bookings accurately contributes to the smooth running of an operation. It is essential that all information is accurately recorded and related back to the customer. This avoids mistakes and helps to maintain good customer relations. Copy this blank booking sheet and complete it using the information supplied below.

Restaurant:		Day:			Date:			Maximum covers:	
Name	Tel. No.	Covers	Arrival time	Running total		Special requirements		Signature	

- Mr Rushinton, table for 6 people, 2 vegans, window table, 8pm, 020 3780 493
- Jane Hibbert, e-mail hibbert@farlies.com, 4 persons, 9pm, birthday cake – Happy Birthday Tom.
- Mark Brown, 3 people, 7.30pm, 07890 23 45 98
- Captain Peppard, 5 covers, wheelchair space, one coeliac, 01895 422633
- Mrs Kumar, 6 people at 8 pm, 02459 674593
- Mr Brahma, 6 people at 8pm, 02459 674593
- Jackie King, Touch Phone Ltd. Retirement dinner, 25 persons, three-course set menu, 3 vegetarians, 1 no pork. Includes one glass wine and one glass Champagne per person, £35 per head

Once you have completed the form ask someone else to check that you have entered all of the information correctly.

Annex A: Cocktails and mixed drinks recipes

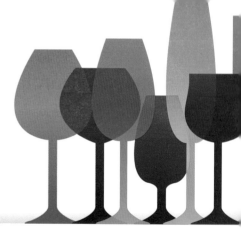

The alphabetical listing of cocktails and mixed drinks below is drawn from various sources including previous editions of this book, the official listings of the International Bartenders Association and the United Kingdom Bartenders' Guild.

A list of non-alcoholic cocktails follows the list of alcoholic cocktails.

When making cocktails and mixed drinks it is important to check the definition for permitted alcoholic liquor measures for your country, including any licensing restrictions on sales to minors.

Examples of glasses for the service of cocktails are shown in Figure 17.2 (page 271).

Alcoholic cocktails

Name	Ingredients	Method
Americano	3 cl Campari 3 cl red vermouth soda water	Place the Campari and sweet vermouth over ice into a Highball glass. Stir well to chill. Top up with soda water to taste. Garnish with twists of orange and lemon peel
B&B	3 cl brandy 3 cl Bénédictine	Pour brandy into a brandy balloon and gently float the Bénédictine over a bar spoon on top
B52	2 cl Kahlúa 2 cl Baileys Irish Cream 2 cl Grand Marnier	Build all the chilled ingredients, in the order listed, into a medium shot glass. Serve with a stirrer
Bacardi Classic	5 cl Bacardi white rum 3 cl fresh lemon or lime juice 0.5 cl grenadine syrup	Place all ingredients on ice into a cocktail shaker. Shake well. Strain into a cocktail glass. Garnish with a maraschino cherry on a cocktail stick across the glass
Bellini	5 cl fresh white peach purée 10 cl well-chilled dry Champagne	Prepare in a Champagne flute by pouring in the fresh peach purée first and then topping up with the well-chilled Champagne or sparkling wine. Garnish with a slice of fresh peach
Between the Sheets	3 cl brandy 3 cl Cointreau 3 cl white rum ½ fresh lemon juice	Shake all ingredients well on ice and strain into a cocktail glass
Black Russian	5 cl vodka 2 cl coffee liqueur	Pour all ingredients into an Old Fashioned glass filled with ice cubes. Stir gently
Black Velvet	Guinness chilled dry Champagne	Half fill a Champagne flute with Guinness and top up with the chilled dry Champagne. Sometimes served in silver tankards

Name	Ingredients	Method
Bloody Mary	6 cl vodka 15 cl tomato juice (or as required) 1 cl lemon juice	Place ingredients in a cocktail shaker and shake well on ice. Season and serve in a Highball glass
	Variations: To make tomato juice spicier, add salt, pepper and Worcestershire sauce to taste. Any of the following may also be added to enhance flavour: dash of Tabasco, fresh lemon juice, pepper from a peppermill or cayenne pepper. Garnish may also be varied by the use of a stick of celery, carrot stick or a wedge of lemon. A *Virgin Mary* excludes the vodka	
Blue Lady	3 cl Cognac 3 cl blue Curaçao 3 cl lemon juice 1 egg white	Put all the ingredients together into a cocktail shaker with ice. Shake vigorously. Strain into a cocktail glass
Bramble	4 blackberries fresh lime juice 1 teaspoon caster sugar or gomme syrup 5 cl gin crushed ice soda water 1cl Crème de Mûre (blackberry liqueur)	Place the blackberries in a small bowl or a mortar and pestle. Add the lime juice and sugar and muddle quickly. Strain through a cheesecloth into an Old Fashioned glass. Add the gin and crushed ice. Top up with soda. Add the blackberry liqueur. Stir. Serve with a straw, a slice of lime and a blackberry in the drink
Brandy Alexander	3 cl brandy 3 cl fresh double cream 3 cl brown Crème de Cacao	Put all ingredients into a cocktail shaker with ice and shake well. Strain into a chilled cocktail glass. Sprinkle the surface with fresh ground nutmeg
Brandy Cosmopolitan	5 cl cognac 1 cl Cointreau 1 cl fresh lemon juice 1 cl cranberry juice	Pour all ingredients into a shaker with ice and shake. Strain into a cocktail glass. Garnish with a wedge of lime
Bucks Fizz	5 cl fresh orange juice 10 cl well-chilled Champagne	Prepare Champagne flute by first pouring in the fresh orange and then top up with the well-chilled Champagne. Decorate with a curl/twist of orange peel
Caipirinha	1 small fresh lime 1½ teaspoons caster sugar 5 cl Cachaça (Brazilian spirit distilled from fermented sugarcane)	Wash the lime and slice off the top and bottom and cut into small segments from top to bottom. Add the lime segments and the sugar to an Old Fashioned glass. Crush the lime to make juice and muddle to make sure the sugar has dissolved. Add ice cubes and the Cachaça and stir. Serve with a stirrer and an optional straw
Champagne Cocktail	½ sugar cube 2 dashes Angostura bitters 25 cl Champagne (well chilled) or sparkling wine 0.5 cl brandy	Place the sugar cube soaked in Angostura into a Champagne flute. Pour over the well-chilled Champagne and float the brandy on the surface by pouring over the back of a teaspoon. Garnish with a slice of orange and a maraschino cherry
	Note: This cocktail may be made with any sparkling wine but should then be called by the name of the wine used and not Champagne Cocktail, as the name Champagne is protected	
Cosmopolitan	5 cl vodka 1 cl Cointreau 1 cl fresh lime juice 1 cl cranberry juice	Place all ingredients into cocktail shaker filled with ice. Shake well and strain into a large cocktail glass. Garnish with a slice of lime
Cuba Libre	5 cl white rum 10 cl cola	Pour the white rum into a Collins glass with ice. Garnish with a lemon/lime wedge. Top up with cola to taste

Name	Ingredients	Method
Daiquiri	4.5 cl white rum 2 cl fresh lemon/lime juice 0.5 cl gomme syrup	Place all ingredients on ice into a cocktail shaker. Shake well. Strain into a cocktail glass. Garnish with a wedge of lime
	Variation: Frozen Daiquiri – ingredients as above but with the addition of one scoop of vanilla ice cream. Pour all ingredients into blender with crushed ice. Blend until slushy and smooth and pour into chilled goblet	
Gin Fizz	5 cl gin 3 cl fresh lemon juice 1 cl gomme syrup 8 cl soda water	Shake gin, lemon juice and gomme syrup with ice cubes in a cocktail shaker. Strain into a Highball glass. Top up with soda water. Garnish with lemon and add straws
	Variations: Make with Sloe Gin; *Golden Fizz* – same as Gin Fizz plus egg yolk; *Royal Fizz* – same as Gin Fizz plus whole egg; *Silver Fizz* – same as Gin Fizz plus egg white only	
Golden Dream	3 cl Galliano 1.5 cl Cointreau 1.5 cl fresh orange juice 1.5 cl single cream	Shake all ingredients vigorously over ice in a cocktail shaker. Strain into a chilled cocktail glass
Grasshopper	3 cl Crème de Menthe 3 cl white crème de cacao 3 cl single cream	Place all ingredients over ice in a cocktail shaker. Shake thoroughly. Strain into a chilled cocktail glass.
Harvey Wallbanger	5 cl vodka 15 cl orange juice 2 cl Galliano	Pour the vodka and orange juice directly into a Highball glass containing ice. Float the Galliano on top by pouring over the back of a teaspoon. Garnish with a slice of orange and a straw and stirrer
Highball	5 cl whiskey Dry ginger ale	Place ice in a Highball glass. Add the whiskey and stir to chill well. Add the dry ginger ale to taste. Decorate with a twist of lemon peel
John Collins	6 cl gin 3 cl fresh lemon juice 1.5 cl gomme syrup 6 cl soda water	Pour all ingredients directly into a Highball filled with ice. Stir gently. Garnish with lemon slice and maraschino cherry. Add dash of Angostura bitter (Note: Use 'Old Tom' gin for a Tom Collins)
Kamikaze	4 cl vodka 2 cl Cointreau 2 cl lemon juice	Add all ingredients into cocktail shaker filled with ice. Shake well and strain into a cocktail glass. Garnish with a lime wedge and stirrer
Kir	1 cl Crème de Cassis 12.50 cl white wine (dry white Burgundy)	Place the Crème de Cassis in a chilled wine glass. Add the well-chilled white wine. Stir thoroughly
Kir Royale	1 cl Crème de Cassis 12.5 cl dry Champagne	Place the Crème de Cassis in a chilled Champagne flute. Add the well-chilled Champagne. Do not stir
Mai-Tai	2 cl golden rum 2 cl dark rum 1 cl triple sec/Cointreau 1 cl orgeat syrup (almond) 2 cl fresh lime juice 3 dashes grenadine	Add all ingredients into a cocktail shaker filled with ice. Shake well and strain into a goblet glass. Garnish with a wedge of lime. Serve with a straw and a stirrer
Manhattan	6 cl American rye whiskey 3 cl sweet vermouth 1 dash of Angostura bitters	Pour ingredients into a mixing glass over ice and stir until well chilled. Strain into a cocktail glass. Garnish with a maraschino cherry

Name	Ingredients	Method
	Variation: Dry Manhattan – substitute sweet vermouth for 2 cl dry vermouth. Garnish with a thin twist of lemon or an olive	
Margarita	3 cl tequila 3 cl fresh lemon juice 3 cl Cointreau or triple sec	Place all ingredients on ice into a cocktail shaker. Shake well. Strain into a cocktail glass rimmed with salt. Garnish with a wedge of lime
Martini	9 cl gin 2–3 drops of dry vermouth	Pour the gin into a chilled cocktail glass. Float 2–3 drops dry vermouth on top of the gin. For a Dry Martini squeeze oil from lemon peel on to the drink. Garnish with either an olive on a cocktail stick or a twist of lemon
	Variations: *Sweet Martini* – basic method as for Dry Martini but using red (sweet) vermouth instead of dry and garnish with a maraschino cherry. For a *Vodka Martini* replace the gin with vodka	
Mint Julep	mint leaves 1 teaspoon caster sugar soda water to moisten 5.0 cl Bourbon whiskey crushed ice	Place mint leaves and sugar into a Highball glass. Moisten with soda water and muddle the mixture to dissolve the caster sugar. Add the Bourbon whiskey and fill the Highball glass with the crushed ice. Stir and decorate with mint. Serve with straws
Mojito	3 sprigs of mint 1 teaspoon sugar 2 cl fresh lime juice 5 cl white rum soda water/sparkling mineral water	Muddle mint sprigs with sugar and lime juice in a Highball glass. Add ice and rum and top with soda water/sparkling mineral water. Garnish with sprig of mint leaves. Serve with a straw and a stirrer
Moscow Mule	5 cl vodka 1 cl fresh lime juice Ginger beer to taste	Fill a Highball glass with ice. Add the vodka and fresh lime juice. Stir well to blend and chill. Top with ginger beer to taste. Decorate with a twist of lime and a stirrer
Mulled Wine *(Serves 20)*	whole orange studded with cloves (clouted) 2 cinnamon sticks 5 g (¼ oz) mixed spice 2 bottles of Burgundy or Rhône red wine ½ bottle Dubonnet ½ bottle drinking water 25 g (1 oz) sultanas 2 lemon halves 1 × 400 g (1 lb) jar of clear honey ¼ bottle dark rum	Heat the clouted orange for 10 minutes in the oven to bring out the flavour. Tie the mixed spices in a muslin bag to prevent clouding the wine. Place all of the ingredients with the exception of the rum into a large pot. Hold some of the honey back so as to be able to adjust the flavour later. Place the pot on a low heat and stir occasionally. Bring the mixture to boiling point but do not allow it to boil. When ready to serve add the rest of the honey to taste. Finish with the rum just before serving into small Paris goblets or similar. Sprinkle a little grated nutmeg on to the top of each drink
Negroni	3 cl gin 3 cl sweet vermouth 3 cl Campari dash of soda water	Stir all ingredients over ice in the bar mixing glass. Strain into a Collins glass filled with crushed ice. Add the soda water to taste. Garnish with a slice of orange and a stirrer
Old Fashioned	1 sugar cube 1 dash Angostura bitters 1 splash soda water 5 cl Bourbon, Scotch or rye whiskey	In an Old Fashioned glass saturate one lump of sugar (or one heaped teaspoon of caster sugar) with Angostura and add a dash of soda water. Gently shake to dissolve caster sugar and then add whiskey and top up with soda water. Fill glass with ice, stir and garnish with a slice of orange and two maraschino cherries and a twist of lemon

Name	Ingredients	Method
Pimm's	5 cl Pimm's No 1 cup 9 cl lemonade/tonic water/ginger ale.	Pour Pimm's into a Worthington or Highball glass. Add ice and top up with lemonade or alternatives. Decorate with slice of apple, orange, lemon and lime and a twist of cucumber peel. Alternatively just use mint leaves. Stirrer and straws are optional
Pina Colada	5 cl white rum 5 cl coconut cream 10 cl pineapple juice	Shake or blend all ingredients vigorously on ice until smooth or place into a blender until smooth. Strain into a chilled Highball glass. Garnish with fresh pineapple wedge and a maraschino cherry. Add straws
Pink Gin	2 or 3 drops of Angostura bitters to taste 5 cl gin	Fill a Paris goblet or Rocks glass with crushed ice to chill it. Remove the ice and place the Angostura bitters in and swill around. Tip out the excess and pour in gin
Red Snapper	1 cl Canadian rye whisky 1 cl amaretto 2 cl cranberry juice	Pour all the ingredients into a cocktail shaker with ice cubes. Shake well and strain into a chilled cocktail glass
Round the World	3 cl banana liqueur 3 cl Scotch whisky 0.5 cl Cointreau 0.5 cl orange cordial	Put the banana liqueur and whisky into a shaker with plenty of ice. Add Cointreau and undiluted orange cordial. Shake and strain into a cocktail glass. Add orange to garnish and serve
Rusty Nail (or Kilt Lifter)	6 cl Scotch whisky 3 cl Drambuie	Pour all ingredients directly into an Old Fashioned glass filled with ice. Stir gently. Garnish with a lemon twist
Salty Dog	4 cl vodka 4 cl grapefruit juice	Shake vodka and grapefruit juice in cocktail shaker. Strain into a salt-rimmed Highball glass filled with ice
Sazerac	1 white sugar cube dash Angostura bitters dash Peychaud bitters dash soda water 5cl bourbon 1cl Pernod	Place a sugar cube in an Old Fashioned glass and soak with the Angostura and Peychaud bitters. Add enough soda to cover the sugar and crush it with the back of a bar spoon. Add ice and the bourbon. Stir. Float the Pernod over the top. Garnish with a twist of lemon
Screwdriver	5 cl vodka 10 cl fresh orange juice	Place all ingredients on ice into a Highball glass. Stir gently. Decorate with a slice/twist of fresh orange
Sea Breeze	5 cl vodka 10 cl cranberry juice 5 cl grapefruit juice	Build all ingredients in a Highball glass filled with ice. Garnish with a lime wedge
Sex on the Beach	3 cl vodka 1.5 cl peach schnapps 5 cl orange juice 5 cl cranberry juice	Pour all ingredients into a Highball glass filled with ice. Stir. Garnish with a wedge of lime. Serve with a stirrer
Sherry Cup	5 cl dry sherry 9 cl medium cider	Use very chilled ingredients. Put sherry into a Highball or Worthington glass and top up with cider. Garnish with freshly cut cucumber slices
Sidecar	3 cl Cognac 2 cl Cointreau 2 cl fresh lemon juice	Pour all ingredients into a shaker with ice. Shake. Strain into a cocktail glass. Garnish with a maraschino cherry
Singapore Sling	4 cl gin 2 cl cherry brandy 2 cl fresh lemon juice soda water	Place gin, cherry brandy and lemon juice into a cocktail shaker filled with ice cubes. Shake well. Strain into a Highball glass and top up with soda water. Garnish with a lemon slice and a maraschino cherry

Name	Ingredients	Method
Tequila Sunrise	5 cl tequila 15 cl orange juice 1.5 cl grenadine	Place the tequila and fresh orange juice on ice in a Highball glass. Stir well to chill and blend. Add grenadine. Do not stir again. Garnish with an orange spiral, maraschino cherry, straws and a stirrer
Whiskey Collins	5 cl American rye whiskey 2 teaspoons caster sugar 2 cl lemon juice soda water	Pour Whiskey, sugar and lemon juice into a cocktail shaker filled with ice. Shake well. Strain into a Highball glass, add ice cubes and top up with soda water. Garnish with a slice of orange add straws
Whiskey Sour	5 cl Bourbon whiskey 2 cl fresh lemon juice 1 teaspoon egg white powder dash of gomme syrup	Pour all ingredients into a cocktail shaker filled with ice. Shake well. Strain into a cocktail glass. Garnish with a slice of orange
	Variations: *Gin Sour, Bourbon Sour, Rum Sour* (dark rum), *Scotch Sour, Daquiri Sour* (light rum)	
White Lady	3 cl gin 3 cl Cointreau 3 cl fresh lemon juice	Place all ingredients on ice into a cocktail shaker. Shake well and strain into a cocktail glass

Non-alcoholic cocktails

Name	Ingredients	Methods
Fruit Cup	3 cl orange juice 3 cl grapefruit juice 3 cl apple juice lemonade/soda water	Pour all ingredients, with the exception of the lemonade/soda, on to ice in a glass jug. Stir well to blend and chill. Add sliced fruit garnish. Top up with lemonade or soda water. Serve well chilled in Highball or Worthington glasses
Saint Clement's	4.5 cl orange juice 4.5 cl bitter lemon	Mix the orange juice and bitter lemon on ice in a Worthington or Highball glass. Stir well to blend. Garnish with a slice of orange and lemon
Shirley Temple/ Roy Rogers	0.5 cl grenadine 9 cl ginger ale	Place ice in a Highball glass and add grenadine. Pour in the chilled ginger ale. Decorate with full fruit garnish and add straws
	Variations: Ginger ale and fresh lime juice or ginger ale and lime cordial to taste	
Tropicana	3 cl coconut milk 7 cl pineapple juice 7 cl mango juice 1 small banana, peeled and diced	Place all ingredients into a blender and blend for a few seconds. Add a scoop of crushed ice. Blend again. Pour into a goblet. Serve with a straw and garnish with a Cape gooseberry set on the rim
Virgin Mary	Made as for a *Bloody Mary* (see above) but without any alcohol	

Glossary

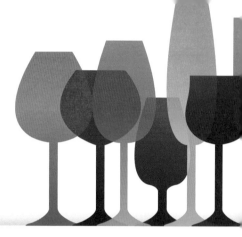

A

À la carte – a type of cover in which the cutlery for each course is laid just before each course is served

À la carte – menu items individually priced

Aboyeur or barker – the person who is in charge of and controls the hotplate during the service period

Active listening – head nodding, gestures and repeating back phrases that are heard to ensure confirmation of understanding

Aerated water – a beverage that contains carbonic gas Examples are tonic water, soda water, dry ginger, bitter lemon, cola and lemonade

Allergen – something that causes an allergic reaction such as swelling, itching or rash

Appetiser – starter courses

Arabica – a mild coffee species

Aromatised wine – wine that has been flavoured and fortified

Assisted service – the customer is served part of the meal at a table and obtains the other part through self-service from some form of display or buffet

B

Bacteria – organisms harmful to humans

Beer line – plastic hose connecting the keg or cask (barrel) to the beer engine or dispensing unit

Blend – a tea composed of a variety of different types of tea

Bouquet – aroma/smell

Broaching head – fitting that connects the beer gas lines on the keg

Buffet – customers select food and drink from displays or passed trays; consumption is either at tables, standing or in lounge area

Built – ingredients and ice are put into the glass one after the other

C

Captive market – the customer does not have a choice of operation

Carvery – some parts of the meal are served to seated customers; other parts are collected by the customers

Catering – offering facilities to people, especially the provision of food and beverages

Cider – alcoholic beverage obtained through the fermentation of apple juice, or a mixture of apple juice and up to 25 per cent pear juice

Cocktail – a short drink up to 10 cl Often used to describe all types of mixed or long drinks

Commercial sector – includes hotels, restaurants, bars and clubs These businesses need to make a profit so that the business can survive and grow

Consortium – a group of independent hotels that make an agreement to buy products and services together

Contracting/outsourcing – to obtain services from an outside supplier

Control measures – ways of minimising risks and hazards

Cost provision – a budget that an organisation must work within

Cost-provision sector – businesses in the public sector that do not need to make a profit Includes hospitals, schools, colleges and prisons

Costs – of materials and providing the service

Cover – place setting

Covering letter – accompanies a CV and explains why you are suitable for the job on offer

Covers – number of people to be served

Cross-contamination – when bacteria are transferred from contaminated food (usually raw food), equipment or surfaces to ready-to-eat food

Crumbing down – removing bread crumbs and other debris from the customer's table

Curriculum vitae (CV) – lists your contact details, educational qualifications and work history, your interests and any other activities in which you participate It is used when applying for a job to demonstrate your skills to potential employers

Customer process – the experience the customer undertakes

Customer relations – the relationship between customers and the food and beverage service staff

Customer service specification – written statements of both technical and service standards, sometimes referred to as 'service offer' or 'customer contract'

Cutlery – now refers to all items used as eating implements – spoons, forks and knives

D

Danger zone – temperatures between 5°C and 63°C It is possible for bacteria to multiply between these temperatures

Decanting – the movement of wine from its original container to a fresh glass receptacle, leaving the sediment behind

Demographic changes – differing patterns of population statistics

Distillation – process used to increase the alcoholic strength of a liquid

Due diligence – ensuring that a business has taken reasonable care and did everything it could to prevent food safety problems

E

Employee – a person who works for the organisation

Environmental health officer (EHO)/environmental health practitioner (EHP) – responsible for food safety standards and enforcememnt

External customers – customers from outside the organisation

F

Fanning – a lower grade of tea, mostly used in tea bags

Farinaceous dishes – pasta and rice dishes

Feathered game – birds such as partridge, grouse, wood cock, quail or pheasant

Fermentation – the conversion of sugar into alcohol and carbon dioxide

Fixed costs –

Flatware – spoons and forks

Flush – a picking of tea

Fobbing – excess foaming of beer

Food intolerance – when a person reacts to eating certain foods

Food poisoning – an illness of the digestive system that is the result of eating foods contaminated with pathogenic bacteria and/or their toxins

Food safety – putting in place all of the measures needed to make sure that food and drinks are suitable, safe and wholesome through all of the processes of food provision

Foodservice – means the same as catering This word is becoming used more often

Fortified wine – wines such as sherry and port, which have been strengthened by adding alcohol

Franchise – an agreement where a person or group of people pay a fee and some set-up costs to use an established name or well-known brand

Franchisee – the franchise user

Franchisor – the branded company franchise provider

Frappé – served on crushed ice

Furred game – includes venison and hare

 G

Grade – particle size of a tea leaf This is used to describe the quality of tea

Guéridon service – a movable service table or trolley from which food may be served

Gyle cap – dated label or plastic cap that shows the date when the beer was brewed and tagged or casked

 H

Hazard – anything that can cause harm

Hollow-ware – items other than cutlery, for example teapots, milk jugs, sugar basins and serving dishes

Hors-d'oeuvres – traditionally a selection of salads, fish and meats

Hospitality – the friendly and generous treatment of guests and strangers

Hotplate or pass – the meeting point between the service staff and the food preparation staff

 I

Infusion – hot liqueur production method using herbs, peels and roots to extract flavour

Internal customers – staff in other service areas, such as kitchen staff, bill office staff, dispense bar staff and still room staff

 J

Just in Time (JIT) – only ordering stock when it is needed

 K

Keystone – disc in the base of a beer cask in which the beer tap is installed

L

Layered or poured – liquids with different densities are floated one on top of the other

Level of service – can be between limited and high level of personal attention

Limited liability company – the amount that the owners of the business will have to pay to cover the business's debts if it fails or is sued is limited to the value of the shares each shareholder (owner) owns Company documents are available to the public

Liqueur – sweetened and flavoured spirit

Low alcoholic beverage – containing between 05 and 12 per cent alcohol

M

Maceration – cold liqueur production method using soft fruits to provide flavour and aroma

Management staff – responsible for making sure the operation runs smoothly and within budget and may be responsible for future planning Examples are head chef, restaurant manager and reception manager

Maturation – period of time to allow cheese to develop and ripen

Mis-en-place – preparation for service

Mixologist – a person who makes cocktails

Mixology – cocktail making

Muddled – some ingredients (for example fruit, leaves and sugar) are crushed at the bottom of the glass before other ingredients are added

Mutuality of obligation – employer and employee have specific rights and responsibilities

N

New World wines – wines produced outside of Europe, in countries such as the USA, Australia, Argentina, Chile and South Africa

Non-alcoholic beverage or soft drink – not containing any alcohol

Non-captive market – the customer has an open choice of opportunities

O

Old World wines – wine produced in Europe

Operational staff – practical, hands-on staff, including chefs de partie, section chefs, commis chefs, waiters, apprentices, reception staff and accommodation staff

Outside catering – off-premises catering

P

Par stock – set level of stock

Partnership – two or more people working together as the proprietors of a business

Patent still (continuous, column or Coffey still) – method used to produce light spirits,

Pathogen – harmful bacteria

Perry – obtained from pear juice and up to 25 per cent apple juice

Personal development plan – measuring, improving and monitoring own performance

Personal protective equipment (PPE) – protective clothing and equipment used for tasks that may pose a risk or hazard

Personal selling – when food and beverage service staff contribute to the promotion of sales

PESTLE – stands for Political, Economic, Sociological, Technological, Legal, Ecological A model used to classify influences on a business

Physical contamination – when something gets into food that should not be there

Post-mix – aerated water served from a dispensing gun; the carbonated water is added to the syrup after the syrup leaves the container

Pot still – method used to produce heavy flavoured spirits, eg brandy

Poultry – includes chicken duck, goose and turkey

Private companies – a company that cannot sell shares

Private sector – organisations that aim to make a profit

Professional bodies – draw membership from various professions at various levels and provide a range of support for both their members and the industry

Profit – difference between revenue and cost

Public limited companies (PLCs) – a company that can sell its shares to the public

Public or secondary service sector – industries where the provision of accommodation, food and beverages is not the principal business; provision by the state or local authority

R

Requisition – complete an order for stock from the stores

Revenue – the amount of money taken (sales)

Risk – the chance of somebody being harmed by a hazard

Risk assessment – identifying hazards and actions required

Robusta – a harsher, bitter species blend that contains more caffeine

S

Semi-captive market – customers may choose, but once the choice has been made then the food and beverage available becomes limited to that provided by the location

Service plate – used by the server during service

Service salver – a round, silver or stainless steel tray used to carry glasses and cutlery

Service sequence – stages in the service of a meal

Shaken – the ingredients are placed in a cocktail shaker with ice and shaken

Shive – wooden disc placed within opening of a beer cast

Silver service – presentation of food by waiting staff, using a spoon and fork, onto a customer's plate, from food flats or dishes

Single point service – the customer orders, pays and receives the food and beverages at one point

Small to medium-sized business enterprises (SMEs) – companies with fewer than 250 employees

Social responsibility – concerns about sustainability and the environment

Sole trader – an individual who owns the business, takes all the risks, is liable for any losses and keeps any profits

Spear head – external fitting on a keg in which the broaching head is attached

Spile – peg that fits the air hole of the shive

Spore –protective shell which allows cells to protect themselves from heat of freezing

Standards of service – how well the level of service is achieved

Stillage – wood or metal rack, on which a barrel is stored so that sediment settles to the bottom

Stillroom – provides items of food and beverages needed for the service of a meal not found in other major departments such as the kitchen, larder and pastry

Stirred – the ice and ingredients are placed into a mixing glass and stirred

Straight-line counter – all foods are displayed on one long counter and customers move along the counter in order

Sub-contractor – a company or person who carries out work on behalf of the company

Supervisory staff – oversee the work of the operational staff

T

Table d'hôte – a type of cover in which the cutlery for the whole meal is laid before the first course is served

Table de hôte or menu du jour – menu with for specific set price number of food courses

Table service – the customer is served at a laid table This type of service, which includes plated service or silver service, is found in many types of restaurant, cafés and in banqueting

Table theatre – a service enhancement in which food and beverages are served from trolleys These can include cheese, sweet carving or drinks trolleys and also guéridon service

Target – something to be achieved

Tender – when companies compete to win a contract

Tisane – a flavoured tea or herbal infusion

Toxin – poison

Trade bodies – associations of employers or specific types of suppliers

Trancheur – a specialist carver

Tuber – vegetable grown beneath the soil

Turnover – the amount of money a company makes

U

Ullage – unable to be sold Collected from drip trays or left in the bottom of kegs or casks

Underflat – also called an underliner

Up selling – another name for personal selling

V

Variable costs –

Vinification – wine making

Vintage – wines grown and made in a particular year

Viticulture – the process of cultivating grapes

W

Wave service – service of whole tables, one at a time and proceeding across the room

Worker – someone who works within the organisation, but is employed by another company

Index